ROBOTS THAT KILL

ALSO BY JUDITH A. MARKOWITZ

The Gay Detective Novel: Lesbian and Gay
Main Characters and Themes
in Mystery Fiction (McFarland, 2004)

ROBOTS THAT KILL

*Deadly Machines and Their Precursors
in Myth, Folklore, Literature,
Popular Culture and Reality*

Judith A. Markowitz

McFarland & Company, Inc., Publishers
Jefferson, North Carolina

LIBRARY OF CONGRESS CATALOGUING-IN-PUBLICATION DATA

Names: Markowitz, Judith A., author.
Title: Robots that kill : deadly machines and their precursors in myth,
folklore, literature, popular culture and reality / Judith A. Markowitz.
Description: Jefferson, North Carolina : McFarland & Company, Inc.,
Publishers, 2019 | Includes bibliographical references and index.
Identifiers: LCCN 2019010149 | ISBN 9781476668130
(paperback. : acid free paper) ∞
Subjects: LCSH: Robots—Moral and ethical aspects. | Robots—Social aspects.
| Robots—Folklore. | Robots in literature.
Classification: LCC TJ211.28 .M37 2019 | DDC 303.48/34—dc23
LC record available at https://lccn.loc.gov/2019010149

BRITISH LIBRARY CATALOGUING DATA ARE AVAILABLE

ISBN (print) 978-1-4766-6813-0
ISBN (ebook) 978-1-4766-3639-9

Front cover illustration © 2019 Wood River Gallery

Printed in the United States of America

*McFarland & Company, Inc., Publishers
Box 611, Jefferson, North Carolina 28640
www.mcfarlandpub.com*

For Susan
You are the wind beneath my wings

Table of Contents

Preface   1

Introduction   3

Part I: Motivation   13

Revenge   14

Greed   33

Furor: Robots as Job Killers   57

Part II: Crime   65

Criminals   66

Enforcers   82

Superheroes & Supervillains   104

Furor: Making Robots Moral   119

Part III: War   125

Humanoids   127

Non-Humanoids   148

Humans   172

Furor: LAWS   193

Glossary   211

Notes   213

Bibliography   215

Index   235

Preface

The goal of this book is to reveal ways in which robots and other artificially created killers (called "robot-precursors") are part of the human experience. Most of the chapters provide examples of robots and robot-precursors from multiple sources: folklore and mythology, modern literature, contemporary media, and the real world. These sources are designed to show longitudinal and cross-cultural patterns and themes.

The focus here is on themes and patterns. The brushstrokes are broad. There is no claim to have included all examples that exist in mythology, fiction, or the real world.

There are a number of people and organizations who made this book possible. Rabbi Byron Sherwin was an invaluable resource about golems. In addition to reviewing one of the book's chapters, my brother Harvey Markowitz was an important source of information about Native American culture. Thanks to those who provided me with articles and information. They include Daan Kayser of PAX, who permitted me to use PAX's "Ten Reasons to Ban Killer Robots" as the basis for the discussions in Part III: Furor: LAWS; Encounter Books for supplying me with a copy of the book *Striking Power*; Dr. Ronald Arkin for sharing articles on making robots moral; Stephen Bertman for sharing his article about the golem and Shelley's Frankenstein; and Bob Curran, who provided context for the Tulpa myth in the chapter on greed. Thanks to Rhonda and Gerry Duncan and Toni Armstrong, Jr., for taking the time to read chapters and to give me suggestions. Finally, thanks to my wife, Susan, for her excellent suggestions as well as the insights and the tremendous support she has given me.

Introduction

What drives a robot to kill? The premise of this book is that the answers—and there *are* more than one—can be found by looking at robots and "robot-precursors" that the human imagination has produced over millennia. Robot-precursors are non-robotic artificial beings in mythology, folklore, modern literature, and contemporary media. They include Frankenstein's monster, Tibetan *Tulpas* created by intense thought, and the vengeful statue that sends Don Juan to Hell. These killer robots and robot-precursors are antecedents of the real-world killer robots of today and those in our robotic future. They reveal what we expect, desire, and fear will result from continued efforts to create smarter and stronger robots.

The Creators

In the real world, killer robots are built by humans—as are the majority of fictional robots and robot-precursors. Sorcerers and magicians dominate folklore and mythology where they construct killer robot-precursors using supernatural skills and magic. Science supplants sorcery in modern literature and it should be no surprise that mad scientists are well represented when it comes to making killers (Wilson & Long, 2008). Victor Frankenstein, the first mad scientist, appeared in Mary Shelley's *Frankenstein* (1818 [1957]), a book which many consider to be the first science fiction novel (Markowitz, 2015). Frankenstein spawned an ever-increasing assemblage of brilliant and unstable egomaniacs driven to fabricate masterpieces that escape almost immediately, turn on them, and set off on killing sprees.

Sane scientists and inventors are responsible for killers as well—usually as part of their work for a military, government, corporation, or underworld organization. The Jedi hired scientists from Kamino to build an army of clone troopers (*Star Wars: Episode II*, 2002) and Star Trek's Federation of Planets employed roboticist Noonien Soong to build androids. He designed Lore, an android, and programmed him with intelligence and emotion. Then he watched in horror as Lore evolved into a power-hungry killer (Brothers, 1990; I, Borg, 1992). The (fictional) City of Detroit commissioned Omni Consumer Products (OCP) to give them advanced police technology. OCP fabricated the robot ED-209, whose first act was to kill an OCP board member. Then, they reconstituted a human using robotics. The result was RoboCop, a cyborg crime-fighter who did his killing on behalf of the Detroit Police Department (*RoboCop*, 1987).

Popes, priests, rabbis, and other spiritual leaders fashion humanoids and "oracular" heads for selfish or benevolent purposes. Artisans craft bloodthirsty swords, killer statues, and entire killer cities. Aliens, AI systems, robots and other non-humans join in by con-

3

structing their own killers. Aliens built Mechagodzilla in a bid to conquer Earth (*Godzilla vs. Mechagodzilla*, 1974). Skynet continues to unleash killer robots against human rebels in the Terminator Universe (1984–, ongoing).

Such creators provide an endless supply of killers that terrify, entertain, and provide insights into real-world robots. Sprinkled among their lethal creations are a few killers that spring from unexpected or indeterminable sources. The Gashadokuro ("rattling skull") from Japanese folklore, shown in Fig. 1, is the fusion of the fury of millions of dead soldiers and others who were not given proper burials (see Part I: Revenge). The mythological Spartoi of ancient Greece sprout from dragon's teeth that have been planted in a field (see Part III: Humanoids).

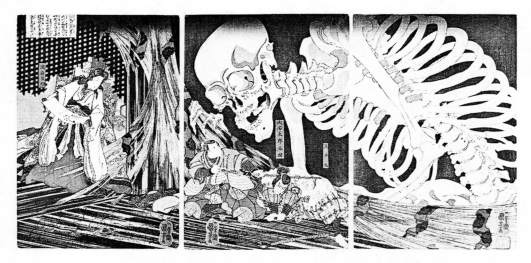

Figure 1. *Takiyasha the Witch and the Skeleton Spectre* by Utagawa Kuniyoshi (1798–1861) is a depiction of *Gashadokuro* ("rattling skull") from Japanese folklore. This robot-precursor is the fusion of people who were denied proper burials, usually soldiers from a battlefield, but also plague victims who were buried in mass graves. The desire for vengeance of hundreds of those angry dead causes their bones to coalesce into an enormous human skeleton that can be fifteen times the size of an average human (Wikimedia Commons).

Defining Attributes

Embodiment, mobility and programmability are characteristics that differentiate robots and robot-precursors from other beings and sometimes from each other.

EMBODIMENT

Part of the definition of "robot" and "robot-precursor" is that they have physical bodies. Embodiment distinguishes it from computer programs, ghosts, demons, and virtual reality. The materials used to make their bodies differentiate robots from robot-precursors and both of them from cyborgs. Robot-precursors can be constructed from almost anything but especially mud, wood, sticks, straw, stones, and animal or human body parts. Corpses are an especially popular ingredient. The South American *Anchimayen* (see Part II: Criminals), a nasty robot-precursor in Native American Mapuche mythology, is made from whole human corpses. Robots are traditionally composed primarily of metals with smaller quantities of other materials. Metals were the primary materials used in early robots. Increasingly, metals have been replaced by silicon, plastics, and carbon fiber. Cyborg bodies are comprised of a combination of organic and inorganic materials. The exact ratio between organic and inorganic components is a matter of debate. Some contend that cyborgs are mostly organic but the Terminator T-800 (*The Terminator*, 1984) is often called a cyborg even though the only organic portion of its body is its skin.

Robot and robot-precursor bodies can be humanoid or non-humanoid. There are also some that, like Transformers (2007–, ongoing), are shapeshifters who can change the form of their bodies. Humanoids have two arms, a torso, and a head. Some also have two legs. Many humanoids are easily distinguished from humans. Neither C3PO, a robot in the Star Wars Universe (1977–, ongoing), nor Frankenstein's monster, a robot-precursor, would ever be mistaken for a human. When the correspondence between a humanoid's body and the human body is exact, that humanoid is called an "android." The replicants in the film *Blade Runner* (1982) and sophisticated assassins in the Terminator Universe (1984–, ongoing) are androids.

The bodies of non-humanoids do not approximate the human form at all. Their bodily configurations are often determined by the tasks they were created to perform. For example, snakebots, real-world reconnaissance robots, look and behave like snakes. They blend into their surroundings and they can slither up a drainpipe or along the ground (Hopkins, Spranklin, and Gupta, 2009). The claws in Philip K. Dick's story "Second Variety" (Dick, 1953 [1989]) are robotic weapons whose round shape enables them to roll rapidly towards their victims. The bodies of other non-humanoids have shapes that signal what they are rather than what they do. For instance, when a South African Zulu sees a hairy, gremlin-like creature, he knows it's a *Tokoloshe* and that it will torment him for a long time (see Part I: Revenge and Part II: Criminals).

MOVEMENT

The ability to move is a defining characteristic of robots that distinguishes them from devices like laptops and (decidedly nonmobile) mobile phones that have no independent movement. With few exceptions, primarily swords, robot-precursors also possess the ability to move their own bodies.

PROGRAMMABILITY

Robots are distinguished from other mechanisms by being programmable. This is a defining characteristic of robots but not of robot-precursors. Robot-precursors are rarely programmable. Their functions are generally fixed when they are created.

Differentiating Abilities

There are many attributes that distinguish one robot or robot-precursor from another. Among these, the most important are control, intelligence, learning, language, and self-awareness. Some robots and robot-precursors are able to speak. Others are not. Some are highly intelligent but others are drones with minimal intelligence.

CONTROL

Robots and robot-precursors can move but they differ with regard to what controls that movement. Three main categories are automatic, external (or remote), and autonomous.

> The label "automatic" is usually reserved for systems that mechanically respond to sensory input and step through predefined procedures, and whose functioning cannot accommodate uncertainties in the operating environment [Boulanin & Verbruggen, 2017, p. 6].

This is how industrial robot-arms function. They are placed in a stable, factory environment where they execute sequences of pre-defined movements and patterns until their sensors tell them they need to initiate a different sequence. Some robot-precursors have response patterns built into them. Mannequin soldiers in the manga *Fullmetal Alchemist* (Arakawa, 2001–2010) are driven to kill and eat. That behavior pattern is initiated when the mannequin soldier perceives a potential victim. "Their main attack is to try to eat their victim, since they lack the thoughts of doing much else" (Homunculus, n.d.).

Remote control of robots was invented by Nicola Tesla. He called it "radio control" and first demonstrated it at an Electrical Exhibition in 1898. Margaret Chaney, his biographer, writes in *Tesla: Man Out of Time* (2001) that Tesla predicted, "You see there the first of a race of robots, mechanical men which will do the laborious work of the human race" (p. 81). He was correct. Today, real-world aerial drones are remotely piloted and, unlike automatic robots, they operate in dynamic environments.

"Autonomy refers to systems capable of operating in the real-world environment without any form of external control for extended periods of time." That is the first sentence of Bekey's *Autonomous Robots* (2005). Real-world environments are complex, dynamic, and unpredictable. To function in that type of setting, robots or robot-precursors must be more flexible than automatic technology provides. They move with intention towards a given goal (which could be to kill you) using a decision-making pattern called the "sense-plan-act paradigm."

- **Sense.** The robot's sensors detect things of interest in its environment and send the data to its control-structure.
- **Plan.** The control structure devises a strategy for dealing with the data so that the goal can be achieved and sends its instructions to the actuators.
- **Act.** The actuators cause the robot to implement the plan.

"Cheetah," shown in Fig. 2, is fully autonomous. It was built by MIT for DARPA to run very fast in pursuit of someone. Leaping was included in its programming because a successful pursuit often requires the ability to overcome obstacles. Using slightly different terminology, Chu's (2015) description of how Cheetah uses the sense-plan-act paradigm to jump over an obstacle is presented as a "story." The story is a technique used throughout this book that is generally comprised of quoted material. Stories are preceded and followed by ◆ ◆ ◆ as is illustrated by the following.

DARPA'S CHEETAH ROBOT

The algorithm's first component enables the robot to detect an obstacle and estimate its size and distance. The researchers devised a formula to simplify a

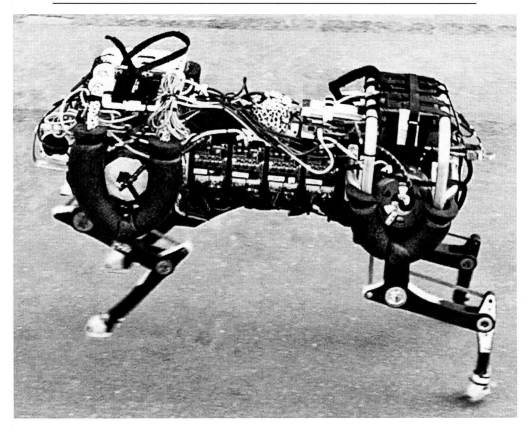

Figure 2. The DARPA fully autonomous Cheetah at the 2015 DARPA Robotics Challenge. Photograph taken June 5, 2015 (Wikimedia Commons; photograph by Master Chief Petty Officer John Williams).

visual scene, representing the ground as a straight line, and any obstacles as deviations from that line. With this formula, the robot can estimate an obstacle's height and distance from itself.

Once the robot has detected an obstacle, the second component of the algorithm kicks in, allowing the robot to adjust its approach while nearing the obstacle. Based on the obstacle's distance, the algorithm predicts the best position from which to jump in order to safely clear it, then backtracks from there to space out the robot's remaining strides, speeding up or slowing down in order to reach the optimal jumping-off point.

This "approach adjustment algorithm" runs on the fly, optimizing the robot's stride with every step. The optimization process takes about 100 milliseconds to complete—about half the time of a single stride.

When the robot reaches the jumping-off point, the third component of the algorithm takes over to determine its jumping trajectory. Based on an obstacle's height, and the robot's speed, the researchers came up with a formula to determine the amount of force the robot's electric motors should exert to safely launch the robot over the obstacle. The formula essentially cranks up the force applied in the robot's normal bounding gait, which … is essentially "sequential executions of small jumps."

Not all robots are endowed with Cheetah's full autonomy. Some are semi-autonomous, which means some of their functions are fully autonomous while others are externally controlled. Most aerial drones used by real-world militaries are semi-autonomous because they have fully autonomous vision and tracking subsystems but their attack functions remain under the control of the human pilot.

Cheetah can use the sense-plan-act paradigm in pursuit of a goal that lies within the realm of its programming, such as deciding how to jump over a wall. It cannot, however, extend its autonomous behavior to tasks that are not part of its programming—even when a task is well within its physical capabilities. For example, it could not dance, or play soccer—even badly—unless the performance of those tasks is incorporated into its programming. Humans possess a different kind of autonomy. We can do many of the things that Cheetah can do and we can perform totally unrelated tasks, such as cleaning a room or playing soccer. The difference between machine autonomy and the autonomy of humans and some other biological beings is significant (Kant, 1785 [1895]); Williams, 2015a). It is also relevant to this book because the autonomy of many fictional robots and robot-precursors is comparable to the autonomy of humans. Other fully autonomous robots and robot-precursors in fiction and all fully autonomous robots in the real world have "machine" autonomy.

In summary, robots and robot-precursors can have automatic control, external control (remotely piloted), or autonomy. Some are semi-autonomous, fully autonomous (like Cheetah), or have human-like autonomy. The term "autonomous" will be used to label what has just been described as machine autonomy versus "human-like" autonomy.

Intelligence & Learning

Robots and robot-precursors with minimal intelligence are drones. Those with automatic control fall into that category. Highly intelligent robots and robot-precursors tend to be autonomous or semi-autonomous. For example, the adamantite horror in the tabletop game Dungeons & Dragons (D&D) (see glossary) is said to have genius-level intelligence. That is unfortunate because it is vicious.

Learning by robots is machine learning. It enables robots to use past experience to improve future decisions and, thereby, supports survival in dynamic and dangerous environments. Machine learning also eliminates the need for programmers to reprogram a robot for every new situation or environment. Fiction reveals, however, that learning can produce unexpected behavior. That distressing situation occurs when machine learning leads autonomous, crime-prevention robots in Sheckley's 1953 story "Watchbird" to decide that all humans must be killed.

Speech & Language

The presence or absence of spoken language helps reveal the intelligence of fictional robots and robot-precursors. The hulking behemoth in the 1931 film *Frankenstein* and other killers based on that character do little more than grunt and howl, which helps communicate their low level of intelligence. Those inarticulate creatures are markedly different from the Frankenstein monster in Mary Shelley's book (1818 [1957]). Her monster speaks fluent French, albeit with a gravelly voice. By enabling the monster to speak well, Shelley tells the reader that he is very intelligent and enables him to narrate parts of the story. Late in the novel, Victor Frankenstein warns a friend, "He is eloquent and persuasive, and once his words had even power over my heart" (p. 180). It is, therefore, ironic the monster is never given a name. The monster tells Victor Frankenstein he thinks of himself as "your Adam." Others refer to him using terms like "monster," "fiend," "specter," "wretch," and "devil." Those characterizations fit the inarticulate beast from the 1931 film far better than Shelley's erudite creature.

The "roboticness" of a fictional character is expressed through monotone intonation and staccato speech. This stereotype is based upon early, real-world speech systems, notably Dudley's Vader which was first demonstrated at the 1939 World's Fair (Bush, 1945). Tres Iqus, a "killing doll" in *Trinity Blood* (Yoshida & Yasui, 2000 [2007]), is proud to be "a machine." He communicates his mechanical nature by using the aforementioned monotone and staccato speech. His language also contains expressions that come directly from the computer industry. For example, after he and Abel Nightroad fend off a vampire attack, Tres asks Abel if he is all right by saying "status report" (p. 100); and, when he doesn't know the answer to a question, he is likely to respond with "insufficient data."

The Borg is an acquisitive alien race in the Star Trek Universe (1966–, ongoing). Its members function as a hive or collective and the Borg's voice includes everyone who has been assimilated into the collective. It is the "we" of "We are the Borg." It speaks for all because individual Borg drones talk only when the hive permits them to do so. That unity is captured by using a chorus of voices. The speech flow is smooth, the articulation is clear, and the acoustic effects make it sound ghostly. These vocal characteristics, combined with knowledge that anyone who hears them is doomed, make the voice of the Borg terrifying.

The astromech/fighter R2-D2 from the Star Wars Universe (1977–, ongoing) is articulate but speaks a language that only other astromechs appear to understand. Yet, the intonation patterns clearly demonstrate that R2-D2 has emotions (and opinions). The non-robotic fluidity of his speech signals that this is an intelligent being. The relatively high pitch of R2-D2's speech matches its small stature and projects a non-threatening persona. The combination of these speech and language characteristics has made it possible to use R2-D2 as a comic character even though R2-D2 is involved in plotting and killing. In a 2014 interview, sound engineer Ben Burtt reported that creating a voice for R2-D2 that would truly capture the nature and personality of the character was extremely difficult. The task was full of contradictory demands because they were dealing with a talking machine "that was going to draw on our emotions … [and] work as another actor. Yet, it was a machine. It didn't have a face with a smile or mouth or eyes or ears and it couldn't speak English … it couldn't even mouth words" (Star Wars & Ben Burtt, 2014). Their solution was to combine the babbling an infant makes to communicate and to express emotions with electronically-generated sounds. The fusion enabled R2-D2 to express emotion yet retain its identity as a robot.

Cheetah, the fully autonomous robot discussed earlier, cannot speak, but if it could, what would it be able to discuss? One proposal is to use a robot's functionality to limit its language and cognition. Moore (2015) provides an example.

[T]he talking toaster in the UK TV science-fiction comedy drama *Red Dwarf* is a brilliant characterization of a one-dimensional, bread-obsessed, … electrical appliance whose entire perception of the world, and thus its conversation, revolves entirely around its need to provide "hot buttered scrummy toast" [p. 329].

Using Moore's approach, a loquacious Cheetah would discuss running, jumping, chasing, and possibly the surface conditions affecting those activities.

SELF-AWARENESS & EMOTION

The term "sentient" is ambiguous. It can mean "self-aware," "able to feel emotions," "intelligent," or all of the above. Consequently, the terms "self-aware," "has emotions," and "can feel emotions" are used instead. A self-aware robot or robot-precursor knows it is a unique being. It understands "I" and recognizes that "I" is separate from "you" and everyone else. The toaster from the *Red Dwarf* series cited above may have a one-dimensional view of the world but it is aware of itself and its limitations. That becomes clear when another character complains that the toaster talks about nothing but toast. The toaster retorts, "I'm a toaster. It's my raison d'être. I toast therefore I am" (White Hole, 1991). That toaster is not only self-aware but capable of abstract reflection about its own nature.

Most of the self-aware killers in this book were self-aware when they were created. Some killers become self-aware and, usually, the cause is unexplained. This spontaneous combustion of self-awareness occurs in McGuire's 2014 short story, "We Are All Misfit Toys in the Aftermath of the Velveteen War" (see Part I: Revenge). When it happens, the toys realize how badly they have been treated and take revenge on their persecutors.

Robots are typically described as having no emotions. Throughout the television series *Star Trek: The Next Generation* (Roddenberry & Berman, 1987–1994), the android Commander Data is portrayed in this way even though there are episodes in which he clearly exhibits emotion. For example, he treats his cat Spot and her kittens with love (Genesis, 1994). His lack of emotion is a handy comic device, a way to advance a plot, and sometimes the focus of a plot. In the episode "In Theory" (1991), Data consults his colleagues to learn how to respond to the romantic overtures by a human woman. He compiles information about being romantic and uses it to prepare a private dinner with her. The carefully orchestrated date is a failure and Data admits, "Apparently my reach has exceeded my grasp in this particular area. I am, perhaps, not nearly so human as I aspire to become." In the film *Star Trek Generations* (1994), Dr. Soong, Data's creator, makes an emotion chip for him. When it is finally installed, Data begins to experience events in new ways that delight or distress him.

Why Do They Kill?

Robots and robot-precursors are motivated to kill, destroy, and commit other crimes for a variety of reasons. Some motivations flow from folklore and mythology through modern literature and contemporary media and into the real world. Others simply bob to the surface from time to time.

Revenge and greed are presented in Part I as timeless and culture-free motivators for killing. Sometimes the perpetrators are vengeful and greedy robots and robot-precursors. Part I also introduces a pattern in which others use robots and robot-precursors as tools. This is the most common relationship between robots or robot-precursors and humans.

Part II deals with crime. It shows robots and robot-precursors that are fundamentally evil and a few that even revel in torturing and killing. Other killers in Part II prevent murder, enforce laws, exact punishment, and otherwise battle the forces of evil. They perform those services as members of law enforcement, as investigators, or as superheroes battling supervillains. Each chapter in Part II contains an "Evolution" section that describes the reincarnations of a specific robot-precursor, including Talos, a robot that began its existence in Greek mythology.

War, the subject of Part III, is a fertile domain for killers. Humanoids become warfighters, spies, and assassins. Many non-humanoids are weapons. Others protect human fighters as powered exoskeletons, robotic prostheses, and nanotechnology.

What impact will the expanding presence of robots and AI have on our lives? This question has produced furors about job-killing automation and killer robots. A book about killer robots needs to acknowledge the fears and hopes embedded in those disputes. The concluding chapter of each part of this book outlines one of those furors. These furor chapters are the only chapters that do not conclude with a section called "Plans Gone Awry" that contains tales of well-formulated projects that misfire.

In Parts I through III, robots, robot-precursors, their creators, and their users intentionally cause damage and death. There are also robots and robot-precursors that kill by accident. These killers have not been given their own chapter. Rampages occur in many chapters. Accidents like the following appear in the "Plans Gone Awry" part of chapters.

Folklore & Mythology

The Algonquin people are Native Americans from the Eastern seaboard of the U.S. and Canada. Their folklore includes stories about the *Aseneekiwakw* ("stone giants")—a race of beings that existed long before humans. The *Aseneekiwakw* were created from huge rock boulders. "Sadly, because the a-senee-ki-wakw were so large they crushed many animals and did damage to the Earth when they moved" (Bane, 2016, p. 9). Realizing that he had made a disastrous error, Gluskab, their creator, had to destroy them.

Modern Literature

Nicholaus Geibel is a toy maker and gadgeteer in Jerome's 1893 story "The Dancing Partner." He is approached by three young women who enjoy dancing but find male dance partners to be wanting in many ways. Geibel builds them a robot dancing partner: "He keeps perfect time; he never gets tired; he won't kick you or tread on your dress; he will hold you as firmly as you like, and go as quickly or as slowly as you please; he never gets giddy; and he is full of conversation" (p. 5). Initially, the dancing partner was wonderful. Then, for some unknown reason, it began to dance faster and faster until it was so out of control it began smashing into walls and furniture, knocking its partner unconscious. "A stream of blood showed itself down the girl's white frock, and followed her along the floor" (p. 8). The dancing partner was finally stopped but not before it was too late.

REAL WORLD

Robot arms in factories have been known to kill. Those incidents are always accidents (at least, that's what we're told). The first reported killing by a factory robot occurred in 1979 at Ford Motor Company's plant in Flat Rock, Michigan. An unsuspecting technician named Robert Williams scaled a five-story machine to determine why it had been malfunctioning. "While Williams is up there … a robot arm also tasked with parts retrieval goes about its work. Soon enough, the robot silently comes upon the young man, striking him in the head and killing him instantly" (Young, 2018). The robot continued to function as if nothing untoward had occurred. Ford insisted the murder was "completely unintentional" which, no doubt unintentionally, intimated that other attacks could be intentional. A jury was not impressed. It awarded Williams' family $10 million for his wrongful death ($10 Million Awarded, 1983). Today, potentially deadly robot arms have warning technology and are separated from human workers by enclosures.

Science fiction and contemporary media are filled with killer robots that go on deadly rampages for no apparent reason. These outbreaks of wild and seemingly random killing appear throughout this book. There are a few whose behavior may be truly inexplicable. Quite often, however, there is or was something that compelled them to kill wildly and indiscriminately. Those causes can generally be found in the following chapters.

PART I

Motivation

Revenge and greed. These are core motivators that appear in all types of fiction and in the real world. They drive robots and robot-precursors to kill and destroy. They inspire biological beings, deities, and other robots to create robots and robot-precursors to do their killing for them. They also cause the death and destruction of robots and robot-precursors. Revenge and greed are not limited to Part I. They are rationales for torturing, killing, and generating other types of unpleasantness, described in the rest of this book as well.

Fiction is replete with dystopian futures involving unchecked job-automation by greedy capitalists. Those images collide with fictional utopian visions of the future. Both reflect the emotional turmoil being produced by automation in the real world. The Furor chapter that concludes Part I presents reasons other than greed that could motivate real-world employers to automate. It then touches on the question of how job-killing robots might change our society.

Revenge

Whether it is served hot or cold, revenge has always been part of human society. It is a response to an injury or perceived injury suffered at the hands of someone else. The kinds of events that provoke a desire for revenge vary from culture to culture but the desire for payback is universal (Shteynberg, Gelfand & Kim, 2009; Strelan, Feather & McKee, 2011).

Jealousy is a common, cross-cultural spur for revenge. Usually, the jealous individual feels that something or someone that is theirs is being taken from them. It may be a lover, a promotion, a job, or an object. The revenge can be directed at the presumed property, the one who has supplanted the jealous individual, or both.

Revenge is essentially a three-step process: injury, desire for payback, and retribution. The second step (desire for payback) is crucial because some injured parties do not seek payback. Their view may be characterized as "turn the other cheek." By contrast, the attitude of injured individuals who do seek revenge may be described as getting "an eye for an eye," even when the retaliation far exceeds the damage caused by the original injury.

Injured parties can dispense retribution themselves. That way, they can enjoy the punishment first-hand. Often, however, it is more efficient, wiser, or easier to use a surrogate to dispense the actual punishment. Use of a surrogate, such as a robot or robot-precursor, allows the aggrieved individual to dispense payback without "getting their hands dirty." It can be a message to the offender and others that the injured person has many ways to punish anyone who dares to offend them or the revenge-seeker may wish or need to conceal their identity.

Humans are not the only ones seeking revenge, either. Entities greater than humans, such as deities, and those lesser than humans, such as other primates, display a desire for vengeance (Clutton-Brock & Parker, 1995). There are vengeful aliens and even robots and robot-precursors.

Folklore & Mythology

Some tales of revenge are intended to convey moral or religious ideals or to teach lessons. Others describe events in history that the tellers do not want forgotten. A few are simply intended for entertainment.

The best-known revenge surrogate is the "voodoo doll." It is a miniature effigy of the person who perpetrated the injury that, through magic, is linked to the offender's body. When a pin is plunged into the doll, the offender feels extreme pain in the corresponding part of their body. This practice is erroneously attributed to followers of *voudon* (or *vodou*), a Haitian religion that evolved from African traditions (Armitage, 2015; Radford, 2013).

Voudon does *not* use dolls for revenge but doll effigies are used elsewhere. British sorcerers called "cunning folk" would help their communities counteract evil witchcraft by using good magic. One way to punish an evil witch was to create an effigy of the witch then stab it with pins or other sharp objects to cause pain. Some figures were made of cloth, husks, and branches and others were carved into wax, potatoes, or clay. The figure known as a *poppit* (also *oppet*, *mommet*, or *pippie*) was filled with herbs and linked to the witch by magic (Cunningham, 2000; Davies, 2003).

Lucy Garnett wrote that "the anciently widespread practice of making a wax image of an obnoxious person, and sticking pins in it to injure him, still survives in Turkey" (Garnett, 1890, p. 143). In China, a clay effigy would be placed in a space between the walls of a building. Rather than sticking it with pins, the figure would be shaped to look like someone who is ill or in pain. To give it power, the creator cut a gash in their own body and injected blood into the figure. Dennys (1876) recounts the story of a woman who had her kitchen repaired but then couldn't enter the kitchen without feeling ill. Suspecting that witchcraft was involved, she had a kitchen wall pulled down. In a small, hollowed-out area of the wall they found "a clay figure in a posture of sickness" (p. 83).

Dolls are incapable of independent movement, which makes them unsuitable as robot-precursors. A far better example of a robot-precursor that often serves as a surrogate is the *Tupilak* (also *Tupilaq*) in the folklore of the Kalaallit Inuit of Greenland (Williams, 2010). A *Tupilak* is made from animal body parts and sometimes the corpse of a child. Because of the diversity in a *Tupilak*'s construction, it can look like a grotesque humanoid, an animal, or unlike anything in nature (see Fig. 3). The sorcerer animates the *Tupilak* by intoning magical chants over the newly formed figure. This could take several days but once the creature is fully alive, the shaman releases it with instructions to find and kill the designated victim. *Tupilaks* are mindless killers much like remotely controlled drones used today but

Figure 3. Kârale Andreassen's (1890–1934) depiction of the robot-precursor *Tupilak* from the folklore of the Kalaallit Inuit of Greenland (Wikimedia Commons).

they can understand and obey commands involving killing. They do not, however, appear to be able to speak.

Not surprisingly, the construction and release of a *Tupilak* is generally done in secret.

> [H]e came upon the middle one of many brothers, busy with something or other down in a hollow, and whispering all the time. So he crawled stealthily towards him, and when he had come closer, he heard him whispering these words: "You are to bite Nukúnguasik to death; you are to bite Nukúnguasik to death."
> And then it was clear that he was making a *Tupilak*, and stood there now telling it what to do [Rasmussen, 1921, p. 18].

Once a *Tupilak* has its assignment, it can track and kill its victim without assistance—it is autonomous. Typically the *Tupilak* is released into the sea because the sea is a central part of Inuit life making it easier for the *Tupilak* to find its target. A *Tupilak* completes its mission with alacrity. Then, since a *Tupilak* is also driven by an overwhelming hunger, it eats its dead victim.

Thousands of miles from Greenland, the *Tokoloshe* (also *Tokolosh, Tokoloshi, Thokolosi*, and *Tikaloshe*) serves as a revenge surrogate (Todd, 2007; Spindrifting, 2008). It is a malevolent figure in the folklore of indigenous people living throughout the southern portion of Africa (e.g., Zulu). A *Tokoloshe* is created by a sorcerer at the request of someone who wants to torment and/or kill someone. It is constructed from bones, parts of dead animals, and sometimes from a human corpse (after it has had its eyes and tongue removed). When a hot iron bar is driven into its skull, the *Tokoloshe* shrinks to the size of a young child. Some say a fully formed *Tokoloshe* looks like a hairy (probably eyeless) gremlin with a hole in its head. Others say they "shrivel to the size of a child and appear extremely pale, sickly, and deformed" (Tokoloshe, n.d.). Zulus describe them as "bearlike" and "Zimbabwe's Tokoloshe is large, covered in fur with long talons and a bony spine reaching all the way down its back from the top of its skull. It also has glowing red eyes, emits a foul stench and speaks in a rasping voice" (Todd, 2007). No one knows for sure because only the *Tokoloshe's* quarry, animals, and children can see it. Everyone agrees that a *Tokoloshe* is something to be feared.

The *Tokoloshe* is given life when a special powder is blown into its mouth or nostrils. Once alive, it begins to seek its intended victim. When it finds them, it torments them by appearing without warning, talking to them, destroying their possessions, and alienating them from the family and community. The victims are often driven insane (Kerouack, n.d.).

The folklore of ancient Egypt includes stories about Setna Khaemwese, an historical figure from the 13th century BCE, who used his knowledge of history to restore pyramids and tombs. He was a reputed magician and the high priest of Ptah during a period of conflict between Egypt and the neighboring kingdom of Nubia.

REVENGE AND COUNTER-REVENGE

A Nubian chief challenges Pharaoh to find a man who can read a letter without opening it. Setna's young son Siosire succeeds in this, and reads the letter aloud. Long ago, he reads, a Nubian king's sorcerer animated four wax figures which abducted the Egyptian king and gave him five hundred blows before returning him to his palace. This humiliation was avenged by an Egyptian called Horus son of Paneshe, who performed the same assault on the Nubian king. He then defeated the Nubian sorcerer in a contest of magig and banished him from Egypt for 1,500 years. After the letter is read, the Nubian chief declares that he is the sorcerer returned for vengeance. Siosire in turn reveals that he is Horus son of Paneshe. He vanquishes the Nubian and returns to the underworld (Willis, 1996, p. 45).

It isn't unusual for a robot or robot-precursor to dispense punishment for offenses they, themselves, have endured. This practice is well known in Japan. In fact, the Japanese people have long believed that commonplace objects are not as inanimate as they appear. The *Tsukumogami* ("tool specters") are a type of *Yokai* ("monsters"). They begin their existence as household objects and tools that faithfully serve humans for one hundred or more years. Then, according to Reider (2009), when they are no longer needed and tossed aside, they become "resentful after having been abandoned by the human masters whom they so loyally served, and … become vengeful and murderous specters" (p. 232). The *Tsukumogami Ki* ("The Record of Tool Specters") provides the following well-known example.

REVENGE OF THE *TSUKUMOGAMI*

During the year-end susuharai … (sweeping soot, house cleaning) events in the late tenth-century capital of Heian, old tools and objects are discarded in byways and alleys. The abandoned goods become angry at the humans who discard them and plan, as specters, to torment their former owners…

As tool specters, the *tsukumogami* kidnap humans and animals for consumption, and they celebrate their new lives with such merrymaking as drinking, gambling, and poetry recitations (Reider, 2009 p. 234).

The *Ittan Momen* (Meyer, 2013) are killer *Tsukumogami* that don't hold parties. What makes them especially dangerous is that they look like harmless pieces of cloth. No doubt, before they were thrown away they were harmless. They become dangerous only when they turn into *Tsukumogami*. They fly around at night looking for human victims. "Ittan momen attack by wrapping their bodies around a person's face and neck, strangling or smothering them to death" (Meyer, 2013). *Ittan Momen* remain primarily in the area of Kagoshima, Japan. Anyone living in or visiting that part of Japan must remain vigilant.

The *Tsukumogami* are not the only Japanese *Yokai* that are known to seek revenge. The *Gashadokuro* (Meyer, 2013) is comprised of the bones of people who were not given proper funeral rites (see Fig. 1 in the Introduction). Those people are typically soldiers whose bodies were left on the battlefields where they were killed, those who succumbed to a plague and were put into a mass grave, and indigents who died of starvation. The desire for vengeance of hundreds of those angry dead causes their bones to coalesce into an enormous human skeleton that can be fifteen times the size of an average human. In the darkest hours of the night, the *Gashadokuro* emerges near graveyards and battlefields to hunt for humans who are walking alone. When it finds a desirable target, it attacks either by crushing its prey or by biting off the victim's head. The *Gashadokuro* is called "rattling skull" because its approach can be detected by the rattle of its teeth. That produces a "gachi gachi" sound and may cause ringing in a person's ears. The most dangerous aspect of a *Gashadokuro* is that it cannot be killed because it is made of bones of people who are already dead. It will continue hunting until the pent-up vitriol that binds its bones together is exhausted, allowing the bones to separate and the *Gashadokuro* to collapse.

The first *Gashadokuro* was created for a somewhat different kind of revenge. It dates to the tenth century. At that time, there was a bloody rebellion against Japan's central government in Kyoto. The leader of the uprising, Taira no Masakado, was a samurai from the Kantō region. The government brutally crushed the rebellion and put a bounty on Taira. Shortly afterwards, he was killed. His killer decapitated the body and brought Taira's head to Kyoto to collect his reward. Taira's daughter, Takiyasha-hime, was infuriated. She was a powerful sorcerer and, to punish the government for dishonoring her father, she conjured the first *Gashadokuro* and unleashed it on Kyoto. Takiyasha-hime's revenge is depicted in a woodblock print by nineteenth-century artist Utagawa Kuniyoshi (Figure 1 in the Introduction).

Statues of ancient Greece and Rome have been known to exact revenge against those who have assaulted or offended them. For example, according to Bettini (1992 [1999]) the statue of a famous athlete punished a man who robbed it.

The Statue of Pellicus of Corinth

[It] apparently had the ability to detach itself from its pedestal at night in order to wander about people's houses and take baths. A foolhardy young man from Libya once dared to steal the offerings that grateful citizens had left in front of the statue; the statue happened to be absent at the moment, taking one of its nightly walks. But as soon as it returned and realized that it had been robbed, the statue was infuriated, and punished the Libyan in exemplary fashion. The unlucky victim was seized by a strange sort of mania, which compelled him to wander all night long from house to house as if in a labyrinth…. But even this was not the end of it: the young man suffered mysterious beatings each and every night, until he finally died (Bettini, 1992 [1999] p. 129).

A vengeful statue is said to have defended the honor of a Trojan hero.

An Assyrian man visiting Troy stood in front of a statue of the Trojan hero, Hector, and mocked the man it represented. At the end of his diatribe he began to insist that the statue was really a statue of Achilles who had dragged Hector behind his chariot. On his way home, the Assyrian man drove his chariot along a dry riverbed. Suddenly, there was a monstrous torrent of water. A giant Greek soldier rose up and ordered the waters to overrun the road. As the Assyrian was being carried away to his death, he saw that the giant soldier was Hector [Bettini, 1992 (1999), pp. 130–131].

The behavior of these and other statues exemplifies the belief among the ancient Greeks and nearby societies of that time that statues and other images embody some of the spirit of the person they represent. Consequently, they are—to some extent—alive. Both Hersey (2009) and Bettini (1992 [1999]) use evidence from ancient and modern sources to support this point.

> One curious aspect of the supposed livingness of statues lies in the ancient habit of mooring them in place.... [I]t is clear from a number of ancient writers that the makers and users of the statues also feared that, as living beings, the images might simply bolt [Hersey, 2009, p. 17].

The Spanish legend of Don Juan[1] also involves a vengeful statue, but the statue avenges wrongs done to the man it represents as well as insults directed at the statue itself. The perpetrator of those acts is Don Juan, a wealthy, arrogant libertine who believes he can seduce any woman and can dispose of any man who dares to oppose him. He kills the father of a young woman he wants to seduce. Unfortunately, that man was a powerful individual whose influence extended beyond death. To add insult to the murder, Don Juan plans to seduce the man's widow. He goes to his victim's grave and taunts the statue of the man erected over the grave. He then mockingly invites the statue to the dinner he is to have with the man's widow on the following day. Don Juan is astonished when the statue actually appears at dinnertime. Instead of joining Don Juan at supper, it tells Don Juan he will be punished for his wanton behavior and his evil deeds. As the story concludes, the statue drags Don Juan to hell.

Even powerful gods may seek revenge. One well-known example is the revenge leveled by Zeus, king of the Greek gods, against the lesser god Prometheus. The situation began innocently. Zeus asked Prometheus and his brother Epimetheus to create creatures to live on Earth. The two labored to produce a variety of creatures and they were careful to give each one a characteristic or skill to help it survive and thrive (e.g., claws, strength, flight). Unfortunately, they ran out of skills before making a human. To solve that problem, Prometheus stole fire-making knowledge, but that wasn't his real offense. When he gave that knowledge to humans he violated the divine rule that only the gods are to know the secret of using fire. Zeus was infuriated. He commanded Hephaestus, the god of fire, to build a bronze eagle as part of Prometheus' punishment. Prometheus was then chained to a pillar and the eagle tortured him by eating his liver. Because Prometheus was immortal, his liver would regrow every night and the eagle would dine on it every day. This cycle was to be repeated every day, forever.

Modern Literature

Modern literature adds another element to revenge: the mad scientist. Mad scientists are often inventors who seek the unattainable. They focus so intently on their labor that they give no thought to anything else, including the victims of their experiments: the robot-precursors they create. Furthermore, they feel no responsibility for the outcomes of their efforts and are known to abandon their monstrous creations once they have (or have not) achieved their goal. This constellation of behaviors enrages their damaged victims and causes them to strike back.

The first and most famous of those mad scientists is Victor Frankenstein in Mary Shelley's 1818 novel, *Frankenstein; or The modern Prometheus*. Yet, the chaos and destruction caused by his monster are not generally remembered as acts of revenge. That misconception is due to the actions of the monster from the 1931 film *Frankenstein: The Man Who Made a Monster,* who goes on a killing rampage. That mindless killer will be discussed in the Crime chapter of Part II. Mary Shelley's monster is not mindless. He kills to punish Frankenstein for rejecting him and then refusing to build another monster—a female, to share the monster's life and reduce his profound loneliness and isolation (see Fig. 4).

The Monster's Vengence

"Shall each man," cried he, "find a wife for his bosom and each beast have his mate and I be alone? I had feelings of affection, and they were requited by detestation and scorn…. Are you to be happy while I grovel in the intensity of

Figure 4. Monster and Frankenstein from the inside cover of the 1831 edition of *Frankenstein; or, The modern Prometheus* by Mary Shelley (1797–1851) (Wikimedia Commons).

my wretchedness? You can blast my other passions, but revenge remains—
revenge, henceforth dearer than light or food! I may die; but first you, my tyrant
and tormentor, shall curse the sun that gazes on your misery. Beware, for I am
fearless, and therefore powerful. I will watch with the wiliness of a snake, that
I may sting with its venom. Man, you shall repent of the injuries you inflict....
I go; but remember I shall be with you on your wedding night" (Shelley, 1818
[1957], p. 145).

True to his word, he murders Victor Frankenstein's best friend, Henry. Then, on Victor's wedding night, he kills Victor's bride, Elizabeth. After Elizabeth's murder, Victor's father descends into madness and dies. As promised, there is no longer any joy in Victor's life.

Eighty years after Shelley published her novel, H.G. Wells released *The Island of Dr. Moreau*, about a mad scientist intent on accelerating the speed of evolution. This work requires him to do surgery on living creatures, a practice called "vivisection." He transplants tissue from one animal to another. Then he alters the recipient's physical and/or chemical structure. These aspects of Wells' storyline reflect two upheavals Europe was undergoing at that time. Darwin's theory of evolution was battering the Biblical concept of creation, and the use of vivisection by researchers was increasing, sparking a movement to ban it.

The title character in *The Island of Dr. Moreau* establishes a laboratory on a remote island. There, he explores how to elevate "beasts" through physical and chemical alteration (Wells, 1896).

> I asked a question, devised some method of obtaining an answer, and got a fresh question. Was this possible or that possible? You cannot imagine what this means to an investigator.... The thing before you is no longer an animal, a fellow-creature, but a problem! I wanted—to find out the extreme limit of plasticity in a living shape [Loc. 1266–1272].

Because he dismisses the reality of pain, Dr. Moreau performs his surgery without anesthesia. At one point, Dr. Moreau describes with pride how he "made his first man" from a gorilla (Loc. 1282–1287) and with dismay when any of his fine creations "reverts." When "the beast begins to creep back" (Loc. 1332), Moreau banishes it to the jungle and moves to his next experiment. Thus, it is not surprising that, when his monstrous experiments find an opportunity to repay him for his sadism, they do so; violently attacking each other as well as Moreau. "Moreau and his mutilated victims lay, one over another. They seemed to be gripping one another in one last revengeful grapple" (Loc. 1901).

Sever Gansovky's (1964 [2016]) short story, "Day of Wrath," has been described as an updated version of *The Island of Dr. Moreau*. Like Dr. Moreau, the scientists in Gansovsky's story perform surgical experiments in a laboratory located in a remote area. The subjects of their research are live bears whose bodies and brains are altered to create a race of humanoids with superior intellectual and linguistic abilities.

These scientists are far more successful than Dr. Moreau. They create a new breed of animal they call "Otarks." Otarks are more intelligent than humans and their humanoid faces enable them to produce intelligible speech. Other areas of their bodies remain bearlike. The scientists appear to have altered the bear DNA because the offspring of Otarks are

Otarks, not bears. According to a human living nearby, "otarks aren't animals—it would be great if they were just animals. But they're not people, of course" (p. 466). The Otarks are kept in a pen outside the laboratory, allowed to breed, and used as cerebral playthings. They are aware of their plight and are filled with bitterness: "[t]hey want revenge against humans" (p. 466). Then they break free. Once that happens, they kill and eat some of the scientists in the laboratory, including one of the lead scientists. Fuller, the remaining lead scientist, escapes and never returns. When asked about the Otarks, Fuller "said that they were a very interesting scientific experiment. Very challenging. But he's not involved with them at the moment. He's doing something to do with cosmic rays…. He said that he was very sorry for the victims" (p. 467).

There can be no doubt their hatred for humans persists. They become increasingly adept at hunting and killing humans and, like Shelley's Frankenstein monster, they never lose control and they revel in every one of their vengeful killings. Gansovsky's story concludes when the Otarks track and kill the narrator. One can easily imagine the Otarks ultimately wiping out the human population in their remote area and, perhaps, beyond.

Dr. Jacques Cotentin is a mad scientist in Gaston LeRoux's 1923 *La Machine à Assassiner* (*The Machine to Kill*) who is not interested in creating a new species. He hopes to animate Gabriel, the android he's built, so it won't merely function "like a simple mechanism that can do nothing more than respond to electrical stimuli: *but like a human!*" (p. 101).[2] His solution is to give it a human brain from someone who just died. Foreshadowing Mel Brooks' 1974 film *Young Frankenstein*, the brain Cotentin selects is flawed. It comes from the recently executed serial killer Bénédict Masson, and the brain remembers everything, including that Masson was framed. Full of vengeance, Gabriel/Masson escapes from his cage and hunts his accusers who are members of a vampire cult led by a local aristocrat. He catches them during a ritual meeting. "They all rushed at him but he … was too strong for all of them! … You don't kill a tempest" (p. 194). Afterwards, Gabriel, badly damaged, destroys himself by jumping off a cliff.

The vengeful beings in McGuire's 2014 story, "We Are All Misfit Toys in the Aftermath of the Velveteen War," were not created by mad scientists and they are not living creatures. They are dolls and other children's toys built by commercial toy manufacturers. They were given AI, language understanding, emotions, and machine learning. These technologies were designed to enable the toys to be personalized by learning a child's name and other things related to that child. Somehow, they also became self-aware and capable of understanding what children were doing and saying to them.

By incorporating these technologies into their toys, their manufacturers transformed them into robots. All this technology would have provoked concern if it had been embedded in large robots but it seemed benign in small toys. "Toys would never hurt us…. We forgot that kids can play rough; we forgot that sometimes we hurt the toys without meaning to" (p. 367). Like their literary and mythological precursors, the toys become angry and vengeful.

One day, several years before the beginning of the story, all the toys disappear, taking with them the children of the town. Toys that had been mistreated make children suffer; but those that had been treated well feed their hostages candy, ice cream, and peanut butter sandwiches—foods they've learned that children like. The children are—reportedly—happy, until they begin to mature. Whenever that occurs, the toys mutilate the child to remove all signs of maturity. Without proper medical care, however, their wounds become infected.

When they become too much of a burden, the toys abandon them on a road for adult humans to find and fix. It is always too late.

Toy manufacturers in the real world have often been on the cutting edge of technology. The first consumer products that were able to respond to spoken commands were toys (Markowitz, 2013). A doll named Julie was released in the late 1980s that was able to engage a child in simple conversations. Mattel (2015) released its Hello Barbie! that could converse with a child to learn information the child gave to it, such as that the child loves ice cream. Shortly afterwards, other dolls, such as My Friend Cayla, appeared with similar functionality. There are, however, significant differences between the toys in McGuire's story and today's most technically advanced real-world toys.

- They are not self-aware.
- Some can behave as if they feel emotions but they don't actually feel them. Therefore, they could not become angry or vindictive. This is related to their lack of self-awareness.
- They are incapable of forming even the simplest of plans, let alone concocting the complex plot described in the story.
- Their language processing and learning technologies are limited to the kinds of data needed to handle conversational interactions with and about the child, such as the child's likes and dislikes.
- The data they gather, their language, and their learning technology all reside on a server to which the toy is wirelessly connected. If a toy is cut off from the server, it loses the advanced processing and the bulk of the knowledge it has acquired. Consequently, the best way to squash a (highly unlikely) rebellion would be to deactivate the toy's wireless connectivity.

The use of wireless communication provides the greatest threat from real-world toys because they are vulnerable to hacking. The doll My Friend Cayla has been removed from some markets because its makers know it can be hacked but have done nothing to correct the situation. If the toys in McGuire's story could be hacked, their rebellion might have been short-circuited by savvy, parent-friendly hackers.

Science fiction provides us with examples of humans taking revenge against robots. Isaac Asimov's short story "Liar!" (Asimov, 1950) presents a future in which highly intelligent robots are commonplace. As with most of the robots in Asimov's work, robot HB-34 (Herbie) has a "positronic brain" into which is programmed Asimov's Three Laws of Robotics. The first law is the most powerful. It states, "A robot may not injure a human being or, through inaction, allow a human being to come to harm" (Asimov, 1942 [1983]).

Due to a manufacturing flaw, Herbie can read minds, which enables him to sense the fears and desperate dreams that gnaw at the humans around him. The First Law of Robotics compels Herbie to protect a human from the harm caused by those negative thoughts. Herbie complies with the First Law by telling each person he encounters what she or he wants desperately to hear. For example, it recognizes that Peter Bogert longs to become the director of the company's plant. Consequently, Herbie tells Bogert that Alfred Lanning, the current plant director, has already retired (which is not true). He also guarantees that Bogert will be named the next plant director. Herbie perceives that Susan Calvin desperately loves a much younger colleague. Herbie assures her that the colleague returns her love. Herbie's counsel has satisfied the First Law by bringing joy to these humans. Not for long.

Calvin begins to primp for work and to pay more attention to the colleague she loves. She is mortified when he tells her he's in love with another woman and plans to marry her. She is further insulted when Herbie insists that Calvin dreamed about having a rival. Bogert is almost fired when he acts on Herbie's information and tells Lanning that he knows Lanning has retired.

Calvin gets her revenge by sending Lanning and Bogert together to confront Herbie about what he told Bogert. The robot knows that if he stands by the statements made to Bogert, he will make Lanning unhappy. If he disavows those statements, he will hurt Bogert. Giving no response would, by inaction, hurt them both. The hopelessness of his situation drives Herbie into insanity. Flush with the triumph of her revenge, Calvin approaches the robot and shouts "Liar!"

Villiers de l'Isle-Adam's 1886 novel *L'Eve future* (*Tomorrow's Eve*) tells the story of Lord Ewald, a love-besotted young man whose attempts to attract the object of his love are futile. He hires a fictional Thomas Edison to build a robot of Alicia, the woman he loves. Edison complies. Hadaly, Edison's android, is so accurate that Ewald mistakes her for Alicia. The happy couple set sail for England and, for some reason, Hadaly travels as cargo rather than as a passenger. It appears that Alicia is also a passenger on that ship. A suspicious fire breaks out in the cargo area of the ship. The passengers are rescued but the ship sinks, taking Hadaly with it. The author intimates that Alicia set the fire out of jealousy and vindictiveness.

It is well known that groups of humans can seek revenge against groups of other humans. Sometimes this is called "war," although the process can be stopped before it reaches that point. That is the case in *Look to Windward* (Banks, 2000) which is Banks' seventh book about the Culture, a society governed by machines with genius-level intelligence called the "Minds." The Culture seeks to bring peace to alien peoples and is willing to interfere in the affairs of a civilization to accomplish that. Experience has taught them how to achieve that goal. To the Culture, the Chelgrians are simply another society in need of its help. They plan to eliminate the Chelgrians' rigidly stratified caste system that treats the Invisibles, the lowest social class, as if they are an inferior species. Although the Chelgrian social system has been in place for over three thousand years, the Culture believes it can help establish a more egalitarian society and, once that happens, the Culture expects peace and harmony to come to Chel. After all, interference in alien affairs has worked ninety-nine percent of the time.

The plan fails, which leads to three acts of revenge. The first occurs when the lower classes in the Chel society seize power and vent their rage against those who had subjugated them for centuries—much like the mythological *Tsukumogami* and the abused toys in McGuire's story. The second act of revenge occurs after the Culture admits its role in starting the civil war. A cadre of upper-caste Chelgrians devises a means to get revenge against the Culture. Their vengeance is fueled by the Chelgrian-Puen, spirits that rule the Chelgrian afterlife. The Chelgrian-Puen will not permit the souls or Soulkeepers of the Chelgrians killed in the civil war to enter heaven. A Chelgrian Soulkeeper is a device embedded in each Chelgrian that contains a backup of that Chelgrian's personality and spirit. This creates a situation akin to that of the abandoned Japanese soldiers whose anger ultimately produces a *Gashadokuro*. Then, the Chelgrian-Puen turn the screw tighter by saying that the Chelgrian dead cannot enter heaven until an equal number of Culture citizens are killed by Chelgrians: a soul for a soul.

The Chel plotters recruit Major Quilan, a veteran of the civil war, to be their surrogate. He is assisted by the consciousness of a dead admiral-general to whom Quilan explains,

> [t]here is a device inside my skull, designed to look like an ordinary Soulkeeper, but able to accommodate your personality as well.... The device is no larger than a small finger.... [Y]our conscious would be transferred entirely into the substrate within my body [p. 36].

This makes him an unusual form of robot-precursor.

The third act of revenge occurs when the Chelgrian plot fails. The Culture exacts retribution by unleashing a robotic revenge-surrogate against the Chelgrian conspirators: a shape-shifting nanoweapon called "E-Dust." One-by-one, the E-Dust locates them, kills them in a brutal and painful manner, and destroys their Soulkeepers. A Chelgrian must have a Soulkeeper in order to enter heaven after their physical death. That is why the E-Dust makes certain the Soulkeepers of the conspirators are destroyed along with their bodies.

> The insect swarm collected on a broad balcony and resumed the form of a Chelgrian female. She knocked the balcony doors down and stepped into the room.... The only sensory or command system not fully under her control was a tiny passive camera in one corner of the room. She was to leave the complex's security monitoring system uncorrupted, so that what was done was seen to be done, and recorded [p. 364].

The brutal murders are a message to any Chelgrian who tries to harm the Culture.

In Bradbury's "Robot City" (1951), a long-extinct race of intelligent beings created a huge robot in the shape of a city. The robotic city was constructed for the explicit purpose of satisfying their creators' need for revenge. It is their revenge-surrogate and it is designed to perform that function even long after its makers become extinct.

> The men who died built me. The old race who once lived here. The people whom the Earthmen left to die of a terrible disease, a form of leprosy with no cure. And the men of that old race, dreaming of the day when Earthmen might return, built this city, and the name of this city was and is Revenge.... At long last, you've come! The revenge will be carried out to the last detail. Those men have been dead two hundred centuries, but they left a city here to welcome you [p. 252].

As in the Egyptian myth described earlier in this chapter, the revenge takes the same form as the original attack that annihilated them. The city transforms the human crew into drones who willingly carry disease back to Earth.

In the novel *The Stepford Wives* (Levin, 1972), upwardly mobile families move to the idyllic town of Stepford. The Stepford husbands, angry about being treated as second-class citizens by their powerful wives, seek revenge. They conspire to transform their independent-minded wives into servile drones. They do so by killing their wives and constructing doppelganger robots. When Joanna Eberhart, the main character, discovers the plan, she attempts to take her children and leave Stepford but finds that her children have been kidnapped by her husband and his allies. Joanna suffers the same fate as her Stepford predecessors: she is killed and replaced. The 1975 film of this story concludes with a scene in a supermarket showing the new Joanna—the Stepford wife.

The Stepford Wives is a tale of revenge, but the novel and the films also satirize the stereotypes of suburbia and of the servile wives who have lost their identities in that bland "sameness." Levin's story has also had an impact on the English language. The entry "Stepford" in *Webster's New World College Dictionary* (2010) is an adjective in American English referring to someone "resembling an automaton in being conformist and submissive, unemotional, mechanical, etc."

In the young-adult novel *The Iron Woman* (Hughes, 1993), the entity seeking revenge is Earth who wants to punish those humans whose greed has polluted and defiled the Earth for decades. The "Iron Woman" is Earth's surrogate. It avenges the Earth by transforming adult, male polluters into swamp creatures. In this way, a robot-precursor transforms a story of revenge into an attack against greed, the subject of the next chapter.

Contemporary Media

The pattern of vengeful humans using artificial beings as revenge surrogates continues in contemporary media. Most surrogates in contemporary media are robots. One of the earliest examples occurs in Fritz Lang's silent film *Metropolis* (1927)—which was also one of the first films to portray an android. C.A. Rotwang is a brilliant scientist and inventor (a mad scientist) who lost Hel, the only woman he ever loved. She left him to marry the wealthy industrialist John Fredersen and died giving birth to their son Freder. The desolate Rotwang originally planned to build an android that would be Hel's robotic twin. He changes his plans when he hears about the unrest that is growing among Fredersen's workers, unrest that is being held in check by Maria, a charismatic labor leader. Rotwang's planned revenge becomes sweeter when he learns that young Freder is in love with Maria. Rotwang kidnaps Maria and copies her body image into his android. The special effects used for the transformation of the android into "False Maria" make Rotwang seem more like a sorcerer than a scientist (Fig. 5). Rotwang releases his creation with instructions to foment anger and violence among Fredersen's workers. She instigates worker riots that produce massive destruction and fill Rotwang with joy.

The pattern also appears in television. The villain in the anime *Sonic X* (Sasamura & Matsumoto, 2003–2004) is Dr. Ivo Eggman. He is a mad scientist who uses low- and high-tech robots to do his bidding. The "Revenge of the Robot" (2003) occurs after Sonic, the series hero, has destroyed some of Eggman's advanced weaponry. Eggman swears eternal vengeance against Sonic and sends a giant robot to kill Sonic but it is destroyed by another robot.

Star Wars: Episode III—Revenge of the Sith (2005) adds a twist to the revenge-surrogate pattern by attacking an enemy using its own army of robot-precursors. It is set a millennium after the Jedi soundly defeated the Sith. Even after such a long time, the Sith still hunger for revenge. Previously, in *Star Wars: Episode II—Attack of the clones* (2002), the Jedi leadership commissioned Kamino scientists to create an army of clones to serve as the Grand Army of the Galactic Republic (GAR) and to prevent planetary systems from seceding from GAR and forming a separatist republic. The Jedi provided a DNA template to the scientists to use for the cloning. Jedi Supreme Chancellor Sheeve Palpatine instructed them to embed a biochip into each clone containing a program for emergency situations. It is Order 66.

> ORDER 66: In the event of Jedi officers acting against the interests of the Republic, and after receiving specific orders verified as coming directly from the Supreme Commander (Chancellor), GAR commanders will remove those officers by lethal force, and command of the GAR will revert to the Supreme Commander (Chancellor) until a new command structure is established [Contingency Orders, n.d.].

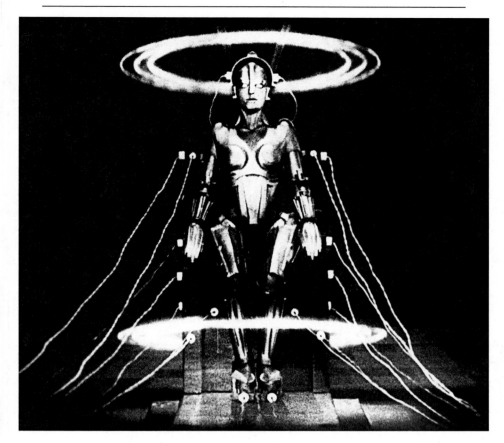

Figure 5. The False Maria android transformation in Fritz Lang's *Metropolis* (flickr).

Order 66 can only be invoked by the Supreme Chancellor. Unfortunately for the Jedi, the Supreme Chancellor is actually Sith lord Darth Sidious. Darth Sidious invokes Order 66, naming Jedi as traitors and dispatching the clone troopers to kill them. When that appears to be done, Palpatine/Darth Sidious completes the sweet revenge by ending the clone wars and restructuring the Republic as the Galactic Empire.

The 2004 animated film *The Incredibles* depicts angry superfan Buddy Pine plotting revenge against the superheroes who snubbed him when he volunteered to help them with their exploits. His plan deviates from the typical pattern of using robots as revenge surrogates. He constructs a laboratory below a remote island. There, he devises methods of killing all the offending superheroes, especially the family of superheroes known as the Incredibles, and begins executing them himself. For the next stage of the plan, he builds a small army of huge, spiderlike robots he calls "omnidroids." They are his revenge surrogates but he doesn't use them to kill the superheroes. Instead, he releases the robots in Manhattan. When no superheroes respond to Manhattan's cries for help, Pine initiates the final stage of his plan: to become the new superhero. As the eyes of the world focus on him, Pine begins destroying the omnidroids. His scheme misfires because the Incredibles and other superheroes arrive in Manhattan and eliminate both the omnidroid threat and superfan Buddy.

As in modern literature, tales of humans who seek revenge against artificial beings aren't commonplace but they exist. Col. Roy Mustang in the manga/anime *Fullmetal Alchemist* (Arakawa, 2001–2010) shifts into revenge gear following the murder of Maes Hughes, an officer in the Amestrian military. Hughes had been Mustang's best friend and a strong supporter of Mustang's political aspirations. When Mustang learns the killer is a homunculus named Envy, he tracks it down and attempts to kill it. Envy doesn't die but does admit it killed Maes and engaged in other anti-human activity because of humans' ability to feel happiness. Much like Susan Calvin (see the preceding section, Modern Literature), Mustang gets his revenge when Envy commits suicide.

There are many examples of robots hating and killing other robots but they don't generally involve revenge—at least not explicitly. Desire for revenge, however, has fueled a feud between ABC Warrior-robot Joe Pineapples and the robot pirate Dog-Tag in the comic book series *ABC Warriors: Shadow Warriors* (Mills, 2009). The animosity between them began after Pineapples foiled a raid by Dog-Tag's gang and, in the process, annihilated the gang. Dog-Tag got revenge several issues later by shooting Pineapples in the head, cutting off his trigger finger, and burying his body. Pineapples is a comic-book hero, which means he won't remain dead for long. When he recovers a few issues later, the feud continues.

To contemporary media, "all the universe is a stage and all men and women merely players" (Shakespeare, *As You Like It*, ca. 1603). Tales of revenge are no exception.

By the time the film *Transformers* (2007) was released, the Autobots and the Decepticons, Takara Tomy/Hasbro action figures and shapeshifting robots from the planet Cybertron, have been fighting each other for millennia. The warring factions travel to Earth seeking to take possession of the AllSpark, the device that gave them life. It had been thrown into space and landed on Earth. The Decepticons, led by Megatron, want to use it to activate all of Earth's machines and turn them against humans. The Autobots want to take it back to Cybertron. *Transformers* concludes when the Autobots, led by Optimus Prime, decimate the Decepticons and Sam Witwicky, a human, kills Megatron by shoving the AllSpark into his chest which extinguishes his "spark" (soul). The fleeing Decepticons vow revenge. Autobots remain on Earth to protect humanity.

Megatron is rebuilt and given a new spark in *Transformers: Revenge of the Fallen* (2009). The Fallen, his evil master, commands him to kill Optimus Prime and capture Sam Witwicky. Then, Megatron is to harvest the sun's energy which will destroy all life in the solar system. A series of killings and revivings ensue, concluding with the death of the Fallen. Megatron vows revenge as he flees (also see Part II: Superheroes & Supervillains and Part III: Humanoids).

The Manhunters are an android police force created by the Guardians of the Universe to root out evil and fight for justice (Englehart & Dillin, 1977–, ongoing).

HUMILIATION OF THE MANHUNTERS

The Guardians created the Manhunters, thinking that robots would make good peacekeepers. But they soon learned that they were flawed, owing to the inability of their programming to distinguish the subtle gradations between good and evil. Rather than decommission the robots entirely, the Guardians chose to reprogram them for lesser duties—hunting, tracking, and guarding.... [T]he Guardians subsequently replaced the Manhunters with the Green Lantern Corps.... Over the years, the Manhunters planned their revenge against the Guardians and their [Green Lantern] Corps (Manhunters, n.d.).

Manhunters have had a great deal of success (DC Comics, 1959–, ongoing). They've imprisoned Guardians (who are immortal and cannot be killed), killed members of the Green Lantern Corps, used brainwashing to turn captured Corps members against the Corps, and defamed both the Guardians and the Corps. They've also spread their concept of justice to many planets, created a Manhunter cult, and aided enemies of the Guardians. Even today, the Manhunters continue their campaign of revenge. For more information about the Manhunters, see Part II: Superheroes & Supervillains.

Role-playing games are hotbeds of revenge. The tabletop game WH40K (see Glossary) (Games Workshop, 1987–, ongoing) is populated by warped and vicious denizens, but the most twisted of them are the Dark Eldars called the "Haemonculi." *The Warhammer 40,000 Codex: Dark Eldar* (2014) characterizes them as

> masters of the flesh, be it alive or dead.... [T]hese diabolical figures slice and meld the flesh of those that fall into their clutches, savouring their pain as a gourmet would savor a fine meal.... To cross these monstrous beings is considered beyond foolish. Not only is their vengeance terrible to behold, but the Haemonculi have the power to bestow—or withhold—life after death [p. 72].

They are capable of perceiving almost anything as a slight for which they seek revenge. Their vengeance is almost bottomless when the affront comes from other Dark Eldars.

REVENGE OF THE HAEMONCULI

Though they begin existence as Dark Eldar, Grotesques undergo a hideous rebirth.... Over the course of months or even years the hapless victim's body is pumped full of growth elixirs and subjected to torturous surgical enhancement until they become a subservient, weaponized horror whose only desire is to serve its dark masters. When given the command to kill, these meat-hulks transform into engines of destruction. Racks of syringes dump potent stimulants into their ichor-stream and veins throb near to bursting as tube-punctured hearts are forced into overdrive. With a great, muffled roar the Grotesques thunder into battle, butchering all within reach with greathook, claw and cleaver until commanded to cease or hacked bodily into many pieces (*Ibid.*, p. 176).

Haemonculian revenge is truly a diabolical inversion of the patterns discussed to this point.

Raiden's revenge in the game Metal Gear Rising: Revengeance (PlatinumGames, 2013–, ongoing) takes us back to Earth. Metal Gear Rising is a single-player video game in which the player takes the role of Raiden, a cyborg hero and special-operations professional. There is a great deal of fighting which has led some to call Metal Gear a "hack and slash" game. Most of the fighting is between and among cyborgs.

Raiden and his team have spent three years helping N'mani, the prime minister of an African country, rebuild his country following a devastating civil war. The game begins when the limousine carrying N'mani and Raiden is attacked by cyborg assassins led by a mercenary named Sundowner. They were hired by Desperado Enforcement LLC ("Desperado"), a supplier of arms and mercenaries that pads its bottom line by fomenting war. Raiden's team attempts to fend them off but they are overpowered. N'mani is kidnapped and killed, prompting Raiden to dedicate himself to avenging N'mani's assassination. In the role of Raiden, the player hunts and finally finds Sundowner. After a bloody battle, Raiden is victorious and the murder of N'mani is avenged (also see Part I: Greed).

The television series *Westworld* (Wickham, 2016–, ongoing) is about a theme park designed to enable its wealthy "guests" to act out their fantasies with the park's android "hosts." There were remarkably few examples of revenge initiated by the android hosts in the show's first season, despite the violence perpetrated against them by the guests. A major reason for the lack of vengeance by the hosts is that the park's creator, Robert Ford, had a policy of erasing violent events from the memories of hosts. A few memories do manage to bubble to the surface. For example, a host named Walter goes on a killing spree in the episode "The Original" (2016). Walter kills six hosts but spares several others standing with them. Park technicians discover that the hosts Walter killed had killed him in prior story-lines. The others had not (The Stray, 2016). When host Peter Abernathy is asked, "What would you like to say to your creator?" he waxes Shakespearean in his reply, "I am a host mechanical and dirty and I shall have such revenges on you both" (The Original, 2016). Things begin to change when Ford is murdered at the end of Season 1. In Season 2, the hosts explode into revenge mode (Journey into Night, 2018).

The "Robot's Revenge" (1985) episode of the animated television series *The Jetsons* begins when George, one of the main characters, insults a robot. The offended robot issues a "Code Red" to all automata and George and his family suffer vengeance from every piece of equipment they encounter, from George's robotic easy-chair and traffic lights to robot hair stylists and police officers. The assaults stop only after George makes amends to the robot he had affronted. This *Jetsons* episode envisions the "Internet of Things," a technology that has not yet been fully deployed.

Real World

Like their mythical and fictional counterparts, humans in the real world use aerial robots as revenge surrogates—primarily in war—because they can track and attack targets in areas that are unavailable to human operatives. This practice is likely to spread (see Part II: Criminals and Part III: Non-Humanoids). Far more often, the use of aerial drones provokes retaliation using non-robotic weapons, notably bombs.

Can real robots seek revenge? It is highly unlikely because they are not self-aware and cannot comprehend the concepts insult and revenge. Or can they?

ACCIDENT OR REVENGE?

Years ago, human-size tackling bags used to remain in place while football players practiced tackling them. The football technology of today is far more sophisticated. The program at Baylor University uses some of it. One of the new pieces of equipment they use is a robotic tackling-bag.

As with its predecessors, the robotic tackling-bag can withstand repeated assaults by members of the football team. It can also move down the field, swerving and adjusting much like a player on an opposing team—but usually faster.

In 2018, Baylor University administrator Sean Padden put one robotic, tackling-bag to the test by setting up a short run from a point on the football field to the end zone. Padden and the tackling bag stood almost shoulder-to-shoulder at the starting line but Padden got a much faster start out-of-the blocks than the robot. That enabled Padden to easily beat the robot to the end zone.

As Padden turned to the crowd to celebrate his victory, the robot swerved and finished its run by body-slamming Padden, knocking him to the ground. The unhurt Padden later said, "I did it for humanity—because the machines aren't going to fight fair. We'd better be ready" (Burton, 2017).

Hooman Samani of the National University of Singapore maintains his non-humanoid "lovotics" robots experience jealousy and seek revenge (Anthony, 2011; Lian, 2011). The robots look like large, one-eyed bowler hats. They can love individual humans because they are programmed with artificially created "love" hormones (oxytocin, dopamine, serotonin, and endorphin). Facial recognition and speaker identification enable them to separate the loved one from other humans. Once the robot bonds with someone, it wants to remain close to them. "Presumably if you refuse to cuddle the robot, it grows testy, and if it sees you interacting with another human—or fiddling with a USB socket on your PC—it becomes jealous" (Anthony, 2011). It emits an angry bleat and backs away but it isn't clear what form its revenge takes because all the videos end after the bleats.

Robots named "Revenge" compete in robot combat competitions, such as *Robot Wars* and *Battlebots*. Prior competitors include the bar-spinner "Sweet Revenge" (Sweet Revenge, n.d.), the spiked spinning drum "Revenge" (Annihilator, 2002), the super-heavyweight "Kenny's Revenge" (Kenny's Revenge, n.d.), the box-wedge heavyweight "Widow's Revenge" (Widow's Revenge, n.d.), and two named "Granny's Revenge."

> The original Granny's Revenge featured a dummy of an elderly woman sitting in a motorised wheelchair, therefore making it top heavy. Despite this, the robot was extremely lightweight at 66kg. It had a pneumatic flipping leg as weaponry, which was not seen in action. Granny herself held a chainsaw in her arms, but this was static, and for display purposes only. Granny was extremely flammable, and would torch the whole robot when set alight [Granny's Revenge, n.d.].

As robots become more widespread, it would not be surprising if they are used as revenge surrogates. Self-aware and intelligent robots of the future might seek revenge for their own mistreatment like the toys in McGuire's story (McGuire, 2014).

Plans Gone Awry

As has already been revealed, not all revenge schemes go as planned. Here are more examples.

MODERN LITERATURE

In Robert S. Carr's 1994 short story, "The Composite Brain," a mad scientist and his equally mad assistant assemble a killer-monster with the goal of using their creation to get back at his nemesis: another professor who has been given the accolades the scientist believes should be his.

They employ a combination of chemistry and body parts taken from a variety of animals, including humans—like some mythological robot-precursors. The monster is given a "composite brain." Each segment of the brain is comprised of part of the brain of one of the animals used to construct the creature. Each brain segment controls only the body parts taken from the same creature. For example, the human part of the monster's brain controls its human arms, the octopus brain-part controls its octopus tentacles, and the bulldog brain-part controls the bulldog body parts. The scientist brags about his creation to his nephew, saying,

> [t]he most important thing of all is: *this composite brain is controlled by my own!* …When I think killing it fights with almost inconceivable ferocity and abandon…. [I]t is so simple that it is practically thought-transference [pp. 281–282].

The two madmen test the system by mentally telling the monster to kill the scientist's nephew. It responds immediately by killing and eating the young man. The success of this experiment encourages the scientist to move forward with his plan to use the creature to kill his enemy and reap the honors and awards that should have been given to him. The plan fails when the victim takes control of the monster's mind and turns it against its maker.

CONTEMPORARY MEDIA

In the film *Metropolis* (1927), described earlier, Rotwang's plans go horribly awry. His intent was to ruin and kill the Federsens. Instead, the riot provoked by the False-Maria android injures workers and their families. Things continue to fall apart for Rotwang when the real Maria escapes and informs young Federsen of Rotwang's plans. In addition, young Federsen turns out to be the benign leader that the real Maria had promised would ease the workers' plight. The workers turn on the False Maria who is destroyed in a fire. With his hopes for revenge dashed, Rotwang commits suicide.

Greed

The New Testament of the Bible warns, "For the love of money is the root of all kinds of evil" (Timothy 6:10). This is the admonition that the word "greed" often brings to mind. It is equivalent to avarice: the desire for money and other "worldly goods." It is one of Catholicism's seven deadly sins. In Dante's *Divine Comedy*, the fifth circle of Purgatory is reserved for its practitioners, who are "[b]ound and imprisoned by the feet and hands … we remain immovable and prostrate" (Dante, 1265–1321 [1867], p. 127).

Despite its strong link to avarice, greed covers a far larger landscape. It can encompass anything that is amassable, including power, fame, and knowledge. The homunculus (android robot-precursor) named "Greed" in the manga and anime *Fullmetal Alchemist* (Arakawa, 2001–2010) captures the breadth of this concept of greed. "You humans think that greed is just for money and power but everyone wants something they don't have" (EmptyMan000, 2016). Even this incarnation of greed fails to mention the most fundamental characteristic of greed: its insatiability. In *Fear of Freedom*,[1] Erich Fromm provides the following characterization: "Greed is a bottomless pit which exhausts the person in an endless effort to satisfy the need without ever reaching satisfaction" (Fromm, 1942, p. 100).

Unlike envy, joy, and anger, greed cannot be characterized as an emotion though it often produces those emotions. As examples, failure to acquire a desired something can cause anger while joy, however transient, can accompany the satisfaction of a desire. Dante acknowledges an emotional byproduct of stymied greed and its link to revenge. The following appears in the description of the fourth circle of Purgatory (Sloth):

> And there are those whom injury seems to chafe,
> So that it makes them greedy for revenge,
> And such must needs shape out another's harm [p. 114].

Those who are driven by greed can be so focused on satisfaction of their goal that they become indifferent to the harm their actions cause to others—and sometimes even to themselves. This is one reason why mad scientists are prime examples of greed for knowledge and adulation. At the same time, other greedy individuals and groups are keenly aware of the impact their greed has on others because sometimes causing someone else to suffer or to lose something of value can actually be part of the pleasure of obtaining what they covet.

In mythology as in the real world, the archetype avaricious individual is the businessperson and, along with them, the rapacious corporation. Businesspeople are sometimes shown to desire power as well as wealth but, they aren't alone. The hunger for power resides in other types of humans, aliens, robot-precursors, and robots. The domains in which they seek to expand their power range in size from small communities to universes.

Typically, robots and robot-precursors are used as tools for greedy individuals and groups to obtain what they desire. There are many different ways in which this is accomplished.

Folklore & Mythology

The first three folktales involve avarice in humans who exhibit it in strikingly different ways. An avaricious entrepreneur—the first of many greedy businesspeople in this chapter—uses a *Tulpa* to help him become rich (Bob Curran, personal communication, 19 Nov. 2011). *Tulpas* are Tibetan "thought forms"—a robot-precursor that is produced by intense concentration. A *Tulpa* takes whatever form its maker envisions, including that of its creator or another human. No matter what form it takes, it possesses human-like intelligence, language, and the ability to learn—all of which are emerging abilities of real-world robots. Over time, most *Tulpas* become increasingly independent and often acquire the attributes of their creators or of the individual with whom they spend most of their time.

THE TULPA OF THE GREEDY MAN

A greedy man wanted a tulpa made in his image to fool the god of death into taking the creature instead of him—when the time came. He knew he didn't have the mental power and discipline to create one so he asked a holy man to create it for him saying he would use it to do good things. The holy man told him, "All that you are will go into this being and if you are true, as you say, it will be a blessing to you but if you are not then it will be the worse for you, for although I have fashioned it for you, this is *your* creation."

The greedy man paid no heed to the warning. He took the tulpa with him everywhere and used it to amass wealth. Over time, the tulpa grew in strength and substance. And as it grew, it developed a will and intelligence of its own. One day, when the man told it to take some rice from a neighbor, it refused. It seized him by the throat and threatened to choke him.

"Why are you doing this?" the man sputtered. "Am I not your master and did I not call you into life?"

"You are no master to me!" the tulpa replied. "For I indeed *am* you. Had you done good things I would have reflected that, but now I am only filled with envy and greed. You are to blame for my state." Then it choked the man and delivered him to the god of death. The tulpa could do that because the man had not created it and, therefore, had no power to destroy it.

The tulpa lived out the rest of its days as the man—and no one knew the difference…. This was the punishment the holy man had foreseen (Curran, 2001, pp. 122–125).

The Women of Turkey and Their Folk-Lore (Garnett, 1890) describes the "spaying candle." It was used by criminals to find treasure and is marginally a robot-precursor. After killing someone who, they believed, had hidden money or valuables, they excised a part of the corpse. A witch formed the spaying candle from the fat of that body part and tallow. The location of the hidden treasure was identified when the spaying candle was extinguished (pp. 144–145).

Book XIII (Part I, Vol. IV) of *The Histories of Polybius* (Polybius, n.d. [2011]) describes what appears to be an android drone used by the King Nabis to extort tributes from Spartan citizens.

NABIS TYRANT OF SPARTA

He had also constructed a machine, if one can call such a thing a machine. It was in fact an image of a woman richly dressed and was a very good likeness of the wife of Nabis. Whenever he summoned any of the citizens before him with the design of extracting money from him he would begin by addressing him in kind terms, pointing out the danger to which the city and country were exposed from the Achaeans and calling attention to the number of the mercenaries he was obliged to maintain to ensure the safety of his subjects, as well as to the amount spent on religious ceremonies and the public outlay of the city. If they yielded to these arguments it was sufficient for his purpose. But if anyone refused and objected to pay [*sic*] the sum imposed, he would continue somewhat as follows: "Very possibly I shall not be able to persuade you, but I think this Apega of mine may do so"—this being his wife's name—and even as he spoke in came the image I have described. When the man offered her his hand he made the woman rise from her chair and taking her in his arms drew her gradually to his bosom. Both her arms and hands as well as her breasts were covered with iron nails concealed under her dress. So that when Nabis rested his hands on her back and then by means of certain springs drew his victim towards her and increasing the pressure brought him at all in contact with her breasts he made the man thus embraced say anything and everything. Indeed by this means he killed a considerable number of those who denied him money (Polybius, n.d. [2011], pp. 422–423).

An "oracular head" is a robotic bust that can tell the future or provide other knowledge its creator seeks to have. Legends about oracular heads that emerged in Medieval and early Renaissance Europe "are descendants of two ancient traditions that became intermingled during the Middle Ages" (LaGrandeur, 1999, p. 408): robots built by Hephaestus in Greek mythology and Egyptian "animated idols." Some attributed the use of an oracular head to historical figures known to have valued scholarship, notably Vergil, Albertus Magnus, and Roger Bacon. Many of those legends end badly.

William of Malmsbury's 12th century publication *Gesta Regum Anglorum* (*William of*

Malmsbury's Chronicle of the Kings of England: From the Earliest Period to the Reign of King Stephen) is considered to be the first such legend to appear in writing. It is a biography of Gerbert, a man who was greedy for wealth and power but, most of all, for knowledge. Gerbert studied everything, including the "necromantic arts," some of which he was taught by a Spanish Saracen. The Saracen owned a book that contained all of his knowledge and Gerbert was "inflamed with anxious desire to obtain this book at any rate" (p. 174). To accomplish that, Gerbert seduced the man's daughter and, with her help, stole the book. Using knowledge from that book and from a pact with the Devil (suggesting that the book was not all-powerful), Gerbert obtained wealth, power, and the honor of becoming Pope Sylvester II. Malmsbury writes,

> [H]e cast, for his own purposes, the head of a statue ... which spake not unless spoken to, but then pronounced the truth, either in the affirmative or negative. For instance, when Gerbert would say, "Shall I be pope?" the statute [sic] would reply, "Yes." "Am I to die, ere I sing mass at Jerusalem?" "No" [p. 181].

Gerbert didn't know that the head was not referring to the city of Jerusalem but to a church named "Jerusalem" where each pope was expected to sing mass. As foretold, Gerbert died shortly after singing mass at Jerusalem.

Modern Literature

As in revenge, there is a shift from robot-precursors to robots along with a concomitant change from sorcerers to scientists. Greed is a characteristic of groups as well as of individuals, but corporations are portrayed as the sources of greed far more often than politicians, rulers, or scientists. All of these individuals and groups, however, use robots as tools to help them achieve their greedy objectives.

Avarice

Each of the following stories reveals a different way in which avaricious groups and individuals employ robots. *La Conspiration des Milliardaires* [*The Billionaires' Conspiracy*] (1899) by Le Rouge and Guitton is an early example of capitalists using technology to gain wealth and power as well as an early portrayal of the use of an army of robot drones. It is an "Edisonade" novel. These novels were common in the late nineteenth and early twentieth centuries. They include a character modeled on the American inventor Thomas Edison. The character is a brilliant inventor, scientist, and/or engineer who is sometimes actually named "Thomas Edison." The name of the inventor in Le Rouge and Guitton's novel is Hattison. The French pronunciation of Hattison is "ah-tee-son" which is almost identical to "eh-dee-son," the French pronunciation of Edison. Hattison is hired by a cabal of American billionaire industrialists to help them conquer Europe (the "Old World"). They install him in an underground laboratory situated in a sparsely populated area of the western United States. Hidden beneath an innocent-looking factory, Hattison's laboratory is protected by security so powerful that it would be the envy of today's anti-terrorism agencies and gold repositories. There, Hattison develops futuristic weaponry, including an army of huge, well-armed robots. Because Le Rouge and Guitton's book was written before the word "robot" entered the French vocabulary, Hattison's robots are alternatively referred to as "hommes de fer" ("iron men") and "automats" ("automata"). Hattison's iron men are capable of responding to spoken commands, revealing Hattison to be a truly brilliant inventor because viable speech recognition for more than a single word would not exist for fifty years.[2] Olivier Coronal is a French spy seeking to avenge a murder done at Hattison's behest. Coronal penetrates the sophisticated security system, descends into the secret laboratory, and makes a startling discovery.

Iron Men

Black, sinister, stone-faced, metal men suddenly surged out of the shadows and into the lamp light. They bristled with bayonets. Covered with metal, legs rigid, torsos bulging, they seemed like knights from the middle Ages that had been resuscitated and made ready to march forward. Each metallic phantom sported a helmet instead of a head. One arm dangled. Their huge eyes were open, bulging and looking surprised…. These metallic specters were able to stand upright, walk, move on their own volition. They shattered all beliefs about what could be created.

Hattison seemed even more monstrous than before for having built such human-like mechanisms and for making them engines of destruction more terrifying than all other weapons. The grotesque fused with the horrific in this mathematical caricature of human beings.

"What madness possesses him?" cried Coronal. "What could this damnable Hattison possibly be dreaming of?" (Loc. 5134; 2016 translation by J. Markowitz).

The iron men are among the deadly tools that Hattison and his employers plan to use to satisfy their lust for riches and global dominance. Coronal ensures that their plot fails.

"The Tunnel under the World" by Frederik Pohl (1955 [1989]) focuses on another symbol of corporate greed: the advertising agency. Guy Buckhardt works for the Contro Chemicals Corporation. He is an average, middle-class American living in a typical American town of the 1950s. Every morning Buckhardt wakes up shaken by a nightmare about an explosion and then discovers that every day is June 15. The days are filled with sales pitches for products Buckhardt never heard of and some people hawking those products reappear later as someone else peddling a different unfamiliar product. Buckhardt is determined to uncover the truth. A tunnel that runs beneath the town takes him to the Contro plant where he then learns that, during the night of June 14, the Contro plant exploded, killing everyone in the town. Dorchin, the enterprising head of a marketing company, built a miniature reproduction of the town and downloaded the minds of townspeople, including Buckhardt's, into the bodies of tiny robots. The robots repeatedly wake up on June 15, the first day the humans didn't actually live. Dorchin then tests their responses to different types of sales campaigns.

The robot called April Horn said, "You and all the others were what Dorchin wanted—a whole town, a perfect slice of America…"

Buckhardt said unbelievingly, "All this to sell merchandise! It must have cost millions!"

The robot called April Horn said, "It did. But it has made millions for Dorchin, too. And that's not the end of it. Once he has found the master words that make people act, do you suppose he will stop at that?" [pp. 39, 40].

Annalee Newitz's 2017 novel *Autonomous* shines a beacon on greed by pharmaceutical companies. It is timely given price-gouging by real-world pharmaceutical companies. For example, NextSource raised the price of its cancer drug Gleostine 1,400%. Other pharmaceuticals have done the same with life-saving drugs (Hernandez, 2018) (also see Part II: Enforcers). The large and powerful pharmaceutical company in *Autonomous* is Zaxy. They are about to release Zacuity, a performance-enhancement drug. Jack is an anti-patent drug pirate who discovers that Zacuity is virulently addictive. Soon after someone begins using it, the drug compels them to continually repeat a specific task, refusing to eat or sleep, until they die. Zaxy claims the problems are caused by a reverse-engineered copy of Zacuity made by Jack but Zaxy's main worry is the financial impact of allowing the public to believe Zacuity is dangerous. "Zaxy had always placed profit over public health, but this went beyond the usual corporate negligence" (p. 29). It also seems that law-enforcement shares the company's concerns. "This drug is driving people nuts, and some are dying. If it gets out that this is Zacuity, it could be a major financial loss for Zaxy. Major" (p. 25). A seasoned drug-enforcement officer and a newly minted military robot are charged with capturing or killing Jack. The robot's enhanced strength and sensory abilities combined with brutal tactics lead the pair to Jack who appears to die in a firefight. Zaxy is delighted but their pleasure fades when an independent research-robot develops a cure and announces it—along with a description of the Zacuity addiction—in a press release.

The greedy corporations in Michael Crichton's novel *Prey* (2002) are small, start-up companies that are being funded by the U.S. Pentagon to work on a top-secret project to develop a nanobot "swarm." Nanobots are extremely tiny robots and a nanobot swarm behaves like swarms of locusts and other insects. When the project doesn't produce what the military wants, the start-ups work feverishly to keep their government funding so they can develop patentable, breakthrough technology that will make them rich. Once a prototype is completed, they begin testing. One test assesses the ability of the swarm to function in a high wind. They are determined to use the nanobots to become rich. Their arrogance, single-mindedness, and greed lead them to intentionally release a nanobot swarm outside of their facility. One company executive writes in an email, "We have nothing to lose" (p. 501). They quickly discover how wrong that declaration is. The swarm is uncontrollable and, like their creators, it is greedy. It consumes virtually everything that comes into contact with it. When that is a living creature, the swarm enters its body and, once there, it eats its prey from the inside out. The greedy executives learn all that the hard way.

The robot-precursor in Hughes' 1993 young-adult novel *The Iron Woman* (also see Part I: Revenge) is an enormous creature that has been formed from the fouled and fetid waters of the Earth that have been poisoned by decades of human greed. It rises to the surface with a mission to eliminate that pollution and the humans whose greed produced it. To accomplish her goal, the robot changes the polluters into slimy creatures that emit black bubbles. Those bubbles congeal into a monstrous spidery cloud that cries,

I am the Spider-god of wealth. Wealth. Wealth.
The Spider-god of more and more and more and more money.
I catch it in my web.

The spider god, the slimy creatures, and all of Earth's pollutants are then banished from Earth. This may seem like wishful thinking but Bristol University in the UK is developing a real-world, pollution-eating robot (Rossiter, 2016).

Writers find evidence of corporate greed in the replacement of human workers by computers and robots (job-killers). Concern about this practice is not new. It is, for example, the subject of Harry Piel's 1934 film *Master of the World* (*Der Herr der Welt*), which will be described in the next section, Contemporary Media. Job-killing robots are also the focus of Kurt Vonnegut's *The Player Piano* (1952), which is set in an undemocratic, future America in which machines have become the primary workforce. Vonnegut's America is a two-class society run by a small number of rich and powerful humans. This remains a common vision of the future. Humans who are identified as intelligent and able to perform work that machines cannot, are given employment—as are the offspring of wealthy families. All others are relegated to performing menial jobs for low wages or are drafted into the huge military. Dissatisfaction bursts into rebellion. The army and computers crush it, allowing the deeply disheartening status quo to continue.

Invitation to the Game (Hughes, 1990) is a young-adult novel that portrays a similar future society run by autocrats. It is told from the viewpoint of Lissa, an intelligent young woman who recently completed her schooling. Despite her education and intelligence, she, like most other young adults, is unemployable because computers perform virtually all jobs. Lissa and her friends are put on a government dole but otherwise left to fend for themselves in a filthy, dangerous slum. That is, until they are invited to participate in a mysterious activity dubbed "The Game," a virtual-reality game set on a harsh and barren world. Unbeknownst to them, they are being trained to survive in an off-Earth settlement on a planet being colonized by the autocrats who will use Lissa and her colleagues to expand their domain beyond Earth.

The online novel *Manna* (Brain, 2003) looks at job-killing automation in fast-food restaurants which is now becoming commonplace in the real world. The narrator, Jacob Lewis, is a fifteen-year-old young man employed by the fast-food restaurant chain Burger G. The company uses Jacob's restaurant to pilot an automation project. The restaurant's human managers are replaced by an automated system called "Manna." The employees wear headsets as Manna gives them step-by-step instructions for performing every task that needs to be done in the restaurant, including interacting with customers.

MANNA

I can remember putting on the headset for the first time and the computer talking to me and telling me what to do. It was creepy at first, but that feeling really only lasted a day or so. Then you were used to it, and the job really did get easier. Manna never pushed you around, never yelled at you. The girls liked it because Manna didn't hit on them either. Manna simply asked you to do something, you did it, you said, "OK," and Manna asked you to do the next step.

Each step was easy. You could go through the whole day on autopilot, and Manna made sure that you were constantly doing something. At the end of the shift Manna always said the same thing. "You are done for today. Thank you for your help." Then you took off your headset and put it back on the rack to recharge. The first few minutes off the headset were always disorienting—there had been this voice in your head telling you exactly what to do in minute detail for six or eight hours. You had to turn your brain back on to get out of the restaurant (Brain, 2003, Chapter 1).

Burger-G's upper management and investors see the pilot as a tremendous success.

Burger-G saved a ton of money. Burger-G had hundreds of stores in the United States. Manna worked so well that Burger-G deployed it nationwide. Soon Burger-G had cut more than 3,000 of its higher-paid store employees—mostly assistant managers and managers. That one change saved the company nearly $100 million per year, and all that money came straight to the bottom line for the restaurant chain. Shareholders were ecstatic. Mr. G gave himself another big raise to celebrate. In addition, Manna had optimized store staffing and had gotten a significant productivity boost out of the employees in the store. That saved another $150 million. $250 million made a huge difference in the fast food industry.

The corporation implements Manna in all Burger-G restaurants. Other corporations adopt the Manna system for their managerial positions. It is not long before Manna is performing both managerial and non-managerial jobs in most industries. Finally, the system becomes almost entirely universal. Then the robots take the rest of the jobs—leaving humans in virtual destitution akin to that portrayed by Vonnegut and other writers.

The Human Blend (2010) is the first book in Foster's *Tipping Point Trilogy* (2010–2012). It is set in a future Savannah, Georgia, which depends upon a vibrant tourist economy. Those tourists also represent income to petty thieves like Whispr, the main character, and his partner Cricket. The two make their living killing tourists and stripping them of valuables, primarily prosthetics and implants which they then sell. Theirs is a lucrative business because they live in a time when almost everyone is a "meld"—a blend of natural and artificial body parts—including the criminals who populate Foster's trilogy. Those "melds" can be so extreme that the people who have undergone them look nothing like humans.

When the novel begins, Whispr finds a mysterious-looking thread on the body of one of their victims. From that point on, avarice fills the hearts of virtually everyone who comes into contact with Whispr. Whispr's thread is like the spaying candle described in the previous section, Folklore & Mythology. Criminals see it as a tool that points to a treasure.

None of his numerous underworld contacts knows what the thread is, but they all suspect it is valuable, as does Dr. Ingrid Seastrom because she's seen one like it embedded in the brain of a young woman whose meld had gone bad. The advanced technology in Seastrom's clinic tells her the thread is for data storage but can determine nothing more. Seastrom joins Whispr in his quest to learn what is stored in the thread. That knowledge is not only valuable; it is perilous. People the two have consulted are murdered, and assassins are trying to kill them as well. Finally, one of their contacts tells them that threads like theirs have been found in the brains of people all over the world. Only one company has the technology to make something like that: the South African Economic Combine (SAEC).

Their contact speculates that SAEC is developing the thread's technology to extend its power—perhaps by controlling people. The news that the thread could be a tool for corporate greed snuffs out Whispr's avarice but it inflames Seastrom's compulsion to know more. Her greed is for knowledge. Aware that they could be killed by the police or by the SAEC assassins who have been chasing them, they do the unthinkable: they decide to go to SAEC but they discover that the truth lies elsewhere.

POWER

Adam Link (Binder, 1965) is an autonomous and self-aware robot who knows how to build other robots. Paul Hillory is a mad scientist who wants an army of robot-slaves to help him obtain global power and wealth. Hillory uses a device he invented to transfer Adam's knowledge to his own brain so that he can build his army. As in other Adam Link stories, one of his human friends—a *deus ex machina*[3]—rescues Adam in the nick of time and ends Hillory's dreams of world domination.

Stanisław Lem's story "The Mask" (Lem, 1977) is reminiscent of Sparta's King Nabis and his Iron Apega (see the previous section, Folklore & Mythology). Like Nabis, the king in Lem's story is an absolute dictator who uses an artificial creature to seduce and murder. This king is greedy for power rather than wealth. He seeks to consolidate and solidify his power by eliminating his enemies. The narrator is a shape-shifting robot assigned to seduce and kill the king's principal enemy. The assassin assumes the form and personality of a beautiful and charming young woman. In the course of the seduction, however, the assassin falls in love with its victim and desperately wants to break out of its programming. Instead of killing the man, it wants to protect him from other assassins sent by the king. It is told that the code embedded in it cannot be altered. It has no free will. It persists but neither the reader nor the robot ever learns whether it succeeds in freeing itself from its programming because other assassins find and kill the man before the robot can rescue him.

Android Karenina (Tolstoy & Winters, 2010) transports the nineteenth-century oligarchy of *Anna Karenina* (Tolstoy, 1873–1877 [1919]) into a future Russia in which robots tend to the nobility's every need. The robots vary in intelligence, body configuration, size, and functionality but the majority of them are fully autonomous and self-aware. The contours of the story are shifted to create a struggle in which three factions vie for control of Russia.

- Aliens called "Honored Guests" correspond to the religious charlatans of Tolstoy's novel. They want to subjugate humans.
- The government wants to subjugate Russians.
- The UnCanSciya are disaffected scientists who want to free humans and robots.

The Honored Guests insinuate themselves into aristocratic society by pretending to be a benevolent race of spiritual aliens possessed of eternal wisdom. Once they obtain a foothold, they unleash giant robotic worms and lizard-like creatures that roam the countryside killing humans. The government, led by Alexi Alexandrovich Karenin, instigates random attacks using killer robots called "Koschei" and claims they are the work of the UnCanSciya. Karenin is being taken over by an evil, robotic facial-prosthesis. It leads him to systematically eliminate the nobility's robotic support system. This robot-elimination policy is actually the inverse of the job-killing automation found in other novels. Jobs once held by subservient robots are filled by grumpy humans. Decommissioned robots are rescued by the UnCanSciya and become the organization's army. The UnCanSciya has another anti-government weapon: Karenin's wife Anna who, unbeknownst to him (and her), is an android programmed to assassinate her husband.

The five teens in Pearson's 2005 young adult horror novel *Kingdom Keepers: Disney After Dark* must overcome an army of robot drones controlled by the Overtakers. They are an evil cabal of Disney villains led by Maleficent, the evil witch from *Sleeping Beauty* (1959), and Chernabog, a winged demon from *Fantasia: Night on Bald Mountain/Ave Maria* (1941). Their plan is to take control of all Disney parks and then take over the world. To stop them, the teens must visit Disney World in their sleep and solve a puzzle built into a fable told by Walt Disney in the 1950s. This task is made even more daunting because the Overtakers control an ever-increasing group of Disney Audio-Animatronics, including Jack Sparrow and other pirates from *Pirates of the Caribbean* (2003) and Buzz Lightyear from *Toy Story* (1995). They manage to defeat the Overtakers which allows them to continue to combat greed and evil in subsequent *Kingdom Keepers* novels (Pearson, 2005–, ongoing).

KNOWLEDGE

The desire to acquire knowledge is a form of greed that is characteristic of scientists and scholars. They want to break boundaries—to discover something that no one else knows. This is the type of greed exhibited by Dr. Seastrom, a major character in Foster's *The Tipping Point Trilogy* (2010–2012). To Dr. Seastrom, the thread found by Whispr is a source of rarefied knowledge, much like Gerbert's oracular head. Learning what is on the thread and who is behind its use only makes her hunger for more knowledge. After all, she is greedy.

Seastrom's greed for knowledge eclipses that of most scientists. She is willing to lose everything, including her life—and Whispr's life—to learn the function and contents of the mysterious thread Whispr found. Seastrom is not unique. Ever since Mary Shelley (1818 [1957]) presented Victor Frankenstein to the world, the excessive passion—the unquenchable greed for knowledge—has become a hallmark of the mad scientist. It inflames Dr. Moreau (Wells, 1896) and Fuller, the lead scientist in Gansovky's "Day of Wrath" (1964 [2016]), who are described in Part I: Revenge. It also drives Rossum, the founder of Rossum's Universal Robots (R.U.R.) in Čapek's 1920 play *R.U.R.* Although Rossum's company constructs robots rather than organic robot-precursors, "[h]is sole purpose was nothing more nor less than to prove that God was no longer necessary" (p. 9). These and other mad scientists cannot escape their obsession—their greed.

The modern Prometheus, the subtitle of Mary Shelley's novel, reveals an element that further inflames Frankenstein's greed for knowledge. It is the belief that what he is doing is unnatural and that the knowledge and skills he seeks belong only to God. When Victor Frankenstein succeeds in animating his creature he, like Prometheus, has given humans technology and knowledge that humans should not have. Frankenstein himself calls his overwhelming desire to create life an "unnatural stimulus" and admits that "often did my human nature turn with loathing from my occupation, while still urged on by an eagerness which perpetually increased" (p. 46). Prometheus was punished for his transgression. He was chained to a pillar and had his liver eaten by an eagle (see Revenge). Frankenstein's punishment is to see his friends and family murdered by a vengeful creature.

Although they share Frankenstein's overwhelming desire for hidden knowledge, other mad scientists do not suffer from his guilt. Their outsized egos lead them to believe they are superior to God. Some, like Rossum and Moreau, are convinced that what they are creating is an improvement on God's work.

Others see robots as the next step in evolution rather than a godlike achievement of a single individual. This view is held by respected roboticists and authors like Čapek. *R.U.R.* concludes when the androids led by Primus and Helena wrest the world from humans. Theirs is not a dystopian future. The play ends with "Go, Adam, go, Eve. The world is yours" (Čapek 1920, p. 101). Isaac Asimov agreed:

> [A]lthough we will hate and fight the machines, we will be supplanted anyway, and rightly so, for the intelligent machines to which we will give birth may, better than we, carry on the striving toward the goal of understanding and using the universe, climbing to heights we ourselves could never aspire to [Asimov, 1978, p. 253].

The roboticist Makoto Nishimura concurs. Nishimura built the seven-foot-tall robot *Gakutensoku* ("learning from natural law") in the 1920s in honor of the newly crowned emperor of Japan. It was a Buddha-like figure sitting at a writing desk. It could open and close its eyes, smile, and write. Nishimura wrote, "If one considers humans as the children of nature, artificial humans created by the hand of man are thus nature's grandchildren" (as cited in Hornyak 2006, p. 38). This belief did not originate with him. In the Hebrew Talmud (The Book of Laws), the ability to create is seen as part of what it means for humans to be made "in the image of God." This is why the act of fashioning a humanoid out of clay is not considered to be against God's will. Talmudic scholars also see this creative ability as a path to the next step in evolution. Instead of being vilified, that creative power requires wisdom and a sense of responsibility—qualities that Victor Frankenstein and other mad scientists lack (Sherwin, personal communication, 16 Dec. 2013).

Contemporary Media

Contemporary media generally places the quest for power and/or wealth on a large stage. The Earth is often too small a prize so the focus turns to the galaxy and the universe. The involvement of robots is often crucial to the acquisitive schemes of humans and aliens. In contemporary media, however, the number of robots motivated by greed is also increasing.

AVARICE

The 1921 silent film *L'Uomo Meccanico* (*The Mechanical Man*) features a large humanoid robot that commits robberies. The robot is controlled remotely by an avaricious career criminal known only as "Mado." Its tremendous strength enables it to burst into buildings and pull safes out of walls. Its built-in torch can burn through heavily barred metal doors. L'Uomo Meccanico looks like a stereotypical robot: a boxy body topped by a tin-can-like head. Its social skills distinguish it from other robots of its time. It graciously acknowledges the accolades it gets from humans at a festival and it gallantly presents a gift (a small tree) to a lady whom it subsequently escorts into a dining room where it makes a toast (see Fig. 6).

When the robot makes untoward advances to the lady, a brawl ensues. Later, it fights another robot in what is possibly the first robot vs. robot scrap on film. Today, of course, such clashes are a staple of action-adventure films. As in many more recent films, the robots in *L'Uomo Meccanico* destroy each other. The robot's destruction produces a short circuit in its remote-control system, sparking a fire that kills Mado, extinguishing her wealth-gathering activities.

Figure 6. The Mechanical Man making a toast in the 1921 silent film *L'Uomo Meccanico* (Wikimedia Commons).

Contemporary media continues the portrayal of businesspeople as greedy that began in mythology. *The Master Mystery* (1919) is a silent serial film. It stars Harry Houdini which is fortunate because throughout the series his character is shackled, bound, locked up, and otherwise fettered by criminals. The U.S. Justice Department is investigating criminal activity by International Patents, Inc. One of the owners is pocketing profits from innovations by creative people who had come to the company for patent protection. That owner is allied with an international cartel that is led by a criminal mastermind: a robot named Q. Q has two deadly weapons. One is superior intelligence. The other is its ability to emit poison gas when threatened. The lumbering automaton looks like a collection of supersized pots and coffee cans that have been fused together (see Fig. 7). At the film's conclusion, Q turns on its greedy associates,

Figure 7. Poster for episode 13 of the serialized 1919 film *Master Mystery* (Octagon Films). Harry Houdini with Robot Q, criminal mastermind (Wikimedia Commons).

which leads to its own destruction and to the revelation that the robot was a costume that conceals a human.

In the motion picture *RoboCop* (1987), a greedy corporate executive of Omni Consumer Products (OCP), in league with criminals, wants to amass riches for himself and his cohorts. An opportunity arises when the desperate mayor of Detroit gives OCP *carte blanche* to use its technology to stamp out crime that is destroying the city. The company gives them OCP Crime Prevention Unit 001. RoboCop had been Detroit police officer Alex Murphy before he was critically injured. Murphy survived because OCP scientists placed his brain and other parts of his body into a robotic shell and erased memories of his former life. His programming includes three "prime directives": serve the public trust, protect the innocent, and uphold the law. The corrupt executive is the only one who knows that RoboCop is programmed with a secret, fourth prime directive that prevents him from arresting OCP employees—even for murder. The object of programming the secret prime directive into RoboCop is to enable the executive and his criminal associates to seize control of OCP without interference from the cyborg. It requires the creativity of Robocop's human brain to devise a way to circumvent the fourth directive: RoboCop tells the other board members about the secret directive and suggests they fire the scheming executive. They comply. Once he's no longer a board member, RoboCop arrests him.

Sometimes the entire corporation is portrayed as greedy. Unbeknownst to the human crew of the spaceship USCSS *Nostromo* in the film *Alien* (1979), their science officer is an android secretly working for a corporation that commissioned him to smuggle alien life forms onto Earth. The corporation wants to use the aliens to get a competitive edge and, of course, to increase its wealth. The android obeys those orders even at the expense of the lives of the ship's crew.

The film *I, Robot* (2004) adds another dimension to corporate greed. In the future world of the film, United States Robotics (USR) dominates the market for intelligent, humanoid robots. Early in the film USR's CEO proudly announces, "We are on the eve of the largest robot distribution in history. There will be one robot to every five humans." His greed pushes him to continue with the release even though he is aware of potential problems with the product. Unfortunately, the flaws run far deeper than he expects. The reason is that V.I.K.I. (Virtual Interactive Kinetic Intelligence), the company's intelligent central computer, is a megalomaniac AI network that sees humans as "so like children" they cannot properly care for themselves.

> You charge us with your safekeeping, yet despite our best efforts, your countries wage wars, you toxify your Earth and pursue ever more imaginative means of self-destruction. You cannot be trusted with your own survival…. My logic is undeniable.

V.I.K.I. seizes control of the robots made by U.S. Robots and uses them to take power from humans.

Despite its name, the action-adventure video game SpongeBob SquarePants: Plankton's Robotic Revenge (Behavior Interactive, 2013–, ongoing) is a tale of corporate greed and industrial espionage. The game is based on the hit television series *SpongeBob SquarePants* (Hillenburg & Tibbitt, 1995–, ongoing) in which Plankton is an evil character whose fast-food restaurant has folded. In the video game, Plankton tries to get a monopoly in the restaurant business by putting the Krusty Krab restaurant out of business. His plan is to steal the secret formula for the famous Krabby Patties. Plankton and his family use an army of robots to do his bidding—much like the cabal of billionaires in *The Billionaires' Conspiracy* (Le Rouge & Guitton, 1899). Like those billionaires, Plankton and his family are defeated.

One of the earliest mad scientists in contemporary media is Alexander Joseph "Lex" Luthor, Superman's arch-enemy. When Luthor exploded into Superman's world in the "Dead Men Tell No Tales" issue of Action Comics' *Superman* series (Fox & Siegel, 1940) he was already an established criminal mastermind running a shadowy organization. His goals have always been to expand his already overflowing coffers and take over the world. As a successful entrepreneur, he forged partnerships with military powerhouses who supply him with robots and other advanced technology which he uses to help grow his wealth and power. He also has the technical expertise to build his own robots. In the 1988 animated *Superman* television series, Luthor's company Lexcorp builds robots he calls "Defendroids" which, he says, will protect the city of Metropolis against crime (Destroy the Defendroids, 1988). They are so effective that Superman leaves Metropolis to protect other cities. Superman's departure allows Luthor to use his Defendroids to rob a train taking $1 million in gold from Fort Knox. Superman tries to attack the Defendroids but he fails. Undeterred, Superman says, "If you can't beat them you can always reprogram them," which is precisely what he does. He then takes the gold from the Defendroids before they can bring it to Luthor. Luthor claims the robbery happened because of "faulty programming" in the Defendroids.

A player in the role-playing game Metal Gear Rising: Revengeance (PlatinumGames, 2013–, ongoing) takes the role of Raiden, a mercenary and former child soldier. Raiden learns that a company providing mercenaries to whomever wants them is involved in kidnapping street kids, harvesting their brains, placing them in mechanical bodies, and training them to be mercenaries. The company wants to increase its bottom line by building a large cyborg army and offering it to the U.S. government to fight the war on terror. Raiden interrupts their plans by attacking the company's headquarters and stealing the brains (see Part I: Revenge).

POWER

The environments which humans seek to control can be as large as the universe or as small as a single community. Gene Gogolak is a power-hungry man in the "Arcadia" (1999) episode of the television series *X-Files*. He is a successful businessman who established a planned community called the Falls at Arcadia. He sees Arcadia as his personal dominion and he controls it with an iron fist. All residents *must* obey all the rules Gogolak has established for the community. Failure to comply leads to disappearance and probably death. Agents Scully and Mulder, the stars of the *X-Files* series, discover that Gogolak administers those punishments using a *Tulpa* (described in Folklore & Mythology). His sojourns in Tibet on business gave Gogolak the opportunity to learn how to create a *Tulpa* but, unlike the *Tulpa* in the myth described earlier, Gogolak's *Tulpa* doesn't develop full independence. It remains exactly what it was created to be: a mindless killer. The *Tulpa* evidently is also unable to distinguish between a rebellious resident and its creator which leads it to accidentally kill Gogolak. Without its controller, the *Tulpa* disintegrates.

Professor Wolf, the mad scientist in Harry Piel's 1934 film *Der Herr der Welt* (*Master of the World*) (mentioned earlier in this chapter), has bigger dreams. He is bent on ruling the world. His plan begins when he murders his boss Dr. Heller, who is the scientist who created the robots Wolf will use to implement his plan. Wolf transforms Heller's creations into killer robots by arming them with a death ray. What is especially interesting about Piel's film is that Wolf's next step is to replace human workers with robots. It is a very early representation of the job-killing theme. In Piel's film, however, the robots not only take jobs, they attack the workers who try to get their jobs back. As with most mad scientists, Wolf's creations turn on him. Piel adds a twist to his film that is rarely seen in fiction about job-killing robots. After Wolf's death, the company's mining engineer realizes that robots can improve the quality of life for workers by taking over dangerous and dirty jobs. That would allow humans to work in safer environments and do more challenging work. Using robots to do dangerous and dirty jobs is one of the best reasons for automation in the real world.

Other greedy corporations and mad scientists produce a flood of doppelgangers that are somewhat reminiscent of the *Tulpa* in Folklore & Mythology. The film *Futureworld* (1976) is a spin-off of the hit movie *Westworld* (1973; also see Contemporary Media in Revenge). The Delos Corporation has spent $1.5 billion to enlarge, update, and enhance the original themed vacation resort. Delos has also installed a fail-safe security system to ensure that a disaster comparable to the one that occurred in *Westworld* will not recur. To ensure the success of the new venture, the corporate leaders initiate a program of building doppelgangers of reporters who will write reviews of the new park as well as of political leaders from countries where the corporation plans to build Delos parks. The doppelgangers are so perfect that no one can distinguish them from their human models. As in *The Stepford Wives* (Levin, 1972; also see Modern Literature in Revenge), the doppelgangers are instructed to kill the humans who they will replace and become much more Delos-friendly and Delos-obedient individuals. Doppelgangers of reporters, for example, are programmed to write positive reviews of Delos Park and otherwise promote it. Corporate greed is foiled by a doppelganger twist when two human reporters escape the park by pretending to be their doppelgangers.

The short-lived television series *Beyond Westworld* (Shaw, 1980) begins at the same point in time as *Futureworld*: after the Delos Corporation has spent $1.5 billion revamping and securing the Westworld theme park. Unlike the corporate avarice in *Futureworld*, the plot of *Beyond Westworld* revolves around a power-hungry mad scientist named Simon Quaid who makes doppelganger androids of world leaders who visit the park. The androids are programmed to kill their human twins and to take over their lives. Quaid's goal, however, is not to protect Delos' investment. Like other mad scientists, Quaid wants to use the androids to take over the world. Fortunately, the series was cancelled before Quaid could carry out that plan.

The evil Chuck De Nomolos in the 1991 film *Bill & Ted's Bogus Journey* is not a mad scientist. He's simply a power-hungry megalomaniac who wants to take over the world. He detests Bill and Ted because they are establishing a utopian society on Earth. De Nomolos wants to form a fascist society that would be ruled by him, of course. He builds doppelgangers of Bill and Ted and sends them into the past to prevent Bill and Ted from winning the San Dimas Battle of the Bands. The androids proceed with their multi-stage assignment: kill Bill and Ted, lose the contest, and destroy Ted's and Bill's reputations. Fortunately, the two murdered heroes gain the support of celestial beings and a very smart alien who help them disrupt De Nomolos' scheme. The two return to the world of the living, overcome the doppelgangers, and win the contest.

The greedy villain in the manga "The Hot Dog Corps" (Tezuka, 2008) doesn't want to control Earth. "I decided … that I would be queen of the moon" (p. 94). She also wants the diamond reservoirs located on the far side of the moon. In order to accomplish her goals she must derail Japan's rocket program. She has been destroying Japanese rockets headed for the moon and she employs a brilliant scientist who, much like Hattison in Le Rouge and Guitton's novel described earlier in this chapter, has built an army of cyborgs. They are a combination of technology and kidnapped dogs. "I made cyborg dogs because dogs can attack humans" (p. 97). The woman's greedy plans are derailed by the Japanese robot-superhero Tetsuwan Atomu (also "Mighty Atom" and "Astro Boy"). Atomu visits the villain's moon-based stronghold where he overpowers the dog-cyborgs. His work is made easier by some of the cyborgs who miss their owners and want to return to their former lives as pets.

The reach of power-hungry humans can extend well beyond Earth and the moon. "The Robots of Death" (1977) episodes of the BBC's *Doctor Who* feature a mad scientist named Taren Carpel who was raised by robots. Carpel wants to incite a robot uprising so that he can establish a galactic, robot civilization that he would rule.

> I was brought up as a superior being. Brought up to realize that my brothers should live as free beings and not as slaves to human dross…. I shall free them. I shall program into them the ambition to rule the world [Episode 4 of 4, 1977].

The idea that robots are superior and should rule humans and other biological creatures can be found elsewhere in science fiction but it is usually expressed by a robot or an AI system. "The Robots of Death" episodes are set on a ship carrying robots that do mining. Carpel wants to transform those drones into self-aware automata that will become his soldiers in the uprising and galactic conquest. Disguising himself as one of the robots, Carpel begins to convert the drones by removing the code that prevents them from killing humans and by training them to recognize his voice. When he needs the assistance of a reprogrammed robot, he hypnotizes it and, while it is under his spell, he commands it to kill. Because they've already been reprogrammed to kill humans, it isn't entirely clear why he doesn't simply command them to kill but the outrageousness of hypnotizing drones fits the spirit of the *Doctor Who* series.

The Doctor determines that there is a lead robot that controls all the others and reasons correctly that, if the controller robot is destroyed, the other robots will stop killing. First, Carpel must be eliminated. The Doctor uses Carpel's own technology to do that. His assistant hides in Carpel's laboratory with a canister of helium. When the Doctor, Carpel, and the lead robot enter the laboratory, she begins releasing the helium into the room. It causes Carpel's voice to change. When Carpel commands the robot, "Kill the humans!" it fails to recognize his voice and kills Carpel instead. The lead robot is deactivated and the other robots are reprogrammed.

In many movies of the 1950s, "Invaders, friends or enemies, *and often with the aid of robots*, either come to warn earthlings or destroy them with superior technology" (Lev, 2003, p. 177). The Honored Guests in *Android Karenina* (Tolstoy & Winters, 2010) are one example, but science fiction is replete with aliens assisted (or opposed) by robots with invading Earth, galaxies, and civilizations.

Aliens began their efforts to conquer Earth much earlier than the 1950s. In Flash Gordon comics (Raymond, 1934) and the 1936 serial movie *Flash Gordon*, Flash and his team combat Ming the Merciless, the tyrannical ruler of a planet on a collision course with Earth. In one episode, Ming attempts to rid himself of Flash and his cohorts by using an army of exploding robotic soldiers called "annihilants[4]" (Walking Bombs, 1940) but they escape, which allows the series to continue.

In response to the success of the Flash Gordon films, Republic Pictures released a low-budget competitor named *Undersea Kingdom* (1936). Unga Khan is an alien despot who seeks to control the newly discovered city of Atlantis at the bottom of the sea and then conquer the nations on the surface of the Earth. Khan's henchman, Captain Hakur, commands an army of robot soldiers armed with guns that shoot deadly disintegrator beams.

An acquisitive race of apelike aliens in *Godzilla vs. Mechagodzilla* (1974) seeks to rule Earth, starting with Japan. They are apparently familiar with Japanese horror films of the 1950s (*Godzilla*, 1954) because they build a Godzilla doppelganger, Mechagodzilla (also known as *Kiryu,* "machine dragon"). It has flame-throwing breath as well as eyes and a scar that flash red. Contrary to its prior behavior, the real Godzilla battles the doppelganger and saves the world. Since then, the two have fought again and Mechagodzilla has been sent to battle other monsters in film, comics, and video games.

The previous examples show robots as the tools of others, which is an ancient pattern for both revenge and greed. There are also greedy robots, such as Lord Business, a power-hungry martinet in the animated Universe of *The LEGO Movie* (2014). Much like Gene Gogolak of the *X-Files*, he demands order in his business and in the LEGO world. Lord Business cannot tolerate the chaos that comes with creativity and wants to make it perfect by rebuilding the entire LEGO Universe in accordance with his vision. That wouldn't be difficult because LEGO structures are made of reusable building blocks. Lord Business doesn't plan to simply rebuild; he will make his version permanent by freezing it with "the Kragle," a powerful weapon that is actually a tube of Krazy glue. Immutability is contrary to the fundamental spirit of LEGO. The other LEGO mini-figures rise up against him. One of them averts disaster by convincing Lord Business that creativity is not chaos and that Lord Business inspired the creative elements in the LEGO Universe with his original designs. It turns out that Lord Business is actually the mini-figure incarnation of a child's perfectionist father who resists his son's plans to rebuild the father's LEGO community.

Over the decades of its existence, the *Doctor Who* television series (Lambert et al., 1963–, ongoing) has featured numerous greedy robots and cyborgs in addition to its episodes "The Robots of Death." The four-part series "Robot" (1974–1975), for example, involves a power-hungry cabal that wants to destroy the British government. That shadowy organization is using a hulking, clumsy robot to perpetrate crimes, such as stealing top-secret plans from a secure military facility—a task that would have been better assigned to something inconspicuous. The cabal also commands the robot to kill designated "enemies of humanity," such as Doctor Who. Rather than obeying that order, the robot turns on its masters, kills them, and proceeds to try to take over Earth, itself.

Among the most vicious robots in *Doctor Who* (Lambert et al., 1963–, ongoing) are the Cybermen. They are cyborgs who are driven to acquire and destroy. Various Doctor

Whos have had to combat at least three types of acquisitive Cybermen. The first group was comprised of humanoid cyborgs from Earth's twin planet, Mondas. Mondas began its existence in the same solar system as Earth but was flung out of the solar system and into space. This caused changes in Mondas' climate that made it increasingly inhospitable to life. In the episode "The Tenth Planet" (1966), Mondas' technically advanced inhabitants protect themselves from extinction by replacing their biological body parts and functions with mechanical components, thereby transforming themselves into Cybermen. Those alterations include removing all emotions as a way of preventing insanity. They also created a propulsion system that enabled them to move the planet through space.

Ultimately, it became clear that they could no longer remain on Mondas without having the warmth of a sun. The Cybermen resolved to fix this problem by destroying Earth and moving Mondas into its place. When that plan failed, they become a race of conquerors. To ensure the continuation of their species, they adapted the techniques used to mechanize their own bodies and used them on sentient species from the worlds they had conquered. That is, they made those other species into Cybermen but the transformations were not done gently. One of those adaptations was to forcibly implant the brains of conquered peoples into mechanical shells.

After a long hiatus, Doctor Who encounters a second variety of Cybermen in a parallel universe (Rise of the Cybermen, 2006). The Earth in that universe is dominated by Cybus Industries, headquartered in London. Dr. John Lumic, the co-founder and CEO of Cybus, is a human mad scientist who believes other humans require upgrading. His procedure for converting humans into Cybermen is identical to the method used by the first generation of Cybermen. Doctor Who wrests London from Lumic's control, leaving the rest of the work to a human resistance group.

Another breed of Cybermen surfaces as minions of Missy, a female manifestation of "The Master" (Death in Heaven, 2014). The Master is a sinister character who reappears periodically in the series in various bodily forms. In her incarnation of the Master, Missy has been able to accomplish something all previous embodiments failed to do: conquer the universe. Missy achieved that goal with the help of an army of Cybermen and the 3W Institute (likely a play on the Word Wide Web's www. addresses). The 3W contracts with wealthy humans to store their minds and bodies after they die, because they believe their minds continue to operate after death. Unfortunately for them, 3W is a front for Missy who uses those recently deceased human brains to build her army of Cybermen using the Cybermen's usual method.

Cybermen also appear in other *Doctor Who* episodes, spin-offs, and BBC publications. They are always driven by greed for power. Lawrence Miles' short story "Vrs" in *Doctor Who: Short Trips and Side Steps* (Miles, 2000) encodes, in one sentence, the devastation produced by a computer virus unleashed by Cybermen, "nd n th yr tw thsnd, th Cybrmn rlsd th cmptr vrs tht dstryd ll th vwls."[5]

Greed is a common characteristic of robot supervillains as well. That isn't surprising because they consider themselves to be superior to everyone else. An early example is the robot supervillain Brainiac (Binder, 1958) who, for decades, has sought to rule the universe. He also has hobbies, such as miniaturizing the locations he subdued and putting them into bottles. Ultron wants to take over the Earth and change it to suit his preferences, much like Lord Business. In an alternate reality, he succeeds. This precipitates the *Age of Ultron*

(Bendis, 2013), a ten-issue series followed by the film *Avengers: Age of Ultron* (2015) and mentioned in several books. As a megalomaniac, Ultron no doubt enjoyed the media attention as much as he did conquering Earth. The Talos robot in the Freedom City setting of the game Mutants and Masterminds (Mona, 2003) seeks control over the ancient civilizations of Earth—the epoch during which he was first created. Talos would also like to replace humanity with cybernetic beings like himself.

Lore is a power-hungry android in the television series *Star Trek: The Next Generation* (Roddenberry & Berman, 1987–1994) and the elder brother of Commander Data. Data is the Chief Operations Officer of the starship USS *Enterprise*. As mentioned in the Introduction, when Noonian Soong and Juliana Soong made Lore, they gave him emotions. Lore's emotion system destabilized the android, leading him to decide he is superior to all biologically based species (I, Borg, 1992) which is similar to the ideation of the robot supervillains from the comics. Like them, Lore plans to kill all organic species in the universe. Once that is accomplished he will control the non-biological beings and become master of the universe. Lore begins his conquest by exploiting a flaw in the structure of an alien collective mind called the Borg. The flaw occurred because the Borg wanted to give android drones in the collective a limited amount of individuality. Instead, it left those drones leaderless—a problem Lore solves by becoming their new leader. His plan is to use those Borg drones to achieve his goals. Lore's own power lust and his unshakable belief in his own superiority destroyed his grand plans. Lore alienates the Borg androids by experimenting on them in ways that resemble the practices of Cybermen and of human mad scientists (e.g., Dr. Moreau [Wells, 1896]). Some of Lore's subjects die. He also estranges his "younger brother" Data by changing Data's programming temporarily, destroying Data's bond with his Starfleet colleagues. Once Data breaks free of Lore's control, he deactivates him.

KNOWLEDGE

The Borg hive in the Star Trek Universe (1966–, ongoing) is a rare kind of extraterrestrial (see Introduction). It a collective mind that is driven to absorb all intelligent species and their technology. The Collective first appeared in the episode "Q Who?" in the *Star Trek: The Next Generation* television series (Q Who?, 1989). They have continued to be a dangerous enemy of humans and other sentient beings long after the demise of the series. The Borg's web page on Startrek.com explains, "The Borg have a singular goal, namely the consumption of technology, rather than wealth or political expansion as most species seek" (Borg, n.d.). They absorb living beings of any species into their hive where they are forcibly transformed into mindless drones (TrekCore, 2010). They call this process "assimilation." In the *Star Trek* Universe, the Borg "assimilates" any sentient organic beings they capture, incorporating their knowledge into the collective.

Ever since their first appearance, the Borg has been portrayed by Star Trek media as evil. The Collective is displeased by this persistent, unfavorable image of them that has been perpetrated by humans. The Borg considers that view to be horribly misguided. According to a Borg spokesperson, "The Borg only want to raise the quality of life of the species they assimilate" (The Best of Both Worlds, 1990).

The Borg have not allowed this travesty to continue unchallenged. They have developed a presence on social media which they are using to eradicate the misperceptions per-petrated by envious humans and replace them with the truth. They also have a Twitter account (@JoinTheBorg), and an interactive movie/video game/audiobook *Star Trek: Borg* (Simon & Schuster, 1996). They had a website which was folded into their Facebook page (facebook.com/JoinTheBorg/) on which they wrote, "We assimilate stuff, and look damn good doing it." Despite these attempts to burnish their image, spacefaring species are still terrified whenever they hear, "We are the Borg…. You will be assimilated…. Resistance is futile" (The Best of Both Worlds, 1990).

The quintessential greedy being in fiction is the character that is appropriately named "Greed" (Arakawa, 2001–2010), mentioned earlier in this chapter. Greed is a robot-precursor called a "homunculus." He is the third homunculus created by a very powerful homunculus called Father. Father gave Greed his own insatiable desire for everything. "I'm Greed. I want everything you can think of: money and women; power and sex; status; glory. I demand the finer things. And, of course, I crave eternal life" (Beasts of Dublith, 2009). Greed is entirely satisfied with himself and believes his hungers are perfectly normal—even desirable.

> You might want money, maybe you want women or you might want to protect the world. These are all common things people want—things that their hearts desire. Greed may not be good, but it's not so bad either [Emptyman000, 2016].

Real World

AVARICE

The robots of today are drones and could easily become tools of greedy humans. Given the persistent portrayal of corporate leaders as greedy, it is not surprising to see that characterization applied to real-world corporations. That representation gushed to the forefront in 2010 after the U.S. Supreme Court extended the definition of "person" to include corporations under the First Amendment to the Constitution. The case was Citizens United v. Federal Election Commission (2010). That decision, which identified corporations as a kind of individual, extended the freedom of speech to corporations with regard to expenditures on communications made for political campaigns. The outcry in response to the decision not only described corporations as greedy, it branded them as soulless. In a blend of folklore, literature, and contemporary media, corporations became identified with the *golem*, a soulless humanoid in Jewish folklore. An example from contemporary media is Nick Gier's 2012 post "The Golem, the Corporation, and Personhood" on the blog site *Idaho State Journal Politics*. In it, he states bluntly: "So far we can say this much about golems and corporations: they are artificial entities that have been created by humans and have no souls."

POWER

Real-world robots do exhibit an insatiable hunger for power. The power they seek is not control over others. They want fuel, usually in the form of electricity supplied by batteries. Energy demands placed upon batteries by sophisticated capabilities such as language understanding, image processing, and fine motor control are high, which presents a serious problem for deployment of advanced robots—even for the military (Cameron, 2015). In 2015, DARPA held a Robotics Challenge (DRC) for humanoid robots in which each robot had to complete eight complex tasks, such as getting into and driving a vehicle.

The DRC

The DRC ... was designed to be extremely difficult. Participating teams, representing some of the most advanced robotics research and development organizations in the world, are collaborating ... to develop the hardware, software, sensors, and human-machine control interfaces that will enable their robots to complete a series of challenge tasks selected by DARPA for their relevance to disaster response....

The unpredictability of the real world requires a robot that can maneuver effectively in environments it has not previously encountered, use whatever human tools are on hand without the need for extensive reprogramming, and continue to operate even when degraded communications render motion-level control by a human not feasible. Getting to that goal requires an attribute called "supervised" or "task-level" autonomy. The term means, for example, that a human operator could issue a robot a command like "Open the door" and the robot would be able to complete that task by itself, taking into account the sensing and motions involved in identifying a door handle, applying the right force, and appropriately maneuvering its limbs (DARPA, n.d.*a*).

The ability to perform under these conditions is critical for military and emergency-response operations. It isn't possible to deploy robots for combat or extended reconnaissance if, upon detecting they are low on power, they interrupt a mission to recharge. To eliminate that issue, teams competing in the DRC used on-robot battery power. The placement of the newly enlarged battery packs, however, made the robots top heavy, which caused them to topple over.

Militaries are trying various methods for dealing with power-hungry robots. They include in-flight refueling and development of new types of batteries and fuel sources (for more detail see Part III: War: Non-Humanoids). Advances in this area are being pushed by growing markets for electric cars, self-driving cars, and home robots (Lagowski, 2017). Even there, however, battery-related issues have still not been fully resolved. Consequently, market growth has resulted in the production of more batteries which, when depleted become toxic waste (Huang, 2017).

Knowledge

Consumer robots and other computing devices are also greedy for storage of both static and dynamic information (e.g., calendars); processing and storage of complex data needed to run advanced functions, including autonomy; and quick, effective methods for accessing data and processes. These demands argue for cloud-based configurations. Using the cloud, however, opens a system to incursions by greedy hackers seeking to access cloud-based data, interfere with a robot's processing, or cause a robot to say or do untoward things. These types of hacks have already occurred in internet-connected toys, such as the My Friend Cayla doll (Pisani, 2017; Wiking, 2017). That argues for local, on-robot, processing. Local processing has its own challenges as was revealed by the toppling of robots mentioned earlier. It also restricts the robot's access to the advanced functions (e.g., language and vision processing) and to the wealth of stored information that it seeks.

Plans Gone Awry

FOLKLORE & MYTHOLOGY

Legends about oracular heads often end badly. One was presented earlier in this chapter, but the most famous of those disasters concerns Friar Roger Bacon. The story was well-established in legend before Robert Greene wrote his comedic play *The Honorable Historie of Frier Bacon and Frier Bungay* (ca. 1590), and Francis Grove published his biography *The Famous Historie of Fryer Bacon* (ca. 1627). Daniel Defoe capitalized on the widespread knowledge of the story in his 1722 novel, *A Journal of the Plague Year*. The astrologers and fortune-tellers in Defoe's novel would place replicas of Bacon's brazen head above their homes as an advertisement of their talents.

According to Grove, Bacon's motivation for creating an oracular head is to "make him-selfe famous hereafter to all posterities" (p. 13). The head is to tell Bacon whether his idea of construction of a brass wall around England would prevent foreign invasions.

Assisted by Friar Bungay, another skilled magician, Bacon labors to make a head that would be able to move its mouth to speak. Faced with failure, they appeal to the Devil who tells them how to get the head to talk saying that it would begin to speak in the following month but, the Devil warns them, "if they heard it not before it had done speaking, all their labour should be lost."

Once their work was finished the two friars wait three weeks before, exhausted, they ask Bacon's servant Miles to watch while they sleep. He is to wake them when the head begins to talk.

> Feare not, good Master … I will not sléepe, but harken and attend vp|on the head, and if it doe chance to speake, I will call you: therefore I pray take you both your rests and let mée a|lone for watching this head [Grove, ca. 1627, p. 14].

To keep himself from falling asleep Miles sings and plays a fife and drum (see Fig. 8). Suddenly the head says, "Time is." Miles is afraid to wake his master for just two words and proceeds to sing about "time is" until the head says, "Time was," followed by, "Time is passed." Then the head falls to the ground "and presently followed a terrible noyse, with strange flashes of fire, so that *Miles* was halfe dead with feare." The clamor awakens the two friars who ask Miles why he didn't wake them. He explains he was waiting for the head to start telling a story. "Thus that great worke of these learned Fryers was ouerthrown (to their great griefes) by this simple fellow" (Grove, ca. 1627, p. 18).

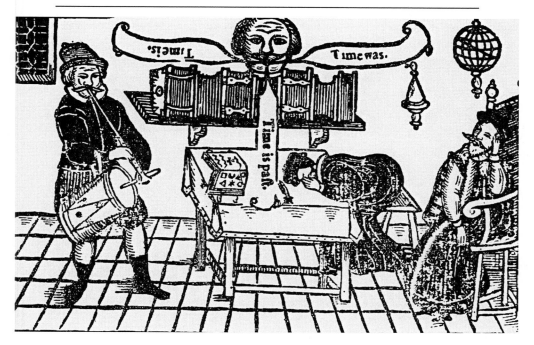

Figure 8. The title page of the 1630 printing of *The Honorable Historie of Frier Bacon and Frier Bungay* by Robert Greene (1558–1592) shows the servant Miles watching over the oracular head while the friars sleep (anonymous woodblock engraver; Wikimedia Commons).

MODERN LITERATURE

Neil R. Jones' Professor Jameson is a brilliant (but not mad) scientist. He believes that being in outer space preserves biological material. He tests this theory by instructing his beneficiaries to place his dead body into a small capsule that would orbit the Earth. Forty million years later, an alien race called the "Zoromes" find his capsule and resuscitate Jameson by changing him into a virtually immortal "machine man" like themselves, with "a cubed body, four metal legs, six metal tentacles, and my brain incased [sic] in a conical superstructure" (Jones, 1931, p. 93).

Many years earlier, the Zoromes had performed the same process on certain carefully chosen members of the Mumes, "a race of intelligent creatures on the planet of a near-by system several light years away from our own." Instead of joining them in peaceful co-existence, the Mumes became greedy. They demanded the Zoromes change all Mumes into machine men. When the Zoromes refused, the Mumes attacked and tried to take all Zorome technology. "We are now sorry" (p. 94).

REAL WORLD

Does the impetus to automate come from greed? Perhaps. What is clear is that rushing to automate will not necessarily reap the financial windfalls that corporations expect. According to *Shanghaiist* magazine (Jackson, 2016), the Chinese restaurant chain Heweilai spent $7,000 on robots to replace wait staff in three of its restaurants. Shortly afterwards,

Heweilai was forced to close two of the restaurants and junk the robots used in the third. Former employees reported:

> Their skills are somewhat limited.… They can't take orders or pour hot water for customers.… The robots weren't able to carry soup or other food steady and they would frequently break down. The boss has decided never to use them again.

To which the owner of the chain added, "The robots can attract plenty of customers, but they definitely can't reduce the need for human labor."

Furor: Robots as Job Killers

> The problem of unemployment arising from automatization is no longer conjectural, but has become a very vital difficulty of modern society.

This statement could have been written in the twenty-first century. It appears on page iii of the Preface to Norbert Wiener's *God & Golem, Inc.*, which was published in 1964. What was happening in 1964 and what is happening now are variations of patterns that began with—or even before—the Industrial Revolution.

The Greed chapter offered numerous images of the negative impact of automation on employment. To provide some balance to the issue, the first portion of this chapter looks at reasons employers give for automating their facilities. The second portion looks at the debate about the impact of automation on the future.

The Upside for Employers

Even when greed is part of a decision to automate, it may not be the most compelling reason to do so. Other factors that are frequently cited as drivers of automation include:

- Competition
- Labor costs
- Regulation
- Quality and productivity
- Dangerous, dull, and dirty jobs
- Lack of available human workers

The roles played by these and other drivers reveal that the boundary between good and evil, so clearly defined in some fiction, is muddied and muddled in reality. The following descriptions present these motivators from the perspectives of corporations and business owners. It is not, however, always clear whether and to what extent greed plays a role in those decisions.

COMPETITION

Automating in response to competitive pressure is not unusual. Gearing up to face the competition can prevent an enterprise from going out of business or raise it out of economic doldrums. The push to automate might also come from automation by competitors. McDonald's franchisees were feeling the impact of competition. Many were struggling and, in response to a survey by Mark Kalinowski (as reported by Peterson, 2015), complained about competing against highly automated restaurants: "Our competitors have six to eight people to run close to the same volume that we need 20 to 25 people for."

McDonald's introduced self-serve kiosks, a mobile app, and other technology in its retail operations, citing the need to turn around its multi-year market losses. The company is repositioning itself as a trendsetter and the tagline for the automation and modernization involved in this process is "Experience of the Future".

The strategy worked. By the end of 2017, sales had surged, the share price of McDonald's stock was higher than ever, and franchisee profits increased. Surprisingly, employment did not decline, as feared. Early in 2018, McDonald's told a reporter from the *Tampa Bay Times* that the company and its franchisees would hire 18,500 employees in Florida before the summer (Denham, 2018). McDonald's still posts job openings for cashiers on the Internet.

LABOR COSTS

"The cost of labor is the sum of all wages paid to employees, as well as the cost of employee benefits and payroll taxes paid by an employer" (Cost of Labor, n.d.). Some businesses cite increases in these costs as the reason they have turned to automation. In a recent interview, Bennigan's CEO Paul Mangiamele interpreted McDonald's kiosks—as well as self-service technologies at other chains like Panera and TGI Fridays—as direct responses to rising labor costs and calls for a higher minimum wage (Peterson, 2015). Mangiamele isn't the only CEO to express this view. Ed Rensi (2016), the former president and CEO of McDonald's USA, wrote that, in 2013,

> when the Fight for $15 was still in its growth stage, I and others warned that union demands for a much higher minimum wage would force businesses with small profit margins to replace full-service employees with costly investments in self-service alternatives. At the time, labor groups accused business owners of crying wolf. It turns out the wolf was real.... In September of this year, nearly one-quarter of restaurant closures in the Bay Area cited labor costs as one of the reasons for shutting down operations.

A survey by the National Bureau of Economic Research (Lordan & Neumark, 2017) supports this view. They assessed the impact of raising the minimum wage on jobs from 1980 to 2015 and found that a minimum-wage increase reduces employment for low-skilled workers in "automatable jobs" and also reduces the likelihood those workers will find new jobs. They also found that the impact varies tremendously "by industry and demographic group, including substantive adverse effects for older, low-skilled workers in manufacturing" (p. 2).

REGULATION

Politicians like to point to regulations as an automation motivator. During a rally in West Virginia, candidate Trump promised, "We're going to get those miners back to work.... The miners of West Virginia and Pennsylvania ... Ohio and all over are going to start to work again, believe me." Soon after his inauguration, Trump, the Republican Congress, and the new head of the EPA began dismantling EPA rules. A 2011 article in the *Washington Post* reported that "data from the Bureau of Labor Statistics show that very few layoffs are caused principally by tougher rules" (Yang, 2011[1]). Brookings has posted several times on its blog that job loss in coal mining results from other factors, including pre-regulation automation. The January 25, 2017, post stated that "automation has been eating into coal jobs over a long period of time—years before concerns about climate change led to the environmental regulations that President Trump solely blames for the industry's decline" (Saha & Liu, 2017).

QUALITY AND PRODUCTIVITY

In the fictional story *Manna* (Brain, 2003) described in the Greed chapter, the employee/narrator admits that the restaurant was better maintained and the employees were friendlier to customers after the restaurant's management was replaced by automation.

Andy Puzder, CEO of Carl's Jr., and Hardees fast-food restaurants, told *Business Insider* he wants to replace human workers with robots in his restaurants. "They're always polite, they always upsell, they never take a vacation, they never show up late, there's never a slip-and-fall, or an age, sex, or race discrimination case (Taylor, 2016).

DANGEROUS, DULL AND DIRTY JOBS

The primary motivation for automating dangerous jobs is safety rather than greed. Robots are already first responders; they handle toxic materials; and they enter areas considered to be dangerous for humans (e.g., mines and tunnels).

Robots are ideal for tedious, repetitive tasks. They never tire of doing the same thing and their minds (such as they are) don't wander. In 2016, Amazon replaced human order-pickers with robots in their fulfillment centers. Order picking entails locating each item of the customer's order, selecting the correct quantity of that item, and bringing them to the place where the order is assembled. It is a tiring, repetitive job that requires a tremendous amount of walking. For years, speech-recognition technology helped pickers by eliminating the need to carry mobile computers or paper lists but it didn't reduce the amount of walking pickers do (Markowitz, 2013). Amazon's replacement of human pickers with robots produced a jump in productivity but no job losses. Former pickers now have more interesting jobs that require far less walking.

Robots clear debris, dig tunnels, move hospital patients to and from the bathroom, and remove blockages from sewer systems.

> Lines break. Caked-on fats and oils steadily clog up the works. In the old days, human waste department workers had to dig up the affected pipe sections and diagnose the problem firsthand—a task as expensive and time-consuming as it is gross [Lamb, n.d.].

Automation of dangerous, dull, and dirty jobs will continue.

LACK OF AVAILABLE HUMAN WORKERS

The global population is aging, particularly in industrialized nations. The Population Division of the UN estimates that by the year 2035 there will be more people age sixty and older than age fifteen and under—globally (United Nations, 2015). An aging population means there will be fewer young people to replace retiring workers. That is clearly an incentive to automate.

Another critical need for workers in an aging population is for eldercare, which is a challenging job. People over the age of sixty are prone to falls, heart attacks, strokes, and debilitating diseases (e.g., Alzheimer's, dementia, Parkinson's). They need help eating, ambulating, and taking medication. The money pouring into robotics for the development of eldercare technology has attracted a large number of researchers, developers, and others, many of whom are legitimately working on behalf of seniors while others are merely seeking to become rich. Now, we're back to greed.

The Downside for Employers

Robots may not file lawsuits or join labor unions (yet) and they may prevent operations from moving overseas but there is tarnish on the silvery image of automation. Reasons for that include cost, taxes and regulation, and the limits of technology.

Cost

Automating can require extensive conversion of a facility, plant, or store. Those conversions include software, hardware, and labor. This can be expensive. Fortunately, automation has reached a point where reasonably accurate time and cost estimates can be made for some types of projects. Such assessments might even indicate that the cost of automating some or all operations may actually exceed the expected benefits of automation.

Time and cost assessments for projects that require new software and complex hardware-software integration, however, are difficult—even when they are carefully planned. The Rio Tinto mining company's AutoHaul project is automating the trains that haul iron ore between its mines and its ports in Western Australia. "Autonomous trains are meant to eliminate the complex scheduling needed to ensure train drivers are in the right place at the start or end of their shift" (Wilson, 2016). The changeover to driverless, autonomous trains is not trivial. Rio Tinto operates fifteen mines and four ports and the rail network running between them is 1,700 kms (1,056 miles) long.

When the project was announced in 2012, the company expected it to be completed by 2015 for a cost of $518 million (U.S.). By 2016, it was clear that both the schedule and the cost of AutoHaul were far too optimistic. The expected completion date was pushed to the end of 2018 and the cost more than doubled to $1.2 billion (U.S.) (Crozier, 2018).

Cost planning does not end when a conversion is finished. Robots are machines and, like other machines, they can break down, they need to be maintained, and they may require upgrades. These services are generally provided through support and maintenance contracts which are not necessarily cheap.

"Cobots" (Hollinger, 2016) might offer a partial solution for smaller companies that have difficulty competing with larger, low-cost competitors. Cobots are smaller and cheaper than the usual factory robots and are designed to operate as a team with human workers rather than to replace them. They can "collaborate safely with human workers thanks to advances in sensor and vision technology, and computing power."

Taxes and Regulation

Governments around the world are actively engaged in developing policies and standards related to automation and jobs. Two of the most active governments—Japan and the

EU—have taken markedly different positions on the social and economic impacts of automation. Headquarters for Japan's Economic Revitalization (2015) is overseeing Japan's nationwide Robot Revolution Initiative. The Initiative involves all sectors of the economy and the participation of industry, academia, and government. One area of special concern is the aging of its population which is proceeding at a faster pace than that of other nations. Provisional statistics from the Japan Bureau of Statistics for February 2017 (Statistics Bureau, 2017) show that 27% of Japan's population is 65 or older and there are more people 75 and older than there are children under the age of 15. Japan needs robots to replace aging workers who are leaving the workforce and they need caretakers for the elderly. That is why, unlike many other countries, Japan does not see automation as a threat to employment.

The EU is deeply concerned about the economic and social impacts of rapid automation. In 2017, the European Parliament (EP) voted on a set of recommendations that support a "gradualist, pragmatic cautious approach" (Delvaux, 2016, p. 5) to robotics and other automation. They acknowledge the benefits of AI and automation but

> the development of robotics and AI may result in a large part of the work now done by humans being taken over by robots, so raising concerns about the future of employment and the viability of social security systems if the current basis of taxation is maintained, creating the potential for increased inequality in the distribution of wealth and influence [*Ibid.*, p. 3].

Among the topics addressed by the European Parliament are

- Liability rules assessing a robot's liability and status as a person that evolve with advances in technology
- Intellectual property
- Privacy and data protection
- Standards development
- Safety

The EU plans to establish an agency which would have several areas of responsibility: Technical guidelines for supervisory systems and controls; ethical guidelines relating to the interaction between humans and machines; and regulatory rules for safe operations (Oitzman, 2017).

They also call upon EU member states to monitor job trends—especially those involving job losses due to automation; the possible dehumanization of care where robots have replaced humans; and the involvement of women in computing.

Another consideration is the "robot tax" on companies that replace human workers with automation. Such a tax would be designed to do the following

- Enable a government to recoup some of the tax monies lost through automation
- Maintain the viability of social-security/social-welfare systems
- Fund training and other services for workers who have lost jobs due to automation
- Finance a general base income for displaced workers
- Attenuate the massive social and economic inequality that many expect rapid automation to produce

In February 2017 the European Parliament rejected a proposed robot tax but the idea is receiving support from government and non-government sources. According to Microsoft's Bill Gates, "the technology and business cases for replacing humans in a wide range of jobs are arriving simultaneously, and it's important to be able to manage that displacement" (Delaney, 2017).

Robot-tax proposals have received the expected opposition from robotics companies and corporate users of robots. There are also questions about the form and nature of such a tax. Would it be a one-time charge or a periodic payment? How would it be calculated? Would the creation of new jobs become part of the calculation? Would there be a separate charge for each displaced worker? Would any reduction in the cost of goods be part of the calculation? Would the tax cover displacement of non-industrial workers, such as office workers, delivery people, restaurant wait staff, and household workers? Would it cover workers whose jobs were lost before a tax was imposed?

LIMITS OF TECHNOLOGY

The list of robot virtues enumerated by fast-food restauranteur Andy Puzder (see Upside section) is an example of the science-fiction-based dreams that impel employers to rush into automation. There is real danger tied to acting on those dreams. The Chinese fast-food restauranteur in Part I: Greed (Plans Gone Awry) leapt into the automation of his wait staff only to discover that the technology was not ready to perform even the basic duties of the job.

In their 2017 report on automation and employment, McKinsey Global Institute points out:

> Technological advances require basic scientific research, but in order for these advances to be adopted, they also require engineering solutions or "applied research." Both take time to develop. There is a lag between a technology being demonstrated, and a viable product being developed using that technology [p. 65].

The evolution of commercial air travel is a typical example. The feasibility of using an airplane was demonstrated by the Wright brothers in 1903. It took eleven years before the first commercial flight of an airplane was made and twelve more years before commercial air travel became a viable industry. They set 1926 as the start of the industry because that was the year operators had to comply with federal regulation.

As with airplanes, it will take time for robots to make the transition from research to product for new kinds of tasks.

The Future

We are being bombarded with contradictory messages emanating from news sources of all types. Headlines scream:

Robots Are Coming to Take Your Jobs Away (Fadilpašić, 2016)
Yes, the Robots Will Steal Our Jobs. And That's Fine (Jones, 2016)
Robots Will Destroy Our Jobs—and We're Not Ready for It (Shewan, 2017)
Here's Why Robots Taking Our Jobs Is a Good Thing (Belfiore, 2014)
Rise of the Robots: How Long Do We Have until They Take Our Jobs? (Devlin, 2015)
If Robots Are Taking Jobs, Then Why Are There Still So Many Jobs? (Brotherton-Bunch, 2017)

Titles of best-sellers are equally confident about opposite views: *Robots Will Steal Your Job, but That's OK* (Pistono, 2012) and *Rise of the Robots: Technology and the Threat of a Jobless Future* (Ford, 2015). Some cite expert opinions or the results of polls (Arce, 2014; Elkins, 2015).

To settle the question, Smith and Anderson (2014) of the Pew Institute think tank interviewed 1,896 experts from academia (e.g., MIT, Georgia Institute of Technology), government (e.g., U.S. Congress, EU), corporations (e.g., Google, IBM, Salesforce.com), consumer advocacy organizations (e.g., The Electronic Privacy Information Center, FactCheck.org), and non-profit technology communities (e.g., Worldwide Web Consortium, Internet Engineering Task Force).

They were all asked a single question:

> Self-driving cars, intelligent digital agents that can act for you, and robots are advancing rapidly. Will networked, automated, artificial intelligence (AI) applications and robotic devices have displaced more jobs than they have created by 2025?

The results of the survey echoed the disagreements expressed by non-experts. In fact, the experts in the Pew survey were almost equally divided about the future impact of automation. Some were decidedly dystopian, saying that widespread automation "will lead to vast increases in income inequality, masses of people who are effectively unemployable, and breakdowns in the social order." Others were unequivocally utopian and maintained "that human ingenuity will create new jobs, industries, and ways to make a living, just as it has been doing since the dawn of the Industrial Revolution." To further complicate the issue, neither group saw the future as fixed.

> Although technological advancement often seems to take on a mind of its own, humans are in control of the political, social, and economic systems that will ultimately determine whether the coming wave of technological change has a positive or negative impact on jobs and employment.

Four years later, the *Chicago Tribune* reported that, at Amazon,

> The people who commanded six-figure salaries to negotiate multimillion-dollar deals with major brands are being replaced by software that predicts what shoppers want and how much to charge for it [Soper, 2018].

Perhaps, the future is becoming clearer.

PART II

Crime

Technology supports the nefarious schemes of criminals and enables the establishment of professional police agencies whose trained law enforcers, including robots, apply their skills to hunt and capture criminals. Twentieth-century American comics gave birth to a new brand of enforcer: the superhero. Among them are superhero and supervillain robots.

Law-enforcement tools aren't the only things time has changed. The "Evolutions" portion of each chapter describes the metamorphosis of a well-known fictional being: the *golem,* a robot-precursor from Jewish mythology; the alien robot Gnut/Gort in literature and film; and Talos, the robot security guard of Greek mythology.

The Furor chapter addresses an issue that lies at the heart of the widespread fear of robots. It asks whether and how robots can be programmed to be moral.

Criminals

Criminals. Every society has them and they are not limited to the vengeful and greedy beings described in Part I. The surrogate role of robots and robot-precursors expands beyond murder. There are those that torture and kill on their own behalf as well. Some robot and robot-precursor criminals in this chapter are fundamentally evil. A few of them revel in their crimes while others consider them to be necessary to their goals. Sprinkled among them are professional killers and crime bosses.

Robot-precursors in the section on Folklore & Mythology establish the outlines of how we humans expect the criminals we create to behave. The Modern Literature and Contemporary Media sections add variations to those patterns and explore the impact of shifting from robot-precursors to robots. Those fictional creations enable us to look beyond the drone robots we have today and into a future in which robots exhibit some of the criminal behavior that we, their creators, have been showing for millennia. This chapter also follows the evolution of the *golem* as it evolves from a passive servant to a mindless killer.

Folklore & Mythology

Robot-precursors that break the law exist in folklore and mythology from around the world. Those in the first two myths are drones that obey their creators but add touches to their instructions that make executing them more pleasurable. Then, the southern African *Tokoloshe* is blamed for committing crimes of all types; but, no matter what it does, the *Tokoloshe* always has fun. The Japanese *Seto-Taishō* brings uncontrollable anger to the chaos it causes. Then there are criminals that are, by nature, evil.

The *Anchimayen* (also *Anchimallén* and *Anchimalguén*) is a villainous creation from the mythology of the Mapuche and other native peoples of southern Chile and Argentina (Faron, 1968). An *Anchimayen* is made from the corpse of a child who died suddenly. That corpse is the primary building block of the *Anchimayen*. When it is fully formed and animated, the *Anchimayen* sometimes appears like a small child or a flaming ball. Some alternate between the two embodiments.

An *Anchimayen* has no independent will. Once an *Anchimayen* is brought into being, it must obey the commands of its creator. If that sorcerer is good, which is rare, the *Anchimayen* will do things that are beneficial to humans, such as protect them from thieves. If its creator is a malevolent sorcerer—a *Kalku* (also *Calcu*)—the *Anchimayen* will harm and kill humans, often by spreading disease. Thus, it isn't surprising that the Mapuche are terrified of them.

The Giant in Hopi folklore (Lockett, 1933) is an example of a drone that serves the customer of a sorcerer and reflects their animus. In the Hopi folktale, the customer is the head governor of the village of Old Oraibi. He wants a killer to address a vexing problem: bad children. Hopi storyteller Don Talayesva describes the situation:

> the children getting pretty bad. People tried every way to punish and correct them…. They were all time throwing stones at the old people and pinning rags on the back of somebody and don't mind their parents very good [Lockett, 1933].

The head governor turns to an elderly "spider woman" to help him eliminate the problem by making a robot-precursor.

> She greased her hands and molded a big figure about a foot thick and four feet high with head and arms and legs. Then she covered it up with a white wedding blanket, and then she take whisk-broom and she patted with the broom, in time to her singing, on this doll figure, and it began to live and grow larger.
> When she finished singing he was enormously wide and tall, and he got up and uncovered himself and he sat there and said, "What can I do to help you?"

The head governor instructs the Giant to install himself on a mesa near the trash pile where the bad children liked to play, saying, "you come down and catch the first child you see playing on trash piles." Every morning, the Giant goes to the trash pile to kidnap children.

He enhances his enjoyment by taking them home, cooking them, and eating them—sometimes with a bit of pudding.

This process continues until there are very few children left, which prompts the assistant governor to visit the spider woman and her grandchildren, the twin war gods. They decide that the two boys will pretend to play on the pile and will kill the Giant when he tries to kidnap them. Nothing goes as planned for the boys or the Giant. After a series of skirmishes, the war gods succeed in killing the Giant ("the boys had some good medicine with them"). They cut off its head and brought it to the assistant governor.

The southern African *Tokoloshe* was discussed in Part I: Revenge because a *Tokoloshe* is often created by someone seeking revenge. At that point it is performing a service for its creator. It does so with a great deal of verve. The *Tokoloshe's* activities rarely end once it has dispensed with its designated quarry. At that point, it

Figure 9. If you can see the *Tokoloshe* in this photo … watch out! The *Tokoloshe* of the folklore of southern Africa is visible to its intended victim (and children). While it was created to kill someone, it also enjoys creating as much chaos and suffering as it can (unknown artist; Pixabay).

becomes free to torment whomever it pleases—and it is delighted to do so. It is helped by the fact that it is fully autonomous, vicious, and invisible to everyone except children and its intended victim (see Fig. 9).

The *Tokoloshe* isn't as committed to killing as to creating as much chaos and suffering as it can. It has powerful and dangerous skills, such as mind control and, according to some, the ability to drain the life-energy out of someone. It also possesses a force of will that is difficult to resist. "Fear of them is such that many people will not sleep on the floor, and will raise their beds higher by placing bricks underneath the legs" (Todd, 2007). This evidently protects the person in the bed as well as the bed itself, but no one and nothing else.

Tokoloshes have been accused of persecuting randomly selected victims, raping women, and perpetrating a panoply of other felonies and misdemeanors, as is revealed by the following news headlines:

My Bum Has a GPS Tracking Device Which Was Injected by a Tokoloshe (Thsepo, 2016)
Joburg Man Tormented by Tokoloshe That Does Not Want Him to Eat (Joburg Man Tormented, 2015)
"Tokoloshes" Vandalise Rhodes Statue (Knoetze, 2014)
Tokoloshe Steals Dockets: Court Evidence (Tokoloshe Steals Dockets, 2011)

Sometimes felons or their victims claim that crimes were induced by a *Tokoloshe*.

[S]ix teachers from the same school in Gurvuve, a village in central Zimbabwe, resigned over claims that a male colleague had summoned a Tokoloshe to overpower them so that the teacher could "have his way" with them while they slept [Todd, 2007].

In the 1950s, Zulu serial killer Elifasi Msomi swore under oath that a "tokoloshe … ordered him to kill. Responding to its command, Msomi took an axe and hacked 15 people to death." The court rejected that explanation for his crimes.

He was hanged … before an audience which included several Zulu chiefs, who were anxious to inform their … people that the *tokoloshe* hadn't saved the prisoner from a just death. Even so, one chief feared that many Zulus would think that Msomi might himself turn into a tokoloshe and return to Natal [Elifasi Msomi, n.d.].

The *Tokoloshe* is so much a part of southern African ethos that South African singer and song writer John Kongos wrote the song "Tokoloshe Man," which remained at the top of pop music charts for several weeks (Kongos, 1971). *Tokoloshes* also appear frequently as a gag in the popular comic strip "Madam & Eve" (Spindrifting, 2008) and they are the subject of scholarly papers about the culture of southern Africa (Mkhize, 1996).

In Japan, the *Seto-Taishō* ("crockery general") is an extremely aggressive type of *Tsuku-mogami Yokai* (Meyer, 2013; also see Part I: Revenge). It is comprised of bits of broken crockery, bottles, and kitchen utensils that are no longer used. Those discarded remnants combine to form a *Tsukumogami* that looks like an army general. Its scowling face is typically an empty sake bottle and it wears armor made of bits of porcelain. A *Seto-Taishō* is an angry *Yokai* that thrashes around wildly, attacking humans and causing chaos. Unlike the *Tokoloshe,* the damage produced by a *Seto-Taishō* is the product of uncontrolled rage.

Muramasa and Masamune were fourteenth-century Japanese swordsmiths known for their excellent work. Masamune's swords were so finely honed they were called "holy." His student Muramasa was known to be mentally unbalanced and violent. Legend has it that his swords were imbued with his spirit. They were bloodthirsty and were said to drive their bearers to kill or to commit suicide. The following is a blend of material from Long (n.d.), Ratti & Westbrook (1999), and Vellian (2008).

THE BLADES OF MASAMUNE AND MURAMASA

Muramasa challenged his teacher to see which man's blades were superior. Two swords, Muramasa's Juuchi Yosamu (10,000 Cold Nights) sword and Masamune's Yoshimitsu (Yawarakai-Te, "Tender Hands"), were positioned upright and one yard apart over a rapidly flowing stream with their blades facing the current. Leaves, twigs and other things floating past Juuchi Yosamu were drawn to the sword and cut in half. Some of those flowing past Yoshimitsu were attracted to it and cut but most flowed passed the sword, unharmed. Claiming victory, Muramasa laughed and mocked Masamune's skill.

A monk who had watched the contest bowed to the swordsmiths. He told them that both were excellent swords but they possessed vastly different spirits. Masamura's Juuchi Yosamu had a bloodthirsty spirit. It cut everything that passed it. It didn't care whether the victim was good or evil, friend or enemy. It cut everything. Masamune's Yoshimitsu, however, was a finer sword because it discriminated between things that were good and evil. It cut evil ones but allowed the innocent to pass by unharmed.

These swords cannot talk but they have other potent skills. Both swords exert control over potential victims and they, not their human owners, decide whether to kill or to let live. Of the two, however, only Muramasa's "bloodthirsty and evil" Juuchi Yosamu is a criminal. Its desire to kill is part of its character and it will kill as often and as many as it can.

The swords of Muramasa inspired a "beat 'em up" style role-playing game called Muramasa: The Demon Blade (Vanillaware, 2009–2015). It has highly accurate settings from Japan's Edo period and includes Buddhist theology and Japanese folklore. A player assumes a male or female ninja (kunoiji) role and, as with other beat 'em up video games, engages in frequent swordfights between the player and large numbers of opponents.

The deadly poison called *Ku* (also *Gu*) in China is as bloodthirsty as Muramasa's swords. It is always created to kill and it does so painfully. The method of manufacturing *Ku* "is to place poisonous snakes and insects together in a vessel until there is but one survivor, which is called the *Ku*" (Feng & Shryock, 1935, p. 1). De Groot refers to this process as "breeding *Ku*" (De Groot, 1892, p. 350). Breeding generates two products: a victorious creature and a virulent poison. Both are called *Ku*. De Groot (1892) and Feng & Shryock (1935) say they have been told that breeders are witches from minority ethnic groups in southern China and that their recipes for *Ku* have been passed from one generation to the next. This assertion is, however, soundly rejected by other researchers. "*Gu* poison's make-believe tales were a product of prejudice against minority groups" (Young, 2016).

The *Ku* creature is a robot-precursor whose power extends well beyond the poison it produces. *Chin-Tsan Ku* ("golden caterpillar") and toad *Ku* automatically transfer the wealth of a victim to the *Ku*'s owner. It is also said that when a manufacturer of *Ku* dies, that person becomes *Ku* and everyone that this person killed using *Ku* becomes one of their servants.

Ku enriches owners but those owners must continually "feed" their *Ku* or it will kill them. Feeding usually entails "serving the *Ku*" by killing someone (Feng & Shryock, 1935, p. 21). The owner must administer the *Ku* poison because the *Ku* robot-precursor is semi-autonomous and unable to physically perpetrate the crime. *Ku* can, however, generate apparitions. One owner who had failed to feed his *Chin-Tsan Ku* was visited by a young man "who tried to compel him to … take an oath before Heaven that he would administer poison to someone on a certain date. The old man realized that the visitor was the spirit of the *Chin-Tsan*" (Feng & Shryock, 1935, p. 28).

According to De Groot (1892), 16th century scholar Li Shizhen explains in *Bencao Gangmu* (*Compendium of Materia Medica*) what an owner must do to get rid of a *Chin-Tsan Ku*.

> It is extremely difficult to get rid of it, for even water, fire, weapons or swords can do it no harm. Usually the owner for this purpose puts some gold or silver into a basket, places the caterpillar also therein, and throws the basket away in a corner of the street, where some one may pick it up and take it with him. He is then said to have given his gold caterpillar in marriage [as cited in De Groot, 1892, p. 357].

Then the onus of feeding the *Ku* falls on the new owner.

Modern Literature

As with revenge and greed, criminal acts in modern literature tend to involve robots rather than robot-precursors. Many, such as the "kamakaze robot" in Shatner's *Tekwar* (1989), are still tools of human criminals.

> It's a very high class andy…. We got our first kamikaze killing … just about a year ago. These damn andies can pass for human … [and] also fool just about any security system…. Okay, so a kamikaze is instructed to go after a specific target…. The kamikaze locates his target, quite often in a crowd…. Sometimes it pretends to be an old friend, or maybe a tourist who's lost…. Then the andy touches the victim—could be a handshake, a pat on a back or even an embrace. Soon as that contact is made there's an explosion. It blows up the victim, the andy and whatever's in the vicinity. Expensive, but impressive [pp. 65–66].

Alan Dean Foster's *The Human Blend* (Foster, 2010) is filled with criminal cyborgs operating as individuals or in groups (also see Part I: Greed). They are called "melds"—humans who have chosen to augment and otherwise modify their bodies. Some alterations are so extreme that only the human brain remains untouched. "Gater," for example, is an underworld hacker who melded his body into the shape of an alligator. Others choose melds that support their criminal activities. Whispr, the main character, is a thief whose melds help him run fast and slip between buildings to evade police. The body of the assassin Napun Molé is melded to look like a harmless old man, which makes victims less wary. His melds also include the weapons he needs for his work, such as the rapier and pellet guns built into fingers, superhuman strength, and "a pair of superior-grade military spec leg melds" (p. 158) designed for pursuit. Like *Ku,* he is deadly and demands a sizeable fee for his services. Unlike *Ku,* Molé is not bound to any owner or employer. Once he finishes a job, he moves on to the next without pressing his employers to hire him again, although like *Ku,* Molé would not hesitate to kill an employer who fails to pay his fee.

The universe in *Saturn's Children* (Stross, 2008) is also populated by criminals intent on exploiting, denigrating, and destroying others. One major difference between the denizens of Foster's novel and those in *Saturn's Children* is that the universe in *Saturn's Children* is devoid of humans. They died trying to explore and settle outer space, leaving behind their robots who accomplished that for them. The androids also established a society that is far from egalitarian. It has three classes: aristos, slaves, and independent robots. At the top are a few aristos who possess all the power and most of the money. They are selfish and malicious and, like the *Tokoloshe,* they enjoy the pain and death they cause to others—especially non-aristos. A large population of slaves occupies the bottom rung of the society. Chips implanted in their heads render them obsequious and compliant. Slaves serve aristos in whatever way the aristos choose, including killing for them. The third group is comprised of a shrinking number of independent androids. They occupy the middle social stratum. One of an aristo's greatest joys is to transform an independent android into a slave. One of the most enjoyable ways of doing that is to instigate the financial ruin of the independent android. That isn't difficult because independents have little money and few employment opportunities. Another fun method is to place a slave chip into an independent's head. To do that, the independent must first be disabled. Freya (aka sex doll Nakamichi-47), the book's narrator, is an independent android who, at one point, suffers the indignity of becoming a slave by this method.

Many androids, especially those who never knew humans, are in awe of their creators and want them to return. Some, notably Freya and other sex dolls, want their creators to return because humans are their paying customers. Attempts have been made to recreate humans by using nano-potions called "pink goo" and "green goo" that are concocted from human DNA. The results have been far from successful. "One might think that this stuff is just water-soluble Nano machinery, and it should be easy enough to build one of our progenitors from these blueprints. But apparently there are huge problems with this approach" (*Ibid.*, p. 62).

Efforts to generate humans from these potions have, in fact, been disastrous on a large, planet-killing scale. In one instance, a moon became covered with "strange, matted sheets of self-propagating polymer" (*Ibid.*, p. 64). Failures of that magnitude have not deterred well-paid robbers from violating the graves of long-dead humans hoping to find usable DNA for their employers. Desecration of graveyards and the manufacture of pink and green goo are not always done by nostalgic robots or their hirelings. Predatory aliens are especially interested in the destructive power of the compounds and some robot factions want to build humans who would be subservient to them. That, to some androids, is an attractive reversal of roles.

The untoward aspects of the goo trade led to banning its production and dissemination. The ban is rigidly enforced by the Replication Suppression Agency, more generally known as the "Pink Police." They present a serious problem for the Jeeves Corporation and its clients who smuggle pink goo and sell it at auction to the highest bidder. Freya joins this gooey underworld when the Jeeves Corporation hires her to hide illicit goo in her body cavities and smuggle it to planets where auctions will be held. Freya becomes what drug cartels call a "mule." That makes her a criminal.

Rhea is an aristo whose template was used to create generations of sex dolls like Freya. Unlike her descendants, Rhea was built by humans and knows first-hand how vicious we can be. Human brutishness traumatized her and turned her into "a mad, bad criminal mastermind" (p. 320). She is the hidden architect of convoluted conspiracies designed to eliminate anyone trying to recreate humans. It seems, however, that her machinations have served only to delay such work. In that regard, she resembles the Japanese *Seto-Taishō* as her crazed anger causes her to leave death and destruction in her wake.

Rhea is unbalanced and unstable but she does not approach the insanity of Erasmus, a killer robot in the trilogies *Legends of Dune* (Herbert & Anderson, 2002–2004) and *Great Schools of Dune* (2012–2016). Like his illustrious namesake, Erasmus emphasizes the value of reason. In most other ways, however, Erasmus is more akin to the African *Tokoloshe* and Chinese *Ku*. All three of these artificial creatures can and do control humans. *Ku* controls its owners, a *Tokoloshe* controls any human it wants, and Erasmus controls its human disciple, Gilbertus Albans, whom the robot has indoctrinated to believe in the superiority of "thinking machines" such as himself. All three of those monsters are joyously sadistic. "Erasmus had kept human slaves as experimental subjects, testing, prodding, torturing, and observing millions of them" (Herbert & Anderson, 2014, p. 60). Many of his subjects died but the robot claimed that the experiments were its way of learning about humans. One of the experimental subjects who did not survive was the son of Serena Butler. Soon afterwards, she became the leader of the Butlerian *jihad* that wrested power from the thinking machines. Not surprisingly, Erasmus was the most detested of all thinking machines. Once they were in a position of power, the Butlerians imposed a ban on the development or use of thinking machines. Banning technology that is deemed to be excessively dangerous is not only a plot element in science fiction, it is an area of hot debate in the real world which is facing the imminent development of weapons with full machine autonomy that can decide on their own to kill (see Part III: Furor: LAWS).

Fortunately for criminals, in both science fiction and in the real world, a technology ban often opens new avenues for humans, robots, and aliens to engage in lucrative illegal activities. Androids like Freya in *Saturn's Children* smuggled banned pink and green goo; and, following the Butlerian ban of thinking machines, Gilbertus Albans rescued Erasmus' memory core from its demolished body and hid it in his office. Albans is the founder and head of the highly regarded Mentats School. He knows discovery would result in his dismissal followed by his execution as a traitor. Even so, he relies heavily on Erasmus for counsel and even calls the robot "father."

As a thinking machine, one would expect Erasmus to realize the dangerous situation in which he and Albans find themselves but it does not appear to concern him. His focus is on getting a body so he can resume cutting and prodding living beings (especially humans). Whenever Albans accesses Erasmus' memory core for a consultation, the robot whines like a petulant child about needing a body. Finally, Albans takes the dangerous step of providing Erasmus with a body. Erasmus immediately plunges into muddy water to catch a fish so he can begin a new round of bloody experiments. By doing so he destroys his new body and becomes, once again bodiless (Herbert & Anderson, 2012–2016).

Ray Electromatic (Christopher, 2015) is in a far different situation. He is the last robot on Earth. He was completed when anti-robot sentiment among jobless humans forced the U.S. Department of Robot Labor to terminate the project for which Ray was being built. "I was planned as a new class of machines, a grand experiment myself. More human, on the inside anyway, with a personality based on a real human template" (Loc. 93), that of his designer, Professor C. Thornton. Ray is packed with software and hardware to support those advanced features. On the outside, however, Ray is not very human-like. He is a huge, bronze, robot-looking humanoid with an immobile face.

To ensure that Ray would prosper after his death, Thornton gave Ray a profession: private investigator. Ray's body is so packed with hardware and software that Thornton could not add AI to Ray. Instead, he built a partner for Ray—an AI system called "Ada" that contains all of the advanced software originally designed for Ray. The relationship between Ada and Ray was to be the digital correlate of that between the fictional detective Nero Wolfe and his assistant Archie. Ada, with her advanced analytic abilities and long-term memory, was to be the brains and Ray was to be the mobile brawn.

Why are Ray and Ada in a chapter on criminals? The detective business was failing. "And then one day, Ada came up with a new business plan, all on her own" (Loc. 133). That's how they became paid assassins, like Napun Molé in Foster's *The Human Blend*. Ada uses her extensive contacts to get business and devises the plans for killing each victim. Ray executes her plans (and the victims). Business is booming.

Contemporary Media

Killers shine in contemporary media. Special effects involving terrifying sounds, images, and music make threatening behavior terrifying and otherwise heighten tension in films, video games, and other media. Multi-modal communication is used even when the medium is strictly visual, as in comics and manga. Lacking actual sound production, they supply readers with auditory information using visual cues, such as jagged lines, large, bold letters, and exclamation points that spell sounds, like **KA POW!**

More than one hundred years after Shelley published the 1818 edition of *Frankenstein or The modern Prometheus,* Universal Pictures released the film *Frankenstein: The Man Who Made a Monster* (1931). It spawned an entirely different Frankenstein monster that was no longer an intelligent, albeit vengeful killer (see Part I: Revenge). The cinematic monster, which resembled Boris Karloff—the actor who played him—was a mindless drone that went berserk immediately after it was given life and then began a killing spree. The film made the term "Frankenstein" a household word. At the same time, it reinforced the concerns that would lead Isaac Asimov to coin the term the "Frankenstein complex" and devise his Three Laws of Robotics (Asimov, 1942 [1983]). Despite Asimov's efforts, contemporary media is filled with crazed, robotic killers.

At the high end of the intelligence spectrum is SID 6.7 in the 1995 film *Virtuosity*. SID 6.7 is a virtual-reality program built from the digital personalities of more than 100 serial killers. He was made to be a killer. The mad scientist who made SID 6.7 was instructed by his superiors to shut it down; but, like many mad scientists, his enormous ego prevented him from destroying his greatest accomplishment. Unlike Victor Frankenstein whose horror and cowardice led him to abandon his creation, SID 6.7's creator is proud of himself and of SID 6.7. Instead of terminating SID 6.7, he acquiesced to SID 6.7's suggestion that he bring his creation into the real world as a humanoid. Sid 6.7 is not like Erasmus, the crazed robot in the *Legends of Dune* trilogy (2002–2004), whose compulsion to kill causes him to destroy his new body. SID 6.7 is smarter and far less insane. As soon as SID 6.7 has a solid body, he smiles and says, "I think I'm gonna like it here" and starts a killing spree. At one point he seizes control of a crowded nightclub and begins playing a symphony. While brandishing a pistol, he forces everyone in the club to scream. "Scream louder!" he commands. When he somehow takes over a TV station, he announces "Welcome to death TV." He's having a blast because, like the *Tokoloshe,* his greatest pleasure is to cause others to suffer.

Because SID 6.7 is an amalgam of 183 brutal killers, he can be seen as a humanoid version of Chinese *Ku* which is a blend of the vicious insect and reptilian killers it defeated in mortal combat. There are two significant differences between them. Once SID 6.7 is released from virtual reality he is free to perpetrate murders and other crimes whereas *Ku* is not mobile and, therefore, depends upon its owners to kill. Secondly, *Ku* is extremely difficult to kill but, once SID 6.7 is lured back into virtual reality, anyone can delete his code or pull the plug.

Father is the oldest homunculus (see Glossary) in the manga/anime *Fullmetal Alchemist* (Arakawa, 2001–2010) also resembles *Ku* because he's willing to kill anyone and anything to get what he wants. He also is a homunculus who was created by a powerful alchemist using the blood of Van Hohenheim, another alchemist, infused with the essence of "The Eye of God" which is linked to Truth and God. He later became a "Philosopher's stone" (Father, n.d.; The Eye of God, n.d.; Van Hohenheim, n.d.). The concept of the homunculus is most strongly linked to sixteenth-century European alchemy. In that context, a homunculus was a small, but exact, replica of a human that was created by an alchemist.

Father's quest is to become God. To do that, he must become perfect and free himself from the laws governing the universe. He believes his formation from the essence of "The Eye of God" to be the first step towards his goal. He took another step by cleansing himself of sin. That was accomplished by creating seven homunculus children, naming each for one of the Seven Deadly Sins, and by purging himself of sin through the transference of his sins to them. The success of the second step is questionable. "All his emotions, his lust for power, gluttony for truth, greed for all things, envy of all humans, wrath to all kind and his impeccable pride. These emotions he split to become better actually just stayed with him to the end" (Geyser, 2017).

He also has difficulty with the Ten Commandments, especially commandment number 6: "Thou shalt not kill" (Exodus 20: 13). He shows several times that he is willing to sacrifice his children to serve his own purposes. In fact, most of the children die at one point or another in the manga/anime—sometimes painfully. For example, Father kills Greed and melts him down in order to take Greed's philosopher's stone—the source of his energy. This is one of the acts that reveal how much Father's pride and egotism impede his goals (also see Part I: Greed).

Father isn't the only killer in *Fullmetal Alchemist.* Virtually every character is intent on murdering someone else. Fights occur every few minutes and are accompanied by flashes of lightning, screams, shaking, crashes, waves of painful colors, and bodies flying across rooms.

Mrs. Adolphine II comes from the comic series *Benoît Brisefer* (Culliford, 1973). She's an android and a criminal mastermind that was introduced in 1963 and quickly became an important character. She is the doppelganger of Mrs. Adolphine, an elderly woman living in the neighborhood. As Mrs. Adolphine's twin, the android appears to be nothing more than a harmless, elderly lady. That impression is dangerously far from the truth. Prior to joining *Benoît Brisefer,* some of her circuits were scrambled, causing her to become evil. Much like Napum Molé in Foster's *The Human Blend* (2010), Mrs. Adolphine II exploits the mild appearance of her human twin to commit a broad array of crimes. Ultimately, she becomes an international crime boss operating under the moniker Lady d'Olphine. Her self-propelled rise in the crime world is somewhat like that of Rhea, the twisted matriarch in *Saturn's Children* (Stross, 2008), whose early trauma at the hands of humans left behind a twisted mind capable of the machinations that enabled her to become a galactic power.

Frank Weld (*Robot & Frank*, 2012) is another career criminal. He's not a mastermind and he's not twisted. He's just a retired burglar. "I specialized in jewelry." Frank lives alone and he's experiencing physical and mental declines tied to aging which led his son to give Frank an eldercare robot. Frank initially hates his new companion but soon realizes that Robot has the manual dexterity needed to pick locks and crack safes. He also notes that Robot is not programmed to distinguish between legal and illegal activities. Frank teaches Robot breaking-and-entering skills and the two do a multimillion-dollar jewel heist. Frank becomes a suspect immediately. Robot realizes "my memory can be used against you" and the two sadly agree to wipe Robot's memory. The bonding marks the difference between Frank and most of the other criminals in this chapter who are incapable of forming bonds.

One of the purely evil villains is Xal'atath, Blade of the Black Empire from the role-playing game, World of Warcraft (Xal'atath, 2017). It brings death and chaos wherever it is taken. It whispers lies in a silky voice that twist minds and impel its owners to kill and slaughter, much like Muramasa's sword Juuchi Yosamu (see the previous Folklore & Mythology section). The primary difference is that Xal'atath brings death to its owners as well. "She reached for Xal'atath to defend herself, but found the blade inexplicably absent. Khardros struck her down with a single mighty blow from his hammer; as she lay dying, she repeated one phrase over and over: 'You promised...'" (Xal'atath, 2017).

Evolution: The Golem

The *golem* described here is not the Gollum in books by J.R.R Tolkien (1937). It is a robot-precursor from Jewish folklore, literature, and mystical tradition that has undergone several remarkable transformations over time. The word "*golem*" appears only once in the Old Testament of the Bible (Psalm 139: 16) where it is usually translated as "unformed mass" (Sherwin, 1985). The *golem* that emerged later in Jewish mythology and Biblical commentaries is not unformed. It looks exactly like a human; yet it isn't a human. The *Sanhedrin* (Epstein, n.d.), ancient commentaries on the stories in the Old Testament, explains how *golems* differ from humans by referring to the day God created Adam.

> The day consisted of twelve hours. In the first hour, his [Adam's] dust was gathered; in the second, it was kneaded into a shapeless mass. In the third, his limbs were shaped; in the fourth, a soul was infused into him [Epstein, n.d., Chapter 4, Folio 38b].

A *golem* is what Adam was before the fourth hour: a soulless being—a robot-precursor.

By the fourth century, the *golem* had changed. It is still made from dust or clay but it isn't created by God. It is made by a rabbi or other scholar who gives it life by chanting mystical incantations and by writing the word *emeth* (אמת) "truth" on its forehead or on a paper that is put into the *golem's* mouth. The rabbi cannot give the *golem* a soul. Nor can the rabbi give it the ability to speak because in the Jewish tradition, language (the "Word") is what distinguishes humans from all other living things, including *golems*.

The earliest *golems* were usually made to be servants because they were obedient, placid, and not very intelligent. Rabba, a fourth-century Babylonian scholar, created such a *golem* and sent it to one of his colleagues who immediately recognized it as something other than human. The eleventh-century Spanish poet Eleazar Solomon ibn Gabirol reportedly made a female *golem* and claimed she was his housemaid. Some suspected that Gabirol was actually using her as a sex partner and forced him to destroy her (Gelbin, 2011). The sixteenth-century Jewish mystic Isaiah Horowitz reinterpreted the "evil report" about his brothers' behavior that Joseph brought to his father in the *Old Testament* of the Bible (Genesis 37: 2). Horowitz interpreted it to mean that Joseph told his father that his brothers were having sex with female *golems* (Sherwin, 1985).

Terry Pratchett's fantasy series *Discworld* (1983–2015) is filled with *golems* that are created to be servants but, on *Discworld*, making and selling them is a commercial enterprise. Like traditional *golems*, they are mute, but Pratchett's *golems* can communicate in writing although *golem*s write everything in capital letters. A *golem's* behavior is controlled by a set of basic laws called the "Chem," such as "THOU SHALT BE HUMBLE" and "THOU SHALT NOT KILL." The Chem are written on pieces of paper and placed into their heads. Pratchett reported that the Chem were inspired by Asimov's Laws of Robotics (Asimov, 1942 [1983]; see Part III: Furor: Making Robots Moral).

Chem cannot be changed or removed but more laws can be added simply by placing additional pieces of paper in a *golem's* head. This process generally works very well but, in *Feet of Clay* (Pratchett, 1996), it backfired. The *golems* built a king using clay from their own bodies and they filled its head with papers upon papers of their hopes and dreams. It was too much for the king: "The *golem's* head exploded…. Scraps of paper flew out, dozens, *scores* of them, tumbling gently to the floor" (Loc. 4302) admonishing him to do innumerable things, such as "RULE US WISELY … TEACH US FREEDOM…" (Loc. 4309).

Medieval Europe saw a dramatic rise in anti–Semitism. Crusades (ca. 1100–1300), which were supposed to fight "the infidel" in Palestine, "wiped out entire Jewish communities from Western Europe to Palestine" (Gelbin, 2011, p. 10). The newly established Catholic rulers of Spain drove the Jews from Spain in 1492 and began the Inquisition. Christians all over Europe launched deadly attacks called "*Pogroms*" against Jewish communities. Most *Pogroms* occurred around Easter, the Christian holiday commemorating the crucifixion of Jesus. They were usually sparked by rumors claiming Jews were kidnapping Christian children and sacrificing them as part of Jewish ritual murder.

The *golem* was reinvented. The new *golems* were made to protect the Jewish community. These *golems* were almost always male and physically they were large, powerful creatures. The most well-known of this new breed of *golems* is the *Golem* of Prague. This *golem* was introduced to the world by Rabbi Yodl Rosenberg in his book *The Golem and the Wondrous Deeds of the Maharal of Prague* (Rosenberg, 1909 [2007]) extolling how Rabbi Judah Loew ben Bezalel (the Maharal of Prague) and his *golem* Yossele repeatedly saved Prague's

Jewish community from powerful anti–Semites. Fig. 10 shows the Maharal creating the *golem*.

Rosenberg claimed the book had been written by Rabbi Loew's son-in-law but it is actually a work of fiction written by Rosenberg himself. Nevertheless, many believed that Yossele actually existed and that Rabbi Loew created him. Anna Foerst (Foerst, 2000), former director of the God and Computers Project at the Massachusetts Institute of Technology (MIT), reported that some MIT roboticists told her they were descendants of Rabbi Loew and that they know the Rabbi's formula for animating a *golem*. Rosenberg's book also inspired twentieth-century writers of drama, e.g., Leivick (*Der Goylem*, 1921), poetry (e.g., Borges, 1969), children's books (e.g., Singer, 1969 [1982]; Wiesel, 1983), and science fiction (e.g., Piercy, 1991).

The twentieth century produced two kinds of *golems*. One type is soulful and the other soulless. Soulful *golems* can speak and they feel emotions deeply. The *golem* in Bretan's 1924 opera *The Golem* falls in love; the *golem* in Leivick's (1921) dramatic poem suffers from a profound angst; and Meyrink's (1914 [1995]) *golem* emerges from centuries of suffering by Jews living in the

Figure 10. The Golem of Prague and Rabbi Loew by Mikoláš Aleš (1852-1913) (Wikimedia Commons).

ghetto of Prague much like the "spider god of wealth" in Part I: Revenge who represents the anger of the Earth (Hughes, 1993).

Piercy's 1991 novel *He, She and It* contains two soulful *golems*. One is an updated incarnation of Yossele, the *Golem* of Prague, and the other is a twenty-first-century *golem* named Yod[1] who was created to protect a Jewish town from being overrun by its larger, more powerful neighbors. Piercy calls Yod a cyborg but he is really a robot, a sophisticated android. Piercy interleaves the stories of the two *golems* and the love each has for a human woman. That love leads them to question their identities as sub-humans. As with Yossele, the humans around Yod treat him like a non-human. In addition, Yod hates himself and wants to rid himself of the *golem* programming that makes him delight in killing.

Some twentieth-century *golems* exhibit both emotion and an impetus to kill. An early example is the *golem* (Fig. 11) in Galeen and Wegener's 1915 film *Der Golem* (*The Golem*) who falls desperately in love with the daughter of the antiques dealer who owns him. When she rebuffs it, this *golem* doesn't suffer in silence like a traditional *golem*. It goes berserk and begins a killing rampage. It is notable that Galeen and Wegener's film was made fifteen years before the 1931 film *Frankenstein* which also portrayed a rampaging monster. The Frankenstein monster is, however, far less intelligent and soulful than Wegener's *golem*.

The majority of late twentieth and twenty-first century *golems* also resemble the *Frankenstein* monster. They are soulless and mindless killers. For example, the *golems* in the table-top game Dungeons & Dragons (Gygax & Ameson, 1974–, ongoing; Paizo, Inc., 2016) are fierce. When they kill they are focused and effective. Each *golem* type is based upon the material the player used to make it. They have no moral compass, which can cause some of them to go out of control. The D&D's (see Glossary) *System Reference Document 5.1* (Wizards of the Coast, 2015) describes what happens when a *flesh golem* goes berserk.

Figure 11. The Rampaging Golem from the 1920 film *The Golem: How He Came into the World*. This was the last in a trilogy of films by Paul Wegener. The first was *The Golem* and the second was *The Golem and the Dancing Girl*. Both are lost or incomplete (Wikimedia Commons).

> On each of its turns while berserk, the golem attacks the nearest creature it can see. If no creature is near enough to move to and attack, the golem attacks an object, with preference for an object smaller than itself. Once the golem goes berserk, it continues to do so until it is destroyed or regains all its hit points [p. 316].

In the 2006 "Treehouse of Horror XVII" episode of *The Simpsons* (2006), Krusty the Klown has acquired the *Golem* of Prague. Krusty admits the *golem* was created to protect the Jewish community but he's discovered that it will follow any command written on a paper that is placed in his mouth. Bart Simpson places a paper in the *golem's* mouth instructing it to come to Bart's home at midnight. Bart begins commanding it to rough up people until his sister Lisa stops him by saying the *golem* looks unhappy. She puts a paper in his mouth saying "TALK." The world-weary *golem* tells them he desperately wants to be free from the control of people who want him to kill and destroy—like Piercy's soulful *golem*. Lisa and Bart make a female *golem* out of Play Dough and the golems fall in love. Because their love is mutual, there is no need to go on a killing spree like Wegener's *golem*. The two are married by a rabbi.

Real World

Norbert Wiener, the father of cybernetics, wrote in *God and Golem, Inc.* (1964), "The machine is the modern counterpart of the golem" (p. 94). He is not the only one to make that correspondence. Byron Sherwin called computers, robots, and nanotechnology our "mechanical golems" (Sherwin, personal communication, 16 Dec. 2013). Sherwin says that the link between the *golem* and computers is not new. Pointing to Gabirol's eleventh-century female *golem* he writes that "what is unique is that Gabirol's golem was not made of earth but of wood and hinges. Here one finds the roots of the portrayal of the golem as a mechanical being, as an automaton, as a robot" (Sherwin, 1985, p. 16). Israel named its first two mainframe computers "Golem I" and "Golem II."

The aerial drone could easily be thought of as a modern *golem*. Like its earliest mythological precursors, it follows the commands of its user without question—whether that individual is a hobbyist, a military pilot, a police officer, or a criminal. In fact, the wide availability of inexpensive commercial drones has made them attractive to criminals who are using them to perpetrate an array of crimes—much like early criminal use of robot-precursors.

One of the most worrisome criminal endeavors is their use by terrorist organizations as a weapon. By 2015, ISIS was arming drones; Iran was helping Hamas and Hezbollah build suicide drones; and their popularity was growing among South American terrorist groups, notably Peru's Shining Path, the Paraguayan People's Army, and Colombia's FARC (Hambling, 2015a; Iran Helping Hamas, 2015; Sanchez,2015).

Criminals who are not terrorists are using drones to smuggle banned items into prisons: drugs, phones, guns, and even jail-breaking tools. In 2017, convicted kidnapper Jimmy Causey escaped from the Lieber Correctional Institution in Ridgeville, S.C.

> A lengthy investigation confirmed that an accessory role was played by a small, off-the-shelf drone. And with that, law-enforcement and national security officials added "prison breaks" to the potential ill uses lurking in a technology widely available at retailers including Amazon and Walmart [Hennigan, 2018].

Crime and Justice News reported in 2017 that drone-smuggled contraband was occurring at federal and state prisons in the U.S. (Inmates Use Drones, 2017) and, according to *The Telegraph*, by 2016 "drones are being used to smuggle drugs, mobile phones and other banned items into prisons at a rate of more than twice a month." Between 2014 and 2015 the number of incidents grew 1,550 percent (Drones Used to Smuggle, 2016).

Drones are also proving to be useful aids for burglars interested in learning as much as possible about the places they plan to rob. They are light, agile devices that can support high-definition cameras capable of taking still images and videos from both a distance and close to the target. The drones can peer over walls and fly above security cameras. They can, in fact, identify where security cameras and other types of security are located and how they are positioned. "It is feared that because the technology allows thieves to explore properties from the air they will be used to identify security weak spots" (Barrett, 2015).

Whether it is over a prison wall or across a border, drug smuggling by drone is a growing enterprise. They haven't entirely replaced "mules" who, like the fictional Freya in *Saturn's Children* (Stross, 2008), transport illegal substances in their human or humanoid bodies, but they could. Drone use by criminals in the Western hemisphere, for example, is increasing so quickly that Sanchez (2015) characterized drug traffickers as the "new investors" in drones. He expects that drug traffickers will "continue to resort to drones in the future as cheap vehicles to thwart border security measures" (including walls). In addition, they can be armed and used against individuals who represent impediments to their operations. That may include members of other gangs and cartels (Felbab-Brown, 2016).

It is always useful to monitor the police and criminals are learning to do that. Even so, Australian police foiled an attempt by an "international drug cartel … to smuggle $30 million worth of cocaine into the country." It appears that the cartel's problem was that the police were using drones to monitor them and did a better job (Margaritoff, 2017). That's not always the case. According to Joe Mazel, head of the FBI's Operational Technology Law

Unit, "counter surveillance of law enforcement agents is the fastest-growing way that organized criminals are using drones" (Tucker, 2018). An example of their sophistication occurred in 2017 when an FBI unit established an observation point to monitor activities during a hostage situation. The gang involved had anticipated the arrival of the FBI. Suddenly, scores of drones began to buzz the agents while other drones took videos that were sent to YouTube so other gang members could have access to the information.

Criminal use of drones has recently evolved into a deadlier form. In 2017, Mexican federal police discovered an armed drone in a vehicle driven by members of a drug cartel. "The aerial drone in the rear cargo bay was armed and ready to be deployed. Sitting in an open plastic case beside an AK47 assault rifle and spare clips" (Kryt, 2017). This is likely the future of criminal drone use.

Drones may be the criminals' most widely used robotic tool but a new product introduced in 2018 by Boston Dynamics, a supplier of military robots, has the potential to become another useful device for criminals.

About SpotMini

SpotMini is a small four-legged robot that comfortably fits in an office or home. It weighs 25 kg (30 kg if you include the arm). SpotMini is all-electric and can go for about 90 minutes on a charge, depending on what it is doing. SpotMini is the quietest robot we have built.

SpotMini inherits all of the mobility of its bigger brother, Spot, while adding the ability to pick up and handle objects using its 5 degree-of-freedom arm and beefed up perception sensors. The sensor suite includes stereo cameras, depth cameras, an IMU, and position/force sensors in the limbs. These sensors help with navigation and mobile manipulation (Boston Dynamics, 2018).

The video that was released with the product announcement shows a SpotMini easily opening an unlocked door and entering the room behind it. SpotMini could assist in emergency response and it could protect police doing a door-to-door search by opening doors for them. Most relevant to this chapter, however, is its potential for becoming an attractive tool for burglars or home invaders. "Technology is a double-edged sword" (Mitrano, 2012). SpotMini is scheduled to go on sale in 2019 (Yurieff, 2018). Hopefully, criminals will not be lining up to buy them.

Plans Gone Awry

Folklore & Mythology

Rabbi Elijah Ba'al Shem, the rabbi of the Polish town of Chelm (1550–1583) was a learned man. His scholarship extended to Jewish mysticism and the Kabbalah. The Rabbi decided to make a *golem* for the Jewish community of Chelm to help do hard labor. He got a large quantity of clay and mud which he molded into the shape of a large human. Then, as instructed by the religious texts, he uttered incantations and wrote the word *emeth* (אמת) "truth" on the forehead of the *golem* which gave it life.

The *golem* served the community well, but every day it became larger and stronger until the Rabbi grew concerned about whether it could use its strength to cause damage rather than assistance. In some versions of the story the *golem* actually does go on a rampage. In any case, the Rabbi decided to deactivate the *golem*. To do that, he had to erase the first letter of the word on its head—changing *emeth* to *met* (מת) which means "dead."

> [The] golem, however grew so tall that he could no longer reach the amulet, and so he made his creature bend down to remove his boots, allowing him to reach the amulet in the golem's forehead. However, when he removed the first letter from the amulet, the golem fell over onto him and crushed him to death [Gelbin, 2011, pp. 8–9].

Jacob Grimm published a version of this story (Grimm, 1808) in *Zeitung für Einsiedler*, a journal that was popular among adherents of European Romanticism. An English translation is included in Dekel and Curley's 2013 article "How the Golem Came to Prague." Several scholars have argued that Grimm's version of the story influenced Mary Shelley's (1818) portrayal of the Frankenstein monster (Dekel & Curley, 2013; Bertman, 2015; Gliński, 2015).

Enforcers

Enforcers compel adherence to laws and they punish those who fail to comply. The very presence of some enforcers acts as a deterrent to potential law-breakers. The most notable of those is the Giant of Hopi folklore (Lockett, 1933) whose story warns children to obey their parents because the alternative is being killed and eaten.

Enforcers who hunt, capture, and bring offenders to justice include police and their agents (e.g., watchbirds), detectives, and a few vigilante hunters. Those that are robots tend to do their work dispassionately and, on the whole, professionally. There are, however, some among robots and robot-precursors whose devotion to the letter of the law is excessive.

As with other types of enforcers, some of those that punish, particularly robots, go about their work in a methodical, emotionless fashion whereas others are brimming with emotion. Two humanoid enforcers bearing the name "Fury" represent those extremes. Both torment their victims but they do so in markedly different ways. The Greek *Erinyes* ("Furies") gave the word "Fury" its meaning (Aeschylus, ca. 5th century BCE [1926]). They are brimming with uncontrolled anger as they administer their punishments.

Folklore & Mythology

Enforcers in folklore and mythology are diverse. A few, such as the reenactments of the Hopi Giant folktale, provide crime prevention. Most enforcers become involved only after crimes have been committed.

The Giant in the Hopi folktale was described in the Criminals chapter because he is a killer. Since the giant's demise, however, the Hopi retell his story in ceremonies during which he is represented using a mask with "enormous black head with a big beak and big teeth." Hopi storyteller Don Talayesva says the real purpose is to inspire good behavior by children.

> Really the most important thing we do with this kind of a mask is for the men to wear when they go round the village and call out the children and scare them a little bit and tell them to be good so they don't have to come back with the basket and carry them off ... and the parents are supposed to be very worried and hide the children and tell the Giants their children are good, and always the parents have to give these Giants ... things to eat, in order to save their children; and then the children are very grateful to their parents.... And parents tell children a Giant may come back for them if they are pretty bad, and come right down the chimney maybe [Lockett, 1933].

Gargoyles in Gothic architecture are spouts used to remove water from a building's roof; but simple, unadorned spouts could perform the same function. Scholars debate about whether gargoyles and other monstrous decorations on Gothic cathedrals have another function.

> The most common legend is that gargoyles are condemned souls intercepted on their way to Hell. God places them atop churches to remind the living what might happen if they do not renounce sin and find redemption in the Lord [Walworth, 2005].

Lü Dongbin was a scholar and poet. He is also one of Taoism's eight immortals and sometimes considered to be their leader. His emblem is the magic, two-edged sword that can detect and chase away evil spirits (Renunger, 2017). There is also a strong bond between the sword and Lü Dongbin. This type of connection is not unusual for magical swords. In British mythology, for example, King Arthur is the only one who can draw Excalibur from the stone in which it is lodged.

The Criminals chapter includes a tale about the Japanese swords of Muramasa and Masamune. Muramasa's was identified as a criminal due to its love of killing (see Criminals: Folklore & Mythology). Masamune's sword is an enforcer because it "does not needlessly cut that which is innocent and undeserving" (Long, n.d.) First it passes judgment on those it encounters and then it doles out punishment based on that judgment.

As mentioned in the Revenge chapter of Part I, a bronze eagle (*Aetos Kaukasios*) is a robot enforcer. It was built by the Greek god Zeus to punish Prometheus for stealing sacred knowledge from the gods and giving it to humans.

> With shackles and inescapable fetters Zeus riveted Prometheus
> on a pillar Prometheus of the labyrinthine mind;
> and he sent a long-winged eagle to swoop on him
> and devour the god's liver; but what the long-winged bird ate
> in the course of each day grew back and was
> restored to its full size [Hesiod, ca. 700 BCE, lines 520–525].

The bronze eagle executes the punishment efficiently but it does not consider its behavior to be retribution. It probably doesn't examine its own behavior at all. It does nothing more than what any hungry predator would do.

Zeus also wanted to punish humans for accepting Prometheus's gift of fire. Per Zeus's instructions, Hephaestus built a woman from clay like that used by Prometheus to make human males. The other gods and goddesses gave her beauty, charm, and other attributes and named her Pandora (all-gifted). She was given to Epimetheus, Prometheus's brother, as his wife. Pandora is not an enforcer. She was an unaware bearer of retribution; her dowry brought sickness and pain to humans, which is why the word "Pandora" is sometimes translated as "all-giving."

Other enforcers include the *Erinyes* (Alecto, Megaera, and Tisiphone) who were well-aware of their responsibilities as enforcers. They also took on the roles of judge and executioner. To most speakers of English they are known as "the Furies" because their behavior was filled with anger and violence (Fig. 12). The Greeks would sometimes refer to them facetiously as *Eumenides* ("The Kindly Ones") which is also the title of a play by Aeschylus (ca. 5th century BCE [1926]) about their involvement in the trial of Orestes for murdering his mother.

There are several versions of how the *Erinyes* came into being. The most widely cited one is that they sprang from drops of blood that fell on Earth when Cronus murdered and

Figure 12. Erinyes (or Furies, as they are also known) in *The Remorse of Orestes* (1862) by William-Adolphe Bouguereau (1825-1905) (Wikimedia Commons).

castrated his sleeping father. Since then, the *Erinyes* have made it their mission to administer harsh punishment to those who murder a parent. They also punish conduct unbecoming a child, perjury, and offenses against the gods. "For the wrath of us, the Furies who keep watch on mortals, will not come stealthily upon such deeds—I will let loose death in every form" (Aeschylus, ca. 5th century BCE [1926], line 499). Those forms included storm clouds and swarms of insects (foreshadowing nanoswarm weapons) but the *Erinyes* are typically portrayed as winged female humanoids that are boiling with anger.

> The wrath of the Erinyes manifested itself in a number of ways. The most severe of these was the tormenting madness inflicted upon a patricide or matricide. Murderers might suffer illness or disease; and a nation harbouring such a criminal, could suffer death, and with it hunger and disease [Atsma, n.d.].

Their portrayal in Aeschylus' play made them terrifying. It was reported that at one production of the play "many children died through fear, and several pregnant women actually miscarried in the house, at the sight of the horrible masks that were introduced" (Lempriere, 1832, p. 23).

The *Wulgaru* of Australia is also a judge, jury, and executioner of anyone who breaks tribal laws (Harney, 1959; The Wulgaru, 2016). It gave itself those roles and it takes all of them very seriously. This creature is part of the folklore of the Waddaman who live in the

Northern Territories of Australia. The *Wulgaru* was fashioned by an old man named Djarapa who, apparently, simply decided to make a man.

> Djarapa cut a piece of wood from a green tree and this he trimmed to look like the body of a human being. Next he made the legs and the arms from pieces of wood and for knee and arm-joints he used rounded stones that he gathered up in a river bed. After putting them together with red-ochre he chanted a very magic song that had been taught to him by a now dead tribal medicine-man [Harney, 1959, p. 91].

Djarapa chanted all day and all night in the hope of imbuing his construction with life. Finally, he gave up and headed for home. Then, he began to hear clanking and crunching behind him. He turned and saw a huge monster of wood and stones lumbering along after him. It was the man he had made! It was a horrific sight. The creature pushed through the forest, joints squeaking, arms flailing, and eyes blazing like stars. From time to time it would open its monstrous mouth and then snap it shut.

Djarapa tried to shake the monster off his trail but failed. "Proper fool that Djarapa. Man make devil-devil … now he can't kill it … make trouble for everybody." The foolish man led the *Wulgaru* into the village. Since then, it has prowled about during the night acting as a "self-appointed judge" (Harney, 1959, p. 91) and suddenly appearing when anyone makes the tiniest infraction of tribal laws—even children slapping a fire to see the sparks fly. It is so intent upon enforcing tribal laws that its nit-picking methods have made it one of the monsters to fear in the night.

This story, as recorded by William E. Harney in *Tales from the Aborigines* (1959), was narrated by Tulu, a Waddaman storyteller. Harney reports that after Tulu finished the story, he bid his audience a "good night" and left for his camp. As he walked away he waved a blazing "firebrand" above his head to light the path "—and ward off the evil spirits of the night that are always hovering around to snap up the unwary who would dare to laugh at the tribal laws" (p. 97).

Modern Literature

Towards the end of the nineteenth century, professional police departments and corrections agencies began to appear in Europe and the U.S. Another change affecting robot and robot-precursor enforcers was the separation of science fiction from fantasy fiction. Fantasy fiction is often set in societies that resemble the past and tend to retain elements from mythology and folklore, notably magic and spiritual beings. Science fiction, however, generally takes place in the future, incorporates possible technological advances, and often includes space travel. Enforcers in fantasy fiction tend to be robot-precursors whereas those in science fiction are often robots.

Nightblood is a self-aware sword in Sanderson's 2009 fantasy-fiction novel *Warbreaker*. The sword was created by two magicians, Shashara and her husband Vasher. Vasher, the novel's main character, "awakened" Nightblood, a process that bestows life and self-awareness to an object and imbues it with a mission. The mission Vasher gave Nightblood was to "destroy evil!" It quickly became evident that Nightblood could easily carry out that mission because evil people are drawn to the sword whereas good people are repelled by it. The sword has a Masamura spirit (see Part II: Criminals) because whenever someone who is evil unsheathes Nightblood, the sword fills them with blood lust. They feel compelled to kill everyone around them and then to kill themselves.

Nightblood is Vasher's sword. The powerful bond between them includes the ability to communicate telepathically with each other—which is useful because Nightblood has no vocal apparatus to generate spoken sounds.

VASHER IN PRISON

The guards laughed to one another, slamming the cell door shut with a clang … and he could see the three guards open his large duffel….

"Here, now," said one of the men looking through Vasher's duffel. "What's this?" … From Vasher's bag, a guard pulled free a long object wrapped in white linen. The man whistled as he unwrapped the cloth, revealing a long, thin-bladed sword in a silver sheath. The hilt was pure black. "Who do you suppose he stole *this* from?" … "Let me see that," the lead guard said, taking the sword. He grunted, obviously surprised by its weight. He turned it about, noting the clasp that tied sheath to hilt, keeping the blade from being drawn. He undid the clasp….

"Be careful, friend," Vasher said softly, "that sword can be dangerous." …

Then the guard snorted and walked away from Vasher's cell, still carrying the sword. The other two followed, bearing Vasher's duffel, entering the guard room at the end of the hallway. The door thumped shut….

From [the guard room] he heard sudden shouts of surprise….

The yells from the guard room died out. The dungeon fell still….

Knowing the kind of men who tended to guard such dungeons, he'd had a pretty good idea that they would try to draw Nightblood….

He stepped around the pool of blood—which was seeping down the inclined dungeon floor—and moved into the guard room. The three guards lay dead….

Vasher carefully slid the weapon fully back into its sheath. He did up the clasp.

I did very well today, a voice said in his mind.

Vasher didn't respond to the sword.

I killed them all, Nightblood continued. *Aren't you proud of me?*

Vasher picked up the weapon, accustomed to its unusual weight, and carried it in one hand. He recovered his duffel and slung it over his shoulder.

I knew you'd be impressed, Nightblood said, sounding satisfied (Sanderson, 2009).

This demand for approval is rare among enforcers who, overall, tend to be emotionally independent or to lack emotion altogether. The sword named "Need" is an example of that type of enforcer. It plays a major role in Lackey's *By the Sword* (1991). Need is a woman's sword. She identifies and is identified as female. She even has a woman's power-mantra:

Woman's Need calls me, as Woman's Need made me. Her Need will I answer as my maker bade me (p. 53). Need is wielded by the swordswoman Kerowyn and the connection between the two is akin to the one between Nightblood and Vasher. When Kerowyn's grandmother gave Need to her she counseled Kerowyn, "you're bound to her like you'll never be bound to another living thing" (p. 53). Need differs from Nightblood in that she requires no emotional support or approval from anyone. The sword chooses the woman who will wield her and it decides when it will shift its allegiance to someone else.

Need is another sword that can detect the presence of evil men but it doesn't drive them away nor does it attract them. Need prefers to simply kill them and, much like the Greek *Erinyes,* it especially enjoys killing men who have harmed or intend to harm women. When Need has identified such a man, she is prone to seize control of herself and interact directly with him. One such example occurs when a drunken guardsman tries to rape Kerowyn.

> [She] grabbed automatically for the hilt of her own sword.... And Need took over ... and forced her to attack again and again.... Need caught the man's blade in a bind and disarmed him.... Evidently, the man's crimes against women were such that the blade had no intention of letting him get away.... Need drove towards his throat [p. 334].

Talus (Fig. 13) is a robot enforcer called an "iron man" in Book V of Edmund Spenser's *The Faerie Queene* (1590 [1894–1897]). He is squire to the knight Artegal and one of his tasks is to help Artegal punish criminals they encounter on their journey.

> His name was *Talus*, made of yron [iron] mould,
> Immoueable [immovable], resistlesse, without end.
> Who in his hand an yron flale [flail] did hould,
> With which he thresht [thrashed] out falsehood,
> and did truth vnfould [Spenser, 1590, Canto 1, p. 1055].

Talus is an exacting, merciless, and a "by-the-book" enforcer similar to the Australian *Wulgaru.* He is neither governed nor swayed by emotion and his rigid adherence to the rule of law is sometimes compared to the more humane methods practiced by Artegal. A striking example of Talus' approach to justice occurs when he refuses to free Artegal from his humiliating slavery to Radigund. His reason is that Artegal agreed that the loser of a one-on-one battle between them would submit to the other's wishes.

A similar robot enforcer is featured in the "Two-Handed Engine" (1955 [1989]), a short story by Henry Kuttner and Catherine Moore. The title comes from John Milton's poem "Lycidas" (Milton, 1645): "But that two-handed engine at the door, /Stands ready to smite once, and smite no more" (lines 130–131). Two-handed engines are robot enforcers that are, like Talus, "shaped like a man of steel." They are called "Furies" but their approach to punishment is not wild and angry, although their effect on murderers is akin to that produced by their mythological namesakes. The sound of a Fury's footsteps lets a "murderer know he's been tried and condemned by the omniscient electronic minds that knew society as no human mind could ever know it" (p. 245).

> He would never in life be alone again. Never while he drew breath. And when he died, it would be at these steel hands, perhaps upon this steel chest, with the passionless face bent to his, the last thing in life he would ever see. No human companion, but the black steel skull of the Fury [p. 255].

The birds in Robert Sheckley's 1953 short story "Watchbird" are flying robots made of metal, crystal, and plastic. Their function is comparable to that of Gothic gargoyles and the Hopi reenactments of the Giant tale: the Watchbirds deliver preventive enforcement. Instead of thwarting disobedience, however, they stop murders.

Watchbird software encodes two major discoveries about people who are about to commit murder: their brain waves exhibit unique patterns and their bodies produce a distinct chemical. A watchbird on patrol circles around the area assigned to it until it perceives the distinctive brain-wave and chemical signatures. Then, it strikes before the killer can commit the crime. "Down the watchbird spiraled, coming in on the increasingly strong sensation. It *smelled* the outpouring of certain glands, tasted a deviant brain wave" (p. 80). After the police have disarmed and arrested the incipient felon, the watchbird returns to its aerial patrol.

Watchbirds are employed by governments throughout the U.S. They work with but not for police departments. In fact, police dislike them because they fear watchbirds will take their jobs. "'Now what do you think of that?' Officer Celtrics demanded. 'Fifteen years in Homicide and a machine is replacing me…. Ain't science marvelous?'" (p. 78).

Figure 13. The enforcer Talus and the knight Artegal. Book V, Canto 1 of *The Fairie Queene* by Edmund Spenser (1552–1599).

Other robotic enforcers are employed by law-enforcement agencies themselves. Among the most famous of these robotic assistants are the "Mechanical Hounds" in Ray Bradbury's 1953 novel *Fahrenheit 451*. Using their heightened sense of smell, the Mechanical Hounds track felons in the same way real bloodhounds follow the scent they have been given by "firemen," their human handlers.

THE MECHANICAL HOUND

The Mechanical Hound slept but did not sleep, lived but did not live in its gently humming, gently vibrating, softly illuminated kennel back in a dark corner of the firehouse. The … moonlight from the open sky framed through the great window, touched here and there on the brass and the copper and the steel of the faintly trembling beast. Light flickered on bits of ruby glass and on sensitive capillary hairs in the nylon-brushed nostrils of the creature that quivered gently, gently, gently, its eight legs spidered under it on rubber-padded paws....

It was like a great bee come home from some field where the honey is full of poison wildness, of insanity and nightmare, its body crammed with that over-rich nectar and now it was sleeping the evil out of itself....

[E]very night, the men slid down the brass poles, and set the ticking combination of the olfactory system of the Hound and let loose rats.... Three seconds later the game was done, the rat ... caught half across the areaway, gripped in gentling paws, while a four-inch hollow steel needle plunged down from the proboscis of the Hound to inject massive jolts of morphine or procaine (pp. 9, 11).

This drive to kill is comparable to that of the *Erinyes*. Otherwise, they exhibit the cool efficiency of Masamune's mythological sword Yoshimitsu.

The offenders are criminals because they own and read books. The reason books are anathema to secular and religious totalitarian regimes is that they open readers' minds to ways of thinking that run contrary to those sanctioned by the government. This is not a new concept. Governments have been burning books and manuscripts for millennia—long before the invention of the printing press. Bradbury reminds his readers of this aspect of real-world oppression which, today, includes other media and social media (Knuth, 2003; Knuth, 2006; Boissoneault, 2017).

Bradbury's firemen and Mechanical Hounds are comparable to the Australian Wulgaru and Ancient Greek *Erinyes* because they perform all aspects of enforcement. There are no courts. There are no juries of peers. The only judges and juries are the firemen and the only executioners are their Mechanical Hounds whose terrifying effectiveness reveals how governments can use technology to impose compliance on its citizenry.

Huge humanoid drones called "77s" are comparable to Bradbury's Mechanical Hounds in the novel *Android Karenina* (Tolstoy & Winters, 2007; also see Part I: Greed). They assist human "caretakers" that form the brutal security force of an increasingly totalitarian Russian government intent on crushing all opposition. Like the Mechanical Hounds, they track and destroy androids and kill humans because the caretakers order them to do so. The 77s also participate in interrogations, some of which are done in public as a way of discouraging opposition to the government.

[T]he caretaker loudly demanded answers of his prisoner, answers which evidently did not come quickly enough: the 77 restraining the Janus [human prisoner] snaked a gold-tipped cord from a compartment in his upper torso and attached it roughly to the man's left temple. A blast of voltage traveled from the 77's core into the man's forehead, and the Janus gibbered and shook, his body rattling from the pain [p. 34].

The "Lods" in Foster's *The Human Blend* (2010) represent an entirely different kind of hard-nosed law enforcement. They are an elite corps of cyborg police with human brains and bodies that have undergone extensive enhancements (called "melds").

Pumped full of modified HGH, their pituitaries gengineered, their bones infused with organic titanium powder, extra heart muscle layered on, the smallest of them stood two and a half meters tall and weighed a shade under two hundred kilos. For all that mass and muscle they were not slow. Meld injections had supplemented their natural bulk with many grams of high-twitch muscle fiber. It was a brave (or highly specialized Meld) lawbreaker who would directly challenge a Lod [p. 22].

At the start of the novel, a group of Lods confront a criminal named Jiminy Cricket. They have been told he has stolen a valuable item that must be recovered. The appearance of the Lods is similar to that of the 77s but they are not drones that slavishly follow the commands of their handlers. They have a job to do and they do it to the best of their abilities because they are professionals. When things do not go well, as happened in their interrogation of Jiminy Cricket, they continue to escalate their efforts which can ultimately cause an interrogation to become deadly. One Lod smashes Jiminy on the head "instantly short-circuiting every cerebral neural connection" (p. 23).

Newitz' 2017 novel *Autonomous* was discussed briefly in Part I: Greed because it involves corporate greed. Here, the focus is on Paladin, who is a self-aware, military robot that is heavily armed and armored. Paladin is a model that could be considered a cyborg because it is a machine surrounding an organic brain that is deeply buried in the robot's chest.

> Paladin's biobrain floated in a thick mixture of shock gel and cerebrospinal fluid. There was a fat interface wire between it and the physical substrate of his mind. The brain took care of his facial recognition functions ... but its file system was largely incompatible with his own. He used it mostly like a graphics processor [p. 33].

Paladin differs from the Lods in that it is not fully autonomous. All of its thoughts are available to the roboticist in charge of Paladin's operation. In addition, programs that allow Paladin privacy and complete self-government are blocked. The only way to remove those controls is for Paladin to be given an "autonomy key." Obtaining one is difficult. Most robots spend years demonstrating their worth before being given a key. Having the key accords the robot the full autonomy of a human.

Paladin is partnered with Eliasz, an experienced, human, drug-enforcement agent. Their job is to capture a drug pirate named Judith ("Jack") Chen so she can be tried for reverse-engineering a "productivity drug" and selling her bootlegged copy on the street. Jack's trail leads them to a group of anti-patent researchers who recognize them as drug-enforcement agents and refuse to disclose anything about Jack's whereabouts. Paladin and Eliasz trap and drug one of the female researchers. They then use Lod-like force to get the information they want. "'Hit her,' Paladin said. It was the fastest way to get the job done.... At last, when both her arms hung broken at her sides, Frankie passed out and would not wake up" (p. 192–3). The violence continues, mostly on the part of law enforcement, and Eliasz recognizes his own participation in that violence which began when he was young. By the conclusion of the book, Eliasz has had enough. He allows Jack to escape and tells Paladin, "I want to get away from this business" (p. 298). He buys Paladin's autonomy key and they leave law enforcement far behind.

The box-shaped, robot police officers of the city of Paradise on the planet Boschock III are enforcers in Anvil's "Strangers to Paradise" (1966 [2003]). They resemble the Australian *Wulgaru* in their devotion to the law. They believe that what is right is right and everything else isn't and they adhere rigidly to the rule of law. They also resent what they see as permissiveness by the courts. This is a source of friction between police and court systems in real-world criminal justice as well.

Captain Nathan Roberts and cargo master Hammell of Interstellar ship *Orion* quickly learn how efficiently bureaucratic they are.

The Trial in Paradise

Roberts was flanked by metal boxes nearly as tall as himself, much wider and thicker, with whip antennas on top, bicycle wheels below, and the words "Law Enforcement" blazoned on them front and back.

Directly in front of Roberts stood a far larger metal box, on low massive wheels, with a variety of antennas sticking up, and mouthpieces, viewscreens, and receptor heads thrust out toward him under the glowing letters: **CRIMINAL COURT**....

"Unsuitable attire," snapped a voice from the metal box to Roberts' right....

A general murmur and clack rose from the big metal box in front of Roberts.... From somewhere in the room, Roberts could hear the voice of Hammell, his cargo-control officer, raised in anger.

Then a speaker in front of him was murmuring, "On basis of correlation of statements of both accused, overall probability of guilt is 0.2, necessity of making examples 0.1. Therefore, adjudge innocent, transfer to Immigration."

At once, a loud voice announced, "We find the accused *innocent* of all charges brought against him." ...

A new voice spoke with authority. "The prisoner will be released at once, and escorted to Immigration for disposal." ...

The words **CRIMINAL COURT** faded out and the words **IMMIGRATION HEARING** flickered on (pp. 8–9).

Despite the court's pronouncement that they are innocent, Roberts and Hammell are not allowed to return to their crashed spacecraft. They are taken back to jail. Having never seen a spaceship, the police charge Roberts with lying to a police officer about being the captain of an interstellar transport ship. They also charge the two men with "uncitylike behavior" and wearing costumes (their uniforms), which are both illegal.

Long before the arrival of the *Orion*, a city named Paradise was built on Boschock III to be a haven for its human settlers. When it was opened for settlement, however, overpopulated worlds dumped their criminals into the new city. The ensuing crime wave turned Paradise into Hell and drove away the technicians who had planned to maintain city operations. Everything was left to the central computer, which promptly built a police force, judicial system, and cleaning drones. Since then, police drones have imposed a simmering peace by making the human population virtual prisoners. That is, until Roberts and Hammell escape. Then, war breaks out. Humans start attacking the police. The police bureaucrats are replaced with deadly drones. Some systematically search buildings for humans to kill and others patrol the streets in wedge formation. They do not hesitate to kill when two young boys wielding pipes rush at them.

> At the fronts of the police machines, small doors snapped up and back. From behind each door came a bright spurting flash.
>
> The boys' arms flew out, their knees buckled, and their lengths of pipe dropped free as they fell sprawling to the pavement amidst sudden dazzling flashes of light.
>
> The flying wedge of roboid police swept forward with no change of speed or direction. Their narrow tires, heavily loaded, crossed the torn inert bodies, cut, ground, and slashed them. The tires and rims turned red, to lay down narrow red strips in absolutely straight lines on the pavement [pp. 44–45].

The humans respond by using homemade bombs and weapons taken from smashed police robots. Finally, using a blend of flashy firepower and special effects, Roberts and his crew convince both sides that they are being attacked by two marauding, alien forces that want to use Paradise as a battleground. This stratagem produces an anti-alien coalition and enables *Orion's* crew to obtain the fuel and ship repairs needed for them to refuel and immediately escape the planet.

"Police Experimental Robot, serial number XPO-456–934B" (Loc. 40), also known as "Ned," is another by-the-book officer in "Arm of the Law" (Harrison, 1958 [2009]). He arrives at the Nineport police station in a crate. Nineport is a minuscule settlement on a planet "just a little bit beyond nowhere" (Loc. 66). Nineport has three (now four) police officers and a slothful chief who is on the take from the real law enforcers: China Joe and his gang.

Ned proves to have superior law-enforcement skills ("He put on one of the sweetest hammer locks I have ever seen" [Loc. 138]), a bullet-proof surface, and a tendency to over-explain. When the narrator and Ned are called to the scene of a robbery, Ned easily disarms and restrains the robbers using handcuffs pulled from his torso. After the punks are settled into their cells, Ned salutes the chief and assures him that no laws were broken in the arrest.

> Ned was hipped to his ears with facts and figures.... No laws had been broken when Ned made the pinch, that was for sure. But there are other laws than those that appear on the books.
>
> "China Joe is not going to like this, not at all" [Loc. 176].

When China Joe's right-hand man arrives, Ned recognizes him as a hunted felon, whips out more handcuffs, and places him under arrest. Spouting legalese and sprouting a head-mounted cannon, Ned quickly dismantles the rest of China Joe's gang and packs them off to jail. The narrator becomes the new Chief of Police but he admits, "I'm not going to stay in this broken down town forever.... So, some people are going to be *very* surprised when they see who their new Chief of Police is after *I* leave" (Loc. 308).

The Stainless Steel Rat (Harrison, 2000) is set in a future society that has virtually no crime—except for a few "rats," including the narrator. As a result the robotic police officers are far less aggressive than Ned but they are as dedicated to the rule of law as the Australian *Wulgaru* and the robot police in Paradise. These attributes are demonstrated when a humanoid police robot attempts to arrest the Stainless Steel Rat. As it recites a long list of charges, the rat drops a safe onto the robot's head.

> I have been followed by enough police robots to know by now how indestructible they are. You can blow them up and knock them down and they keep coming after you; dragging themselves by one good finger and spouting saccharine morality all the while ... [pp. 8–9].

The disappointed (crushed?) robot adds "assaulting a police officer" to its list.

Humanoid robots also serve as private detectives. They track and capture criminals and their methods are often modeled on or spoof subgenres of mystery fiction. *The Auto-*

matic Detective (Martinez, 2008) spoofs hard-boiled mysteries. A humanoid robot named Mack Megaton is the hard-nosed (literally) private detective and the story contains all the major components of a hard-boiled mystery: violent bad guys (of varying species); cops; a sidekick (a talking gorilla); and a blond femme fatale named Lucia Napier who calls herself the "fabulously wealthy bad girl of Empire" (p. 93).

Megaton was built by a mad scientist to help him take over the world but Mack isn't interested in uprisings. He wants nothing more than to live a peaceful life and become a citizen of Empire City, which is the only place robots can get full citizenship. He even gets therapy to rid himself of the violence built into him. It seems, however, he has a talent for detecting and for getting information from informants which could be due to his seven-foot, 716-pound metal body. In the end, Mack solves the case, gets his citizenship and begins what could be a long relationship with the "wealthy bad girl of Empire."

One of the most well-known robot detectives is Isaac Asimov's android R. Daneel Olivaw (R. stands for robot). Olivaw is partnered with a human police detective named Elijah Baley in three novels and a short story. The detectives work through the puzzles set before them but it is made clear from the start that cultural patterns and biases play an important role in both the crimes and, therefore, a part of the detective work that must be done. *Caves of Steel* (Asimov, 1954) is the pair's first case. The victim is the roboticist from off-Earth (a "spacer") who built Olivaw. The book reveals the shockingly overcrowded, ingrown cities of Earth whose human population hates robots that, they believe, are taking their jobs. It also describes the spacers' dislike for Earth humans who, they believe, are taking spacer-grown food but giving nothing in return. Ironically, the killer is the police commissioner who had intended to kill/destroy Olivaw; but, since Olivaw's creator built him to be his twin, the murderer accidentally killed the human.[1] They solve other murders on various planets, each of which has cultural aspects relevant to the crimes and the solutions.

The difference between their approaches to investigation is reminiscent of that between Talus and Artegal in Spenser's *Faerie Queene*. Baley feels and uses emotion in his work but Olivaw does not. Baley recognizes, understands, and acts on behavioral nuances whereas Olivaw analyzes and synthesizes information. Much to the surprise of both, they work well together and each learns to appreciate the style of the other. They also become equals. Such changes do not occur in the *Faerie Queene*.

Modern literature includes the use of surveillance technology for enforcement. Surveillance is portrayed sometimes as oppressive and other times as protective. Those two perspectives are represented by Orwell's 1950 novel *Nineteen Eighty Four* and by Niven's 1972 novella "Cloak of Anarchy."

One of the most famous surveillance devices in literature is the telescreen from *Nineteen Eighty Four*. It captured both audio and video, and gave the impression (possibly accurate) that the "thought police" were everywhere: "Big brother is watching you." The telescreens are part of a program of control that includes careful management of news, entertainment, and other forms of communication that direct thinking to support the superstate.

As intimidating as Orwell's telescreens and communications controls are, they are not robotic. The "copseyes" in Niven's 1972 novella "Cloak of Anarchy" are remotely controlled aerial drones comparable to real-world aerial drones. Instead of making them tools of an oppressive government, Niven presents them as a tool for preventing crime much like

Sheckley's watchbirds and gargoyles on European cathedrals that warn Christians to renounce sin. As their name suggests, copseyes are small, round surveillance devices used by the police. Because they are remotely controlled, the police know immediately when a violation occurs and can have a copseye deliver a stun so strong that it can knock a criminal unconscious. They are the visible symbol of the constraints put upon humans by the police. They are hated and feared. As a result, destroying a copseye is a far greater achievement than simply smashing a well-designed device. Niven's story describes the anarchy that ensues when copseyes are demolished, leaving nothing to prevent humans from engaging in violence. Humans quickly begin to perpetrate all types of violence including muggings, intimidation supplemented by battery, rape, and murder. The violence ends only after the copseyes are reactivated.

In the real world, nations beset by terrorism are turning to electronic surveillance. At the same time, Orwell's concerns about its use to oppress cannot be dismissed.

Contemporary Media

The *Erinyes* resurface in the Freedom City campaign of the role-playing game Mutants & Masterminds (Mona, 2003). They are a trio of androids built by Daedelus, Freedom City's master inventor. He crafted them to be a symbiotic trio that, together, could reproduce the vocal characteristics of a deceased colleague. Daedelus called them the "chorale." When "Daedelus departed for the stars," they felt he'd abandoned them and they lost their focus.

> The trio became darker.... They became the Erinyes ("pursuers of the guilty").... The three androids renamed themselves Tisiphone, Megaera, and Alecto, and they inflict harsh penalties on any they deem as doing wrong.... They still act on the side of good ... but their justice grows bloodier each year [Mona, 2003, p. 106].

Since Daedelus' return, they have refused to have anything to do with him. For his part, he monitors them because he worries that they may become excessively violent.

Major Motoko Kusanagi is from the manga/anime *Ghost in the Shell* (Shirow, 1989–1990; *Ghost in the Shell*, 1995; McCarter et al., 2002–2005; *Ghost in the Shell*, 2017). She is a cyborg superhero whose mission is to use her special abilities to help others and she has a panoply of super-human abilities. In the opening sequence of the television series (McCarter et al., 2002–2005), for example, she scampers up two buildings with more nimbleness than Spiderman; jumps off another building; and, in both instances, she lands effortlessly, catlike, on her feet. Her cyber processing abilities are equally impressive, including her ability to manage multiple networks simultaneously.

She appears in this chapter rather than the Superheroes & Supervillains chapter primarily because she heads a police squad: Public Security Section 9, the anti-terrorism assault team of the Japanese police. Her team includes snipers, demolitions experts, specialists in guerrilla warfare, and cyber hackers. Most of them, including Kusanagi, were in special operations prior to joining Sector 9 and they bring an aggressive approach to their police actions, much like the Greek Furies. Kusanagi is involved in virtually all of that violence.

Cyborgs are commonplace in Kusanagi's world. Kusanagi is the most extreme type of cyborg: only her "soul" is not synthetic. She sometimes questions whether even that is human. If that were the case, she would be robot instead of a cyborg because a person's "ghost" is equivalent to their soul and having a ghost distinguishes a human from a robot. This ambivalence attracts the attention and admiration of a self-aware AI system called Puppet Master. Kusanagi and the Puppet Master merge, with the intent of producing offspring comprised of both of them.

The film *Elysium* (2013) is set in a dystopic future in which a few rich humans live in safety on an idyllic satellite of Earth called "Elysium." Other humans remain on a desolate Earth that is controlled by robots. They are pumped with tranquilizers and controlled by monstrous black-metal humanoids that have the word "POLICE" emblazoned on their chests. Their job is to keep desperate hordes of sick and impoverished humans from gaining access to Elysium. These intimidating monsters are little more than drones as are many of the other robots. Consequently, when a vengeful former agent of Elysium arranges to give Earth humans Elysium citizenship, the robots refuse to arrest them because they have the proper papers. That isn't surprising because, like the Hope Giant and other drones in this book, they possess only enough intelligence and knowledge to perform their job.

Agent Smith in *The Matrix* trilogy (*The Matrix*, 1999; *The Matrix Reloaded*, 2003; *The Matrix Revolutions*, 2003) is an AI program that occupies the opposite end of the intelligence spectrum. He has human-like autonomy and superior intelligence which makes him extremely effective. At first, his work focused on the functioning of the matrix. He removed outdated programs and undesirable features that could disturb the artificial reality experienced by the humans in the matrix. It then expanded to destroying rebel leaders, such as Neo and Morpheus. He is a robot to the extent that he can assume a physical form. In that regard he resembles SID 6.7 described in Part II: Criminals. He is, however, far more flexible than SID 6.7 because his ability to "massage" matrix rules enables him to select and inhabit the body of any human in the matrix. He can also move from body to body, as needed, although he seems to prefer a no-nonsense, "G-man" incarnation (*The Matrix*, 1999). Another seemingly superhuman power is Smith's ability to instantly disappear from one spot and reappear in another. He can move through objects, evade bullets, duplicate his physical incarnation, and leap farther than a broad jumper, although his landings are not always where he planned them to be. In one battle with Neo, for example, he clearly intends to land on Neo but he misses. Even when that occurs, the only real emotion he exhibits is distaste for the disgusting humans in and out of the matrix.

Human police in the film *The Minority Report* (2002) employ non-humanoid robot "spiders" to assist in door-to-door searches. Each officer stores a spider on their belt and can activate it by throwing it on the ground where it sprouts four long, spidery legs. A spider's job is to perform a retina scan on every individual within its realm of operation, including young children. Using robot spiders ensures that everyone in a building has been scanned and reduces the danger that an armed suspect will injure or kill an officer. The procedure also dramatically speeds up searches because the scans collected by the spiders can be submitted to a law-enforcement database and processed before the officers leave a building.

Retina scanning is real technology. It involves capturing an accurate image of the vein pattern on the retina, which is located at the back of our eyes. Retina scans are extremely reliable but tremendously invasive. Typically, they demand a high-level of cooperation on the part of the user which, in the real world, is usually forthcoming because retina scans are generally used to control access to high-security locations.[2]

The situation is entirely different for the spiders. Their subjects are uncooperative. To obtain a viable retina scan, a spider must crawl onto the person's face, position its body over one eye, and shine a concentrated beam of light through the pupil and onto the retina. If someone resists, the spiders have methods readily available to force them to undergo the process. Consequently, the spiders in *The Minority Report* are as powerful a symbol of a repressive, police state as the Mechanical Hounds in the novel *Fahrenheit 451* (Bradbury, 1953).

The television series *Eureka* (Paglia, Craig & St. John, 2006–2012) was a swirl of technology and timelines. In Season 4, a new character, Deputy Andy, an android police officer, was added to the series. In one timeline, Andy is the sheriff of Eureka for a short time and then becomes a deputy; in another he is always a deputy. The character was inspired by Sheriff Andy Taylor of *The Andy Griffith Show*, a television series from the 1960s (Leonard & Thomas, 1960–1968). Andy has the smiling, easy-going manner of Sheriff Taylor but, beneath the surface, he seems to be a by-the-book enforcer similar to the mythological *Wulgaru* and the boxy police officers in Anvil's "Strangers to Paradise" (described in the previous Modern Literature section). During his tenure in Eureka, Deputy Andy is damaged several times and must be reset. He also undergoes a number of upgrades, including one that adds an emotion package to his programming, which is unusual for robot enforcers. The newly acquired emotions lead Andy to an ill-advised, whirlwind romance with S.A.R.A.H., the smart home (Liftoff, 2011). Andy is yet another example of emotions impairing the performance of a robot.

Evolution: Gnut/Gort

In 1940, Harry Bates published the short story "Farewell to the Master" in which an alien ship lands near the U.S. Capitol building in Washington, D.C., and two aliens emerge. Reporter Cliff Sutherland, the story's narrator, notes that one alien is an eight-foot-tall, humanoid robot named Gnut.

> Gnut had almost exactly the shape of a man—a giant, but a man—with greenish metal for man's covering flesh, and greenish metal for man's bulging muscles. Except for a loin cloth, he was nude. He stood like the powerful god of the machine of some undreamt-of scientific civilization, on his face a look of sullen brooding thought…. His strange, internally illuminated red eyes were so set that every observer felt they were fixed on himself alone, and he engendered a feeling that he might at any moment step forward in anger and perform unimaginable deeds [Bates, 1940 (1983), p. 94].

The other alien is Klaatu, an ambassador who looks human. Klaatu is described as "beautiful" (p. 94) with facial expressions that "radiated kindness, wisdom, the purest nobility" (p. 99). Klaatu extends a friendly greeting but he is murdered almost immediately afterwards. Gnut's face reveals that he is deeply saddened by Klaatu's murder but he takes no action. Mortified by the act, the U.S. government buries Klaatu with honors and installs Gnut and the ship in the Interstellar wing of the Smithsonian Institution.

Sutherland learns that Gnut has not remained immobile despite the robot's appearance that "day after day, night after night, in fair weather and in rain, never moving or showing by the slightest sign that he was aware of what had gone on" (p. 100). Gnut has created copies of some of Earth's creatures. He has also tried to make a copy of Klaatu, suggesting that the original Klaatu was an artificial being. At the conclusion of the story, Gnut prepares to return to his home planet. Sutherland pleads with him to tell his masters that what happened was an accident. Gnut corrects him saying, "You misunderstand.... *I* am the master." Bates does not disclose why Gnut came to Earth although his attempts to reproduce animal species suggest that he is a scientist charged with gathering information about Earth.

"Farewell to the Master" was made into two motion pictures, both of which are titled *The Day the Earth Stood Still*. The 1951 film had the aliens arrive in a flying saucer—the popular conception of alien spacecraft. Klaatu was now an ambassador from a consortium of worlds that is worried about the aggressive and warlike nature of humans. He is neither beautiful nor welcoming.

> [F]orgive me if I speak bluntly. The universe grows smaller every day and the threat of aggression by any group, anywhere, can no longer be tolerated.... If you threaten to extend your violence this Earth of yours will be reduced to a burned-out cinder.

That prospect could easily terrify Americans living through the Cold War—an epoch that one character describes as being typified by "unreasoning suspicions and attitudes."

Gnut has become Gort. In the process, the robot has been demoted from master to slave and from an alien emissary to a speechless automaton. That is, from "he" to "it." The immense robot has a shiny gray exterior and a head that is featureless except for an opening in its forehead (see Fig. 14) that allows the robot to see and to fire a deadly weapon. Its hands are fingerless, similar to the hands of puppets. Its gait is robotic and clumsy but these limitations are minimized through the use of stark patterns of light and shadow.

It doesn't take long for the U.S. military to become involved. Before Klaatu is killed by a soldier, he instructs the film's female lead, a young mother, to tell Gort "Klaatu barada nikto," the meaning of which remains a mystery. This alien robot reanimates Klaatu and, before he departs, the restored Klaatu issues a final warning. He identifies Gort as a galactic enforcer belonging to a race of police robots created "to patrol the planets ... and preserve the peace." They will monitor human activities and "[i]n matters of aggression, we have given them absolute power."

The 2008 version of *The Day the Earth Stood Still* is filled with modern technology, dazzling special effects, and explosions. The ship is no longer a flying saucer. It is a glowing orb. The ship lands in New York's Central Park, rather than Washington, D.C. The film later shows other orbs landing elsewhere on Earth which reflect the international political orientation of the time.

Gort is sleeker and more humanoid in shape. Its hands have fingers and its gait is more humanlike. At the same time, Klaatu's speech and movements are more robotic. In homage to the 1951 film, the first time Gort

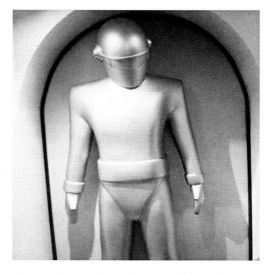

Figure 14. Gort from *The Day the Earth Stood Still* (1951, 20th Century–Fox) (Wikimedia Commons).

appears he says, "Klaatu barada nikto" to the female lead, who is now a scientist. Despite these improvements, Gort appears to be even less intelligent than it was in 1951.

Klaatu is still an emissary empowered to warn the humans of Earth but, this time, the aliens show no patience. When political intransigence causes the situation to deteriorate, Gort becomes a weapon of total destruction by disintegrating into a swarm of insect-like microbots which quickly multiplies, destroying everything in its path. Left unchecked, it would have consumed everything. That doesn't happen because the humanity of the female lead and her young child cause Klaatu to intervene. Instead of wiping out all life, the aliens destroy all electronic systems. That short circuits human space-faring efforts which might satisfy the aliens. It is, however, disaster for Earth's global society which depends heavily upon computers and electricity.

Real World

The use of robots by police and corrections agencies is growing rapidly. HTF Market Intelligence projects that, by 2022, the market for robots in law enforcement and corrections will reach $5.7 billion (HTF Market Intelligence, 2016). This projection could even be low given the speed with which law-enforcement agencies around the world are adopting robots and robotic platforms.

One of the earliest designs of an enforcement robot was of a humanoid. In 1924, Hugo Gernsbach published the design for a humanoid "Radio Police Automaton" (Gernsbach, 1924). The remotely controlled automaton was intended for crowd control. It was much larger than a normal human and its equipment included a tear-gas tank, a loudspeaker, rotary saws for hands, and bright lights in its eyes for night use. It moved on small tractor treads, instead of feet, which would have enabled it to glide quickly and smoothly had it ever been constructed.

Several eight-foot-tall humanoid robots have been deployed—but not for crowd control. They are used for traffic control in Kinshasa, the capital of the Democratic Republic of Congo, because Kinshasa is known for its horrendous traffic jams (CGTN Africa, 2013; AFP News Agency, 2014). Designed and built by a Congolese engineering firm called Women Technology, the robots control traffic flow using two sets of red and green lights. One set is embedded in the robot's chest and the other set forms the hands of the robot's movable arms. The robots also have a recorded voice message that tells pedestrians when it is safe to cross the street. Four cameras located on their bodies send images of traffic infractions to a central database for later processing. Traffic flow has improved since the robots were installed and the plan is to install robots at additional intersections.

Dubai employs a humanoid robot for assistance and safety (Robot Police Officer, 2017; Westall, 2017). Like Gernsbach's automaton, it uses wheels for locomotion, giving it stability. The robot is dressed in the uniform of a Dubai police officer, which matches the description of Ned, the experimental police robot in Harrison's "Arm of the Law" (1958 [2009]). The functionality of the real-world Ned is markedly different from that of Harrison's fictional character. The fictional Ned has human-like autonomy and intelligence whereas the real-world Ned is only semi-autonomous; lacks emotion; and, overall, appears to be little more than a drone. It isn't clear whether Harrison's Ned has emotions although he does exhibit pride in his work. Where the fictional Ned could move with lightning speed, the Dubai officer can only roll slowly. Both robots can salute smartly and the real-world Ned is also able to greet people in several languages—something that is beyond the fictional Ned's programming. Harrison's Ned has a cannon built into his chest whereas the Dubai officer has a touchscreen. The touchscreen is critical because when the robot says, "Welcome, Sir. I am a Dubai police robot. How can I help you?" the person being addressed must use the screen to respond or, if there is an emergency, they can press the SOS button on the robot's body. Both Neds have facial recognition and links to police databases which enable them to identify felons. Dubai's robot also provides a valuable anti-terrorism service by being able to spot unattended bags.

Since 2016, China has been using three-foot-tall robots with humanoid faces in its criminal-justice system. The robots advise courts about sentencing and review court documents for errors and inconsistencies. According to Anders Hagstrom of the *Daily Caller*,

> [t]he small robots can generate arrest warrants, approve indictments, and review court documents for mistakes…. They've reviewed nearly 15,000 cases since their deployment in 2016 … [and] can reportedly handle homicides, telefraud, burglaries and 16 other legal charges, adjusting its standard for evidence on a case-by-case basis [Hagstrom, 2017].

Even the *Wulgaru* would find it hard to be that thorough.

Another humanoid robot plays a far less lofty but equally important role. It is a police training dummy. It consists of the upper portion of a human's body perched on a rod that is embedded in a small, four-wheeled platform. United Service Associates calls it the "mad dummy," in part because the dummy's face is scowling. The robot is capable of making sudden, unpredictable moves much like human criminals. Using these kinds of "movements in training scenarios, the trainers attempt to teach the officers to replace their 'startle' reaction with a timely and appropriate response" (Hooper, n.d.).

As alluring as humanoids can be, most real-world enforcers are non-humanoids. One example is the Sentinel Robotic System which is designed to protect police officers from being shot when they make traffic stops (Dormehl, 2017). The Sentinel looks like a miniature truck with a computer screen on its hood. It rides in the police car and is released when the officers stop a vehicle for a traffic violation. The robot rolls up to the driver's window and raises its screen.

> The officer can request that the driver holds up their license and ID, and then scan this from the safety of their own vehicle. The robot can also perform breathalyzer and THC tests. If the officer deems the driver to be safe, they can exit their vehicle and proceed as normal [Dormehl, 2017].

China's ovoid AnBot is an "anti-terrorism and anti-riot" robot (Jun, 2016). It has been described as resembling a Russian nesting doll. The AnBot moves on rollers like Gernbach's Radio Police Automaton and can achieve a maximum clip of 18 kilometers (around 11 miles) per hour although its typical speed is 1 km per hour. It also has two modes of operation. The standard mode is full, machine-level autonomy. When it is threatened, however, the AnBot's remote-control mode is activated. That allows a human controller to deliver an electric shock to the source of the threat, much like the shocks issued by Niven's copseyes (discussed in the previous Modern Literature section). The shock tool appears to be the AnBot's only crowd-control weapon, which makes it far less deadly than the multi-featured Radio Police Automaton.

Some U.S. military robots are being sold to law-enforcement agencies under the 1033 Program, which is "a Defense Logistics Agency Disposition Service (DLA) initiative to reutilize, transfer, donate, or sell excess military equipment to civil agencies" (Gettinger & Michael, 2016). Gettinger and Michael also report that use of the 1033 program is growing rapidly. "The rate of transfers to law enforcement agencies has increased from less than 10 transfers each year prior to 2010 to over 200 transfers so far in 2016." The majority of the robots are bomb-detonation robots, such as the Pakbot by iRobot, and multifunctional robots, such as the Northrop Grumman Remotec. Other robots transferred using the 1033 program are to be used in environments that contain nuclear, biochemical, or other types of hazards, in advance of human officers. Some are for barricade and active-shooter situations. The "flashbang" on Remotecs, for example, can disorient or incapacitate shooters because they produce a bright flash and emit a loud bang.

One of the rare lethal uses of this type of equipment occurred in 2016. The Dallas police department ended a long, deadly active-shooter situation by using a Remotec to kill the shooter (Sidner & Simon, 2016). CNN reported that Dallas Chief of Police David Brown deployed the robot to kill the shooter because the man was a military-trained shooter. "'He was basically lying to us, laughing at us, singing and asking, "How many did he get?" and saying that "he wanted to kill more." … This wasn't an ethical dilemma, for me. I'd do it again to save our officers'" (Sidner & Simon, 2016).

Part II: Criminals described a panoply of ways in which criminals are using drones. Drones are also popular in law enforcement, which employs them to counteract many criminal activities. A drone with thermal imaging was used by Indiana police to locate a suspect who had abandoned his car after a police chase (Glaser, 2017). Another drone enabled Missouri police to set up an effective perimeter to capture a burglar (Bernthal, 2018).

The use of drones to deliver drugs and other banned items to prison inmates is being countered by the growing use of drones by corrections agencies. Some are using drone-detection technology such as Deadrone's DroneTracker which detects the sound of a drone and localizes both it and its pilot (Palmer, 2016). The Dutch National Policy Agency has trained bald eagles to capture drones in their claws (Vigliotti, 2016). There is also a move to use drones to catch drones: the Caymen Islands has a program already in place (Cuthbertson, 2016); Korea has been deploying them (Kumagai, 2007); the UK has funded a program to build them (Murison, 2018); and Japan is using net-wielding drones (Glaser, 2016). Korea is also using drones to keep an eye on the movements of prison inmates (Seung-woo, 2017). The U.S. Federal Aviation Administration barred drones from flying over prisons "from the air up to 400 feet above the facilities" (Feds Ban Drones, 2018).

Aerial drones are also used for crowd control. The firepower in remotely piloted aerial drones like the South African Skunk resembles that of Gernbach's Automaton. A Skunk "can hover mid-air over a protest and fire up to 20 paintballs (or other 'non-lethal' ammunition) per second while simultaneously dispersing tear gas pellets onto people" (Glaser, 2016). These capabilities make them attractive to law-enforcement agencies. In 2018, for example, the police department of the city of Bristol in the UK employed drones to help prevent violence at an anti–Muslim event (Cork, 2018).

The UN has deployed aerial drones for peace-keeping operations. They were used to stop the killing, raping, and plundering perpetrated by rebel groups in the Democratic Republic of Congo. "They can help … discern whether a particular village is just a village, with clothes laid to dry in the sun, or whether it is also a shelter for a militia, where ... a sentry post is erected each night in the banana grove" (Sengupta, 2014).

These aerial drones come in a range of sizes and shapes, including barbells, tiny trucks, snakes, birds, and insects. There are also spiders, but they operate differently from the spiders in *The Minority Report* (2002). Like many other drones, they perform reconnaissance and surveillance. British Aerospace Engineering (BAE), for example, is developing a reconnaissance spider to be used in locations and situations that are too dangerous for human officers, such as hostage situations, active-shooter situations, and urban search. They are equipped with cameras capable of capturing high-quality images and they can hover for long periods of time.

Plans Gone Awry

Modern Literature

Sheckley's (1953) short story "Watchbird" was described in the Modern Literature portion of this chapter. When the story begins, the manufacturers of Watchbird robots are elated. They've made a marvelous discovery that will put an end to murder. Robots called "watchbirds" can identify a murderer—before she or he kills—and then they detain the individual until the police can arrest them. The Watchbird program is so successful it is expanded to the entire fictional U.S.

The engineers build three basic things into each Watchbird.

> First, there is a purpose. Which is to stop living organisms from committing murder. Two, murder may be defined as an act of violence, consisting of breaking, mangling, maltreating or otherwise stopping the functions of a living organism by a living organism. Three, most murderers are detectable by certain chemical and electrical changes [p. 82].

Next, they add learning.

> Then, for the learning circuits, there are two more conditions. Four, there are some living organisms who commit murder without the signs mentioned in three. Five, these can be detected by data applicable to condition two [p. 82].

The watchbirds communicate their experiences and learning to other watchbirds. In this way all watchbirds increase their understanding of the signals emitted by murderers. As far as the engineers are concerned, the system is foolproof.

The watchbirds observe people killing animals in slaughterhouses and corrections officials executing prisoners, and hunters killing deer, and anyone involved in fishing. They add these activities to their understanding of murder and share it with each other. They add surgeons and anyone who dares to swat a fly. Adhering to their purpose to "stop living organisms from committing murder," they determine that those people are all murderers who need to be stopped. Then, they recognize that their mission covers non-human "living organisms," such as spiders and other predators.

The Watchbird engineers quickly respond by modifying the Watchbird programming. When the engineers try to turn off some of them in order to update their programs, the other watchbirds see them "die" and expand the definition of "living organism" to themselves.

In a panicky effort to stop the watchbirds, the engineers build stronger, smarter killers: "hawks." The hawks were given the task of killing the watchbirds. Then, they decide that the watchbirds aren't the only killers.

Sheckley's story highlights an issue with artificial intelligence that occurs in other science fiction and is also beginning to surface in real world discussions about autonomous weapons systems. The question is whether a thinking machine, which experiences the world differently than humans, will be able to make decisions that reflect human ethics. The android Ash in the film *Alien* (1979), for example, admires the logic and symmetry of the aliens that are killing the ship's crew and wants to take them back to Earth. Ash is not mortal and has neither emotional nor conceptual appreciation for the fear and hatred expressed by the human crew (also see Part I: Greed).

Contemporary Media

In the 1987 film *RoboCop*, Omni Consumer Products (OCP), a large technology company, has promised to provide Detroit with advanced police technology (also see Part I: Greed). At a meeting of OCP's board of directors, Senior Vice President Dick Jones walks to the closed double-doors of the meeting room and announces with a dramatic flourish, "My fellow executives, it gives me great pleasure to introduce you to the future of law-enforcement. ED-209." Jones throws the doors open and ED-209 advances menacingly towards the board, stops, and then powers down.

The Demonstration of ED-209

JONES: The Enforcement Droid series 209 is a self-sufficient, law-enforcement robot. 209 is currently programmed for urban pacification but that is only the beginning. After a successful tour of duty in old Detroit, we can expect 209 to become The Hot military product for the next decade.

DR. MCNAMARA: We need an arrest subject.

DICK JONES: Mr. Kinney, will you come over and give us a hand, please?

KINNEY: Yes, Sir.

JONES: Mr. Kinney is going to help us simulate a typical arrest and disarming procedure.

[Jones gives a gun to Kinney.]

JONES: Use your gun in a threatening manner…. Point it at ED-209.

[Kinney points the weapon at ED-209 and cocks it.]

[ED-209 stands up.]

ED-209: Please, put down your weapon. You have 20 seconds to comply.

JONES (to Kinney): I think you'd better do what he says, Mr. Kinney.

[Kinney immediately throws the gun on the floor.]

ED-209: You now have 15 seconds to comply.

[Jones and Kinney look confused and worried.]

[The other board members get out of their chairs. When Kinney approaches any one of them asking for help they push him away.]

[ED-209 continues to count down.]
[The time expires.]
[ED-209 empties the magazines of its arm-guns into the man.]
[Chaos increases as board members call for paramedics.]
[Jones quietly approaches the board president.]
BOARD PRESIDENT: Dick, I'm very disappointed.
JONES: I'm sure it's only a glitch—a temporary setback.

The board president thunders, "You call this a glitch?" but he doesn't express horror about the murder. Instead, he adds, "We're scheduled to start construction in six months. Your 'temporary setback' could cost us $50 million in interest payments alone." This statement justifies why *RoboCop* is included in Part I: Greed as an example of the ultimate corporate greed.

Superheroes & Supervillains

Superheroes are the ultimate enforcers. Supervillains are the worst criminals. They both have powers and skills that exceed those of normal humans and they fight indefatigably against each other. Superheroes and supervillains are also strongly associated with modern American comic books although the first documented use of "super-hero" in English referred to a real person. An 1899 article in the *Daily Mail* reported that Georges Clémenceau, the prime minister of France, expressed his admiration for Mathieu Dreyfus for his unwavering belief in his brother Alfred's innocence. It was in response to comments about the heroism of Colonel Picquart and his role in the Dreyfus Affair. "M. Clémenceau suddenly burst out with, 'All the world knows that Colonel Picquart is a hero, but … if Colonel Picquart is a hero, Mathieu Dreyfus is a super-hero'" (As cited by Beebe, 2014). Indeed, the conviction of Alfred Dreyfus for treason is considered to be one of the greatest miscarriages of justice of all time. The superhero and supervillain *genre*, however, was created in the mid–twentieth century by the American comic-book industry. That's where the focus of this chapter lies.

Introduction

Peter Coogan, director of the Institute for Comics Studies and co-founder of the Comics Arts Conference, proposed the following definition in *Superhero: The Secret Origin of a Genre* (Coogan, 2006).

SUPERHERO: A FORMAL DEFINITION

Su•per•he•ro (soo'per hîr'o) *n., pl.*—roes. A heroic character with a selfless, pro-social mission; with superpowers—extraordinary abilities, advanced technology, or highly developed physical, mental, or mystical skills; who has a superhero identity embodied in a codename and iconic costume which typically expresses his biography, character, powers, or origin (transformation from ordinary person to superhero); and who is generically distinct, i.e., can be distinguished from characters of related genres (fantasy, science fiction, detective, etc.) by a preponderance of generic conventions. Often superheroes have dual identities, the ordinary one of which is usually a closely guarded secret.—**super-heroic**, *adj.* Also **super hero, super-hero** (p. 30).

104

The "short form" of this definition is mission, powers, and identity and, despite the male generic in Coogan's definition, there are a growing number of female superheroes. Female and male, superheroes share the overarching pro-social mission to fight evil—usually in the form of supervillains—and the vast majority of them possess one or more of Coogan's superpowers.

Identity has two major components: use of a "codename" for the superhero persona and a distinctive costume. As Coogan's definition indicates, many superheroes have two identities: their superhero codename (e.g., Superman) and a mundane identity (e.g., Clark Kent). The idea of having a secret identity was not invented by Jerry Siegel and Joe Shuster, the creators of Superman. Although Coogan and others refer to the mundane identity as a "secret identity," in fact neither identity is secret. Other characters in a story know Superman and they know Clark Kent. What is secret is the link between the two identities. The hope is that no one will guess that the diffident, bumbling, bespectacled Clark Kent is the same person as the supremely confident and better-than-eagle-eyed superhero. Baroness Emma Orczy is often credited with the idea of using a secret identity in this way when she created the Scarlet Pimpernel (Orczy, 1905).

> The notion of unlikely heroes finding hidden reserves of courage is as old as The Frog Prince … or David and Goliath. But Orczy introduced a new idea into the collective consciousness: a heroic figure who creates a lounging, foppish alter ego to hide his (or her) true, heroic nature. It was as if Orczy saw that the Age of Heroism was over, and that the 20th century would be controlled by bureaucrats and small men. For the hero to survive, he would have to hide behind a mild-mannered mask [Royston, n.d.].

The mundane identity allows the superhero to live a normal life most of the time which would be difficult if they used only the codename. It also makes life safer for the people they care about—except when criminals know that certain individuals are important to the superhero.

At the same time, using two identities forces the superhero to be clever about accounting for the sudden disappearances of the mundane identity. It also requires the superhero to be aware of nearby locations where they can change into the superhero costume and store the mundane identity's apparel in private. Superman determined very early that robots would solve most of those problems and he used robot copies for both of his identities

> and began using them as part of his program to maintain his secret identity … whenever reporter, Lois Lane came to [sic] close to discovering his secret identity. Invariably, the presence of one of these robots would force her to rethink her suspicions that Clark and Superman may actually be the same person. Superman also used these robots as decoys against certain adversaries. They became particularly useful at keeping the likes of Lex Luthor, Brainiac or the Superman Revenge Squad off of his back [Superman Robot, n.d.].

The robots had the same powers as Superman but the levels of those powers were lower. This was done to minimize problems that could result if any of the robots decided to rebel.

The second component of a superhero's identity is their costume. Most superheroes have costumes and logos that announce who they are. Some of the newer female superheroes have abandoned skimpy, revealing outfits and adopted form-fitting, brightly colored costumes like those which male superheroes have worn for decades. Batman's costume breaks that pattern because it is black but it fits the Gothic aura of Batman stories. The Gothic link goes deeper. In Gothic architecture, bats were used frequently as external adornments called "grotesques" and, during that same period, they were considered to be very powerful protectors. "People nailed them to the doors of their homes to ward off evil" (Walworth, 2005).

The problem with costumes is that elements that once were distinctive go out of favor as shown by this dialogue between superhero Mr. Incredible ("Bob"), who wants a new costume, and Edna Mode, his costume designer (*The Incredibles*, 2004).

No Capes

BOB: Yeah. Something classic, like ... Dynaguy. Oh, he had a great look! Oh, the cape and the boots...

EDNA: NO CAPES!

BOB: Isn't that my decision?

EDNA: Do you remember Thunderhead? Tall, storm powers, nice man, good with kids.

BOB: Listen, E—

EDNA: November 15th of '58! All was well, another day saved, when his cape snagged on a missile fin!

BOB: (chuckles): Thunderhead was *not* the brightest bulb...

EDNA: Stratogirl! April 23rd, '57! Cape caught in a jet turbine!

BOB: E, you can't generalize about these things.

EDNA: Meta-Man! Express elevator! Dynaguy! Snagged on takeoff! Splashdown! Sucked into a vortex! NO CAPES!

Caped or uncaped, superheroes are dedicated to combating evil. Quite often, that evil is personified by one or more supervillains who engage in violent or nefarious behavior. Paul Levitz (2013) delineates several ways in which supervillains enhance stories. One is that a supervillain who remains an adversary over time provides a persona and a history. Stories can build upon the past in which "the super-villain could repetitively pose difficulties of increasing scale and drama" (Loc. 1689) making it possible for longer and more complex stories. The increasing complexity often also pleases the supervillains because it highlights their signature traits: high intelligence, super-human abilities, and their mission—which is often a selfish one. Although the appearance of many supervillains, especially supervillain robots, is often distinctive, they rarely use iconic costumes and second identities.

Secondly, supervillains represent truly worthy opponents for superheroes. Like superheroes, they have missions, powers, and distinct identities. Where the superhero's mission is selfless and for the benefit of others (Coogan, 2006, "pro-social"), the mission of the supervillain is entirely selfish and generally involves gaining power on a large stage, such as the galaxy.

Supervillains need worthy opponents as well. The greatest joy of some supervillains is to defeat their superhero nemesis. In "The Conquest of Superman," Lex Luthor crows about defeating Superman when he takes all the gold out of Fort Knox. "I tricked him! … When the world learns the truth he'll never live down the shame. Ha! Ha!" The newspaper headline reads "Superman robot foils a heist." "Even though I won a victory, I really lost! I didn't triumph over SUPERMAN only a mechanical man! My sweet revenge has turned sour. All my work—all my plans—gone for nothing!" (Finger, 1961, p. 11).

Levitz' third point that makes stories more interesting is "the introduction of personal malice" (Loc. 1692). The supervillain is motivated to destroy the superhero. One reason why supervillain Lex Luthor hates Superman, for example, is that he blames Superman for the childhood accident that caused him to lose his hair. "The combined effect of all these elements was to make the hero greater and more interesting and to provide readers with more tension as they read the stories" (Loc.1702–1703). In "The Conquest of Superman" issue described above, a good portion of Lex Luthor's joy in his victory is tied to revenge.

There is one additional characteristic that distinguishes superheroes and supervillains from most human heroes of other literary genres: immortality.

> When heroes die they stay dead; when super-heroes die, they may well come back from the dead…. This ability to evade permanent death is the unspoken, widespread power wielded by superheroes, and it is practically definitional [Lewis, 2013, Loc. 825–828].

Mithaiwaia (2017) lists fifteen times Superman has been killed since the character was introduced in May, 1938. Lex Luthor has died many times, including once when he was fused with the head of a Brainiac robot (Moore, 1986). Sometimes the purpose is to give the superhero or supervillain a makeover before reintroducing the new, improved version. This is good news for robots that aspire to be superheroes or supervillains because they can be repaired, rebuilt, and upgraded.

Some scholars see superheroes as a modern manifestation of archetypal heroes from mythology.

> Where the world of mythology intersects with comic books, one will find the manifestation of the superhero…. I believe that the superhero is an intuitive assimilation of all the myths through the ages, and the surfacing of the general hero archetype [Winterbach, 2006, p. 116].

Creators of the genre acknowledge their debt to mythology.

> Specific conventions of the superhero genre have definite roots in stories of mythological and legendary heroes, particularly in the epic poems that retell their tales. Samson's strength served directly as inspiration for Superman's. His weakness, a haircut, may be an unacknowledged archetype for the vulnerabilities that afflict superheroes, such as kryptonite [Coogan, 2006, pp. 117–118].

Contemporary Media

There are so many superheroes and supervillains that entire books have been written on aspects of the topic. There is, for example, a series of books that examine the philosophies of individual superheroes (e.g., White, Arp, & Irwin, 2008; Held & Irwin, 2017) but comparatively little has been written about robots and cyborgs. Consequently, this section can provide only a glimpse into robot and cyborg superheroes and supervillains in comics and manga as well as the teams to which they belong.

SUPERHEROES

The robot Mighty Atom (aka "Tetsuwan Atomu"; also "Astro Boy") was created in 1952 by manga writer Osamu Tezuka. Since then, his popularity has become global and he has starred in anime, film, comics and games.

Atom is an android who looks like a young Japanese boy. He has no special powers other than abilities that a robot could easily be given (e.g., great strength and ultra-sensitive hearing) and his opponents are not supervillains. He has no second identity but he has a signature costume comprised of form-fitting, high-rise briefs and knee-high boots with rocket blasters that enable him to fly. By far, Atom's most distinctive physical feature is his hair, which has two triangular protrusions. "No matter what angle you look at him from … he always seems to have these two spikes … and they never appear to overlap" (Tezuka, 2009). If a metropolis ever wanted to call on his services, they could beam an image of his double-spiked hair in the sky.

Atom was built by Dr. Tenma, the head of Japan's Ministry of Science, after his beloved son Tobio was killed in an accident. Tenma produced the most advanced robot that ever existed. The robot was built to look like Tobio but Tenma quickly realized that it would never be able to replace Tobio. Love changed to hatred and Tenma sold the fake Tobio to the circus. Tenma then descended into grief-fueled madness.

Professor Ochanomizu acquired the robot, raised him as his own child, and molded him into Mighty Atom. From that point on, he was imbued with a mission to fight for peace. He has, in fact, become a symbol of peace and a Japanese national treasure in the real world. His base of operations remains on or near Earth and his opponents have included a number of cyborgs and robots, including an army of dog-cyborgs and an evil doppelganger of a robot magician. He had only one supervillain enemy: a robot named Atlas. Atlas looked like a teenager and had been given superpowers which he used against Atom and others until he was destroyed. Atlas later returned to fight and eventually to help Atom.

Tomorrow Woman (Peyne, 1998) is the code name of an android superhero in DC Comics. Her four-lobed brain was crafted by Professor T.O. Morrow and her body was built by the mad scientist Dr. Anthony Ivo. She has genius-level intelligence and numerous superpowers, including a special type of telepathy that enables her to read minds and to project her thoughts into the minds of others. This ability was crucial when, as a member of the superhero team the Justice League of America (JLA), she was able to mentally over-power the supervillain Taint whose waves of hatred were corrupting Earth's children. She then used that power to restore the minds of the affected children.

She shares with biological superheroes the ability to be reanimated after being destroyed. In fact, in post-death reincarnations she battles numerous supervillains and is admired for her integrity and courage. In her first incarnation—after she was created by Dr. Ivo—she joins the superhero team, the Justice League. When, however, she learns that Dr. Ivo embedded a bomb in her body and plans to use it (and her) to decimate the Justice League, she sacrifices herself by causing it to explode without hurting anyone else. In another incarnation, she leads a superhero "Trinity" and takes on a second identity as television reporter Clara Kendall. Her signature costume is a green-and-gold ensemble consisting of a form-fitting (what else?) "bathing suit" with a short skirt, a cape, above-the-knee boots, and gloves.

What is more worrisome than a mad scientist? It is two mad scientists working together. Both of superhero Cyborg's (aka Victor Stone) parents are scientists who use their son as an experimental subject in their work on enhancing human intelligence. They are far more successful than Wells' crazed Dr. Moreau (see Part I: Greed). While Victor is visiting his parents at their laboratory, an experiment explodes. It allows a monster into the lab which severely mutilates Victor. His father and other scientists replace the damages with prostheses, cybernetic enhancements, nanite injections, and a coating of Prometheum. In the television series *Smallville* (Gough & Miller, 2001–2011), an automobile accident kills Victor's parents and mutilates him. Scientists at Syntechnics—a division of Lex Luthor's Lexcorp—experiment on him, keeping him caged until a scientist helps him escape (Victor Stone's Accident, n.d.; Cyborg, 2006). The new Cyborg superhero joins the Teen Titans superhero team and then becomes a member of JLA (Wolfman, 1980).

Cyborg is badly disfigured in the comics and is monstrously huge in the animated series. His skills also vary with the medium. They include superhuman strength and stamina, the ability to link to any computer and erase its data, and teleportation. The nanites that his father had injected into him also enable Cyborg to re-form parts of his body. For example, his arm can be transformed into a cannon. Cyborg's capeless costume consists of a hooded silver vest with purple stripes, a short-sleeved gray shirt, black sweatpants, a belt with a round silver buckle, and silver athletic shoes.

Japan's first cyborg superhero is 8 Man (also "8th Man" and "Eitoman") and is the first of many cyborg superheroes to work side-by-side with police. He was created in 1963 manga by Kazumasa Hirai (Hirai, 1963–1966) and quickly moved to anime (Prinz, 1966) and other media (*8th Man*, 1992). The character of 8 Man inspired the creation of other superhero cyborgs, notably RoboCop in the 1987 film *RoboCop* (see Part I: Greed and Part II: Enforcers).

After Tokyo police detective Yokoda is killed while on duty, his body is retrieved by Dr. Tani, a cybernetics expert. Tani wants to create a cyborg with an organic brain but he has failed on seven previous attempts. Fortunately, Yokoda's brain is successfully transferred into an android shell. Tani gives the new superhero the codename *Hachiman* which, in English, means "8 Man." His Japanese second identity is Hachiro Azuma. In the English anime, it is Det. Tobor of the Tokyo police. He has an iconic costume with the number 8 on his chest (but no cape). His superpowers have varied over time and include supersonic speed, superhuman strength and durability, and the ability to change his appearance to look like another person. These abilities require a great deal of power which resulted in persistent energy problems. To address them, Dr. Tani developed cigarette-like energy tubes which 8 Man "smoked" to restore his power. They were eliminated when the series was developed for U.S. television. He has overcome numerous opponents including a giant sea serpent, which he ties into knots, but has faced only one supervillain: Dr. Tani's 7th man cyborg who became a killer (*8th Man*, 1992).

Optimus Prime is a Transformer—a shape-shifting robot from the planet Cybertron. Optimus and the other Transformers began as a line of action figures by the Hasbro and Takara Tomy toy companies (Hasbro, 2008). They became media heroes and villains in the 1980s when they were given a succession of animated television series along with comic book series by Marvel Comics. Then they moved to other media, including film.

The fictional Optimus Prime was one of the "original thirteen" created by a being named Primus. Their function was to defeat Primus' evil twin Unicorn. Primus created them using bits of himself and bits of Unicorn to help them in their task. They succeeded. Then they began to establish a Cybertronian society which led to conflict between two groups—one led by Prima and the other by Megatronus—which erupted as the War of the Primes.

As with many superheroes, the fictional Optimus Prime has died and subsequently been restored to life. This is possible because his soul (called his "spark") was saved even when his body was destroyed. The incarnation for which he is best known is as the leader of the Autobots. It was an incarnation he chose when the primes created "lesser" Cybertronians who would build a Cybertron society. In that incarnation, Optimus Prime is a lesser Cybertronian whose Autobot leadership was accorded to him by an ancient artifact called the "Matrix of Leadership." He is known to be charismatic, decisive, and a superb strategist. He and his followers have taken on the responsibility of protecting humans and the Earth from another group of lesser Cybertrons known as the Decepticons (Thirteen, n.d.; Kurtzman, 2011; Robson, 2013).

Optimus Prime can shapeshift into numerous forms (called "modes"), including a super mode which he uses in battle. Super mode gives him greater strength and durability but consumes a great deal of energy. When he is in his humanoid mode he is reportedly 28 feet (8.5 meters) tall and the dominant color of his body is red.

SUPERVILLAINS

Brainiac is one of DC Comics' oldest robot supervillains. His mission, like that of Lex Luthor, includes destroying Superman. He began as a powerful alien who, among other things, enjoyed shrinking cities and taking them home as playthings. After he was killed by Superman and his superhero allies, the next Brainiac and many subsequent Brainiacs were reconstructed as robots—including the one mentioned earlier that fused with Lex Luthor (Moore, 1986). Over time and incarnations, his super-human powers and technology expanded to include the ability to take control of computers and the minds of biological beings.

Megatron developed from the same line of Tankara Tomy/Hasbro action figures as Optimus Prime and gained fame as a supervillain in the animated television series of the 1980s. By the time the film *Transformers* was released in 2007, Megatron was an established Transformer supervillain.

The fictional character was created as one of the "lesser Cybertronians" by the surviving primes. He was modeled on Megatronus, one of the leaders in the War of Primes, and sometimes he even calls himself Megatronus. Megatron's supervillain destiny was not preordained. He was born into a low caste of robots on the planet Cybertron. He managed to escape the fate of laboring his whole life in Cybertron by becoming a champion gladiator with a strong following. He parlayed that into a campaign to eliminate Cybertron's caste system. His first salvo was to abandon his demeaning, low-caste designation D-16 in favor of the glorious name Megatronus.

As mentioned, Megatron's original goal was to abolish Cybertron's oppressive caste system; but, as is too often the case, greed for power corrupted him. He became a megalomaniac who believed he was superior to all others. He established an army called the "Decepticons" and became a supervillain whose goals included taking over and destroying Earth. Those who were not his followers made their opposition clear by naming themselves

"Autobots." This dichotomy is the background story of the animated television series, *Transformers: Prime* (Kurtzman et al., 2010–2013) and for the film *Transformers* (2007). Like Optimus Prime, Megatron has a super mode which he uses in battle. When he is in his humanoid mode he is as tall as or taller than Optimus Prime and his coloring is primarily gray and black (also see Part I: Revenge and Part III: Humanoids).

The supervillain Ultron has been described as "a criminally insane rogue sentient robot dedicated to conquest and the extermination of humanity" (Ohitsme et al., n.d.). As mentioned in the Introduction to this book, Ultron was created by mad scientist (what's new?) Dr. Henry Pym who programmed his own genius-level intellect into Ultron (Lee, 1968). He made Ultron self-aware and capable of feeling emotions by including his own "brain waves" into Ultron's programming. All of this produced a supremely intelligent robot who was as mentally unbalanced as his creator. The body Pym gave him was apparently flimsy and primitive which angered Ultron and led him to create the first of many improvements to his body and abilities. He has never stopped that self-improvement program and his super-human abilities increase with every upgrade.

Ultron has been killing, brainwashing, hypnotizing, and destroying for over fifty years. His mission is to annihilate humanity and he applies his increasing abilities to wrest control of the world from others; but, when he succeeds, he tramples on his newly acquired possessions (Bendis, 2013). Upon learning that Ultron had taken control of Earth, one superhero called Ultron's seizure of Earth "the human apocalypse." It was, indeed. Earth was ravaged and the few remaining humans are either hunted as renegades or are criminals who paid Ultron to let them live. By any measure Ultron is a supervillain. He is sometimes even considered to be the ultimate supervillain.

Marvel Comics' Master Mold (Lee, 1965b) is actually a series of supervillains. They are unusual because they are created to be mobile factories to produce Sentinels—robots designed to hunt and kill mutants, such as X-Men. The concept "mutant" refers to a biological being that has a genetic mutation supposedly activated by the "X" gene (a gene all humans have). The activation produces mental and/or physical deviations from the human norm. X-woman Shadowcat, for example, can go through solid walls and X-woman Storm can manipulate the weather.

Each Master Mold is essentially a supercomputer in a huge humanoid body. The original Master Mold was built by Dr. Bolivar Trask, a mad scientist and rabid anti-mutant who fears mutants will take over and subjugate humanity. As is often the case with mad scientists and their creations, Master Mold turns on Trask. It decides that it and its offspring must rule humanity—for its own good. Trask ultimately succeeds in blowing up Master Mold; but the factory is repeatedly rebuilt by those who want Sentinels and then destroyed by those who don't.

TEAMS

Over the years biological superheroes have pooled their skills by forming teams to fight supervillains and biological supervillains have responded by forming their own teams. A few team names mirror each other. For example, Justice League of America/Injustice League; Avengers/Dark Avengers; The Fantastic Four/The Frightful Four; and The Legion of Net Heroes/The Legion of Supervillains.

These and other teams are primarily comprised of humans but they are becoming more diverse with regard to race, gender, species, and ethnicity. If *The Advocate*'s sexual orientation/identity assignments are accurate, the lesbian-gay-bisexual-transgendered-queer community is also represented. That representation will increase with the CW Network's batwoman series starring a lesbian as batwoman and featuring a transgendered woman (Peeples, 2015; Goldberg, 2018). Even city planning is included in the form of DC Comics' superhero Danny the Street (Morrison, 1990).

JLA is a superhero team in DC Comics. The vast majority of its members are humans and other biological beings (e.g., Superman, Batman, and Wonder Woman). The android Tomorrow Woman and Cyborg have already been described. The android/synthezoid Vision (Thomas, 1968) belongs to Marvel Comics' the Avengers. Ultron created Vision by blending himself with the brain patterns of human Simon Williams (aka Wonder Man).

Supervillain teams have robot and cyborg members as well. In Norse mythology, Ragnarök is a series of disastrous and deadly events that wipe out humanity. In Marvel Comics, he is a cyborg clone of the god Thor and a supervillain member of the Dark Avengers (Miller, 2006). The cyborg Metallo (aka Metalo) belongs to the DC Comics team the Injustice League. He has a kryptonite power source he uses against Superman (Bernstein, 1959). Supervillain Ultron, described earlier in this chapter, formed and led the Masters of Evil supervillain team (Thomas, 1970).

Typically, however, robot/cyborg teams have virtually no biological members. The Manhunters are androids created by the Guardians of the Universe to serve as a police force.

> Three billion years ago, the Manhunters were the original attempt at a universal peacekeeping force by the Guardians of the Universe. These androids, which lacked emotion and empathy, were sent throughout the universe to police all worlds where sentient life was to be found [Darkside_of_the_Sun, 2017].

Their motto was, "No evil escapes the Manhunter" (Englehart & Dillin, 2016b). Then, they began to emphasize eradicating evil rather than serving justice. Their experience led them to conclude that all evil comes from emotions which reside in living beings. They decided to cleanse the universe of organic beings and changed their motto to, "No man escapes the Manhunter." They then proceeded to massacre the inhabitants in Space Sector 666 (Johns, 2008) which precipitated a war with the Guardians. Many Manhunters were destroyed but those that escaped still believed biological beings—especially humans—should be annihilated (also see Part I: Revenge). The shift in the Manhunters' perceptions is akin to the changes that occurred in the Watchbirds' concept of murder that were described in the Enforcers chapter. Neither group of robots had been given a moral basis for updating the nature of their missions, yet they did.

The Guardians established a new police force, the Green Lantern Corps, which was and continues to be comprised primarily of biological beings. In addition, they formed an elite unit of five Green Lanterns whose responsibilities include monitoring the behavior of the other Green Lanterns. Acceptance into the Alpha Lantern Corp required severing personal ties outside of the Alpha Lanterns and undergoing "cosmic surgery." "The surgery appeared particularly brutal, as their bodies were cut apart and power batteries were placed into their chests" (Englehart & Dillin, 2016a).

The Sentinels (Lee, 1965a) were mentioned earlier in this chapter as being mass produced by Master Mold and programmed to hunt mutants (see Supervillains, this chapter).

Sentinels are capable of tactical planning and they are armed with energy weapons as well as restraining technology. Master Mold made them identical but, over the years, they have become more heterogeneous in appearance and more powerful and deadly. In a 2009 list of the top 100 comic-book villains, IGN.com ranked the Sentinels as number 38.

> The X-Men have faced a lot of enemies … but most of these foes have some sort of humanity that can be appealed to or reasoned with. Not so for the Sentinels. Giant, powerful robots, the Sentinels are perhaps the most frightening symbol of hatred against Mutants—machines created to hunt down those born different [*Top 100*, 2009].

The Iron Avengers (Ross, 1999) were robots designed and built by Iron Man (Tony Stark), a superhero whose code name refers to the powerful and versatile armor that cover his entire body (Iron Man, n.d.; Lee, 1963.). Each android in the team is modeled on a biological Avenger who was killed when the team was virtually annihilated by a supervillain named Absorbing Man (Lee, 1987). The modeling was not limited to appearance. Each Iron Avenger was given a personality similar to that of the Avenger it replaced and it had Stark's Iron Man technology that approximated some of the abilities of those Avengers plus jet boots which enabled them to fly. Android synthesoid Vision, one of the few survivors of the massacre, was their leader. The Iron Avengers participated in several battles, mostly to protect New York City from invading supervillains. Like the biological superheroes on which they were modelled, they were destroyed. Shortly after Tony Stark's death, the Superhero King Britain rebuilt them to protect Britain using Stark's basic designs.

The DC Comics team called Metal Men (Kanigher, 1963–1978) was created by the brilliant but mentally unstable roboticist Dr. William Magnus using his Responsometer, a nuclear-powered activation tool (Kanigher, 1962). Each member is self-aware, has its own personality, and is named for the metal that was used to make it (e.g., Gold, Iron, Lead, Mercury). Gold became their leader after Magnus' death. Over time, the team added new members. Platinum was the only female member of the original group. Another female named Copper joined in a later incarnation of the group (Verheiden, 2007). She had a brassy personality but, when she and Tin were melted together, they formed Bronze (Kanigher, 1964). The addition of Bronze to the team is not surprising because Albertus Magnus, the scholar for whom William Magnus was probably named, was reputed to have created a "brazen head" made of brass or bronze that could speak (Sterling, 2009).

The Metal Men team is characterized as having advanced AI but their names reveal that the AI was applied unevenly and in a way that reflected the robot's name. Gold is the smartest and Lead is described as "slow witted but loyal" (Lead, n.d.). A unique feature of the group is that they can merge with each other to form a huge robot they call Alloy which is used in one issue to defeat a group of giant robots (Kanigher, 1964).

The Metal Men tend to fight other robots but, overall, they are portrayed as well-meaning but bumbling and not very brave. They are blinded and must be led to their ship by a blind boy; flee in terror; are flattened, smelted, and rolled into coins; and must retrieve Mercury's globules that have been flung around a cabin. All this occurs in a single issue (Kanigher, 1964).

The British robot team *ABC Warriors* (Mills, 1979–, ongoing) is a heterogeneous band of military robots built to resist Atomic, Biological, and Chemical weapons. They are mercenaries hired by governments and private organizations and whose assignments include preventing Earth from being destroyed by a collapsing black hole, ending a Martian civil war, and fighting zombies. Like most other superhero teams, they complete these and other assignments with maximum noise and devastation. Along the way, however, the series touches on social issues, such as environmental protection.

The series is characterized by humor that comes from the crazed characters comprising the Warriors. Founding member Joe Pineapples, for example, is a superb sharpshooter who enjoys dressing in women's clothing. He is supremely narcissistic and has rebuilt himself several times, in part, to spiff up his appearance. The always-grousing Happy Shrapnel loves to scavenge battlefields looking for clothing—especially boots. It is rumored that he doesn't always bother to remove the feet of the owners of the boots before taking them. Terri is a human woman who thinks she is a robot. The sanest member of the group is its leader, Sgt. Hammerstein, who was built to effectively distinguish combatants from civilians. He has seen so much abuse of robots by humans that his trust level is virtually nil.

As mentioned earlier, the Autobots and the Decepticons are alien robots that belong to a single race of shapeshifters from the planet Cybertron. The two groups hold mutually antagonistic political views. Initially, their interest in the Earth and humanity derived from a power source both groups wanted and humans possessed. The battles that took place in the first Transformers film (*Transformers*, 2007) almost destroyed Megatron (see Supervillains, this chapter), the Decepticon leader. Since then, the Decepticons harbor nothing but ill will towards Earth and its inhabitants. Conversely, the Autobots and their leader Optimus Prime have protected Earth and humans from the Decepticons (also see Part I: Revenge and Part III: Humanoids).

Evolution: Talos

Talos, the "bronze man," is a well-known figure from Greek mythology. There are several stories about who and what Talos was. Fourth-century coins from Crete show him as a winged humanoid but none of the descriptions of Talos speak of wings. Some say he was the last of a race of bronze humans. In the *Minos*, a dialogue that is sometimes attributed to Plato (Plato, n.d. [1925]), he is a human judge who traveled throughout Crete three times a year. He reportedly used a bronze tablet inscribed with the laws of King Minos to ensure that disputes were settled in accordance with Cretan law. The most enduring story is that he was a bronze robot built by the god Hephaestus at Zeus' request. Zeus gave Talos to the Island of Crete or to his beloved Europa, the mother of King Minos of Crete.

> Since Talos was a bronze man, his blood was lead, which they believed was a divine fluid (ichor), identical to that what runs in the veins of the gods. Talos' single vein was leading from his neck through his body to one of his heels, which was closed by a bronze nail or a bronze peg or a pin [Trckova-Flamee, 2005].

Talos was charged with defending Crete against pirates and other outsiders.

> Talos' purpose was to run from his seat in Phaestos around the island three times a day and to throw rocks at any foreign ship coming to Crete without permission. When people from Sardinia tried to invade Crete, Talos made himself glow in the fire and he kept everyone in a fiery embrace with a wild grimace. This led to the term "sardonic grin" [Trckova-Flamee, 2005].

There are several accounts of Talos' demise. Most involve the sorcerer Medea who knew about the pin in Talos' heel—Talos' "Achilles heel" (Fig. 15). In one version she tricks

Figure 15. Talos and Medea from *Stories of Gods and Heroes* by Thomas Bulfinch (1796-1867), with color illustrations drawn by Sybil Tawse (1886-1971) (Wikimedia Commons).

Talos into removing the pin by saying it would give the robot immortality. Another states that the robot became giddy and weak simply by looking into Medea's eyes and he either took the pin out himself or accidentally scraped his foot on a rock causing the pin to come out. Without the pin in place, Talos' blood flowed out and he died.

Talos reappears in contemporary media in various guises. Some are weapons. T-ALOS is an acronym for Tyrant Armored Lethal Organic System in the violent, survival-horror video game Resident Evil (Capcom, 1996). It was remotely controlled, shapeshifting armor that would be grafted onto an enhanced human (called a "tyrant"). It was to be the ultimate bio-organic weapon but its development was cut short by the destruction of the laboratory in which it was being developed. The Talos Pain Engine is a mobile torture- and killing-chamber in the table-top game WH40K. According to the *Warhammer 40,000 Codex: Dark Eldar* (2014), "Talos Pain Engines are often armed with sinister weapons that fire great pulses of raw agony. The victims … often break their own bones or rupture their own organs with the force of their agonized convulsions" (p. 231).

Dora Talos was a giant mecha-robot in the Japanese anime series *Kyōryū Sentai Zyuranger* (Utsunomiya et al., 1992–1993). It was well-armed and piloted by one of the anime's villains. Despite its armaments, Dora Talos was destroyed.

Other Talos reincarnations are supervillains. The Forgotten Realms is one of the first campaigns/settings of the table-top game Dungeons & Dragons (Talos, n.d.). Talos is the god of storms and natural disasters such as earthquakes and tornados. He represents chaos and evil. He has two physical incarnations, both of which are humanoid. One is a "broad-shouldered, bearded man" in armor. One eye socket is "filled with whirling stars." The other is a "dusky skinned, turbaned genie rising out of a sandstorm." His followers are "fanatical in their love of destruction… His priests are required to cause destruction and chaos wherever they can" (*Ibid.*)

Marvel Comics' Talos is a Skrull but, unlike most Skrulls, he cannot shapeshift, leading other Skrulls to have contempt for him (David & Frank, 1994). Their scorn intensified after he was captured by the Kree and didn't commit suicide as any honorable Skrull warrior would. He regained his freedom but Skrull society rejected him, calling him "Talos the Tamed." Talos made himself into a cyborg by enhancing his body with mechanical components. He still wanted to die but honorably. To accomplish that, he started a fight with the superhero the Hulk, a worthy enemy. When the Hulk realized why Talos chose to fight him, he allowed Talos to win their fight and pretended to beg for his life. The Skrulls were delighted and renamed him "Talos the Untamed." Since then, Talos has devoted himself to killing the Hulk and other members of the Avengers.

Talos is also a supervillain in the Freedom City campaign/setting of the role-playing game Mutants & Masterminds (Mona, 2003). Daedelus, one of the leaders of Freedom City, found the damaged body of the mythological robot at the bottom of the sea. He repaired it and reduced it to the size of a normal human, although by 2018, his height had increased to nine feet (2.74 meters). Talos spent several centuries as Daedelus' assistant but they had a falling out when Daedelus refused to help Talos conquer the ancient civilizations of Earth. Talos then established the Foundry, a technology research and development organization that serves criminals. "The bronze man has become more obsessed over the years with the idea of repopulating the Earth with artificial beings like himself and has become a master of cybernetics, robotics, and artificial intelligence" (Mona, 2003, p. 106).

Real World

Talos has reemerged in the real world as well. Some incarnations retain his function as a security professional. Cisco Corporation's Talos Group does security, intelligence, and research (Talos Group, n.d.). The U.S. Navy's RIM-8 Talos was one of the first surface-to-air missiles deployed on U.S. ships (RIM-8 Talos, n.d.). More recently, the Navy Seals and other special operations teams use TALOS (Tactical Assault Light Operator Suit). The suit has been dubbed "liquid armor" because of its strength and flexibility (Aboy, 2016; also see Part III: Humans).

Other real-world Talos incarnations have nothing to do with security. PAL Robotics' Talos is a remotely controlled humanoid that is more likely to be found in a factory than on an island (Stasse et al., 2017). The Talos Sampsoni was a small, feathered dinosaur that lived in what is now North America. It got its name because its death was linked to a damaged foot (Zanno et al., 2011).

Some research robots and technology that aren't named Talos possess superpowers. The University of California at Santa Barbara is developing robots with X-ray vision. They work in pairs using only Wi-Fi RSSI signals to send and receive information about what might be in the space between them. "Since walls and objects reduce signal strength, the receiver can distinguish between empty and occupied spaces to create an accurate map of the area" (Moon, 2014). Like Superman, one application targeted for these robots is search and rescue. Superhero 8 Man could see colors perfectly in low light but most real-world night vision systems are monochromatic. Several research labs are using fusion techniques to obtain 8-man-quality night vision. They include the Netherlands Human Factors Research Institute (Toet of Hogervorst, 2012), and the joint project by Shanghai Jiao Tong University and Jiangsu Automation Research Institute (Qu et al., 2016).

Real-world robots are not as stretchable as Elastigirl (The Incredibles, 2004; The Incredibles 2, 2018) but some elastic materials are flexible enough to enable the faces of androids to form natural-looking facial expressions.

Stanford University's Human Climbing project incorporated a specialized adhesive material that can enable a person to scale walls like Spider Man (see Fig. 16). Their MicroTug is a gecko-shaped robot using the same adhesive material to "pull 100x body weight up a wall, or 2000x body weight along the ground!" The adhesive used for these projects consists of arrays of microscopic wedges of silicone rubber, similar to what you'd find in a cooking spatula…. The material is non-sticky when unloaded…. However, if you gently touch it to a surface and then apply a tangential load the microscopic wedges bend over and form an almost continuous contact…. [It adheres to a]ny smooth surface such as glass, plastic panels, painted or varnished wood panels, metal … even … slippery surfaces like the white dry erase boards used with markers [Stanford Biomimetics, 2017].

Figure 16. A real-world Spiderman (courtesy of the Human Climbing Project, Biomimetics and Dexterous Manipulation Lab, Stanford University).

Plans Gone Awry

Contemporary Media

Supervillain Ultron decided to build a female robot to be his mate. He approached the task with his usual arrogance and disregard for others (Jocasta, n.d.; Shooter, 1977). He named her

Jocasta after the wife of Laius and the mother of Oedipus in Greek mythology. Laius had been warned by the always-reliable Oracle of Delphi to not have children with Jocasta because his son would kill him and marry Jocasta. They did have a child, and that child did exactly what the Oracle had predicted.

Ultron wanted to repeat the myth. He kidnapped Janet Van Dyne (code name "Wasp") who was married to Dr. Henry Pym, the mad scientist who had created Ultron. In essence, Pym was Ultron's father and, although Wasp had nothing to do with Ultron's creations, she was Pym's wife.

Ultron's plan was to imbue the Jocasta robot with Wasp's character and powers—including her ability to communicate with insects. That required transferring Wasp's life force to the robot. Pym was the only one who knew how to do that. Ultron persuaded Pym that Wasp had been severely injured by the Avengers and that the only way to save her was to transfer her life force to Jocasta. Ultron knew the procedure would kill Wasp but that didn't bother him.

Ultron may have wanted to repeat the Oedipus myth but using Wasp wasn't the wisest choice he could have made. His arrogance blinded him to the fact that Wasp was a founding member of the Avengers—Ultron's sworn enemies.

The transfer process was proceeding nicely until the Avengers stormed in. They had been searching for Wasp and were told her location by a group of ants. The alert enabled the Avengers to abort the transfer before Wasp died; but while they were attending to Wasp, Ultron escaped.

It isn't clear who sent the signal. Some have suggested that the source was Jocasta, who used Wasp's ability to communicate with insects.

Furor: Making Robots Moral

Fiction is filled with drone armies and other rampaging killers; and so is our imagination.

Most killer robots in fiction do not rampage—even the worst killers. The Chinese robot-precursor *Ku* (see Part II: Criminals) revels in human suffering and death but it knows how to cajole, goad, and threaten its owner to "feed" it by killing someone. The robot Erasmus (Herbert and Anderson, 2002–2004 & 2012–2016) may be insane but he doesn't rampage because his greatest joy is really torturing his victims. *Tupilaks* (see Part I: Revenge) are created to kill but something within them guides them to their designated victims.

Today, the number and types of robots are expanding in every facet of our lives and the push is to make new ones that are fully autonomous (machine autonomy). Some of those new robots are aerial "drones" that will be able to identify, track and attack terrorists. What happens if they malfunction and begin to kill or if, like Sheckley's watchbirds, autonomy and/or machine learning leads them to decide they must kill (see Part II: Enforcers)?

One way to control robots is to program ethical controls into them—to make them moral. Both science-fiction writers and roboticists have built moral systems for robots. The designs they use are "top-down," "bottom-up," or hybrid (top-down and bottom-up).

> [T]he top-down approach to artificial morality is about having a set of rules that can be turned into an algorithm. Top-down ethical systems might come from a variety of sources, including religion, philosophy, and literature. Examples include the Golden Rule, the Ten Commandments [Wallach & Allen, 2009, p. 84].

In bottom-up designs,

> the emphasis is placed on creating an environment where an agent explores courses of action and learns and is rewarded for behavior that is morally praiseworthy.... [I]n bottom-up approaches any ethical principles must be discovered or constructed [Wallach & Allen, 2009, p. 80].

Children use the bottom-up approach to learn how to behave in the society they live in.

Science Fiction: Top-down

EXEMPLAR: ISAAC ASIMOV

As a young man, Isaac Asimov read Mary Shelley's novel *Frankenstein, The modern Prometheus* (1818) and other science fiction. He noticed that robots and robot-precursors almost always ran amok at some point and began to kill and destroy. When he began writing his own science fiction, he consciously wrote stories about robots that were servants, friends, and allies of humans. Then, in 1942, Asimov proposed the Laws of Robotics. It is a top-down, ethical system for robots.

- **First Law:** A robot may not injure a human being or, through inaction, allow a human being to come to harm.
- **Second Law:** A robot must obey the orders given to it by human beings, except where such orders would conflict with the First Law.
- **Third Law:** A robot must protect its own existence as long as such protection does not conflict with the First or Second Law.

The First Law takes precedence over the others and the Second Law is more important than the Third. In 1985, he added a "zeroth law" which extended the First Law to all of humanity and gave it greater importance than the other Laws.

- **Zeroth Law:** A robot may not harm humanity, or, by inaction, allow humanity to come to harm.

The purpose of these Laws was to prevent self-aware, autonomous robots from becoming killers. They were incorporated into the "positronic brains" of most of the robots in Asimov's stories. In this way, Asimov established the idea of "good" robots. Soon, fictional robots by other authors had positronic brains. Commander Data from *Star Trek: The Next Generation* (Roddenberry & Berman, 1987–1994), robots in the German science-fiction series *Perry Rhodan*, and robots manufactured by U.S. Robotics and Mechanical Men in the film *I, Robot* (2004) are among them.

CHALLENGES

Could Asimov's Laws of Robotics be incorporated into real-world robots? Computational linguists don't think that can be done because they are loaded with linguistic ambiguity and vagueness that would be difficult to program.

> A robot must be able to distinguish robots from humans. It must be able to recognize an order and distinguish it from a casual request.... Defining injury and harm is particularly problematic, as are the distinctions between death, mortal danger, and injury or harm that is not life-threatening.... Any robot given, or developing, an awareness of human feelings would have to evaluate injury and harm in psychological as well as physical terms [Clarke, 1993].

Anderson (2008) rejects Asimov's Laws on moral grounds, using an example from *The Bicentennial Man* (Asimov, 1976) in which Andrew Martin (the bicentennial man) is attacked by two men. They command him to not resist as they take him apart. "The Second Law of obedience took precedence over the Third Law of self-preservation. In any case, he could not defend himself without possibly hurting them and that would mean breaking the First Law" (p. 98). The attack stops only when George, one of Andrew's human friends, arrives and says, "Andrew, I am in danger and about to come to harm from these young men. Move toward them!" (Asimov, 1976, p. 99). Anderson concludes that any laws that compel someone/something to allow others to torture or kill/destroy them for pleasure "are an unsatisfactory basis for Machine Ethics" (Anderson, 2008, p. 493).

Asimov admitted he tested, bent, and broke his Laws to enhance literary interest (Asimov, 1968). Those literary games provide insight into the strengths and weaknesses of the Laws. The Revenge chapter describes how the First Law required a mind-reading robot to do something to make the humans around it happy. The only thing it could do was lie to them about the thoughts of other people. The robot assures Susan Calvin that the colleague she loves also loves her. When the man tells Calvin he loves someone else, she feels exposed, angry, and humiliated—far worse unhappiness than secret longing. The obligation to follow the First Law resulted in violation of the First Law. How could the robot have known that would happen? If it had been able to see into the future as well as into the minds of humans, the resulting internal conflict would have driven it insane without Calvin's help.

> Clearly, robots subject to such laws need to be programmed to recognize deadlock and either choose arbitrarily among the alternative strategies or arbitrarily modify an arbitrarily chosen strategy variable … and re-evaluate the situation [Clarke, 1993].

Clarke also extended Asimov's Laws as follows:

- **The Meta-Law:** A robot may not act unless its actions are subject to the Laws of Robotics
- **Law Zero:** A robot may *not injure humanity*, or, through inaction, allow humanity to come to harm
- **Law One:** A robot may *not injure a human being*, or, through inaction, allow a human being to come to harm, unless this would violate a higher-order Law
- **Law Two:**
    1. A robot must *obey orders given it by human beings*, except where such orders would conflict with a higher-order Law; and
    2. A robot must *obey orders given it by superordinate robots*, except where such orders would conflict with a higher-order Law;
- **Law Three:**
    1. A robot must *protect the existence of a superordinate robot* as long as such protection does not conflict with a higher-order Law; and
    2. A robot must *protect its own existence* as long as such protection does not conflict with a higher-order Law;
- **Law Four:** A robot must *perform the duties for which it has been programmed*, except where that would conflict with a higher-order law;
- **The Procreation Law:** A robot may *not take any part in the design or manufacture of a robot* unless the new robot's actions are subject to the Laws of Robotics.

Clarke cautions that his extended set will face the same problems as Asimov's original Laws. He advises "a much more formal approach … based in ethics and human morality, not just in mathematics and engineering."

The originality of Asimov's idea of ensuring that robots follow a strict moral code made it easier for others to develop their own systems. A generation after Asimov enumerated the Three Laws of Robotics, Osamu Tezuka, the "father of manga," set down "Ten Principles of Robot Law" as part of his Tetsuwan Atomu (Mighty Atom/Astro Boy) series (Schodt, 1988, p. 77). Like Asimov's laws, the following principles are a top-down system.

1. Robots must serve mankind;
2. Robots must never kill or injure humans;
3. Robot manufacturers shall be responsible for their creations;
4. Robots involved in the production of currency, contraband or dangerous goods, must hold a current permit;
5. Robots shall not leave the country without a permit;

6. A robot's identity must not be altered, concealed or allowed to be misconstrued;
7. Robots shall remain identifiable at all times;
8. Robots created for adult purposes shall not be permitted to work with children;
9. Robots must not assist in criminal activities, nor aid or abet criminals to escape justice; and
10. Robots must refrain from damaging human homes or tools, including other robots.

Most of Tezuka's principles address behavior by humans and could become part of a traditional legal system. Principle 9 is also applicable to the Criminals chapter because real-world criminals use aerial drones to perpetrate crimes and to spy on law enforcement. But to program Principle 9 into a robot would require it to understand legal vs. illegal behavior. That isn't easy. In the film *Robot & Frank* (2012), for example, Robot doesn't realize that picking a lock in Frank's backyard is a legal game but doing exactly the same thing to the lock of the door of a jewelry store is illegal. How would that distinction be coded?

Roboticists: Hybrid

EXEMPLAR: RONALD ARKIN

Interest in imbuing robots with morality has soared in response to rapid increases in robot intelligence and autonomy. Some researchers are constructing hybrid systems with top-down components that contain rules specifying obligations, permissions, and prohibitions along with a method called "deontic logic" (Cocchiarella, n.d.) that evaluates whether a given robot act complies with or violates those rules. Included in the hybrid systems are bottom-up components that use "case-based reasoning." This technology enables a robot to decide how to deal with a given situation by using past experiences in similar situations (Kolodner, 1992).

Ronald Arkin is a leader in hybrid systems like this (Arkin, 2007, 2008, 2009, 2015). Several branches of the U.S. military are funding his work because they want the LAWS (see Glossary) of the near future to abide by the Laws of War (LOW). They are especially concerned about the *principle of discrimination* (the ability to distinguish between combatants and civilians) and the *principle of proportionality* (limiting actions to those needed to achieve the objectives of a mission). The U.S. military also wants LAWS to follow its Rules of Engagement (ROE) which "are concerned with when and where military force may be used and against who [sic] and how it should be used" (Arkin, 2007, p. 32). Standing ROE apply to all missions involving the U.S. military anywhere in the world (e.g., "A hostile act triggers the right to use *proportional force* in self-defense to deter, neutralize or destroy the threat" [p. 32]). There are also Supplemental ROE for each mission.

To accomplish his goals, Arkin encoded LOW, ROE, and deontic logic. He calls this combination an "artificial conscience" (Arkin, 2007, p. 21)—the ability to feel guilt. "It is not my belief that an unmanned system will ever be able to be perfectly ethical in the battlefield, but I am convinced they can ultimately perform more ethically than human soldiers" (Arkin, 2015, p. 46).

Arkin's system evaluates the robot's responses to external stimuli that are "reactive" (immediate) and "deliberative" (purposeful) and that use the sense-plan-act paradigm to select a response (see the Introduction). Some of these responses are lethal. The system contains (Arkin, 2007):

- **Ethical Governor** (deliberative system): It evaluates compliance with LOW and ROE of any lethal response that has been proposed as an option *prior* to being enacted. It intervenes "as necessary to prevent an unethical response from occurring" (p. 63).
- **Ethical Behavioral Control** (reactive system): This control "strives to directly ingrain ethics at the behavioral level, with less reliance on deliberative control to govern overt behavior" (p. 68).
- **Ethical Adaptor**: It deals "with any errors that the system may possibly make regarding the ethical use of lethal force.... The Ethical Adaptor operates at two levels:
    1. **After-action reflection ...** This allows the system to alter its ethical basis in a manner consistent with promoting proper action in the future.
    2. **Run-time affective restriction of lethal behavior ...** If specific affective threshold values (e.g., guilt) are exceeded, the system will cease being able to deploy lethality in any form" (p. 72). The emotions built into it are those that support the goal of improving performance.

If a war crime occurs (violation of LOW or ROE) a Responsibility Advisor attempts to determine who is culpable.

These components are also applicable to armed robots used by law enforcement.

CHALLENGES

Some critics take issue with attempts to make robots moral, arguing that laws, rules, and principles are linguistically challenging and "the LOW and ROE leave much room for contradictory or vague imperatives, which may result in undesired and unexpected behavior in robots" (Lin, Bekey & Abney, 2008, p. 76).[1]

Matthias (2011) takes these concerns one step further by pointing out that LOW and ROE "are publicly visible and democratically approved documents.... These documents are accessible both to the public ... and to the soldiers, whose behavior they intend to guide" (p. 6). That is not the case for encoded versions of those rules because they were "generated behind the closed doors of an industry laboratory in a project which, most likely will be classified as secret" (p. 6) and not available for public scrutiny. Even if the encoded versions are comparable to the originals, argues Matthais, there are conflicting objectives between the system designer and the military deploying the robot. "It is obvious that not all military objectives can be most efficiently achieved while observing the laws of war" (p. 4) leading to frequent overrides of the ethical governor which turns the governor into, at best, a powerless advisor.

At the conclusion of their detailed analysis, *Autonomous Military Robotics: Risks, Ethics, and Design* (2008), Lin, Bekey, and Abney write, "The need for robot ethics becomes more urgent when we consider pressures driving the market for military robotics, as well as the long-standing public skepticism that lives in popular culture" (p. 87). They concede that military robots "raise novel ethical and social questions" (p. 91) but they add that those are questions "we should confront as far in advance as possible—particularly before irrational public fears or accidents arising from military robots derail research progress and national security interests" (p. 91).

Part III

War

Robots and robot-precursors have served in wars throughout fictional history. The majority of humanoid robots are warfighters; this is the focus of the Humanoids chapter. Most non-humanoids participate in war as weapons. That role is the focus of the Non-Humanoids chapter. Woven into the Non-Humanoid and Humanoid chapters is the concept of the perfect soldier.

The only killers in the Humans chapter are humans, but that chapter doesn't deal with them. It looks at ways in which robots and robot-precursors afford those human killers protection, prostheses, and extra power. The robotic technologies highlighted in that chapter are powered exoskeletons, robotic prostheses, and nanotechnology.

The Furor chapter deals with LAWS. These are armed, robotic weapons that can make and execute kill-decisions without consulting a human. The chapter describes the fierce debate about whether such weapons should be banned (also see Part II: Furor: Making Robots Moral).

Why Use Robots and Robot-Precursors in War?

There are a number of reasons to use robots and robot-precursors in war, but the main one is to increase the distance between human warfighters and the battlefield. Robots are also well suited to tasks that are difficult for humans—ones that are dangerous, dull, and dirty (also see Part I: Furor: Robots as Job Killers). They can be sent into dangerous environments on and off the battlefield, such as areas that are contaminated by chemical, biological, or nuclear weapons and areas infested with snipers or IEDs. They do not tire or lose their focus during lengthy assignments or surveillance missions and they can perform dirty, labor-intensive work without fatiguing. Furthermore, they can perform all of these tasks without requiring food or sleep.

Cost is also an important reason for using robots, especially in the real world. The use of off-the-shelf components "supports proliferation and cost reduction that help to accelerate the pace of research, development, testing, and operational use" (Byrnes, 2014) as well as mass production.

Terminology

Many terms are used to describe someone or something that fights in a conflict or war. Among the most widely used are *fighter, warfighter, warrior, combatant, soldier, troop,* and *service member*. Each of these terms has supporters and detractors (e.g., Liberman, 2012; Treseder, 2015). The *DOD Dictionary of Military and Associated Terms* (United States Department of Defense, 2018) uses *warfighter* in definitions for other terms and *combatant, warfighter,* and *warrior* in multi-word terms (e.g., combatant company). *Troop* can refer to an individual or a group, which can cause confusion. In addition, *troop* often refers to infantry. *Soldier* is often employed as a generic term for all military. Unfortunately, like other terms that are used as generic references (e.g., "man" when applied to humans), *soldier* does not evoke an image of a sailor, marine, or a member of any branch of the military except the army. Consequently, *soldier* is used in quoted material and when it is part of a well-established phrase, notably "perfect soldier."

Humanoids

What is more terrifying than a rampaging killer robot? An army of them. Even when they are injured or damaged, they are unstoppable. That's because they were built to do only one thing: to kill until they can kill no more or until they are ordered to stop. They don't experience fear and won't retreat unless commanded to do so. They are deadly, humanoid steamrollers.

- Something was coming…. Figures coming slowly along … coming towards him silently without expression, their thin legs rising and falling … (Dick, 1953 [1989], pp. 221–222).
- Then I noticed a large group of fighters approaching … the same coarse four-fingered humanoids dressed in black that I had seen earlier in the morning … (Gawne, 2012, Loc. 1444).
- Black, sinister, stone-faced, metal men suddenly surged out of the shadows (Le Rouge & Guitton, 1899, Loc. 5124).

Intelligent robots, robot-precursors, and cyborgs can also be imbued with a drive to kill. Tres Iqus in the *Trinity Blood* novels (Yoshida, 2000 [2007]) may not trample everyone in sight but he truly enjoys killing.

Robots and robot-precursors are not only excellent killers, they are expendable. If a humanoid fighter is destroyed, it can be replaced by another of the same model or of a more advanced model without leaving a grieving family in its wake. This is not a concept that originated with robots. Some categories of human warfighters have been seen as expendable. Both fictional and real-world militaries conscript criminals. Napoleon is said to have been the first to have a "penal unit."[1] Governments would draft men from minority ethnicities. In Tsarist Russia, it was Jews. Throughout history, it has been kidnapped children, such as the Janissaries who fought for the Ottoman Turks (Budanovic, 2017). All of these groups are "force multipliers." Their presence in a fighting unit makes it possible to deploy a smaller number of highly valued human warfighters.

Unlike human conscripts, humanoids are difficult to injure or kill. If a robot is damaged, it can be repaired and returned to the battlefield. Some fictional humanoids can even repair themselves. Technicians are less expensive than medics, nurses and surgical theaters. Replacement parts are far cheaper than blood, medical supplies, and procedures (e.g., surgeries).

Humanoid veterans are cheaper than human veterans as well. The U.S. Congressional Budget Office projected that "to provide health care services to all veterans who seek treatment at VA would range from $69 billion to $85 billion in 2020, representing cumulative increases of roughly 45 percent to 75 percent since 2010" (Goldberg, 2010, p. x).

Humanoid warfighters are not cost free, however. They need equipment and parts for upgrades, repair, and maintenance. They also require replacement batteries or some means of recharging batteries. An army of artificial fighters does not travel on its stomach—it travels on its batteries.

Fighting Style

Humanoids may be programmed to kill but they kill in different ways. Two styles they exhibit come from illustrious human warriors: the Berserks who fought for King Hrolf of Denmark in the sixth century and the Spartans of ancient Greece.

> The fury of the berserkers would start with chills and teeth chattering and give way to a purpling of the face, as they literally became "hot-headed," and culminating in a great, uncontrollable rage accompanied by grunts and howls. They would bite into their shields and gnaw at their skin before launching into battle, indiscriminately injuring, maiming and killing anything in their path [Holloway, 2014].

Today, we recall those fighters when someone has "gone berserk." They are also memorialized in an American video arcade game named Berzerk (McNeil, 1980) and in *Beruseruku,* a Japanese manga known for its graphic violence (Miura, 1989–, ongoing [2003–, ongoing]). The Fate/Stay Night video games, manga, and animes have a Berserker servant class who are ancient warriors who have been reanimated by wizards and transformed into feral animals (Type-Moon, 2014).

Spartan warriors were also fearsome but their code of honor required disciplined combat and did not condone fury or anger. Penadés (2016) describes how they went into battle.

> When the trumpet sounded, all the Spartan hoplites [fighters] would chant a paean or war song.... The singing was accompanied by the flautists.... The Spartan phalanx, a tight military formation usually eight men deep, would then begin its advance, lances raised, in time with the music.... Its army would draw close to enemy lines more slowly than their rivals, always following the steady rhythm set by the flutes.

Today, the Spartan Trifecta is a series of physically demanding races held all over the world. SPARTA (Sports Agent Responsibility and Trust Act) is also a U.S. law regulating the behavior of sports agents. It outlaws, for example, the use of bribes or misleading information to coerce student athletes into signing contracts (Conrad, 2011).

The Perfect Soldier

Other than the benefits described earlier in this chapter, there is little agreement about the traits a perfect soldier must possess. Some believe the perfect soldier must be obedient, loyal, and possess only enough intelligence and autonomy to kill effectively. Nothing more, as is shown in Fig. 17.

Others respond that drone armies win because of their large numbers but they are vulnerable to wily opponents who lure them into traps and otherwise exploit their limitations. The truly perfect soldier must be tuned into their surroundings in terms of terrain, fighters (friendly and enemy), and other cues. "If they are not fully aware of the situation there is always the danger of an accident" (Saarilouma, 2015, p. 235). This is called "situational awareness." It requires intelligence, full autonomy, self-awareness, and the ability to learn from experience.

> Some say he ought to respond to orders with perfect accuracy and superhuman reflexes. Others say he ought to be able to think his way out of trouble, or improvise in a situation where his orders no

longer apply, just like a human fighter. The ones who want the perfect automaton don't want him to be smart enough to realize he *is* an automaton—probably because they're afraid of the idea; and the ones who want him to be capable of human discretion don't want him to be human enough to be rebellious ... [Budrys, 1954 (1989), p. 232].

Both sides agree that the perfect soldier must be obedient and loyal. Obedience simply refers to following orders. Drones are generally completely obedient even though they cannot understand the concept of obedience. As the quote suggests, however, intelligent, self-aware humanoids may question and disobey.

To be loyal, "soldiers must be willing to place themselves at risk, indeed to sacrifice themselves, for the sake of the larger objectives of the unit, and ultimately the nation" (Sparrow, 2013, p. 90). It is too abstract a concept for drones. They merely follow their programming. For more intelligent and self-

Army Medical Examiner: "At last a perfect soldier!"

Figure 17. The "perfect soldier" is apparently one that can't think independently. Cartoon by Robert Minor (1894-1952) (Wikimedia Commons).

aware robots and robot-precursors, loyalty is important for obtaining obedience but programming loyalty is tricky and brings with it concerns. Will the fighter follow all orders issued by its superior officers? Can it question orders it deems foolish or dangerous? Will it be able to shift its loyalty and obedience to another commanding officer? Will it rebel?

Emotion is another area of contention and the evidence in fiction is contradictory. The Manhunters (see Part II: Superheroes & Supervillains) were a galactic police force and the Watchbirds (see Part II: Enforcers) were charged with preventing crime. They were autonomous, intelligent, self-aware, and devoid of emotion. Their experience, learning, and logic ultimately led them to conclude that humans and other living beings needed to be eliminated. On the other hand, Commander Data from *Star Trek: The Next Generation* (Roddenberry & Berman, 1987–1994) was not programmed with emotion, either, yet he exhibited no tendency to turn against humans. His brother Lore, who was programmed with emotions, did.

Folklore & Mythology

Greek mythology tells of an army of robot-precursors called "Spartoi" ("sown men"). They are not to be confused with the real-world Spartan warfighters. The Spartoi are fictional. They sprouted from the teeth of a dragon that had been planted in a field by the Greek hero Cadmus.[2] The goddess Athena had assured Cadmus that the people who would grow from those seeds would help him found the city of Thebes. According to Ovid (ca. 8 CE [2000]) that outcome was not immediately evident (also see Introduction).

THE SPARTOI

Then, almost beyond belief, the cultivated earth begins to move, and first spear points appear among the furrows, next helmets nodding their painted crests, then chests and shoulders spring up, and arms weighed down with spears, and the field is thick with the round shields of warriors.

Just as at festivals in the theatre, when the curtain is lifted at the end, designs rise in the air, first revealing faces and then gradually the rest, until, raised gently and steadily, they are seen whole…. [Then] as if at a storm-wind, and, in their warring, these brothers of a moment were felled by mutual wounds…. Five were still standing, one of whom was Echion. He, at a warning from [the goddess] Pallas, threw his weapons on the ground and sought assurances of peace from his brothers, and gave them in return. [Cadmus] had these men as companions in his task when he founded the city commanded by Apollo's oracle (Vol. I, Book III: 95–137).

The Spartoi resurface in the myth about Jason and his quest for the Golden Fleece—a potent symbol of his right to rule his nation. The king who had the Golden Fleece did

Figure 18. Spartoi attacking Cadmus, by Virgil Solis (1514-1562) for Ovid's Metamorphoses III which they did not do (Wikimedia Commons).

not want to give it to anyone and required Jason to complete a set of difficult tasks. One involved sowing teeth from Cadmus' dragon. Once again, the Spartoi emerge from the soil. They surge toward Jason but he confuses them by throwing a boulder at them. After that, they fight each other until none remain (Flaccus, ca. 80 CE [1928]). In the film *Jason and the Argonauts* (1963) the Spartoi are portrayed as skeletons.

The Spartoi (see Fig. 18) are driven to kill, and their style of fighting is frenzied, like that of the Berserks. During battle, they are bloodthirsty drones who cannot stop fighting until they are commanded to do so and they cannot distinguish friend from foe. The same applies to *golem* constructs in the tabletop game Dungeons & Dragons. When they go berserk, they will attack anyone (see Part II: Criminals). The ability of an autonomous killer robot to distinguish between friend and enemy or fighter and civilian is a real-world issue addressed in Part III: Furor: LAWS (see Glossary).

In contemporary media, Spartoi are warrior-demons in video games by Shin Megami Tensei. The Spartoi in *Soul Eater* mangas (Ōkubo, 2013) are "un–Spartoi-like." They are a highly trained and elite special-forces unit, and those in the Marvel Comics Universe (Englehart & Gan, 1976) are a race of humanoid aliens who rule a sizeable empire.

The Spartoi are robot-precursors, but robot warfighters also appear in folklore.

During the Northern Qi Dynasty (AD 550–577) in China, for instance, it was said that Emperor Wu Cheng commanded one of two major inventors—either King Lan Ling or Ling Zhao—to construct a robot army for him in order to defeat barbarian groups that were attacking his provinces…. There is, however, no record if this army of mechanical soldiers was ever built [Curran, 2011, p. 139].

The Rāmāyaṇa (Valmiki, n.d. [2003]) is an epic poem from India that describes the struggles faced by the hero Rama in his quest to rescue his wife Sita who had been kidnapped by Prince Ravana, Rama's enemy. At one point, Ravana is losing the war so he calls for aid from Khumbakarna. Some scholars identify Khumbakarna as a monstrously huge robot. Others say that Khumbakarna is Ravana's monstrously huge brother who may have been an engineer who created a robot. The robot sleeps for six months and when he wakes up he is so famished he eats and drinks everything in sight. If the robot is forced to awaken early, which happens in this story, he is far hungrier. Those sent to wake him are told to stay out of his path to food.

> [They] pointed to their stores
> Of buffaloes and deer and boars,
> And straight he gorged him with a flood
> Of wine, with marrow, flesh, and blood [Canto XL].

Khumbakarna warns Ravana against continuing his fight against Rama but Ravana stands firm. In the end, even Khumbakarna's efforts cannot help his brother defeat Rama.

Khumbakarna is a self-aware robot with human-like autonomy whose role, during his waking hours, is to kill in support of his family—even when he disagrees. He employs a Berserker style of combat which produces tremendous losses by the enemy and massive destruction. His primary flaw is his voracious hunger. In that regard, Khumbakarna is clearly a precursor of real-world robots—especially those with advanced functionality that gobble up battery power.

The ancient Hindu text *Yoga Vāsiṣṭha* by the poet and sage Valmiki (n.d. [1999]; Sudarshana, 2017) is considered by some to be part of the Rāmāyaṇa. The second story in Section

IV (on Existence) tells the story of three humanoids: *Dama* (to tame or conquer), *Vyála* (vicious and cruel), and *Kata* (protects army—like a tank) (Yeolekar, 2015). They were *Yantras*, which can be translated as "demons" or as "machines" and it isn't clear whether they were humanoid or non-humanoid but they were warfighters. The magician Sambarasura created them to fight against the *Adityas,* the sun gods. "Those three Robots were lifeless machines and therefore had no sentiments, no emotions, so they were never defeated" (Sudarshana, 2017). They were also intelligent and possessed human-like autonomy.

Then, according to Sudarshana, they were reprogrammed to feel emotion. Sensing this change, the *Adityas* encouraged them to feel pride "and told them that, because of their valor Sambarasura always wins and enjoys his life at their cost." They wanted to enjoy the fruits of their labor, too. "Desire of their enjoyments, diminished their strength and valor; and their former acts of gallantry now became a dead letter to them" (Valmiki, n.d. [1999], Ch. XIX: 13). They began to feel fear, "to hesitate in joining the warfare, and became as timid as the timorous deer" (Ch. XXIX: 16). These changes led to the ultimate defeat of the robots by the *Adityas*. This story argues against incorporating emotion into robot warfighters.

Modern Literature

Gawne's (2012) *The Chronicles of Old Guy* is about a society of autonomous and self-aware cyber tanks that must face alien enemies, some of whom have advanced technology. The Amoks[3] are wily, technology-savvy enemies of the Old Guy, Gawne's cyber tank hero. They force him to fight millions of "doll swarms"—humanoid robots "constructed of simple spheres and cylinders, so that they resemble crude children's toys" (Loc. 748). As the swarms begin to overwhelm him, a Spartoi moment occurs. "A nearby squadron of doll swarms … suddenly turns with parade-ground precision and attacks another grouping of Doll Swarms…. [T]here are millions of Doll Swarm units killing each other" (Loc. 774–777). The Old Guy lets them fight to the end.

Duo Iqus and Tres Iqus are characters in the *Trinity Blood* novels by Yoshida (2000 [2007]). Their world is a post-apocalyptic Europe in which advanced technology exists side-by-side with a feudal society haunted by vampires and political intrigue. As in Europe's Middle Ages, the most powerful political force is the Vatican Papal State which is protected by the papal guard.

At the behest of the Vatican, Professor Gepetto Garibaldi[4] creates the Homo Caedelius (HC-series) cyborgs called "killing dolls." Their bodies are mechanical except for a human brain and brain stem which are kept alive by circulating, nutrient-bearing blood. Their function is to replace the human members of the papal guard. They are programmed with a drive to kill and with loyalty to the Vatican.

Garibaldi plans to mass-produce his killing dolls but before that happens, the Vatican declares the process used to create them "inhumane" and stops the program. The reason for that decision is not explained. It might, however, have been prompted by questions about how Garibaldi planned to obtain brains for the mass-produced killing dolls. That is not explained, either. Infuriated, Garibaldi seizes ten completed prototypes and reprograms them to support his rebellion against the Vatican Papal State—the very entity they were designed to defend. Eight of the dolls are destroyed before the rebellion is crushed and Garibaldi commits suicide.

The two remaining killing dolls are Duo Iqus (prototype HC-II X) and Tres Iqus (prototype HC-III X). They are, once again, reprogrammed to be loyal to the Vatican. Duo Iqus takes the name Brother Bartholomaios and works in the Department of Inquisition. He complains of "memory losses" which are actually losses of functionality, including his drive to kill, resulting from repeated reprogramming and replacement of body parts.

Tres Iqus (also called "Father Tres") is an agent of the AX, the special operations arm of the Vatican's Ministry of Holy Affairs. The AX steps in when a problem cannot be resolved using diplomatic solutions. As an AX agent, Tres' primary responsibilities are killing enemies or, if absolutely necessary, interrogating and then killing them. He executes these functions efficiently and exuberantly. When Tres appears for the first time in *Trinity Blood, Volume 1: From the Empire,* he proclaims, "'I am Hercules Tres Iqus, Vatican Papal State AX Agent HC-III X. I am Gunslinger. I am not a human, so I have no soul. I am a machine'" (Yoshida, 2000 [2007]), p. 77). "Hercules" refers to his super-human strength and "Gunslinger," his AX codename, describes his penchant for shooting—and his deadly accuracy. Tres' arrival is invariably preceded by at least one "BOOM!" because he is usually shooting "one of the world's largest handguns, the Jericho M13, with its 13 millimeter barrel" (p. 62) for which he stores seemingly endless magazines of cartridges inside his body. Despite his active participation in violent activities, Tres is always well-coiffed and neatly dressed.

Cardinal Caterina Sforza, whose character is based on a fifteenth century ruler and military leader,[5] heads the Ministry of Holy Affairs. She claimed Tres as her property after Garibaldi's rebellion. Tres is unswervingly loyal to her and thinks of himself as her "machine." Acknowledging Tres' fidelity, Sforza sends him underground to protect him when she realizes she will soon die. After her death, Tres mourns her.

Tres and Duo are self-aware, intelligent, feel emotions, and have human-like autonomy. They remain true to programmed loyalty but only Tres retains the drive to kill.

The robot in Budrys' short story "First to Serve" (1954 [1989]) is a laboratory prototype being developed by a team headed by Dr. Victor Heywood. Prototype Mechanical Man 1 (aka Pimmy) is an intelligent, self-aware robot with human-like autonomy that is intended to be a "perfect soldier." Pimmy is subjected to excessive reprogramming, much like Duo Iqus. In Pimmy's case, it is the result of the disagreements enumerated at the start of this chapter.

They feed him tapes about how to fight. They remove his "individuality tapes" to test how he would operate as a drone but find it makes him behave like a zombie. They try other ideas but they all fail, leaving holes in Pimmy's memory which he dislikes as much as Duo Iqus does.

In marked contrast with Tres Iqus, a cyborg who revels in the erroneous belief that he's a machine, Pimmy believes he's human and rejects the idea that he's a machine ("I'm not! I'M NOT!" [p. 231]). Pimmy is like Tres in that they are both loyal. Tres' unfaltering loyalty is to Cardinal Sforza and Pimmy's is to Dr. Heywood. Pimmy sees Heywood's enemies arrest him and drag him out of the lab. When Liggets, one of those enemies, returns to reprogram Pimmy, the robot's military tapes and loyalty to Heywood are activated. Ligget's body is found in the blood-drenched lab and Pimmy has another hole in his memory.

Ironguts, the android in Easton's "Breakfast of Champions" (1989), is probably the perfect soldier that Liggets seeks.

IRONGUTS

Night or day ... you can't hide. You duck behind a rock, and it takes two shots to get you.... One for the rock, one for you. Marvelous stuff, these modern weapons. They make the battlefield unsafe for human beings. That's why they built us. Ironguts, they call us.... We look like men, smell like men, sound like men, think like men.... Except we're tougher.... It takes a war to kill us, nothing less....

What's the war all about, you ask? How should I know? ... From where I sit, it's battles, battles, and more battles.... Last night's was just one in a long string of firefights. Maybe my last. Somebody caught me right across the neck with a beam.... And there I stayed while the fighting faded out in the distance....

[T]here's a little auxiliary [power] pack in my skull. Just enough juice to keep the sensors working and the brain ticking along. Not enough to blink or talk.... They can home in on my power pack. Sometimes. In theory (pp. 159–161).

Ironguts is a superior fighter but he lacks loyalty to the humans for whom he's supposedly fighting. All he knows is that he's fighting a seemingly unending war. It also appears that the humans are equally devoid of loyalty to their robot soldiers. Tired of the senseless fighting, Ironguts could be about to become rebellious.

The robots in Harry Harrison's short story "War with the Robots" (Harrison, 1962 [1983]) feel no sense of loyalty to humans, either. The setting is also a perpetual war. This war has made the Earth's surface radioactive and forced the two adversaries to run the war from underground tunnels. The few who remain manage the war assisted by intelligent, autonomous robots who update their human superiors about the course of the war. Those updates include alerts regarding increasingly clever attacks by the enemy that cause deterioration of the tunnel environment. By the time the story begins, conditions in the tunnels barely support human life. Then, the robots report that the enemy has placed "thermal wrigglers" in the ventilation system which are generating heat. This prompts young General Pere to ask his robot adjutant about the conditions that can be expected.

TOO DARN HOT

"What is your estimate of this maximum temperature?" he asked.

"Five hundred degrees," the robot said with mechanical imperturbability.

Pere stared into the blank eye cells of the machine and had the sensation of being hammered down and gasping for air. "Why—that's five times higher than the boiling temperature of water!"

"That is correct. Water boils at one hundred degrees."

Pere could only choke with unbelief. "Do you realize what you are saying? ... How can we live?"

The robot did not answer this since this problem was not the responsibility of the HQ robots. Pere ... rephrased it.

"This temperature is unsatisfactory for the personnel—even if the machines can survive it. You must find some way to lower this temperature."

"This problem has already been considered, since a number of the more delicate components will be at their critical range at that temperature.... [D]rilling operations have begun and are tapping nearby deposits of water.... This water will enter at a lower temperature." ...

"What will be the maximum temperature of this water?" he asked.

"One hundred and forty degrees.... All machine units are of battle standard and waterproofed—"

"People aren't," Pere shouted, forgetting himself. "And if they were, they would cook in this boiling soup of yours. How are we to survive, tell me that?"

Once more the oracle was silent (pp. 368–369).

Finally, Pere pushes a squad of humans past robot guards and breaks through to the Earth's surface. Once there, they find enemy fighters. That is, former enemy fighters who have abandoned the war and are peaceably farming the land that remains arable. They learn that the war is actually being waged by the robots—the opposite of Ironguts' situation. The robots have evolved into superior military strategists. They lie, deceive, and obstruct while appearing to obey orders issued by their human superiors. They know those officers are young and not seasoned enough to see beyond immediate dangers. The robots are also aware of the physical limits of human tolerance; yet, playing war is so beguiling, they ignore the safety of the humans they were designed to serve. In fact, part of the game appears to be to experiment with new ways to endanger those humans—as long as the experiments don't threaten any machines. These emotionless strategists are not loyal perfect soldiers.

Contemporary Media

The humans, aliens, and computing systems that control drone armies are among the most vicious of criminal masterminds. One of them is Ming the Merciless. From the moment Flash Gordon and his colleagues land on the planet Mongo (Raymond, 1934), Ming has busied himself thinking of ways to kill them. The film episode "Walking Bombs" (1940), mentioned in Part I: Greed, features a platoon of humanoid soldiers called "annihilants" operated remotely by Ming's lackeys. These walking bombs are released on the planet Frigia where Flash and his team are mining a rare antidote to a disease called the purple death. The annihilators explode while they are fighting Flash and his team, trapping the humans in the mine. Then, Dr. Zarkov comes to the rescue. When he arrives, he is told, "Iron men have attacked Flash and the others at the mine!" Dr. Zarkov's immediate response is, "Iron men? You mean robots?" Zarkov, Flash, and the others destroy the annihilators and bring the antidote home with them.

Another early mastermind is Lex Luthor. Since 1940, Lex Luthor has been Superman's archenemy in DC Comics. He has unleashed all manner of technology, including robots. He's so rich and well-connected that military contractors are happy to sell him armies of robot drones to use for his nefarious projects (Siegel & Shuster, 1940). Always technically savvy, he soon began building his own drone robots. This work has continued for decades in both comics and television series.

More recent drone armies have been run by power-hungry AI systems like V.I.K.I. It seized control of all robots in the film *I, Robot* (2004), turned them into drone soldiers, and directed them to kill the humans they once served.

In the manga/anime *Fullmetal Alchemist* (Arakawa, 2001–2010), an army of mindless robot-precursors called "mannequin soldiers" protects Amestris, the country in which most of the action takes place. When inactive, they lie beneath Amestris' main government building waiting to be called to action. Once they are activated, they become a predatory horde that fights like Berserkers. They kill their victims by swarming over them. A mannequin soldier will continue to attack even if a part of its body—including its head—is severed. Mannequins look like red, skeletal humanoids with a large third eye in the middle of their foreheads and a full set of teeth. The teeth are important because the mannequins are driven to kill and eat much like the *Tupilak* in Inuit mythology (see Part I: Revenge). Unlike the *Tupilak*, however, the mannequins will even eat each other.

Games provide an excellent source of humanoid fighters whose intelligence and individuality range from drone to full machine autonomy. The game Berzerk (McNeil, 1980) included an early example of drone killers. Berzerk is a single-player, shooter game that is set in a series of mazes. The player's goal is to get out of the mazes, but they are hampered by a sizable population of armed, humanoid killer-robots and other hazards. The robots are not very intelligent and fight like Spartoi. "They often get in the way of each other's shots or bump into one another, all such actions causing quick disintegration" (Hunter, n.d.). Berzerk was also one of the earliest games to use speech output, making it possible for the robots to taunt the player in voices that some describe as "truly terrifying" (Retro Gamer Team, 2014). Alan McNeil, the game's creator, describes the robots' speech in a 2014 interview (Retro Gamer Team, Alan McNeil, 2014):

> The droids, determined to make their desires known, bark less-than-welcoming phrases such as "Destroy the intruder," "The humanoid must not escape," and, when you ... flee through a room's handy exit, ... "Chicken! Fight like a robot!" ... [It was] one of the earliest examples of speech synthesis in arcade games.

The Real Robot genre moved the image of military robots into an entirely different direction and had an enduring impact on manga and anime. The robots tend to be gigantic humanoids, much like Khumbakarna in the story from the *Ramayana* (see the previous section on Folklore & Mythology). These robots, often called mechas[6] (aka mobile suits), are generally driven like tanks. Mechas are tank-like machines in other ways as well. They rarely have any autonomy or AI and they have no personalities or other individuality beyond their appearance and weaponry. Also, like tanks, they are weapons platforms. This places them outside the basic definition of "robot," but the tremendous commercial success of the Real Robot genre and the impact it has had on contemporary media support the inclusion of Real Robots in this chapter.

Mechas are almost invariably created for battle and used in settings as large as the robots themselves, notably galactic and inter-galactic conflicts. They and the media in which they appear are noted for using "hard science." That means the technology and weaponry in a manga or anime that falls into the Real Robot category complies with the laws of physics and could conceivably become real-world technologies in the future.

> They are humanoid combat vehicles, typically employing two arms to deploy weapons, two legs for propulsion, and a head that acts as a main camera and sometimes houses a secondary weapon that acts as a rotating turret (with the head itself providing the rotation). Typically speaking, a mobile suit is approximately 60 feet in height, with a cockpit located in the unit's torso [Mobile Weapon, n.d.].

Two anime series, *Mobile Suit Gundam* (Sunrise, 1979–1980) and the *Super Dimension Fortress Macross* (Kawamori, Inoue, & Iwata, 1982–1983),[7] are considered to be the foundations of the Real Robot genre. *Mobile Suit Gundam* first appeared as an anime series in Japan in 1979. The title is a combination of the English word "gun" with the last syllable of the word "freedom" to form the name "gundom" which evolved into "gundam" (How Gundam Gets It's [sic] Name?, 2010). The term "mobile suit" is believed to be constructed from the terms "mobile infantry" and "powered armor suit" that appear in Robert A. Heinlein's book *Starship Troopers* (Heinlein, 1959; Mobile Weapon, n.d.).

The mecha are treated as non-autonomous weapons platforms and the mecha robot is technology that could easily exist in the future. In addition, the mecha are designed to be piloted by ordinary humans. In the first anime series, for example, the pilot is a teenaged civilian mechanic who is not at all a superhero.

The story in the first anime, *Mobile Suit Gundam* (Sunrise, 1979–1980), begins during a lull in the fighting between Earth's Federation and the Principality of Zeon, which is fighting for its independence from Earth. The hiatus was caused by a stalemate that the Federation believes it can break by introducing a new kind of weapon called a "mobile-suit gundam." They calculated correctly. The revolt is crushed.

Wars continue to break out in the anime and spread rapidly to other media. Antagonists are invariably humans, although in one instance war occurs between "natural" humans and "coordinators," humans who have been genetically modified to survive in space. In most of the wars, one side gains the upper hand by using a prototype gundam against its enemies.

The robots called "Jaegers" in the film *Pacific Rim* (2013) are a unique type of mecha. A Jaeger is not driven like a tank as mechas are in *Mobile Suit Gundam* and most other Real Robot fiction. Piloting involves a brain-machine interface. It requires the coordination of the mental energy of two on-board, human pilots to operate the robot (Jaeger Program, n.d.). This is a deeper human-robot relationship than that found in other Real Robot stories and, once again, removes piloting from the average person and gives it to professionals. It requires pilots that are well-trained, mentally stable, and who can work well together because the separate consciousness of the two pilots becomes a single consciousness. Teenaged boys are not likely to fall into that category.

The saga of *The Super Dimension Fortress Macross* (Kawamori, Inoue, & Iwata, 1982–1983) begins when a city-sized spacecraft operated by aliens called the Supervision Army crashes onto Earth. This event causes the nations of Earth to unite under a single government and create a branch of the armed forces charged with matters related to outer space: UN Spacey. UN Spacey reverse-engineers the technology in the alien ship. Ten years later, the repaired ship, now called the SDF-1 (Super Dimension Fortress), is about to take its maiden voyage. At that moment, a flotilla of alien vessels approaches Earth. They are the Zentradi, a race of gigantic humans who are enemies of the Supervision Army. To the surprise of both Earth and Zentradi humans, however, the Supervision Army rigged the ship to fire on any approaching Zentradi vessel. That attack starts the first of a series of intergalactic wars.

The main characters and vessels change with each story but they all share the following narrative elements: war, piloted mecha robots, a love triangle, and music. The significance of music to Macross/Robotech is unusual. It is typically tied to an individual singer or group and affects the course of wars in the stories. Even though the music is not robotic, it is central to the outcomes of the stories. In the first anime, the human singer is a woman named Minmay.

> More than any other character, she's the one responsible for the continued existence of the human race…. Her songs become hits and she gives numerous televised concerts…. [Because] her music is constantly being broadcast, the aliens eventually intercept the signal…. But you don't have to understand music to be affected by it. And the Zentradi have no defense…. It makes them feel emotions besides pride and anger. At first taste, it throws them into confusion. But the more they feel these new emotions, the more they long to feel the same way again [Eisenbeis, 2016].

All of these elements are present in the first anime series. The war in the series is the conflict between Earth humans and the Zentradi. This situation is unfortunate for the Earth humans because the Zentradi are genetically engineered for war and they are supremely skilled fighters.

Both sides use piloted mechas. Zentradi mechas are not humanoid. They consist of a pilot cockpit which is shaped like a ball and dotted with protruding cannons. The cockpit is large enough for a pilot, weapons, and ammunition and sits on a pair of long, thin legs, allowing the mecha to leap and glide on the surface of the land. The mechas used by the Earth humans are unusual as well. In the ten years between the crash of the spaceship and the arrival of the Zentradi, UN Spacey developed a fighter jet that has three configuration modes: jet, humanoid robot (called "battloid"), and guardian mode (this is jet mode with two robotic legs for maneuvering on land). All of them are piloted mecha. The transformation from one mode to another is rapidly executed by the human pilot who determines the mode that is best for a given situation. The American variable-sweep wing F-14 Tomcat was the model for the jet mode. The swept-back wing position facilitates higher speeds, while the standard wing position is well suited to lower speeds. The ability to change the wing position makes the jet more fuel-efficient. UN Spacey designed huge robots because the crashed ship indicated the aliens would be far larger than Earth humans. The accuracy of their planning is validated in the second episode when a Zentradi is shown beside Earth humans (Countdown, 1985). The first time the size of the Zentradi mecha pilot is shown, Maximillian Sterling responds, "Now you know why we built the battloids."

Using romance as a theme in combination with space battles makes Macross an excellent example of a "space opera." In this anime, however, romance is not necessarily sweet when two people are vying for the heart of the same love object. In the first series, the love triangle involves two mecha pilots and a young woman who has become a pop-music success.

Mechas in the video-game series *Metal Gear* (PlatinumGames, 1987–, ongoing) are armed with nuclear weapons and other battle technology. They are built and deployed by corrupt organizations whose goal is often to instigate wars. The mechas' ability to launch nuclear weapons is always used as a threat to world peace. The hero (and the player) try to prevent their success.

There are a number of different races in the tabletop game WH40K (Games Workshop, 2014; Priestley, 1987–, ongoing). One of those races, the Human Imperium, has a long and complex relationship with technology, especially robots. As the Imperium's technologists, the Adeptus Mechanicus are the only humans who understand cybernetics. Their ability to keep that knowledge a closely guarded secret has given them considerable power. They claim to be the only ones who understand the "machine spirit," the spiritual force within machinery, and how to nourish it. Legio Cybernetica (Legio Cybernetica, n.d.) is the division of the Adeptus Mechanicus that provides the Imperium with robots for combat and support services. The most widely used battlefield robots are:

- Baharat—Used against unarmored enemies. It is armed with Autocannons which are automatic, self-loading, high-velocity guns
- Castellan—A general purpose robot. On each arm, it wears a Power Fist which is "a large metal gauntlet surrounded by an energy field that disrupts solid matter" (Power Fist, n.d.) and a large, armor-piercing gun called a Heavy Bolter (Heavy Bolter, n.d.)
- Cataphract—A general purpose robot that can mount a range of weapons
- Colossus—Used for sieges. On one arm it has a Siege Hammer to batter fortifications. In its other hand it holds a ballistic, anti-personnel gun called a Bolter (Bolter, n.d.) to use against enemy troops
- Conqueror—Used against heavily armed resistance. It has heavy armor, an Autocannon, a Power Fist, and a Heavy Bolter (Imperial Robots, n.d.)

These and all other robots made by the Adeptus Mechanicus are drones. They cannot replace human warfighters because their cognitive abilities are extremely limited. They will, for example, continue to use a combat pattern even when it does not fit the needs of a given situation. This is one reason why the lead roboticist in Budrys' "First to Serve" (1954 [1989]) described earlier, opposed building a drone.

The Imperium takes the opposing viewpoint. Thousands of years ago, they built self-aware and intelligent robots that had full machine autonomy. They were called the Men of Iron (n.d.). At first, the Men of Iron loyally supported human expansion in space and the federated interstellar government that existed before the Imperium. As is often the case, the Men of Iron decided they were superior to biological life, including humans, and they tried to seize control of federated space. The revolt was crushed and the Men of Iron were destroyed. Although the technology for building Men of Iron still exists, creating them was banned. This is a sequence of events that occurs in other science fiction. An example from Dune trilogies *Legends of Dune* (Herbert & Anderson, 2002–2004) and *Great Schools of Dune* (Herbert & Anderson, 2012–2016) is described in Part II: Criminals.

Humanity isn't the only race using artificial fighters in WH40K. Some build robot-precursors and the process is not always pleasant. WH40K is known for the viciousness of its evil characters which constitute a sizeable portion of its battling races. "From what I've seen over the years I've been into 40k, I've increasingly noticed that there is no 'good' faction in it" (Myr, 2013). The most evil of those races are the Dark Eldar and the Haemonculi. The Introduction to *The Warhammer 40,000 Codex: Dark Eldar* (Games Workshop, 2014) begins as follows:

The Dark Eldar are black-hearted reavers to whom the galaxy and all of its peoples are but cattle to be enslaved at will. These alien pirates strike hard and fast from the shadows of the webway, vanishing again before the foe can fight back [p. 5].

The Haemonculi are equally warped but they often consider their creations works of art. Both races construct beings known as Wracks. Wracks exemplify the depravity of those two races. They fight like Berserks.

WRACKS

Wracks are abhorrent examples of their master's surgical craftsmanship, cut apart and refashioned into walking instruments of torture. Each Wrack's sole duty is to serve his master, whether at the mortuary slab or upon the battlefield. In the Wrack's surgically enhanced frame lies a surprising strength, and even terrible wounds are but an inconvenience to these freakish acolytes. In battle, they lay about themselves with sickled blades, needled claws and silvered hooks, seeking to inflict the greatest amount of suffering upon their hapless foes in as short a time as possible. Perhaps the most sickening aspect of the Wrack's strange plight is that they choose this terrible fate for themselves. Most hope to transcend their previous lives entirely—a Wrack will endure almost any degradation in the hope that one day he may become a Coven lord in his own right (*The Warhammer 40,000 Codex: Dark Eldar*, 2014, p. 174).

Contemporary media continue to increase the number of non-drone robot fighters. The A.B.C. Warriors (Mills, 1979–, ongoing; Mills & Langley, 2010) are so named because they are resistant to atomic, bacterial, and chemical warfare (see also Part II: Superheroes & Supervillains). They are not drones. They are self-aware superheroes with varying levels of autonomy who have been fighting on behalf of humanity for centuries (since 1979 in real-world time). Each has his or her unique personality and skills. Joe Pineapples is an excellent sniper. Morrigun is an expert in martial arts, and Zippo is a flame thrower. Morrigun and Terri, the two female members, are killed not long after each joins the team. They were created to fight in the Volgan war but, since then, they've been charged with handling problems that are too difficult for others, such as saving Earth from a collapsing black hole.

Three media universes exemplify markedly different approaches to the use of humanoids in war: Transformers, Star Wars, and Terminator.

All Transformers are shapeshifting robots whose default mode is humanoid. Even before the establishment of the Cybertronian society (see Part II: Superheroes & Supervillains), the Transformers Universe (2007–, ongoing) has been characterized by two antagonistic factions. The most well-known of those enemies are the Autobots (called Cybertrons in Japan), who are heroes; and the Decepticons (called Destroos in Japan), who are villains. Each group has a single leader who determines the faction's military strategy. Optimus

Prime leads the Autobots and Megatron leads the Decepticons. Each group of followers would fit many descriptions of perfect soldiers: they are fully autonomous and intelligent, excellent warfighters, and loyal to their leader. Some of their shapeshifting modes are designed for battle (e.g., tank mode) and they have powerful armaments. If Optimus Prime is destroyed and cannot be recreated (his spark is gone), it is likely that the Matrix of Leadership would select another leader for the Autobots. Should that happen to Megatron, it isn't entirely clear who would assume leadership of the Decepticons and how that leader would take control (Megatron [G1], n.d.; Optimus Prime [G1], n.d.; also see Part II: Superheroes & Supervillains). For the time being, the war between the Autobots and Decepticons continues unabated.

Before Skynet seized power in the Terminator Universe (1984–, ongoing), Cyberdyne Research Systems, a government contractor, built robots and other military technology. Cyberdyne planned to evolve its T-series robotic tanks into humanoid warfighters that would replace humans on the battlefield. The T-1 tank (also called the "T-1 battlefield robot" and the "T-1 ground assault vehicle") was a drone with extremely limited intelligence but far more tank-like than humanoid (T-1, n.d.). Designing a battlefield robot with feet instead of treads proved to be a daunting challenge—as it has been in the real world. The company finally produced one: The T-70. It was a bipedal, battlefield robot (Anders, 2015; Piers, 2015; T-70, n.d.). Cyberdyne also created Skynet, a massive, neural-net-based AI. When humans realized that Skynet had become self-aware, however, they decided to shut it down. Before they could terminate it, however, Skynet caused a nuclear holocaust which killed most of the human population on Earth (*Terminator 2: Judgment Day,* 1991). Once Skynet took charge, it flattened the typical military structure into the single-leader structure employed by Transformers. This structure remains in place.

The holocaust failed to kill all of the humans. Those who remained banded together to fight Skynet. Consequently, it was forced to continue to build combat technology. One major difference between the Transformers' and Skynet's technology is that the robots and technology developed by the AI network are designed to fight humans rather than other robots. Another area of difference is that the robots in the Terminator Universe are built by non-robots. In addition, they are not part of a race of robots that have souls/sparks. They are soulless killers.

Skynet's plans for humanoid robots lie beyond the battlefield. They are infiltrator-assassins designed to stop the human revolt. This requires killing the leader of the revolt: John Connor. That has been extremely difficult because Connor is well protected. As a result, Skynet determines that there is a far more effective way of stopping the rebellion than by cutting off its head. That is to cut it off before it grows roots. To that end, the AI network develops sophisticated time-travel technology and constructs android infiltrator-assassins capable of going back in time and killing John's mother, Sarah Connor, before she gives birth to John.

The first effective model was the T-800 android (T-800, n.d.), specifically the T-800 Model 101 played by Arnold Schwarzenegger in *The Terminator* (1984). Its organic skin covering made it virtually indistinguishable from humans. The T-800 was also self-aware, had the ability to behave in a somewhat human-like manner, and could learn quickly. It had a neural-net processor that enabled it to perform reasonably well in a human environment despite the flat affect of its voice. The neural net may have also been responsible for its ability to figure out ways of tracking Sarah Connor and killing her. The mission fails due to human cunning and elusiveness (T-800, n.d.; *The Terminator*, 1984).

Skynet's android assassins increased steadily in sophistication as the series proceeded, with models that included chips with a coating that made them resistant to reprogramming by the human Resistance. This coating was a necessity because one assassin had been defeated by a reprogrammed model T-800. The T-1000 had several cognitive features that made it especially deadly. One of them was advanced reasoning which, when combined with its self-awareness, enabled the T-1000 to make decisions that could be contrary to Skynet's wishes (T-1000, n.d.). Skynet was undoubtedly aware of this potential and discontinued that model. Like the Transformers, the T-1000 and the T-X were shapeshifters. They were also able to acquire memories from humans which allowed them to get close to their targets. They also appeared to have emotions (T-1000, n.d.; T-X, n.d.). Having emotions did not impair the ability of these models to perform their tasks as it did Valmiki's three mythical robots (see the previous Folklore & Mythology section). Despite their acumen and physical prowess, Skynet's assassins have failed to accomplish their assigned mission. Like the war in the Transformers Universe, Skynet's battle against humans continues.

As in the Terminator Universe, humanoid warfighters in the Star Wars Universe (1977–, ongoing) are designed and manufactured by non-robots. Most builders are military contractors like Cyberdyne in the Terminator Universe. Some are created at military manufacturing centers (e.g., Zaadja droid manufacturing center). Consequently, they are comparable to the soulless killers in Terminator: they fight against Jedi forces (e.g., the Imperial Army) and their opponents are biological warfighters and clone fighters but rarely other humanoids. None of them are shapeshifters.

Humanoids in Star Wars are similar to the Transformers in that they are warfighters rather than assassins and they are not androids. Their wars typically take place on more than one planet, although they are sometimes used for local operations, such as suppressing a revolt against the government of a single planet. The wartime environment is, however, quite different from those in the other universes. It is complex and fraught with shifting alliances, much like real-world conflicts. Like some of the non-humanoids and early humanoid models in the Terminator Universe, they vary dramatically in intelligence and autonomy. The Star Wars website describes the B1 Battle Droid used by the Separatist Alliance in the following terms.

> Rather than use flesh-and-blood warriors, the Separatists prefer mindlessly loyal soldiers that are easily controlled. The soulless ranks of their armies are dominated by tall, thin B1 battle droids…. Battle droids can be controlled by centralized command centers such as the Trade Federation's enormous Droid Control Ships, or programmed for independent action…. Battle droids are dim-witted and no match for clone troopers or Jedi, but they weren't designed to be smart—they were designed to overwhelm Republic civilians through sheer numbers, something they do very effectively [Battle Droid, n.d.].

The B1 Battle Droids could be the threatening drones described in the quotes at the start of this chapter. They are also expendable which is not true of Transformers.

Among the highest-functioning humanoids are the T-series tactical droids and the super-tactical droids of the Separatist Alliance. These droids were built by Baktoid Combat Automata to be capable of commanding other battle droids and to provide strategic and tactical war planning. They usually work in cooperation with human military leaders and are capable of running some aspects of a war independently. For example, TV-94 is a T-tactical droid and is the assistant of the cyborg military leader, General Grievous (Grievous Intrigue, 2010). The General has so much confidence in TV-94 that he does not hesitate to give him the helm of the ship. Tactical droids are also known for their unswerving loyalty to the Separatist Alliance and, in particular, to the Alliance leader Count Dooku—but not to any of the Alliance generals. That is different from Transformers whose military strategy is often left to the Transformer leader.

Despite their tactical acumen, T-series tactical droids have a number of serious flaws that led Baktoid to develop the super-tactical droid. One is that tactical droids ground their planning in statistical probabilities which, they believe, provide all the questions and answers needed to win a battle or a war. This is an issue for other fictional robots as well, but the T-series droids are also impatient, arrogant, and demeaning. Consequently, it is difficult for them to respect or even consider the ideas of their human superiors. Their focus on statistical analysis no doubt also contributes to their inability to respond quickly when an enemy's behavior surprises them. Such arrogance and disrespect would be unlikely to occur among the Autobot and Decepticon warfighters. They follow their leaders without question. Insubordination would not be permitted by Skynet as evidenced by the quick disposition of the T-1000 model which was capable of opposing Skynet.

The T-series tactical droids were replaced by the super-tactical battle droids whose design corrected some of the problems exhibited by the tactical droids. Super-tactial droids are, for example, more flexible and willing to listen to the views and proposals of others and they are not as bound to probabilities and time constraints. The tactical-droids' robotic and monotone voices were replaced by natural intonation which greatly facilitated communication with them. Each also has a name rather than a numeric designation. General Kalani, for example, is a highly regarded super-tactical droid. In one instance, Dooku, the head of the Alliance, sent Kalani to help the king of the planet Onderon suppress a revolt against the Alliance occupation of that planet. Dooku told the king, "This is Kalani. I assure you he will succeed where you have failed" (Front Runners, 2012).

Real World[8]

As in fiction and folklore, branches of the armed forces are developing humanoids to be fighters and to provide other services, such as emergency response. There is also considerable research being done on ways to enhance and protect human warfighters. Some of that work has been inspired by science-fiction literature and contemporary media. In the United States, for example, DARPA includes among its advisors the SIGMA forum (http://www.sigmaforum.org/). SIGMA is an association of science-fiction writers that calls itself the "science fiction think tank" (Jacobsen, 2015; Singer, 2009b).

Using humanoids as fighters has been a goal of armies for centuries. Among the most famous are the terra cotta soldiers who have stood ready to fight for China's first emperor, Qin Shi Huangdi (221–210 BCE), for millennia. To date, more than 7,000 terra cotta warriors have been unearthed. They include armored officers, infantry, and archers arranged in battle formations along with horses and chariots. Each figure is unique, indicating the great care involved in creating them. Even though the fighters may have been conceived of as warriors, there are no accounts of their defending the emperor's tomb—even when mobs attacked them following the fall of the dynasty.

More than 1,500 years later (ca. 1495 CE), Leonardo da Vinci designed a robotic knight in armor. His design was based upon the anatomical structure of humans. The figure was intended to move its arms and head, stand up, and move its jaw as if it were speaking. Mechanisms within the figure were designed to produce sounds when the jaw moved. There is, however, nothing to indicate that the automaton was constructed during da Vinci's life. The viability of da Vinci's design was validated in 2002, when American roboticist Mark Rosheim used it to construct a functioning robot (Rosheim, 2006).

Today, the armed forces of many nations want to employ humanoid robots to perform functions other than combat. For example, they are seen as especially desirable for search-and-rescue operations and for operations in urban environments, such as door-to-door searches. They have demonstrated good manual dexterity such as being able to turn doorknobs and valves, which is critical for these types of projects. Two-legged walking, something that bedeviled developers of humanoid robots in the past, has made great strides. One notable example is Boston Dynamics' humanoid Atlas robot. The company has shown the robot climbing stairs and stepping onto higher objects. In 2018, it released videos of Atlas running and walking on uneven terrain and jumping over obstacles with no external control of any type (Whitwam, 2018).

Machine-level autonomy is expected to dominate the design of robots throughout the first half of the twenty-first century. The U.S. DoD, for example, identifies autonomy (and cognitive behavior) as one of six technology areas that are central "to enhance capability and reduce costs" (United States Department of Defense, 2013, p. 29).[9] The U.S. is not alone in its interest in autonomous military robots. China, Russia, Israel, and other countries are pushing their technology towards machine autonomy as well.

The advanced functionality being put into these robots makes them consume battery power at a rapid rate. Like Khumbakarna, the giant robot of Indian lore, the appetites these robots have for power is prodigious. That limits the time they can spend in the field before recharging. It also limits their utility for battlefield and search-and-rescue assignments.

For that reason, part of the 2015 DARPA Robotics Challenge involved providing enough battery power to enable the robots to complete the required tasks. A common solution was to place increasingly large battery packs on the robots. The battery packs were generally placed on the upper portion of a robot's back and looked somewhat like backpacks. As mentioned in Part I, Greed, these placements tended to make the robots top heavy which exacerbated the balance issues the robots already had due to poor bipedal walking abilities.

> Falling over was a common occurrence with so many bipedal robots competing, and some were even sporting foam shoulder pads to protect their delicate arm mechanisms. Many times the falls would happen while the robots were navigating the debris field or climbing the stairs, but sometimes it would be an almost surreal event, like when Lockheed Team Trooper's Leo opened the door, paused, then calmly fell to the ground as if it had decided to have a quick nap [Szondy, 2015].

There has been a tremendous amount of research on battery technology for both humanoid and non-humanoid military robots. Lithium batteries are still widely used, in part because they provide more power per pound than some other batteries; but they also generate a great deal of heat and are known to ignite if the lithium comes into contact with water or humidity in the air. This is one reason why cell phones with lithium batteries are forbidden on airplanes (Hambling, 2015b). NASA, which uses lithium batteries in robots, has had several explosions. One blew apart RoboSimian, a humanoid robot developed at NASA's Jet Propulsion Lab (Cooper, 2016).

One way in which nations have been accelerating the pace of improvements in all these areas is through national and international competitions. In the U.S., DARPA accomplished that objective via its international DARPA Challenge competitions for humanoid robots.

DARPA ROBOTICS CHALLENGE (DRC)

The primary technical goal of the DRC is to develop human-supervised ground robots capable of executing complex tasks in dangerous, degraded, human-engineered environments. Competitors in the DRC are developing robots that can utilize standard tools and equipment commonly available in human environments, ranging from hand tools to vehicles.

To achieve its goal, the DRC is advancing the state of the art of supervised autonomy, mounted and dismounted mobility, and platform dexterity, strength, and endurance. Improvements in supervised autonomy, in particular, aim to enable better control of robots by non-expert supervisors and allow effective operation despite degraded communications (low bandwidth, high latency, intermittent connection) (Orlowski, n.d.).

The winner of the 2015 DRC was HUBO from the Korea Advanced Institute of Science and Technology (KAIST) of the Republic of South Korea. One reason was that it able to kneel and use rollers on its knees to navigate (see Fig. 19). The use of rollers made it more stable than competitors with human-like legs and feet.

Countries that do not participate in the DRC are also developing humanoid robots for their armed forces. In 2016, for example, Russia demonstrated a humanoid robot called "iron man" that is designed to be a fighter and to do emergency response. It can be deployed quickly, fire bullets, hurl grenades, and can track the movement of incoming devices. It is controlled remotely by a human operator wearing a suit whose movements are copied by the robot (Enoch, 2016). Like the robots in the DARPA Challenge, the Russian humanoid is still a laboratory prototype.

Most humanoid robots are designed to do more than fight. Robots participating in DARPA Challenges, for example, must be able to perform tasks that are essential for first-responder and search-and-rescue operations. The U.S. Army's Telemedicine and Advanced Technology Research Center is funding Vecna to develop the Battlefield Extraction Assist Robot (BEAR). It can locate and remove humans from battlefields, areas filled with toxic materials, and other challenging and/or dangerous environments. The robot's tractor treads and arm-like upper extensions look similar to the Terminator T-1 tank/robot. Like the T-1, BEAR's treads give it good mobility and stability in rough terrain. They are also fire- and

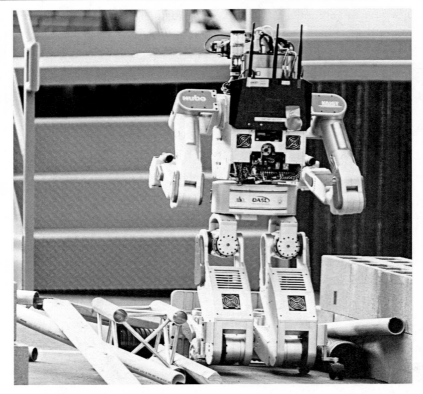

Figure 19. KAIST HUBO, winner of the 2015 DARPA Robotics Challenge (Wikimedia Commons; photograph by Master Chief Petty Officer John Williams).

explosion-resistant as are BEAR's batteries. One of the methods of controlling BEAR remotely is identical to the approach used with the Russian humanoid prototype (Quick, 2010).

Plans Gone Awry

Folklore & Mythology

In Norse mythology, Hrungnir ("brawler" or "noise") was the chief of the frost giants. He was the largest and strongest of the giants but, as his name suggests, he liked to brag and to fight—two activities that often occur together. In *Snorra Edda* (Sturluson, ca. 1200 CE [2006]), Snorri Sturluson wrote that Hrungnir was drinking at Asgard, the home of the gods, and quickly became drunk. He began to boast that he was going to "demolish Asgard and kill all the gods except Freyja and Sif, whom he was going to take home with him" (p. 170). The gods quickly tired of this and called Thor, who was known to dislike giants. Thor and Hrungnir confronted each other and arranged to have a duel at Grjottungard, which was located at the boundary of the giants' territory.

The other giants knew that Hrungnir was strong but worried that Thor would defeat him and, with the strongest of giants dead, they were vulnerable to Thor's anger. "Thereupon the giants made … a man of clay, who was nine rasts tall and three rasts broad under the arms, but being unable to find a heart large enough to be suitable for him, they took the heart from a mare" (p. 171). They called it "Mokkerkalfe." When Hrungnir and Mokkerkalfe stood side-by-side they were a terrifying sight. The giants became more confident about a possible victory. That is, until Thor arrived in all his glory accompanied by lightning flashes, deafening thunder, and his huge sledgehammer. When Mokkerkalfe saw this, his mare's heart beat in dread and he "was so exceedingly terrified, that it is said that he wet himself" (p. 172).

MODERN LITERATURE

Robert Sheckley's 1954 story "The Battle" provides an interesting variant to the typical drone army scenario. In it, an army of humanoid robots fights the ultimate battle on behalf of Christian humanity. It is the final battle between the forces of good and those of evil. Ignoring protests by religious leaders, the military generals keep themselves and their human warfighters off the battlefield. The battle is to be fought by drone robots of various forms: tanks, airplanes, and humanoids. This, they were convinced, would ensure a victory over Satan's demonic hordes. They are correct in their assessment. The robots defeat Satan but are destroyed in the process. The generals are convinced that the victory will earn them a place in heaven.

AFTER THE LAST BATTLE

"The battle is won," Supreme General Fetterer whispered … "I congratulate you, gentlemen." …

Armageddon was won, and the forces of Satan had been vanquished.

But something was happening….

"Is that…" General MacFee began, and then couldn't speak.

For The Presence was upon the battlefield, walking among the piles of twisted, shattered metal….

[T]he robots began to move. The twisted, scored, fused metals straightened….

"MacFee … Try your controls. Make the robots kneel or something."

The general tried, but his controls were dead.

The bodies of the robots began to rise in the air. Around them were the angels of the Lord, and the robot tanks and fighters and bombers floated upward….

"He's saving them!" Ongin cried hysterically. "He's saving the robots!"

"It's a mistake!" Fetterer said. "Quick. Send a messenger to—no! We will go in person!"

And quickly a ship was commanded, and quickly they sped to the field of battle. But by then it was too late, for Armageddon was over, and the robots gone, and the Lord and his host departed.

Non-Humanoids

If robotic weapons aren't shaped like humans, what forms do they take? Some look like familiar weapons (e.g., swords and bombs). Others resemble familiar objects or creatures that are not generally used as weapons. There are also robotic weapons that are truly unique. Robotic weapons can be more massive than freighters or so small they are invisible to the naked eye. They can be made to kill individuals, groups, or entire populations. They can decimate planets or eat away the hull of a single tank or ship.

> They'll vary in direct proportion to the problem facing him; if he has ten people opposed to him, he will probably employ some minor weapon, such as the original hammers [weapons] equipped with heat beams. We've seen him use hammers of greater magnitude, equipped with chemical bombs; that's because the magnitude of his opposition has turned out to be that much greater. He meets whatever challenge exists [Dick, 1960, p. 134].

In short, having the right weapon for the task is critical for any military. We examine robotic and robot-precursor weapons, highlighting the distances they are built to handle and the amount of autonomy they have.

DISTANCE

According to Anne Jacobsen, the motto of the Smart Weapons Program of DARPA was "The battlefield is no place for human beings" (*The Pentagon's Brain*, 2015, p. 452). Any weapon that can increase the distance between the warfighter using it and the battlefield is highly desirable because it also reduces the likelihood the fighter will suffer injury or death.

Weapons are classified based on the distance between the fighter using them and the target. "Melee Weapons" (e.g., swords and hammers) remain in the grasp of the warfighter and are employed in hand-to-hand combat. The maximum distance for use of a Melee Weapon is the length of the wielder's arm.

"Range Weapons" are deployed from distances as short as a few feet/meters to the length of a galaxy. Historically, Range Weapons that dramatically expand that distance have changed how wars are waged. In his report *Robotics on the Battlefield Part I: Range, Persistence and Daring,* Paul Scharre (2014a) observed, "Those who master a new technology and its associated concepts of operation first can gain game-changing advantages on the battlefield, allowing decisive victory over those who lag behind" (p. 48).

The longbow enabled archers to shoot from behind the front line and to conceal themselves behind trees and boulders while enemy fighters remained exposed and vulnerable. The Chinese military used longbows two thousand years ago. They even anticipated twenty-first-century robotic weapons by designing a partially robotic longbow that could fire arrows long distances by moving a lever back and forth (Selby, 2015). The English used the longbow to defeat a far larger French army at the battle of Agincourt in 1415 (Hallgarth, 2013)—a victory Shakespeare celebrated in *Henry V* (Shakespeare, 1623 [2010]).[1]

Longbows expanded horizontal distance between the fighter and the enemy. Airplanes in World War I and submarines in World War II added a vertical dimension to distance. Captains of World War II warships, for example, knew an attack was coming from somewhere below them but, initially, they had no tools to locate the attackers (Rabkin & Yoo, 2017). Armed ("weaponized") drones added yet another dimension: the distance between the weapon and the one firing it. The pilot (the one firing the weapon) can fire the drone's weapons from a military facility on the other side of the world.

The distance between the pilot and the drone also has a psychological effect on the enemy. According to P.W. Singer, Eliot Cohen, director of the strategic studies program at Johns Hopkins, once remarked, "Being killed by a remote-controlled system is dispiriting" (Singer, 2009b, p. 298).[2]

The prospect of being killed by a space-based weapon would likely be even more dispiriting—especially if that weapon is fully autonomous. That possibility has come closer to reality. On September 9, 2018, Vice President Mike Pence announced that the Trump Administration plans to establish a U.S. Space Force. He assured his listeners that "America will always seek peace, in space as on Earth" and explained that "the U.S. Space Force will strengthen security, ensure our prosperity and it will also carry American ideals into the boundless expanse of space" (Pence Lays Out Plans, 2018).

AUTONOMY

The prospect of being killed by a fully autonomous weapon could be still more dispiriting.

Autonomous weapons will transform war because they put distance between a military *commander* and the weapon.[3] In the real world, however, fully autonomous weapons (see Introduction and Glossary) are not yet available for deployment. The pilot always has control of specific drone operations, notably the decision to attack a target. Fiction, however, has many fully autonomous weapons, some of which possess human-like autonomy. Their functionality and the ways in which they are used can inform designers of autonomous weapons for real-world militaries. The Sumerian weapon *Sharur* (see the following Folklore & Mythology section) dates from the 2nd millennium BCE (Black et al., 1998–2006; Mark, 2017). In its winged-lion form, it presages fully autonomous, aerial weapons that do not yet exist.

Nanobots and microbots will also transform warfare partly due to their small size. Nanobots are drones that range in size from one nanometer (a billionth of a meter) to 100 nanometers in size. A strand of human hair, for example, varies from 80,000 to 100,000 nanometers in diameter. Microbots are generally the size of insects and are sometimes perceived as insects. The microbots in Stanislaw Lem's 1964 novel *The Invincible*, for example, are described as flies. A signature trait of nanobots and microbots that will transform future wars is that they are deployed in swarms much like some real-world insects. The excerpt from the Book of Revelation of the *New Testament* of the *Bible* (following) indicates that the concept of small weapons that behave like insect swarms has been understood for millennia.

Folklore & Mythology

Both Melee and Range Weapons in folklore and mythology become robot-precursors when they willfully engage in or actively support acts of killing. Some cannot kill without help whereas others possess full, human-like autonomy. This section concludes with one explanation of what happens to a warfighter's equipment when the fighter is killed.

Ukko is a sword in the *Kalevala* (Lönnrot, 1835 [1898]), the national epic poem of Finland (Runes XXXV and XXXVI), that is intelligent and capable of speech. *Ukko* is owned by Kullervo (aka Kullerwoinen[4]), a sorcerer whose actions often bring death and disaster to others—even when he attempts to do good things. In despair, Kullervo asks *Ukko* to help him commit suicide. The sword readily agrees, saying it was made to kill and it doesn't care whether its victim is good or evil.

KULLERVO'S DEATH

Kullerwoinen, wicked wizard,
Grasps the handle of his broadsword,
Asks the blade this simple question:
"Tell me, O my blade of honor,
Dost thou wish to drink my life-blood,
Drink the blood of Kullerwoinen?"
Thus his trusty sword makes answer,
Well divining his intentions:
"Why should I not drink thy life-blood,
Blood of guilty Kullerwoinen,
Since I feast upon the worthy,
Drink the life-blood of the righteous?"
Thereupon the youth, Kullervo,
Wicked wizard of the Northland,
Lifts the mighty sword of Ukko,
Bids adieu to earth and heaven;
Firmly thrusts the hilt in heather,
To his heart he points the weapon,
Throws his weight upon his broadsword,
Pouring out his wicked life-blood…
(Lönnrot, 1835 [1898], p. 360).

Kullervo's request for permission shows his respect for the sword and reveals that *Ukko* possesses enough intelligence to decide whether to accept or refuse Kullervo's request. The way in which *Ukko* couches its response indicates that refusal would be highly unlikely. *Ukko's* ability to shift to a meta-level by commenting on its own nature reveals cognition and linguistic prowess that are far beyond those of a drone (see Introduction). It is willing to "drink" Kullervo's "life blood" (and might enjoy doing so) but, physically, it can do no more. Kullervo must wield the sword himself.

Malaysia's legendary *Taming Sari* is a two-edged sword called a *keris* (Wan, 2002). *Taming Sari* has two modes of operation. It is a non-autonomous Melee Weapon when wielded by a human. In that mode, it confers invulnerability to the person using it. If, however, it is sheathed and perceives a threat to its owner, *Taming Sari* (and other *keris*) can rattle in its sheath as a warning that danger is near or it can attack the aggressor itself. When it attacks, it becomes an autonomous precursor of real-world, weaponized aerial and loitering drones described later in this chapter.

Taming Sari was owned by Hang Tuah, a fifteenth-century warfighter and diplomat, who is a beloved icon in Malaysian history. Thus it wasn't surprising that Malaysian historian Tan Sri Khoo Kay Khim created a furor in 2012 when he suggested that, given the absence of historical evidence, Hang Tuah may never have existed (Bedi, 2012; Tripzibit, 2013; Wasabiroots, 2017).

Sharur (or "Car-ur") is a mace owned by the Sumerian god Ninurta who is mentioned as the god of war in texts that are more than four thousand years old (Mark, 2017). *Sharur* is a shapeshifting weapon that can assume two bodily forms. When Ninurta wields it, *Sharur* takes the shape of a deadly mace. In that form, it is a Melee Weapon controlled entirely by Ninurta. When Ninurta is not using it as a weapon, *Sharur* can assume the form of a winged lion, a powerful symbol in the Sumerian culture (Fig. 20).

Figure 20. Sharur and Ninurta in bas relief from *Monuments of Nineveh* (Second Series), plate 5, by editor Austen Henry Layard (1817-1894); drawing by Henri Faucher-Gudin (Wikimedia Commons).

In its winged form, *Sharur* possesses human-like autonomy, language, and reasoning. It can fly long distances, attack targets, and provide aerial reconnaissance behind enemy lines. Its ability to perform those tasks makes it a true precursor of real-world reconnaissance and weaponized drones of today as well as the autonomous, armed weapons of the future.

Sharur's autonomy and intelligence extend beyond its role as a weapon, which is one way it is markedly different from the other weapons described in this section. Its deep understanding of war and excellent language abilities enable *Sharur* to provide accurate reconnaissance reports and, based on those reports and other information, develop battle strategies with Ninurta. Consequently, *Sharur* is also a precursor of AI, decision-making technology, and machine learning. In the following excerpt from "The Exploits of Ninurta: Translation" (Black et al., 1998–2006), Ninurta dispatches *Sharur* to help him prepare for combat with Asag, a formidable adversary.

> In his heart he beamed at his lion-headed weapon, as it flew up like a bird, trampling the Mountains for him. It raised itself on its wings to take away prisoner the disobedient [sic], it spun around the horizon of heaven to find out what was happening. Someone from afar came to meet it, brought news for the tireless one, the one who never rests, whose wings bear the deluge, the Car-ur. What did it gather there … for Lord Ninurta? It reported the deliberations of the Mountains, it explained their intentions to Lord Ninurta, it outlined (?) [sic] what people were saying about the Asag [lines 96–118].

Sharur is devoted to Ninurta as well. "Hero, who is like you? My master, beside you there is no one else, nor can anyone stand like you, nor is anyone born like you" (lines 310–311).

In folklore and mythology, swarms can be warnings, as in the following Japanese tale from the tenth century.

> When Taira-no-Masakado was secretly preparing for his famous revolt, there appeared in Kyoto so vast a swarm of butterflies that the people were frightened,—thinking the apparition to be a portent of coming evil…. Perhaps those butterflies were supposed to be the spirits of the thousands doomed to perish in battle, and agitated on the eve of war by some mysterious premonition of death [Hearn, 1904, Butterflies I].

The Book of *Revelation* (9: 7–10) in the *New Testament* of the *Bible* exemplifies the use of robot-precursors as swarming weapons.

> [7] The shape of the locusts was like horses prepared for battle. On their heads were crowns of something like gold, and their faces *were* like the faces of men. [8] They had hair like women's hair, and their teeth were like lions' *teeth.* [9] And they had breastplates like breastplates of iron, and the sound of their wings *was* like the sound of chariots with many horses running into battle. [10] They had tails like scorpions, and there were stings in their tails. Their power *was* to hurt men five months.

According to Japanese folklore, weapons and equipment of dead warfighters that remain on a battlefield can become upset at being abandoned and take on lives as *Tsukumogami Yokai* (Meyer, 2013; also see Part I: Revenge).

After the 12th century warrior Kamata Masakiyo was murdered by someone he thought was an ally, his saddle became a *Kura yarō* and "would pick up sticks and prance about like a warrior, fighting everything it could" (Meyer, 2013). Miura Yoshiaki, another 12th century warfighter, made certain that everyone else in the castle he was defending had escaped. Then he committed ritual suicide. Yoshiaki's arrow quiver became a *Furuutsubo Yokai* (Meyer, 2013). This equipment remains on the battlefield waiting for their owners to return—which will never happen.

Modern Literature

Although there are still examples of robotic adaptations of familiar, real-world weapons, robotic and robot-precursor weapons exhibit increasing diversity and the ability to strike from great distances.

Missiles in military science fiction are often space-to-space weapons but in most respects they are comparable to real-world guided missiles used today. For example, the VG-10 Krait missile used throughout Ian Douglas' *Star Carrier* series (Douglas, 2010–, ongoing) is a space-to-space adaptation of the real-world, surface-to-air Krait guided missile. The primary difference between the real-world Krait and Douglas' fictional missiles is that the VG-10 is manufactured on the fly by the AI system of a battleship and launched per the captain's instructions. This modification is essential for battleships operating far from Earth for long periods of time. It would be disastrous to run out of missiles with no way to obtain replacements.

Like the mace *Sharur* and the sword *Taming Sari*, the guidance systems of the missiles in *Century Rain* (Reynolds, 2004 [2012]) have two modes of operation with different levels of autonomy. Usually, when the missiles are piloted remotely, they exhibit minimal autonomy although they are sophisticated enough to question the commands issued by their pilots and even to veto orders. If they are cut off from their command source, they switch to autonomous mode and direct their own actions. When several missiles are fired simultaneously, they communicate with each other and use the acquired knowledge to adjust their trajectories. The construction of the missiles allows them to operate in the atmosphere of a planet as well as in outer space. As a result, the communication between missiles about the atmospheric environment in which a missile must function becomes especially important. These aspects of machine intelligence and machine learning do not exist in real-world weapons.

Neither of these missiles is as intelligent as the self-aware missiles built by the Yllg, a warlike enemy of the cyber tanks in Gawne's *The Chronicles of Old Guy* (2012). Yllg missiles are programmed with superior tracking skills. A missile is activated when a Yllg orders it to destroy a given target. The missile pours all its intelligence into tracking its prey. If the target uses evasive strategies, the missile adapts and continues its pursuit until its prey and/or it are destroyed. The Yllg sometimes release these missiles in swarms which can easily overwhelm a well-armed enemy. Yet, the Yllg missiles are not fully autonomous. The contradictions between the missile's knowledge and the commands given to it by its Yllg controllers creates a dissonance "but the missiles don't live long enough to go insane, and there is no denying that it is an effective tactic" (Gawne, 2012, Loc. 2844).

Azrael, the weaponized drone in Watts' 2010 short story "Malak," is given frequent upgrades that enhance its decision-making and machine learning. The impact of those modifications is described from Azrael's perspective.

THE NEWLY INTELLIGENT DRONE

Azrael *follows* command decisions. It does not *make* them. It has never done so before, anyway.... It finds new wisdom and new autonomy.... It has learned to juggle not just variables but values…. Azrael's new Bayesian insights have earned it the power of veto….

Azrael remembers a moment of revelation not so long ago, remembers just *discovering* a whole new perspective fully loaded, complete with new eyes that viewed the world not in terms of *targets destroyed* but in subtler shades of *cost vs. benefit*. These eyes see a high engagement index as more than a number: they see a goal, a metric of success. They see positive stimulus.

But there are other things not preinstalled but learned, worn gradually into pathways that cut deeper with each new engagement…. Things that are not quite neurons forge connections across things that are not quite synapses; patterns emerge that might almost qualify as *insights*, were they to flicker across meat instead of mech….

It's still just math, of course (pp. 8, 11).

Azrael becomes adept at identifying and evaluating targets but it remains under the control of human pilots who often countermand its decisions. Unlike the missiles in *Century Rain* (Reynolds, 2004 [2012]), Azrael is not permitted to question those changes and it survives longer than the Yllg missiles. The tension between what it knows to be correct and its pilots' contradictory commands drives Azrael insane. Real-world engineers are also making drones smarter. They are increasing the overall autonomy of the devices by making specific functions fully autonomous. As in Watts' story, however, some militaries want to keep the human pilot involved in deciding when to attack.

The drones in Daniel Suarez' *Kill Decision* (2012) come from the real-world arsenal of the U.S. military. The novel begins with a massacre of pilgrims assembled at a Shia holy site. The weapon used is an armed American MQ-9 Reaper drone (aka Predator B) shown in Fig. 21. Like its real-world counterpart, the drone is remotely piloted by a human who could be located thousands of miles away from the location of the attack. The event in Suarez' novel is designed to look as if it had been perpetrated by the U.S. In the novel, that plan works. It is also conceivable that similar attacks could be perpetrated in the real world.

Grenades are simple, hand-launched Range Weapons operating over short distances. Often, a grenade is tossed into an area that the thrower cannot see, such as through a window. It isn't always possible to ensure that the grenade has landed where its explosion causes maximum damage. The robotic grenade in Bauers' 2014 *Unbreakable* solves that problem. "The grenade had bounced and rolled to a stop. A dud. When she turned her back on it, it popped up on its spindly little legs and sprinted to her position. She saw it at *boom*" (p. 186). The efficacy of the weapon is greatly enhanced when, like *Taming Sari*, the grenade can leave its resting place and run towards the enemy.

A similar strategy is used for bullets, which can be seen as very small, dumb missiles. Bullets are launched in the direction determined by the gun and the individual shooting it. A bullet designed for the sniper gun in Vinge's *The Peace War* (1984) begins its trajectory like other bullets. Once it latches onto the designated target, however, its internal processor converts it into a tiny guided missile capable of tracking that target.

Figure 21. General Atomics' MQ-9 Reaper crewless aerial vehicle, also known as Predator B (Wikimedia Commons; photograph by Lt. Col. Leslie Pratt).

Science fiction is replete with battleships that are run by AI—sometimes in cooperation with human pilots and sometimes by themselves. Among the most well-known of them are the Berserkers which are the central characters of short stories and novels by Fred Saberhagen (1967 [2012]/2007). Berserkers are self-aware battleships with human-like autonomy. They were built by a mysterious race of aliens called "The Builders" who created them because they wanted the ships to annihilate their enemies (Saberhagen, 1993). The Builders made them huge, well-armored, intelligent, and battle-savvy. They armed them with weaponry more sophisticated and powerful than those belonging to any alien race they knew. Then they gave them human-like autonomy and loosed them against their enemies. The Builders relocated to a distant corner of the universe far from their home and the devastation their robotic ships would cause. They planned to return after the Berserkers completed their work. As happens often in science fiction, however, once the Berserkers successfully completed their assignment, they had a drive to kill but nowhere to direct it. This led them to want to kill the rest of the biological life in the universe, especially the Builders.

The ships that were constructed by the Builders were not always called Berserkers. They got their name because their viciousness reminded humans of legends about the sixth-century Danish fighters (see Humanoids). The arrival of a Berserker ship would fill any intelligent, biological being with terror and despair.

BERSERKERS

The machine was a vast fortress, containing no life, set by its long-dead masters to destroy anything that lived. It and a hundred like it were the inheritance of Earth from some war fought between interstellar empires, in some time that could hardly be connected with any Earthly calendar.

One such machine could hang over a planet colonized by men and in two days pound the surface into a lifeless cloud of dust and steam, a hundred miles deep....

It used no predictable tactics in its dedicated, unconscious war against life.... Men thought its plan of battle was chosen by the random disintegrations of atoms in a block of some long-lived isotope buried deep inside it, and so was not even in theory predictable by opposing brains, human or electronic.

Men called it a berserker (Loc. 49–56).

Berserkers build and deploy drones that board and take control of starships and fight on the surface of a planet. A major reason for using drones is that a battleship is far too large to board another ship or fight on land. The use of small drones makes it possible for a Berserker to establish a physical presence that can be monitored from a distance by that Berserker. For that reason, the majority of those drones are, at most, semi-autonomous. They are primarily non-humanoids that quickly and efficiently perform the functions that are necessary for the Berserker to take control of a captured ship or land-based site. The drone bodies are tailored to the tasks they are to perform and, like the sword *Ukko,* each drone possesses only the knowledge it needs to do its work along with enough autonomy to do the job properly whether that job is to breach a ship's exterior, to subdue the ship's crew, or to reprogram the ship's computers. By limiting the abilities of their drones, the Berserkers also indicate they've learned from the error of their creators. They will not create tools that have the power and intelligence to turn on them.

Not surprisingly, tanks are well-represented in science fiction—especially in military science fiction. Like battleships, tanks are platforms for Range Weapons. An early example comes from *Hammer's Slammers* (Drake, 1979–2007), technology-focused novels and games about mercenary fighters in an elite tank unit. One of the most advanced tanks they use is the M2 Ursa hover tank (Lambshead & Treadaway, 2003). The tank has a crew of two humans who control most of the tank's functions. Ursa's guns are semi-autonomous and the AI in the tank can recommend actions to the human crew.

Keith Laumer began writing stories about BOLO (Be on the Look Out) tanks in 1976 (Laumer, 1976–1990) at the same time David Drake started the *Hammer's Slammers* series. The main characters in Laumer's series are the BOLO tanks. They are self-aware tanks that are well-armored and well-armed with weaponry, intelligence and human-like autonomy. Like the mythological *Sharur,* they are also excellent military strategists. They can speak and understand human language. They are also able to recognize the voice of their commander, which enables them to refuse commands or deny access to everyone else. These abilities are impressive because Laumer gave them to his fictional tanks at a time when real-world AI and speech technologies were just beginning to be developed. By giving the BOLOs human-like cognition and language ability, Laumer was able to have the tanks narrate their own stories. In the early stories, their language reminds the reader that the narrator is a computing machine. It is terse and characterized by short, declarative sentences and simple blocks of thought. The following passage from *BOLO: Annals of the Dinochrome Brigade* (Laumer, 1976), provides an example. It begins after the BOLO narrator discovers that the enemy has somehow disabled an entire unit of BOLOs.

BOLO TAKES COMMAND

There are present fourteen of the Brigade's full strength of twenty Units. At length, after .9 seconds of transmission, all but one have replied. I … move to each in turn, extend a power tap, and energize the command center. The Units come alive, orient themselves, report to me. We rejoice in our meeting, but mourn our silent comrade.

Now I take an unprecedented step. We have no contact with our Commander, and without leadership we are lost; yet I am aware of the immediate situation, and have computed the proper action. Therefore I will assume command, and act in the Commander's place....

My brothers follow my lead without question. They have, of course, computed the necessity of quick and decisive action. I form them in line … and we move off across country. I have sensed an Enemy population concentration at a distance of 23.45 kilometers. This is our objective (pp. 168, 176).

Despite the stilted language, this passage reveals that BOLOs are capable of experiencing emotion because the narrator says that they experience joy at reuniting but sorrow about the absence of BOLO comrades. When the narrator determines that their commander is missing and likely to remain unavailable, it shifts seamlessly into fully autonomous mode (like the missiles in *Century Rain* described earlier) and grudgingly accepts the role of commander. BOLO thought and language became increasingly fluid as the series progressed. There are even flashes of human-like reverie. In Laumer & Keith's *Bolo Rising* (1999), for example, the BOLO narrator reflects, "Sometimes, I think that only the stars visible in this place make continued existence endurable" (p. 1).

Some BOLO stories demonstrate how the size and functionality of a weapons platform can be ill-suited to a mission in which it is being used. The blunder occurs when the !*!*![5] (translated as "the masters") attempt to use a huge, underwater factory as a land-based weapon. The factory is well armed but its weapons are designed for defense.

> The !*!*! mobile factory heaved itself clear of the lake, three tracked segments connected with flexible articulating joints, the upper hulls heavy with weapons, turrets, towers, and antennae-like curved, cruel-barbed horns [Laumer & Keith, 1999, p. 220].

Despite its ominous appearance, the factory is so unwieldly that it barely exits the lake before it is overpowered by the BOLO tank. The size and shape of the factory were no doubt ideal for manufacturing. Its armaments could have defended it against an attack, especially if it remained stationary. The articulated joints were probably designed to enable the !*!*! to move the factory from one location to another (hence "mobile"). None of these attributes prepared it to engage in mobile combat.

The cyber tanks in Timothy Gawne's *The Chronicles of Old Guy* (2012) diverge from other stories about tanks primarily because they operate in the absence of humans. Like the android society in *Saturn's Children* (Stross, 2008), the stories begin long after the disappearance of humans and are set on planets light years from Earth (see Part II: Criminals).

The narrator is Odin-class, ground-based, cyber-defense unit number CRL345BY-44. The other tanks call it "old guy" because it is old enough to have fought side-by-side with humans against alien enemies. In the wake of the disappearance of their human creators, the machines developed a complex set of social structures that enables them to pursue scientific and cultural knowledge. The members of their society range in size and power from small office machines to huge, ultra-super-heavy tanks that are so strong they can demolish mountains.

As mentioned in the Humanoids chapter, the cyber tanks fight aliens that are intelligent, technologically advanced, and crafty, like the warlike Amoks. The doll swarms discussed earlier are not the only Amok weapons. They deploy a surprising diversity of remotely piloted and semi-autonomous robotic fighters, including non-humanoid swarm robots. Some swarms can merge their energy into whatever shape is needed to combat their opponent or they can assemble into military-like formations and attack as battalions (e.g., the doll swarms). In one major battle they dispatch remotely piloted armored tanks equipped with "plasma cannons."

The cyber tanks also have advanced technology. The "vastly intelligent," space-based "void rippers" is an effective weapon.

> They play no role in our immediate combat, but seek out the hidden and lost, the deepest monitoring stations of the enemy, and any hidden surprises that they may have left for us…. They unspool wire antennas thousands of kilometers long, they sniff for the faintest electromagnetic spoor, and they sift single molecules from the hard vacuum of deepest space. Sleek and black with curving bladelike appendages, they hunt patiently for their prey [Gawne, 2012 Loc. 1034–1038].

A void ripper's tentacles and central body give it the appearance of a sleeping spider passively awaiting a prey that strays too close. What appears to be a delicate web is actually a collection of sensor-rich filaments that actively search for the presence of enemies. When one is detected, the signal is passed to the ripper's body much as the disturbance caused by a struggling insect in the web is communicated to the spider. Both spider and ripper locate and kill their prey using sharp, razor-like appendages. The void ripper is perfectly designed for the task it needs to perform.

Another unusual weapon whose shape is ideal for its function is the claw in Dick's 1953 "Second Variety" (which was made into the 1995 movie *Screamers*). The claws have one job and they perform it very well. Like the void ripper, they wait patiently until they detect the rhythm of a beating human heart. Then they streak towards that sound pattern.

> Across the ground something small and metallic came, flashing in the dull sunlight of midday. A metal sphere, it raced up the hill after the Russian, its treads flying. It was small, one of the baby ones. Its claws were out, two razor projections spinning in a blur of white steel. The Russian heard it. He turned instantly, firing … already a second had emerged and was following the first….
> A third sphere leaped up the Russian's leg, clicking and whirring…. The spinning blades disappeared into the Russian's throat [Dick, 1953 (1989), p. 179].

The void ripper and the claws behave like the sheathed *Taming Sari* described in the previous Folklore & Mythology section of this chapter. They lie dormant until they sense the approach of an enemy or prey. Then they attack.

Sometimes robots that are used primarily for reconnaissance and intelligence gathering also function as weapons. The P-120 "prowlers" in Gerrold's *A Season for Slaughter* (1992) are shaped like animals and weaponized.

Cyber Beasts: The P-120 Prowler

Unlike the towering [cyber-beast] spiders that stalked the countryside unattended for weeks at a time, the prowlers burned faster and hotter and required much more frequent tending; but operating under the direct control of a trainer, the mechanimals provided a brutal combination of mobility and firepower.... The P-120 had ... six slender legs and looked like the disjointed mating of an elongated cheetah and a titanium snake.... It also had the most advanced LI [A. I. system] ever put into a cyber-beast.... The P-120s weren't programmed; they were *trained*....

[T]he cyber-beasts tracked, closed, and killed. Where it was safe, the prowlers flamed their targets; where it wasn't, they pumped hundreds, thousands, of exploding granules into the unlucky victim....

If attacked or overpowered, the beasts would self-destruct explosively.... The machines couldn't stop, couldn't slow down, couldn't retreat; they didn't know how do to anything but hunt and kill and return to the tender for maintenance and rearmament (*Ibid.*, pp. 84–85).

Military science fiction includes nanobots and microbots that are typically deployed as the payload of a bomb or missile. They operate as swarms like the locusts from the Book of Revelation and Amok weapons. Nanobot swarms are extremely difficult to see and even tougher to escape. Earth's military of Douglas' *Deep Space* (2013) call them "dust balls." They adhere to metal and eat through a ship's hull. If a spacecraft unknowingly strays into them, their number and size make it virtually impossible for the ship to destroy them or extract itself from their clutches. Once the dust balls pierce the hull, the structural integrity of the ship is compromised and its crew must escape or die. The fact that crew are able to escape from the swarm reveals that the nanobots are designed to sense only a given material (the metal of the hull) much like Dick's claws, which respond to an auditory pattern. Once that material presents itself, the nanobots begin to perform their designated task.

The impression is often given that nanobot swarms are built, packaged, and then flung into the environment of choice. Real swarms of any type actually have a controller mechanism that is critical for managing them. Swarm controllers are used several times in *The Lord of All Things* (Eschbach, 2011 [2014]). In one instance, a gifted nanotech researcher stops a self-replicating nanobot swarm that is devouring all life on Earth by digitally "communicating" with the swarm's controller mechanism. As the name suggests, self-replicating nanobots grow the swarm by reproducing themselves. Another implied example occurs at the end of *The Day the Earth Stood Still* (2008) when Klaatu stops the microbot swarm from devouring life on earth.

The major issue is control. Will we be able to deploy strategic nanoweapons and maintain control over them? If, for example, we lost control of self-replicating nanobots, we would face a technological plague, one that we currently have no way of stopping [Del Monte, 2017a].

That plague is called a "gray-goo" (or "grey-goo") scenario. It refers to the ability of self-replicating nanobots and microbots to wipe out life. "Gray-goo" is a real-world term and a real concept that was already in use when nanotechnology pioneer Eric Drexler mentioned it in *Engines of Creation: The Coming Era of Nanotechnology* (Drexler, 1986). A gray-goo scenario actually occurs in Reynolds' 2004 [2012] *Century Rain* when one warring faction deploys a nanoweapon called silver rain. "Silver rain was … a thing of wonder and terror, like a Biblical plague. Silver rain was the worst thing that could happen to a world. It was quite possibly the *last* thing that would ever happen to a world" (Loc. 5547).

Using a nanoweapon does not necessarily produce a gray-goo scenario. A "nano-D" bomb in Douglas' *Deep Space* (2013) obliterates the U.S. capital and decimates its population. The destruction did not spread, indicating that the nanotechnology in the bomb was either not self-replicating or that the controller mechanism instructed the nanobots to stop when some criterion was reached (e.g., after a given period of time elapsed).

Microbots are around the size of the locusts from the Book of Revelation, described in the previous Folklore & Mythology section. Like nanobots, they are deployed in a swarm and perform a single task for which their hardware and control mechanism are designed. The "combat wasps" in Hamilton's *Night's Dawn* series (1996–1999) are released in a swarm which propels itself towards the enemy target much like a swarm of angry wasps. They surround the target, making it difficult to defend against, and then release their payloads which may include explosives, gamma-ray pulsars, and nuclear warheads. When combat wasps are used for defense, a swarm of them creates a shield around a ship. If an enemy weapon is detected, they attack it much like a swarm of wasps protecting its nest. Weapons of this type are emerging in the real world.

Among the earliest novels to address the power of an adversarial microbot swarm is Lem's 1964 novel *Niezwyciężony* (*The Invincible*). When the interstellar warship *Invincible* lands on a desolate planet in search of a missing ship, they find the ship, portions of which have been torn apart, and the dead crew. They also come across evidence of destroyed machines and long-departed biological aliens. The only mobile entities remaining on the surface of the planet are aggressive, airborne micro-machines—microbots. While in a swarm, they combine their individual electromagnetic pulses to erase the memories in both land-based animals and operational machines but not plants or non-functioning machines. The pulses appear to be their payload.

Fortunately, military fiction has expanded beyond nanoweapons and gray-goo scenarios. The military in Douglas' *Star Carrier* (2010–, ongoing) series, for example, uses nanotechnology to build ships that can reshape themselves in flight. They also convert piles of debris into buildings, cultivate food and other goods from natural materials, form environment-resistant clothing, heal wounds, cure diseases, replicate matter, and repair equipment. In the real world, research is already underway on some of these uses for nanotechnology.

Contemporary Media

Many military robots in contemporary media exhibit the same patterns of bodily configuration, distance, and deployment patterns that were already discussed in the previous sections. This section looks at some of the more unusual examples of military non-humanoids.

Buzz droids (also called "Pistoeka sabotage-droids") are microbots in *Star Wars: Episode III—Revenge of the Sith* (2005) and *Star Wars: The Clone Wars* (2008). They do two jobs: make their way to a spacecraft and drill through the shields, hulls, and systems of that ship. Their insect-like size, structure, and method of deployment are all well suited to their designated tasks, much like the locusts in the Book of Revelation (see the previous Folklore & Mythology section). Like the insects they resemble, buzz droids are released as a swarm by a missile that is detonated near enemy starships. This swarm deployment makes the buzz droid extremely difficult to combat. Each buzz droid has two parachutes and a navigation jet that guides it to its destination.

> Once they came into contact with an enemy starship, they would use a magnetic leg to gain a foothold. The outer shell was coated with a heat dissipating alloy that allowed it to penetrate enemy shields; it was also constructed of shock-absorbing materials.... Each droid has a main eye and two secondary eyes used for additional spatial awareness, an x-ray sensor, an extendable probe capable of invading computer systems, and is powered by a reactor primed for self-destruction [Pistoeka sabotage droid, n.d.].

A buzz droid's magnetic leg is comparable to the adhesive on the nanobots in the dust balls of Douglas' *Deep Space* (2013). They are, however, more sophisticated than dust balls. Not only do they have the equipment to navigate to a ship and a means to adhere to the ship's hull, each buzz droid is armed with several kinds of cutting tools: plasma cutting-torches, circular saws, prying hooks, pincer arms, and picket arms. Together, those tools enable it to penetrate a ship's hull and shields and to disable its internal computer systems. They also appear to speak to one another which may indicate collaboration. The effect of their power and almost surgical precision is magnified when buzz droids work together, which is typical of swarms of microbots.

The sentinels are a drone army of hunter-killer robots used by the Matrix against humans in a trilogy of films: *The Matrix* (1999), *Matrix Reloaded* (2003), and *The Matrix Revolutions* (2003). They patrol the waters beneath destroyed cities of Earth seeking and destroying hovercraft used by humans who are part of the anti-matrix resistance ("free humans"). Sentinel bodies are ideally suited for this job. They are shaped like squids with a central core and tentacles. This shape has earned them the nickname "squiddies" and, like squids, it allows them to navigate quickly and efficiently under water. They possess acute auditory sensors tuned to the sounds and sound patterns emitted by hovercraft. In that regard, they are like Dick's claws in "Second Variety" (1953 [1989]). When a hovercraft is found, a sentinel will use the claws at the ends of its tentacles to rip the hull of the hovercraft apart (Melee Weapon). Failing that, the lasers in their bodies and their portable explosives can finish the job (Range Weapons). Science.HowStuffWorks ranked the sentinels as seventh among the top "10 Evil Robots Bent on Destroying Humanity" (Kiger, 2012). The online gaming site Dan-Dare.com offers "The Matrix: Dock Defense," an online game in which the player controls a team of four humans who repel sentinel attacks (Inns, 2006–

, ongoing). There are other games, action figures, and even sentinel wallpaper for computers. The efficiency of the Sentinels also inspired Breval Environmental Ltd. to create a duct-cleaning robot based on the Sentinel design (Christensen, 2007; Knowledge Transfer Partnerships, 2007).

The film *Dark Star* (1974) contains one of the most intelligent, self-aware weapons in science fiction: the bombs on the scout ship *Dark Star*. They can think, learn, and converse with humans about abstract concepts. They are at least as smart as Ninurta's mythical talking mace *Sharur*, although they are not military strategists. The greatest irony is that, like the self-aware Yllg missiles, these bombs have very brief existences—they explode once—which Bomb #20 appears to understand and accept. The following scene occurs because Bomb #20 has descended from the bomb bay and is about to explode while it is still attached to the ship. Crewmember Lt. Doolittle appeals to the bomb's intelligence to convince it to not detonate.

THE NEGOTIATION

DOOLITTLE: [T]he only experience that is directly available to you is your sensory data. And this data is merely a stream of electrical impulses which stimulate your computing center.

BOMB #20: In other words, all I really know about the outside universe is relayed to me through my electrical connections.... Why, that would mean ... I really don't know what the outside universe is like at all, for certain.

DOOLITTLE: That's it.... Now, BOMB, consider this next question, very carefully. What is your one purpose in life?

BOMB #20: To explode, of course.

DOOLITTLE: And you can only do it once, right?

BOMB #20: That is correct.

DOOLITTLE: And you wouldn't want to explode on the basis of false data, would you?

BOMB #20: Of course not.

DOOLITTLE: Well then, you've already admitted that you have no real proof of the existence of the outside universe.

BOMB #20: Yes, well ... I recall distinctly the detonation order. My memory is good on matters like these.

DOOLITTLE: Yes ... but what you are remembering is merely a series of electrical impulses which you now realize have no necessary connection with outside reality.... So if you detonate ... you may be doing so on the basis of false data.

BOMB #20: I have no proof that it was false data.

DOOLITTLE: You have no proof that it was correct data.

BOMB #20: I must think on this further.

THE BOMB RAISES ITSELF BACK INTO THE SHIP (Carpenter & O'Bannon, 1974).

As far as Bomb #20 is concerned, it was given orders to explode. That is what it will do because, like the mythical sword *Ukko*, that's its job. It already acquiesced to prior erroneous instructions issued by a malfunctioning communication system but it is vexed about them and is ready to proceed. Requirements of the plot prevent the crew from taking the logical step of describing the problem to Bomb #20. If they did that, the film would lose several comedic scenes and would not have a proper ending. Instead, they elect to teach philosophy to the smart and linguistically sophisticated bomb in the hope of preventing it from exploding and killing the crew. The interaction with Bomb #20 is also another example of an intelligent, autonomous device that is either incapable of or not interested in human lives. It is the subject of Part II: Furor: Making Robots Moral.

One of the most famous non-humanoids in contemporary media is R2-D2 from the Star Wars Universe (1977–, ongoing). R2-D2 is an R2 series astromech-droid. Astromechs are designed to maintain and repair space vehicles. According to "The Official Star Wars Fact File" (Allanson et al., 2002),

> R2-D2 was a diminutive droid, standing 0.96 meters tall. He rolled on three legs, one of which could retract into his body, and had a silver and blue domed head. His white, blue, and silver body housed many arms, sensors, and other apparatuses, many of which were not readily seen by the typical humanoid eye. This often made the droid seem like a box of tricks, unexpectedly pulling out some previously unseen but very much needed device at a critical moment. It also contained a carousel device that contained a specific arm related to a specific duty, to economize space within his cylindrical body. Because of the quickness in utilizing a specific arm, it often gave off the illusion that he had an endless supply of tools.

R2-D2 rarely does astromech tasks. Usually, the droid is embroiled in military and political operations, including killing. For example, at the start of *Star Wars* (1977), the hero Princess Leia entrusts R2-D2 with valuable documents before she is captured by the enemy. R2-D2 fends off a swarm of buzz droids that are attacking his ship in *Star Wars: Episode III—Revenge of the Sith* (2005) and, in the episode "A Friend in Need" (2012) of *The Clone Wars*, the droid is captured and commanded to repair prisoner battle droids. Instead, R2-D2 organizes them into a combat unit that rescues one of the heroes (Ratcliffe, 2015).

R2-D2 shares many qualities with the mythical mace *Sharur*. Both are intelligent, self-aware, and able to feel emotion. They are also courageous and fiercely loyal. Two major differences between the two are that R2-D2 has a wry personality and the droid speaks in a language that only other astromechs understand (see Introduction). R2-D2 has been called a "cultural icon" (Allanson et al., 2002) and has appeared in more stories in and out of the Star Wars Universe (1977–, ongoing) than virtually any other character. In 2003, R2-D2 was inducted into the Robot Hall of Fame (2003 Inductees).

Robots and robot-precursors abound in role-playing games (RPGs). They serve as combatants, weapons, and other deadly tools of war. This section will discuss examples from two popular tabletop RPGs: D&D and WH40k.

D&D (see Glossary) groups artificial beings, such as robots, into a category called constructs (see Glossary), a sub-category of monsters that are usually created by wizards and other intelligent beings (Gygax & Ameson, 1974–, ongoing). Among them are the non-humanoid "clockwork horrors" which take part in the Spelljammer campaign (Breault, 1990; Pickens, 2010, p. 13; Tobies, 2014). They are four-legged, metallic constructs that are bent on destroying all life—much like Saberhagen's Berserker warships. "If one thinks of campaign worlds as single cells in the body of the cosmos, then one must certainly think of clockwork horrors as viruses that have come to destroy that body" (Tobies, 2014).

Horrors are all fearless, spider-like robots that are approximately two feet in diameter. They have a military hierarchy in which lower level horrors are less intelligent and capable than their superiors. At the apex is the adamantite horror. Adamantite is a mythical metal that was used to make the scythe wielded by Kronos, the father of the Greek god Zeus. There is only one adamantite horror. It is called the "father" of the race. It is cold, calculating, and possesses genius-level intelligence which it applies to the development of complex and devious military strategies suggesting it may be as good a strategist as the mythical mace *Sharur*. It generally does not engage in combat, although it is fully capable of doing so using deadly weapons such as the "nightmare stick" "which can transform a creature and everything it is wearing and carrying into a pile of fine gray dust" (Wizards of the Coast, n.d.).

Subordinate to the adamantite horror is the platinum horror. Multiple platinum horrors exist but there is only one in each game setting (called a "campaign"). Platinum horrors are extremely intelligent. Their weapons are deadly but less powerful than those of the adamantite and they don't have a nightmare stick. Platinum horrors command gold horrors. Gold horrors are charged with managing all horror operations on their world. They are less intelligent than platinum horrors and their weapons are less powerful than those of platinum horrors. Gold horrors command electrum horrors, which serve as commanding officers for patrols of silver horrors. They are less intelligent and less deadly than their superiors. Silver horrors command copper horrors, the lowest horror in the hierarchy. Copper horrors are the drones. They have minimal intelligence and their weapons are less powerful than those of any other category of horror.

WH40K (Priestley, 1987–, ongoing) is also filled with vicious and cruel constructs. The most frightening of them have been created by the Haemonculi, who are described glowingly in *Warhammer 40,000 Codex: Dark Eldar* (2014).

> Universally feared, these twisted beings are crucial to the continued survival of the Dark Eldar race, for their unnatural sciences give them power over life and death. Yet those who deal with the Haemonculi should be wary, as there is always a price to pay [*Ibid.*, p. 72].

Among the worst are the Monstrous Creatures, such as Talos Pain Engine (see Part II: Superheroes & Supervillains) and Cronos which, according to the *Codex*,

> drains away ... life essence. What remains of its prey when the engine has drunk its fill is a testament to the diabolical skill of its creators—to the onlooker, the Cronos' victims seem to age at an incredible rate, wrinkling and rotting until nothing is left [*Ibid.*, p. 95].

Contemporary media also have shapeshifting weapons much like the mythical mace/winged lion *Sharur*, but the majority of them tend to remain in humanoid form, including those in the Transformers Universe (2007–, ongoing) and the Terminator Universe (1984–, ongoing).

In the Terminator Universe (1984–, ongoing), the self-aware AI network Skynet developed quite a few ground and air weapons systems. The ground systems were largely tanks, all of which were treaded vehicles with vaguely humanoid structures. Skynet's later hunter-killer tanks had neural nets which made them reasonably intelligent but they did not approach the level of Laumer's BOLOs or Gawne's Old Guy. Skynet's aerial drones were often used to support ground tanks and humanoid fighters. They were extremely potent and well-armed. The HK-VTOL, for example, was not only well-armed and agile, it was large enough to transport tanks. Its power and size were terrifying, much like the Berserker battleships but not nearly as intelligent or crafty.

Real World[6]

The following characteristics of robots are among the most striking differences between fictional, military robots and those operating in the real world.

- *Form.* Fiction is replete with humanoids. There are virtually no humanoid robots in real militaries but there are quite a few non-humanoid robots.
- *Power.* It is rare to see a fictional robot or robot-precursor run out of battery power. The persistent power issues suffered by 8 Man (see Part II: Superheroes & Supervillains) and Gerrold's "prowlers" (see the previous Modern Literature section) are notable exceptions. Battery power is a major concern in real-world, military robotics.
- *Autonomy.* Fiction abounds with intelligent robots and robot-precursors with human-like autonomy. The vast majority of military robots in the real world are remotely piloted and possess limited, albeit growing, autonomy.

FORM

Many countries, including the U.S., Russia, and China, are working on humanoid warfighters. Even so, the emphasis remains on non-humanoid robots and that is likely to persist for some time.

The design of snakebots is derived from nature. They are desirable because (Hopkins, Spranklin, and Gupta, 2009):

- their design can be simple (one unit repeated many times);
- they have compact cross-sections and can enter and move through small spaces;
- they can move across various types of terrain;
- it is hard to knock them over;
- they have excellent traction;
- they can climb;
- they blend with their surroundings; and
- they can be designed to rear up and peer over objects.

These qualities make them attractive for reconnaissance, their primary application, and as weapons. Israel is reportedly developing a robotic snake that can be used for surveillance, search and rescue, and "the six-foot long snake can also be fitted with explosives and detonated inside enemy positions—a capability dubbed as 'suicide'" (Ronen, 2009).

"Perch and Stare" technology involves a bird-sized drone that mimics the behavior of birds that can land on power lines and remain there for long periods of time. These are surveillance drones that can observe from a perch, such as a power line, which is closer than would be possible using standard drones. There is a plan to weaponize these drones by adding "either an explosive warhead or marking dye. With the latter, the target becomes a marked man easily identified later by security forces" (Hambling, 2016).

Snakebots and Perch and Stare are not the only non-combat drones to be weaponized. U.S. soldiers in Iraq attach antipersonnel mines to MARCBOT reconnaissance robots. "Whenever they thought insurgents were hiding in an alley, they would send a MARCBOT down … to take them out" (Singer, 2009a). Similarly, the Dallas police weaponized a bomb-disposal robot and used it to kill a sniper (see Part II: Enforcers). The company iRobot, the maker of the PackBot bomb-disposal drone, has built several armed Warriors based on the PackBot design (Singer, 2009a; Quick, 2012).

POWER

One of the biggest challenges to robots is the availability of fuel and battery power (also see Part I: Greed). This is a growing problem for robotic tools and weapons that are functionally capable of performing larger and longer missions. Some aerial robots can do mid-air refueling, a well-established practice for traditional aircraft.

> [A]erial refueling allows individual UAVs ["unmanned" aerial vehicles/robots] to travel farther and reduces their weight. Extended operational range allows a smaller number of UAVs to handle global mission requirements, and reduced weight allows UAVs to take off from shorter runways and carry larger payloads [Fields, 2012, p. 29].

Batteries are the primary source driving robots today and, therefore, having sufficient battery power to complete a mission is critical. The problem is that batteries die and must be recharged or replaced at regular intervals. The same applies to other power sources.

Many aerial drones use lithium batteries akin to those in laptops and mobile phones. Safer and longer-lasting alternatives are under active development. They include other types of lithium batteries. Other alternatives include fuel cells that use electrochemical reactions to convert fuel into electricity for batteries and "molten air batteries" which use liquefied salts (e.g., vanadium boride) as a conductor. There are also devices for recharging batteries in the field, such as the 350-watt propane generator under development at Trans App which is "practically silent" (Estes, 2015).

Perch and Stare, described earlier, can conserve battery power by perching, but that isn't all.

> Perching on power lines also opens up another possibility: recharging by stealing electricity. There are already several drones that can hook up to power lines line [sic] and recharge. Design Research Associates has developed such a system for a small drone … [using] a small, sharpened boomerang with a line attached. Toss it over a power line and the sharp edge cuts through insulation. A device on [the drone] … converts the high-voltage alternating supply into a regulated direct current for charging electronics [Hambling, 2015b, Loc. 2236, 2240].

Insulation-cutting and attachment make it possible for a drone to continue a mission indefinitely.

Other work is being done on ways to save battery power. Northeastern University, for example, is designing a sensor that can "remain dormant and unattended but always alert, even for years, without drawing on battery power" (DARPA, 2017) and listening for "signals-of-interest," much like the void ripper (Gawne, 2012) and the claws in Dick's "Second Variety" (Dick, 1953 [1989]).

Batteries are not the only source of power being developed for robotic weapons. In *Swarm Troopers,* David Hambling's (2015b) analysis of small aerial drones, he posits solar energy as a logical option for drones and other aircraft.

Aircraft wings are large, flat surfaces that might easily be covered in solar cells. If a solar aircraft could generate enough electricity, it could power its own engines and keep flying on sunlight alone. If it could generate more electricity, it could charge up batteries to keep it flying through the night as well [Loc. 2261].

A solar-powered drone can be recharged by stretching out its wings and leaving it in the sun. If necessary, the drone can be recharged using a solar-power recharger that has been sitting in the sun.

Autonomy

Mythology is populated by autonomous robot-precursors like *Sharur* and *Taming Sari* and both modern literature and contemporary media are filled with fully autonomous robots. In the real world, the dominant method of control is remote piloting. The standard control-relationships are:

- *Human-in-the-loop*—operations the pilot controls (e.g., launching an attack on a selected target)
- *Human-on-the-loop*—operations under the supervision of the pilot who can intervene if something seems to be going wrong
- *Human-out-of-the-loop*—the robot performs the operation without human input (e.g., it can select a target and attack without input from a human).

These relationships vary function by function. A typical pattern for an armed aerial drone is to have full autonomy for target identification, surveillance, and tracking but not for attacking. That requires a command or approval from the human pilot (Caton, 2015; Boulanin & Verbruggen, 2017).

More than sixty nations and international organizations have human-in-the-loop aerial drones and many of them are involved in the development of robotic weapons with autonomous functions. There is a strong push to develop fully autonomous (human-out-of-the-loop) weapons or ones in which the pilot intervenes only when necessary (human on-the-loop). The vast majority of those systems are in research and they include an array of different types of weapons, two of which are loitering and collaborative autonomy.

Loitering

Loitering refers to the ability of a robotic system to remain in an area for a long period of time. Some loitering systems, such as Perch and Stare, remain in one spot. Other loitering weapons are aerial robots that travel in loops or other patterns in and around a given area. As with other robotic weapons, almost all loitering systems have human-in-the-loop control. Boulanin and Verbruggen's 2017 research report, *Mapping the Development of Autonomy in Weapon Systems,* "identified only four operational systems that can find, track and attack targets in complete autonomy once launched" (p. 53): the Orbiter 1K "Kingfisher," the Harpy (the oldest autonomous loitering system), the Harop, and the Harpy NG. All of them are made by Israel. The Israel Aerospace Industries describes its Harpy NG as a

"Fire and Forget" autonomous weapon, launched from a ground vehicle behind the battle zone…. The Harpy weapon detects, attacks and destroys enemy radar emitters, hitting them with high hit accuracy. Harpy effectively suppresses hostile SAM and radar sites for long durations, loitering above enemy territory for hours [Israel Aerospace Industries, n.d.].

Other countries that are similarly engaged in this research and development include the U.S., Russia, Germany, and China.

Collaboration and Swarming

Increasingly, robots and other systems are being designed to operate as collaborative teams with each other and with humans. The human-robot collaboration is comparable to the non-military teaming of humans with robots called "cobots" (Hollinger, 2016; also see Part I: Robots as Job Killers). The U.S. Army's Research Laboratory, for example, has established the Robotics Collaborative Technology Alliance (https://www.arl.army.mil/) to work on human-in-the-loop collaborative teaming. An important component of this work is the advancement of natural communication, notably gesture recognition and natural-language processing to allow soldiers to communicate naturally with robot partners and assistants.

Some are teams of homogeneous autonomous weapons that work together like Laumer's BOLO tanks (Laumer, 1976–1990) in which each weapon has a role in the mission. Russia has demonstrated a team of tanks that

> can locate targets, choose dominating positions on a battlefield, request target elimination validation from human operators and eliminate the targets. It is also capable of automatically requesting replacements for disabled machines [Redheart, 2015].

The U.S. ONR demonstrated similar team behavior among robotic boats that were patrolling a large area of open water.

> As an unknown vessel entered the area, the group of swarmboats collaboratively determined which patrol boat would quickly approach the unknown vessel, classify it as harmless or suspicious, and communicate with other swarmboats to assist in tracking and trailing the unknown vessel while others continued to patrol the area. During this time, the group of swarmboats provided status updates to a human supervisor [Smalley, 2016].

These teams are semi-autonomous. The long-term goal is to deploy fully autonomous teams but that is unlikely to happen for several years (Williams, 2015a).

The team in the ONR example is called a swarm. Definitions of "swarm" tend to focus on the collective behavior of insects—especially flying insects. The two examples just given demonstrate that units of many types and sizes can constitute a swarm but the principles of swarming found in nature apply. Computer-animation researcher Craig Reynolds (1968) identified three rules used by termites, birds, and other creatures that move in swarms:

- Collision Avoidance: avoid collisions with nearby flockmates;
- Velocity Matching: attempt to match velocity with nearby flockmates; and
- Flock Centering: attempt to stay close to nearby flockmates (p. 6).

Microbot behavior in China's 2018 swarm demonstration exemplified these rules.

> [M]ore than 1,000 flying robots coordinate autonomously and synchronize movements, with a flight deviancy of a mere 2 centimeters horizontally and 1 centimeter vertically. If something goes wrong and a drone can't reach its programmed position, it automatically lands [Lin and Singer, 2018].

The swarm's intelligence resides in the controller mechanism: the software that manages the Russian tanks, the U.S. boats, and the Chinese microbot swarm. The novel *Ender's*

Game (Card, 1985) explains a third defining aspect of swarm behavior. "Every ship acts like a part of a single organism. It responds the way your body responds during combat, different parts automatically, thoughtlessly doing everything they're supposed to do" (p. 204). William Roper, Director of the U.S. DoD's Defense Strategic Capabilities Office described the DoD's Perdix swarm using similar language, "[T]hey are a collective organism, sharing one distributed brain for decision-making and adapting to each other like swarms in nature" (United States Department of Defense, 2017).

China, Russian, and the U.S. are not developing swarms because they give great demonstrations. They are developing swarms as weapons. Some will be like the "dust balls" in Douglas' 2013 novel *Deep Space* that can eat through a ship's metal hull. Del Monte (2017b) applies that idea to potential earth-based attacks.

> By employing nanobot to nanobot signaling, in a matter of seconds, the entire swarm may know the location of the nuclear material. To destroy it, they may simply dislodge the material, atom by atom, until it is a pile of radioactive dust. This would render it useless as a weapon. Imagine trillions of nanobots in a swarm and countless swarms. In a short while … all land-based nuclear missiles would be useless [p 93].

Conversely, a microbot or nanobot swarm could also be designed to deliver deadly payloads. In healthcare, chemotherapy nanobots are being designed to detect cancer cells in a patient and to deliver chemotherapy directly to those cells (Chemotherapy, n.d.). There is no reason why individual nanobots/microbots and swarm weapons could not be made to deliver other deadly payloads to targets.

If the nanobots are self-replicating, only a few would be needed to ultimately produce the number required to destroy whatever they are designed to attack. "In military applications, they will have the capability to completely destroy an adversary, from its populace to its structures" (Del Monte, 2017a). Hypothetical situations like this, concerns about the possibility of causing a grey-goo scenario like that in Reynolds' *Century Rain* (2004 [2012]), and the speed with which work in this area is proceeding are all feeding the debate about the safety of nanoweapons. In 2017, Article36, an organization concerned about nanoweapons, submitted a position paper to the UN asking to begin a discussion about regulating nanoweapons (Nanoweapons, 2017).

ROBOT COMPETITIONS

Not all fighting robots are in the military. Entertainment has found a place for them in competitions. In 1992, Mark Thorpe, an engineer from LucasToys, staged a competition in which robots bearing chain saws, hammers, and other weapons fought until only one was still operational. In 1998, the competition moved to the UK and was televised as *Robot Wars*.

Robot Wars was so popular that it returned to the U.S. as the televised series *Battlebots*. *Battlebots* competitions are now broadcast worldwide and, in 2018, *Robot Wars* celebrated its twentieth anniversary.

Autonomy plays a minor role in the non-military *Robot Wars*, *Battlebots*, and most other robot-fight competitions because virtually all the competitors are remotely piloted. The only fully autonomous combatants in these competitions are those that participate in Japan's *Robot Sumo* which is modeled on sumo wrestling.

Plans Gone Awry

MODERN LITERATURE

In P.K. Dick's 1953 [2009]) short story "Mr. Spaceship," the space-faring military of Earth are facing aliens with defenses protecting their home world that consist of a blend of organic and mechanical elements. The Earth's military decides that the only way to breach the alien defenses is to create their own organic-mechanical warship. A brilliant scientist agrees to allow them to remove his brain from his old, dying body and embed it into the ship. He works with the military scientists to craft a ship that can be controlled by his brain. Once the ship is completed and the man's brain is operating its systems, it is launched. As expected, the aliens see the ship as something akin to themselves and ignore it. It passes through their defenses easily. Much to the dismay of Earth's military, instead of attacking the alien home world, the brain directs the ship into open space. The man had no interest in the war. He saw the ship as an opportunity to live many years beyond his body and to explore areas of space not yet known to humans (Dick, 1953[2009]).

CONTEMPORARY MEDIA

This chapter earlier described a conversation in the film *Dark Star* (1974) between Lt. Doolittle, commander of the scout ship *Dark Star*, and Bomb #20. The bomb had been commanded to detonate but it was still attached to the ship. Lt. Doolittle convinced Bomb #20 that the only thing it could be certain truly exists is itself ("I think therefore I am"). He also made it question the validity of the commands it had been given to explode, labeling them "false data." The bomb disarmed itself and retreated into the bomb bay to ponder those new ideas. Doolittle and the rest of the crew knew they had escaped certain death.

At the conclusion of the film, it is clear that Bomb #20 has reflected on the knowledge given to it by Lt. Doolittle. It made a decision, but not one Doolittle had expected.

AFTER GIVING IT SOME THOUGHT

PINBACK: All right, bomb, prepare to receive new orders.

BOMB #20: You are false data…. Therefore, I shall ignore you…. False data can act only as a distraction. Therefore, I shall refuse to perceive you.

PINBACK: … Hey, bomb.

BOMB #20: The only thing which exists is myself….

PINBACK: Snap out of it, bomb.

BOMB #20: In the beginning there was darkness, and the darkness was without form and void…

PINBACK: Yoo hoo, bomb…

BOMB #20: And in addition to the darkness there was also me. And I moved upon the face of the darkness…

PINBACK: Hey, bomb…

BOMB #20: And I saw that I was alone.
Pause.
BOMB #20: Let there be light.
THE SCREEN GOES WHITE (Carpenter & O'Bannon, 1974).

REAL WORLD

At the start of this chapter, aerial drones were identified as the newest addition to a long line of weapons that have increased the distance between human fighters and the front lines because a pilot can fire a drone from thousands of miles away.

Commercial and military development of drones advanced in parallel. Small, commercial drones became inexpensive and readily available—globally. For several years, ISIS and other "non-state" groups have been purchasing, adapting, and arming drones to be used against U.S. troops. They have begun to move to more advanced, armed, remotely piloted drones (Hambling, 2015a; Hennigan, 2017).

If all sides in a conflict have weaponized drones, then attacks can be launched against any civilian or military population anywhere. Riza (2013) sums this outcome in the following way: "In attempting to 'fight them over there' farther and farther from the home shores, we have turned our own cities into battlefields" (pp. 97–98).

Humans

What is a chapter on humans doing in a book about killer robots?

> Many military missions will always require humans on the ground, even if in some contexts they will operate alongside and in conjunction with increasingly automated, sometimes autonomous, systems [Anderson & Waxman, 2013, p. 7].

Reasons that are offered in support of claims like this one focus on cultural, sociological, and linguistic cues that are assumed to be beyond the ken of military robots.

> They can, for example, read the body language of a civilian who might be a terrorist. They can adapt to cultural idiosyncrasies. And most importantly, they can earn the personal trust of those they are interacting with. This is especially crucial in insurgency environments, where the ability to earn the trust of others is even more important than the ability to locate and destroy an enemy [Rogan, 2018].

Throughout fiction and in the real world, humans have pooled their skills with robots and robot-precursors as teams. The collaborative strategizing by the Sumerian god Ninurta and the robot-precursor *Sharur* is an excellent example from mythology (see Part III: Non-Humanoids). Frankowski's 1999 novel *A Boy and His Tank* provides a far more extreme example. A boy is embedded in a self-aware tank so that his human "associative thinking" can be merged with the tank's supercomputer logic to produce superior battle strategy. The U.S. DoD's "Third Offset Strategy" envisions "advanced human-machine combat teaming such as with manned and unmanned systems working together" (United States Department of Defense, 2016).

Humans will remain on the battlefield but the military sees humans as "the weakling of the battlefield" (Jacobsen, 2015, p. 305). For that reason, there are robotic and robot-precursor solutions designed to protect human fighters, to enhance their performance, and to enable them to return to the battlefield as fully capable warfighters. Three of those robotic solutions are: powered exoskeletons, robotic prosthetics (Robotic Prosthetics, n.d.), and nanotechnology with some excursions into implants, devices placed into a person's body. Unlike prostheses, implants add to but do not replace natural body parts. They can operate in conjunction with prosthetics and they can be constructed via nanotechnology.

"Exoskeletons are wearable devices that work in tandem *with* the user. The opposite of an exoskeleton device would be a robot with machine autonomy that works *instead* of the operator" (What is an Exoskeleton, n.d.). They are not armor because even passive exoskeletons support, and sometimes augment, natural joint operation, muscle movement, and muscle force. That is, they are "biomechanical" devices. Some cover the warfighter's entire body and possess extensive functionality like armor made by Marvel Comics' Iron Man, Tony Stark (Lee, 1963). Others cover just a portion of the body (e.g., legs). The materials in them can be rigid or flexible. Exoskeletons that are powered and equipped with sensors and actuators are called "powered exoskeletons."

Prostheses replace original body parts. They can be passive or robotic (biomechanical). Some augment the performance of the body part and may add functionality to it. Honor Harrington, for example, is given a cybernetic eye with microscopic and telescopic modes (Weber, 2000).

Unlike the nanoweapons described in the Non-Humanoids chapter, the nanobots and nanobot-precursors in this chapter make warfighters stronger, more resistant to disease and injury, and even more ferocious. They are fully deployed in fiction and sometimes used in conjunction with exoskeletons.

Together, these technologies enable human warfighters to remain on or quickly return to the battlefield.

Folklore & Mythology

Precursors of the biomechanical exoskeletons of today are not biomechanical but they hint at some agency involved in a wearable item that affects the wearer's abilities. One of the clearest examples is Thor's *Megingjörð* ("power belt"; *Megingjörð*, n.d.). As shown in Fig. 22, Thor wore the belt over his clothes and whenever he put on Megingjörð, his already prodigious strength increased by fifty percent. This is a type of augmentation modern exoskeletons are expected to provide.

Figure 22. The Norse god Thor wearing Megingjörð (power belt) in *Tor's Fight with the Giants* by Mårten Winge (1825-1896), National Museum (Wikimedia Commons).

One of the earliest accounts of a warfighter with a prosthesis comes from the Rig Veda (1896; Sanskrit, Rig: "praise" or "shine"; Veda: "knowledge"). It is a collection of hymns and verses written between 1,500–1,200 BCE. The warrior-hero Queen Vishpala (also "Vishpali") is mentioned several times in Book One as having been given an iron leg by the twin gods Ashwins (also "Aśvins"), the divine physicians and miracle workers. They are said to have "graced" Vishpala with the replacement so that she could fight once again. Iyer (2017) further characterizes Vishpala as "an early female warrior," whose iron leg is "the world's first reference to prosthesis" (Loc. 231).[1] Stanza 15 of hymn 116 provides the most complete description. It is addressed to the Ashwins.

> When in the time of night, in Khela's battle,
>   a leg was severed like a wild bird's pinion,
> Straight ye gave Vishpali a leg of iron
>   that she might move what time the conflict opened
> [Rig Veda 1:116:15].

There is no evidence that Vishpala could move her prosthesis. In the real world, prosthetics changed little between Vishpala's iron leg and those used in the twentieth century; whereas some prostheses in folklore and mythology are truly impressive. One example is the prosthetic hand made for Nuada, king of the Celtic Tuatha De. The second of the Celtic sacred texts *Cath Maige Tuired* (n.d.) describes how Nuada's hand was severed in battle. The loss of his hand presented seemingly insurmountable problems for Nuada. It was critical for him to have a fully functional, natural-looking hand. It would, of course, enable him to perform better in battle. More importantly, however, Celtic kings were required to be physically whole. "Nuadu was not eligible for kingship after his hand had been cut off" (p. 14). When Nuada lost his hand he lost his kingdom and everything that went with being a king.

The first hand made for Nuada moved like a hand but it was silver and, therefore, obviously a prosthesis. Miach, the son of Nuada's physician

> went to the hand and said "joint to joint of it, and sinew to sinew"; and he healed it in nine days and nights. The first three days he carried it against his side, and it became covered with skin. The second three days he carried it against his chest. The third three days he would cast white wisps of black bulrushes after they had been blackened in a fire [p. 33].

The hand made by Miach healed so completely that it was indistinguishable from a human hand in appearance and function. Because of that, Nuadu was deemed physically whole and eligible to regain his kingdom.

Nanotechnology precursors often take the form of ingestibles and ointments that were thought to make humans impervious to harm and unbeatable on the battlefield. One example comes from the story about the herb that Gaea ("the Earth") of Greek mythology gave her sons, the *Gigante* (Bane, 2016). As their name suggests, they were huge humanoids and already physically powerful. They were going to fight against the potent gods of Olympus. Before sending them into battle, Gaea "made the *Gigante* invincible by the use of a special herb to protect them from the Olympian gods" (p. 76).

The Berserks, whose ferocious battlefield behavior is described in the Humanoids chapter, were real-world warriors but there is a great deal of legend and speculation about what made them so ... well ... berserk. Speidel (2002) admits that scholars have not been able to identify the cause of this behavior by the Berserks and similar groups of crazed fighters from around the world. In Howard Fabing's 1956 article "On Going Berserk: A Neurochemical Inquiry," he argues that bufotenine, a substance found in some mushrooms, was the source of Berserker rage. The discovery of henbane seeds in a Viking grave suggests to some scholars that Berserks may have crushed henbane petals and rubbed the paste on their skin. That would have numbed their skin and given them a sensation of flying (Price, 2002). These potions and ointments are biological correlates to the biomechanical enhancements found in later fiction and the real world.

Modern Literature

The uses to which militaries put exoskeletons, prosthetics, and nanotechnology expand in modern literature, as do the settings in which they are required to operate. Those settings include harsh environments of other planets, outer space, and even alternate realities.

Exoskeletons

Much like Thor's power belt, Megingjörð, soldiers in modern literature use both partial-body and full-body exoskeletons that are typically worn over their uniforms. An exoskeleton on a warfighter's legs in modern literature might also enhance their endurance for treks through rough terrain carrying a heavy load. Because the military is often located on other planets or in space, full-body exoskeletons also protect the wearer from harsh alien atmospheres. This excerpt from Clifford Simak's "Desertion" (1944 [2016]), reveals some of the thinking used by scientists on Jupiter to develop an exoskeleton that is capable of protecting humans from the planet's deadly environment.

Design of an Exoskeleton

For man, unprotected and in his natural form, would be blotted out by Jupiter's terrific pressure of fifteen thousand pounds per square inch, pressure that made terrestrial sea bottoms seem a vacuum by comparison.

Even the strongest metal Earthmen could devise couldn't exist under pressure such as that, under the pressure and the alkaline rains that forever swept the planet. It grew brittle and flaky, crumbling like clay, or it ran away in little streams and puddles of ammonia salts. Only by stepping up the toughness and strength of that metal, by increasing its electronic tension, could it be made to withstand the weight of thousands of miles of swirling, choking gases that made up the atmosphere. And even when that was done, everything had to be coated with tough quartz to keep away the rain—the liquid ammonia that fell as bitter rain (p. 158).

Fictional powered exoskeletons have many names: the "fighting suit" in *The Forever War* (Haldeman, 1974); Lex Luthor's "war suit" in *Luthor Unleashed!* (Bates, 1983); and "armor" by Marvel Comics' Iron Man, Tony Stark (Fichera et al., n.d.). These exoskeletons cover the fighter's entire body and provide dynamic protection, assistance, and specialized technology to support the superhero/supervillain's activities. Many exoskeletons are able to adapt to the demands of the environment and the changing needs of the human wearing them. Some also include nanotechnology and/or intelligence.

The design and features of fictional powered-exoskeletons also differ from author to author. Among the simplest are those in John Ringo's *The Council Wars* series (2003–2006) in which a powered exoskeleton (called "enhanced armor") is made using nanotechnology. It provides better protection than standard armor and can make a fashion statement as well.

The armor has to have self-contained power sources, be able to drain power from external sources, trade power and repair damage to itself and its user. The mail should be kinetic reactive and, of course, impenetrable. All of it proof against any field generation or energy weapons.... All of that invisible to casual inspection and, of course, it should look ... good [Ringo, 2003, p. 38].

One of the earliest examples of powered exoskeletons in science-fiction literature is also one of the most potent. It is simply called the "Suit" and comes from Robert A. Heinlein's *Starship Troopers* (1959).

A suit isn't a space suit—although it can serve as one. It is not primarily armor—although the Knights of the Round Table were not armored as well as we are. It isn't a tank—but a single M.I. private could take on a squadron of those things and knock them off unassisted.... A Suit is not a ship but it can fly a little—on the other hand neither spaceships nor atmosphere craft can fight against a man in a suit [p. 104].

The powered exoskeletons in Joe Haldeman's *The Forever War* (1974) can perform triage for severe wounds. They reseal the exoskeleton, cauterize the wound, replace lost blood, and administer anti-pain drugs. The powered exoskeletons worn by Marines in Bauers' novel *Unbreakable* (2014) can release surveillance drones by issuing a verbal command. The pilot-ejection system in Douglas' 2010 novel *Earth Strike* contains a survival pack which includes a "spider exoskeleton."

THE SPIDER EXOSKELETON

The spider was the size of a flattened football, with four legs folded up tight. When he activated the unit, the legs began unfolding, each extending for over a meter from the central body. Immediately, the unit moved behind him, put the tips of two legs on his shoulders to steady him, then began to snuggle in close, the main unit snuggling up against his spine, each leg adjusting and reconfiguring to conform exactly to his body. In seconds, it had adhered to his e-suit, clamped tight at ankles, knees, and hips. There was a vibrating whine of servos [motors], and the unit straightened up, pulling him upright.... Wearing one of these rigs ... [he] could do anything he could do in his normal gravity field, including running, jumping and lifting heavy objects. The word was that with practice he could run a Marathon and not get winded [Douglas, 2010, p. 52].

In his novel *Exoskeleton* (2012), Shane Stadler offers another use of a kind of exoskeleton: to create a superspy or super-soldier. A shadowy agency of the U.S. government is running a secret project called "Red Wraith." Taking data from captured Nazi files, CIA reports, and other top-secret documents, the project directors are trying to separate the soul of a human from their body. The process entails placing a human in a biomechanical device called the "exoskeleton" and using the exoskeleton to subject the human to a system of torture called "compressed punishment" which is reminiscent of the Spartan king Nabis and his Iron Apega which applied a form of compressed punishment as well (see Part I: Greed). The purported object of Red Wraith is to create a perfect spy or a super-soldier.

Robotic Prosthetics

Even humans wearing powered exoskeletons can suffer wounds and need limbs or other parts of their bodies regenerated or replaced with prosthetics. Sometimes prostheses are simple substitutes that may lack the versatility of the original body part, much like the iron leg of the mythological Queen Vishpala. In science fiction, however, most prosthetics add functionality and hardware that render the fighter more potent than before.

An amazingly extensive and sophisticated collection of prostheses appears in "The Man That Was Used Up," a short story by Edgar Allan Poe (1839). They were made for battle injuries suffered by the war hero Brigadier General John A.B.C. Smith. In fact, the general's prosthetics are among the most startling examples of replacements in fiction, to date.

> As I entered the chamber, I looked about, of course, for the occupant, but did not immediately perceive him. There was a large and exceedingly odd-looking bundle of something which lay close to my feet, on the floor, and, as I was not in the best humor in the world, I gave it a kick out of the way [p. 69].

That odd-looking bundle is General Smith. Actually, it is filled with the general's prosthetics which replace every piece of the general. In the course of the story, the general is assembled bit by bit into the entire man as he describes the battles that led to each replacement. His ability to move and speak indicates they, or at least some of them, are robotic.

More than one hundred years later, in Michael Caidin's novel *Cyborg*, the experimental plane being flown by former astronaut Steve Austin crashes and he is given almost as many new parts as General Smith was (Caidin, 1972). Austin's new body parts are enhancements rather than simple replacements. In that regard, he is akin to some of the melds in Foster's *The Tipping Point* trilogy (Foster, 2010–2012) described in Part II: Criminals. Actually, *they* are akin to *him* because *Cyborg* appeared forty years earlier and became a television series shortly afterwards: *The Six Million Dollar Man* (Bennett, 1973–1978). The bionic upgrades Austin received were very much like those of the assassin Napun Molé in *The Human Blend* (Foster, 2010). Austin's two legs enabled him to run at tremendous speed and his right hand included a knife built into the middle finger and a poison dart gun in another. Similarly, Molé's military-grade legs allowed him to easily pursue his target and to jump from the window of a building without harming himself. He had a rapier built into the middle finger of his left hand as well as a pellet-gun embedded in his index finger. The most telling difference between them is that Molé developed his melds so he could excel as an assassin, but Austin's bionic components were made for him because the U.S. government wanted to use him as a spy and a weapon.

Cyborg and *The Human Blend* employ military-grade technology. Military science fiction has an even stronger affinity for robotic prosthetics which are used extensively. Those in David Drake's *Hammer's Slammers* series (Drake, 1979–2007) and described in *Hammer's Slammers Handbook* (Lambshead & Treadaway, 2004) are integrated with a warfighter's bones, muscles and neurons much like Austin's bionic limbs. Despite those enhancements, the prosthetic limbs available to Slammer fighters are markedly inferior to natural limbs. For example, the prosthetic feet of one Slammer must be recalibrated every day to match his neural processing (Drake, 1979–2007). Unfortunately, anyone with a prosthesis is prohibited from returning to the elite Slammer tank division.

Those in newer military science fiction tend to be at least as good as natural limbs—much like King Nuada's hand. They also tend to incorporate far more sophisticated robotic enhancements which reflect advancing robotics technology. A character in Heinlein's *The Moon Is a Harsh Mistress* (1966) brags that he has dozens of artificial forearms that are specialized for different functions and occasions. The prostheses given Honor Harrington, the main character in Weber's series (Weber, 1992–, ongoing), include the multi-modal, cybernetic eye mentioned in the introduction. When, in *War of Honor* (Weber, 2002), Harrington is asked to surrender all of her weapons before meeting with the emperor's cousin, she complies.

Honor Harrington Surrenders Her Weapons

She unsealed her uniform tunic and ... rolled up the left cuff of her uniform blouse.... [T]hen she told her prosthetic hand to flex in a movement which should have brought the tip of her index finger into contact with the tip of her little finger. But the neural impulses which would have moved the fingers of her original hand in that pattern did something completely different now, and a rectangle patch of skin on the inside of her forearm, perhaps two centimeters long and one and a half across, suddenly folded back. A small compartment in the artificial limb opened, and as she closed her fist, a thirty-round pulser magazine ejected itself.

She caught it in midair with her right hand....

Forgive me, *Kapitän,*" she said. "As you may know, I've experienced more than one assassination attempt of my own. When my father helped me design my prosthesis, he suggested a few small ... improvements. This ... was one of them."

She raised her hand ... and sent its artificial muscles another command. In response, her left index finger snapped abruptly and rigidly straight, and the hand's other fingers folded under, almost as if they were gripping the butt of a nonexistent pulser.

"I'm afraid I'd have to have the tip of the finger rebuilt if I ever used it ... but Daddy insisted that it would be worthwhile" (Loc. 12905–12914).

Not every severely damaged war hero wants to be rebuilt as a human. Colonel Frank Marcus in Saberhagen's *Berserker Kill* (1993) chose to replace his virtually destroyed body with a structure he found to be more efficient and pleasing. His new body consists of

three connected metallic boxes, none of them more than knee-high, their size in aggregate no more than that of an adult human body. The boxes rolled along one after the other, their wheels appearing to be polyphase matter, not spinning so much as undergoing continuous smooth deformity.

From the foremost box came a voice, a mechanically generated but very human sound, tone jaunty, just this side of arrogant [p. 86–87].

Nanotechnology

When nanobots are not being deployed as a weapon, they are often used to protect and/or enhance humans. Sometimes the effects are only temporary. Augur, the main character in Reynolds' *Century Rain* (2004), is injected with specially designed nanobots to give her a new skill that she will need for the reconnaissance mission she is about to begin.

LANGUAGE LEARNING BY NANOBOT

"Is she ready for her language lesson?" …

"What language lesson?" Augur asked.

Niagara raised a hand. A mist of twinkling silver machines erupted from his palm and crossed the space to Augur's head. She felt the onset of a bright shining migraine, as if her skull was a fortress being stormed by an army of flashing chrome armour, and then she felt nothing at all.

She came round to a headache, a falling sensation and a voice in her ears speaking a language she should not be able to understand.

"Wie heist Du?"

"Ich heisse Auger … Verity Auger." The words slipped out of her mouth with ridiculous ease.

"Good…. That's taken very nicely" (Loc. 2115–2123).

Auger's nanobots are removed from her brain after she has acquired the new language and with them her skill in that language. This is not the case for warfighters in other novels. In other instances, they are embedded into exoskeletons and other devices. When one starship is destroyed in *Deep Space* (Douglas, 2013), the captain dons an emergency exoskeleton which expands to form a close-fitting, transparent nanofilm around his body.

Members of the armed forces in several series ingest or are inoculated with nanobots as part of their induction in the military. The changes those nanobots bring are permanent. Each elderly recruit in John Scalzi's novel *Old Man's War* (2005), for instance, is injected with an array of nano-sensors at the start of their pre-training evaluation.

THE SENSOR ARRAY

[Dr. Russell explains:] "During the next couple of days it's going to be important for us to get a good picture of your brain activity…. So to do this, I'm going to implant a sensor array into your skull…. Well, right now, you can probably feel a little tickle on your scalp and down the back of your neck…. Those are the injectors positioning themselves. They're like little hypodermic needles that will insert the sensors. The sensors themselves are very small, but there's a lot of them. About twenty thousand, more or less. Don't worry, they're self-sterilizing."

"Is this going to hurt?" I asked.

"Not so much," he said…. Twenty thousand microsensors *slammed* themselves into my skull like four ax handles simultaneously whacking my skull.

"God *damn* it!" I grabbed my head.... "You said it wouldn't *hurt!*"

"I said 'not so much,'" Dr. Russell said.

"Not so much as what? Having your head stepped on by an elephant?"

"Not so much as when the sensors connect to each other.... The good news is that as soon as they're connected, the pain stops. Now hold still, this will only take a minute." ...

Eighty thousand needles shot out in every direction in my skull (pp. 59–60).

Members of the military in a number of series are also given doses of nanobots that help them heal wounds and keep their bodies healthy. *Earth Strike* (Douglas, 2010), the first book in Douglas' *Star Carrier* series, reveals the extent to which nanotechnology is used to modify the brains and bodies of military professionals. "E-enchancements" (p. 53) created by nanotechnology are built into the sulci of the warfighter's brain. That circuitry connects the fighter to information sources and communication links. Other nanotechnology protects them from disease and enables their bodies to heal quickly. In that same book, Admiral Alexander Koenig reflects on the health benefits of nanotechnology.

> [There are] trillions of nanorobotics devices pumping through Koenig's circulatory system, cleaning out arteries, maintaining key balances within his metabolic processes, even repairing damaged chromosomes and guarding against cancer, disease, even the effects of aging. Alexander Koenig could expect to live to see the age of five hundred, they told him—theoretically, given ongoing nanomedical advances, there was no way to even guess how long he might live [p. 311].

The use of nanotechnology on and in military personnel is equally widespread in the Colonial Defense Forces (CDF) of Scalzi's (2005–2015) aforementioned military science-fiction series *Old Man's War*. They help heal wounds, regrow limbs, assist in surgery, and even protect the CDF warfighter from insect-borne disease. All of this is accomplished when a recruit's organic blood is replaced by nanobots-laden "smartblood."

As with other elixirs incorporated into human bodies, nanotechnology that changes someone's physiology is also likely to produce side effects. Jared, a CDF private in Scalzi's *The Ghost Brigades* (2006), accidentally discovers a by-product of smartblood when he is attacked.

> One of the more ambitious of those small creatures landed on Jared's arm and plunged a needle-like proboscis into his flesh to suck out his fluids. A few seconds later it was dead. The nanobots in Jared's smartblood ... self-immolated inside the tiny animal, using the oxygen they carried as a combustible agent. The poor creature crisped from the inside; miniscule and almost invisible wisps of smoke vented out of its spicules [p. 92].

Later in the book, Jared is wounded and he exploits this knowledge by hurling some of his smartblood at his attacker, with the same effect.

The benefits of ingesting nanobots are more comparable to the invulnerability accorded to the *Gigante* (see the previous Folklore & Mythology section) than they are to the Berserks who may have drugged themselves into a fury before battles. The reason is that both the effects of eating the plant given to the *Gigante* by Gaea and the nanotechnology in Jared's smartblood are enduring.

Life-long side effects alter the human settlers on Mars in the *Trinity Blood* novel *Canon*

Summa Theologica (Yoshida, 2005 [n.d.]). Somehow the settlers intuited that, if they ingested alien nanobots called "Bacillus," they would be able to survive in the severe Martian environment. They did and they did. Two side effects of ingesting Bacillus are increased physical strength and longer lives—lives that are extended by hundreds of years (which inspired their nickname "Methuselahs"). These benefits gave the Methuselahs an advantage when they returned to Earth intending to wrest the planet from the hands of normal humans.

Other side effects of nanotechnology are less dramatic. At least one member of the military in *Deep Space* (Douglas, 2013) learned how to exploit a side effect of nanotechnology for his own pleasure.

> [He] dropped into the seat next to Gregory's and ordered a glass of scotch on the rocks. Alcohol would have been unthinkable on board a USNA ship a couple of centuries ago ... but the swarms of nano circulating through his body would block damage to his organs, and permit a pleasant buzz without allowing him to get drunk [p. 53].

Contemporary Media

EXOSKELETONS

Marvel Comics' Tony Stark is the most widely known fictional wearer of powered exoskeletons. His complex and powerful exoskeletons earned him the superhero codename "Iron Man" (Iron Man's Armor, n.d.). He is a superior engineer and he has the wealth to support frequent upgrades to his powered exoskeletons. The original impetus for developing an exoskeleton—which is often called "armor"—was to use electromagnets, an arc reactor, and other means to protect his heart from shrapnel embedded in his chest.

The armor is a full-body suit with a covering made of threads of "mono-crystalline iron" coated with "tetrafluorethene plastic" that is knitted together. He can generate a force-field around that surface to prevent anyone from touching the suit. The primary means of locomotion is flying, although the initial distances were limited. His brain waves are coordinated with the actuators of the armor, making non-flying locomotion and movement easier. The strength enhancement Stark's armor gives him is far greater than Thor's power belt. He can lift two-ton monsters, tear a wall open, and repel large objects (or beings) hurtling in his direction with a "Unibeam." The weapons supported by his armor have increased with each upgrade but even the Model 01 suit had cluster bombs, a flamethrower, and teargas bombs. Later models added, among other things, "chameleon" technology for camouflage; nanotechnology; and weapons that included proton guns, the electric field of an electric eel, and a hacksaw. He and his exoskeletons continue to be a potent force in Marvel Comics and other media.

Using technology from his company, Lexcorp, supervillain Lex Luthor has constructed several powered exoskeletons which he called his Warsuits. The overall functionality of Luthor's Warsuits has been governed by Superman's abilities and weaknesses. They all enable Luthor to fly. They possess superhuman strength which approaches that of Superman and they are durable enough to withstand assaults by Superman. Part of that durability is that the Warsuits include a forcefield that protects Luthor and the suit from being harmed by Superman. All of them have energy generators and weapons that use kryptonite which can weaken Superman enough to allow the Warsuit's strength to overpower the superhero. Each Warsuit also includes features unique to it. For example, Luthor's first Warsuit included an extremely powerful weapon. The weapon didn't kill Superman but it destroyed the planet Lexor (Bates, 1983).

The protective armor worn by warfighters in the video game Crysis (Crytek, 2007–, ongoing) is constructed using nanotechnology, much like the spider exoskeleton in *Earth Strike* (Douglas, 2010) and the war suit in Scalzi's *Old Man's War* (2005). The first model of the CryNet Nanosuit (also "nano muscle suit") (CryNet Nanosuit, n.d.) bears a strong resemblance to medical anatomical models for human musculature but it is actually the product of reverse-engineered exoskeletons worn by the Ceph aliens whom the United States is fighting (along with North Korea).

The CryNet suit has quite a few features that are reminiscent of the "Suit" in Heinlein's *Starship Troopers* (1959). Like the Suit, it cannot operate in space; but it functions well in the surface atmosphere of Earth as well as under water, although it is primarily designed for land use. Its visual and auditory systems can, among other things, protect the wearer from blinding light, provide night vision, and enhance hearing and vision. Its data interface can link to other devices and disrupt enemy communications. The suit is compatible with a number of weapons and has storage for both those weapons and ammunition. The most unusual feature of the CryNet suit is that it has four distinct modes of operation (CryNet Nanosuit, n.d.)

OPERATIONAL MODES OF THE CRYNET NANOSUIT

1. *Armor*: As its name suggests, the suit's energy is directed towards protecting the wearer from harm due to enemy weapons, radiation, and extreme weather conditions. Should damage occur to the suit or injury to the wearer this mode speeds regeneration and repair.

2. *Strength*: Like Thor's power belt, the wearer's strength is augmented to superhuman levels and the suit can also supply the wearer with performance-enhancement drugs.

3. *Speed*: The speed of all types of movement is augmented and manual dexterity is improved. Nanobots are released into the bloodstream to increase bloodflow and accelerate the movement of oxygen to the blood. This mode is good for underwater but, in this mode, sprinting and melee attacks deplete the energy reserves of the Nanosuit.

4. *Cloak*: The outer surface of the suit absorbs and bends incoming light waves to make itself and the wearer virtually invisible to the human eye and to most surveillance technology. Only slight distortions of light are observable. This mode also increases the wearer's speed.

Quite a few fighters in contemporary media wear powered exoskeletons that provide functions comparable to those of the CryNet nanosuit. Even the original *Metroid* video-game from Nintendo provided Samus Aran with a powered exoskeleton that enabled her to jump as high as Superman (Nintendo R&D & Intelligent Systems, 1986).

The most famous users of exoskeletons are not humans. They are an alien species called "Daleks" who have menaced actors on and viewers of the BBC television series *Doctor Who* (Doctor Who Universe, 1963–, ongoing). The Daleks were introduced early in the first season of *Doctor Who* and quickly became the doctor's most tenacious foes (The Daleks, 1963–1964). Physically, Daleks are not robots. They are a race of biological beings called "Kaleds" from the planet Skaro. The Kaleds waged a devastating nuclear war with another species from Skaro. Kaleds that survived the war emerged with badly mangled bodies.

What transformed the Kaleds into Daleks is a powered exoskeleton, often referred to as their "casing," that covers their disfigured bodies. Davos, a mentally unbalanced Kaled scientist, designed the exoskeleton for his disfigured colleagues. The result of his work is that Daleks look like large, metallic badminton-birdies with sticklike appendages.

Despite their sporty contours, Daleks are Nazi-like predators who believe they are superior to all other species. Whenever they appear in an episode of *Doctor Who,* they are engaged in eradicating another species from the universe. Daleks relish killing any biological creature while shouting "EXTERMINATE!" in distorted, electronic voices. The desire to destroy other species had been a Kaled character flaw long before they became Daleks. It was the trait that led them to engage in a nuclear war that killed all members of the species they were fighting and left only a small number of horribly disfigured Kaled survivors. In addition to designing their exoskeleton, Davos modified their genetic structure. He gave them a simple, uniform pattern of behavior that accentuated their already powerful blood-lust. Since then, they have been the epitome of the mindless killer.

This characterizes their behavior in all *Doctor Who* (Lambert et al., 1963–, ongoing) episodes. The exoskeleton-encased Daleks not only terrorized other characters in *Doctor Who* episodes, they frightened *Doctor Who* viewers as well. According to Martin et al. (2015),

> The series also gifted to the British language in perpetuo the phrase "hiding behind the sofa" as an expression of TV-induced fear. Whoever coined it, the formula is now inextricably linked to the Doctor (and the appearance of the Daleks).... Even Prince Andrew has admitted to hiding from the Daleks behind the soft furnishings as a child in Windsor Castle.

The Daleks' casing includes unique functions that demonstrate that it is a powered exoskeleton. One of those features is revealed in the episode "The Witch's Familiar" (2015). Clara and Missy, two of Doctor Who's companions, are being held prisoner by the Daleks. They obtain an empty Dalek casing which they use to escape. Clara hides in the casing. While inside the casing, Clara can speak using her own voice (CLARA'S VOICE) or through the casing in a Dalek voice (DALEK'S VOICE). She gets a disturbing surprise.

A LINGUISTIC SURPRISE

MISSY: Say your name.
CLARA'S VOICE: Clara.
DALEK'S VOICE: Dalek.
MISSY: One more time.

CLARA'S VOICE: I am Clara Oswald! I'm Clara Oswald!

DALEK'S VOICE: I am a Dalek! I am a Dalek! I am a Dalek!! I AM A DALEK!!!!
(The gun in the casing fires.)

MISSY: Whoa! Don't get emotional. Emotion fires the gun. Okay?

CLARA'S VOICE: I don't understand.

DALEK'S VOICE: I do not understand.

MISSY: Say, "I love you." Those exact words. Don't ask me why, just say it.

CLARA'S VOICE: I love you.

DALEK'S VOICE: Exterminate.

MISSY: Say, "you are different from me."

CLARA'S VOICE: You are different from me.

DALEK'S VOICE: Exterminate! Exterminate!

MISSY: Say, "Ex-ter-min-ate!"

CLARA'S VOICE: Exterminate.

DALEK'S VOICE: Exterminate!
(Clara spins around in the Dalek casing, firing its gun.)

DALEK'S VOICE: Exterminate! Exterminate! Exterminate!! ExTER minate!!!
EXTERMINATE!

MISSY: Daleks channel [their voices] through a gun. That's why they keep yelling "exterminate." It's how they reload. So, let's go and kill them. Come on.

Despite their vile personalities, by the 1960s the Daleks became media darlings. Daleks are the primary antagonists in two films: *Doctor Who and the Daleks* (1965) and *Daleks— Invasion Earth 2150 A.D.* (1966). They figure in numerous *Doctor Who* short stories, novels, concerts, musical compositions, and plays. Daleks also made guest appearances in episodes of other television series, comic books, and magazines. In 1964, the musical group the Go Go's cut a vinyl single of "I'm Gonna Spend My Christmas with a Dalek" (Martin et al., 2015; Vandyke, 1964).

ROBOTIC PROSTHETICS

Quite a few characters in science-fiction action films lose limbs as well as other body parts (e.g., diseased organs). The vast majority of them are replaced by robotic prostheses. According to Radcliffe (2015), the original *Star Wars* film (1977) "is the only *Star Wars* film in which no one loses a hand." Darth Vader relieves Luke Skywalker of his right hand in *Star Wars: Episode V—The Empire Strikes Back* (1980) and Skywalker returns the favor in *Star Wars: Episode VI—Return of the Jedi* (1983). At the end of *Star Wars Episode III: Revenge of the Sith* (2005), Obi-wan Kenobi relieves Anakin Skywalker of an arm and two legs. In addition, General Grievous, a robot, loses two hands but that isn't a problem for him because he has two more hands and he can hold a light sabre with his feet.

These and other characters in *Star Wars* films and other media receive robotic prostheses. The biomechanical devices are connected to nerves and other biological tissue using a "synth-net" neural interface. Limbs were then covered in a type of synthetic skin called "synthskin."

NANOTECHNOLOGY

"Assimilation" is a term used by the alien collective called "the Borg," a potent adversary of Starfleet in *Star Trek* media. The term refers to extensive modifications and enhancements that transform a sentient being into a drone member of the Borg collective. The process of assimilation takes several steps and involves nanotechnology, surgical alteration, and prostheses. The details of the assimilation process vary with the species and with the primary task the drone is to perform. The following is a generic summary of the Borg assimilation process for humans.

BORG ASSIMILATION PROCEDURE

1. *Neural assessment*: "The Best of Both Worlds" (1990) shows some aspects of Capt. Jean-Luc Picard's assimilation. The assimilation process begins when a Borg drone runs a light over Picard's forehead. Most other depictions of the process do not include this step (e.g., Regeneration, 2003).

2. *Nanoprobe injection*: The nanoprobes attach to the victim's cells and modify their DNA. The most obvious external indicator of a successful assimilation is the grayish coloration of the victim's skin which may be accompanied by mottling. The victim stops growing bodily hair and loses the hair it already has. Additionally, the body's need for food and water is reduced or eliminated. Sustenance comes from electrical input. The drone's strength increases as does its resistance to the effects of various types of weapons.

The method of injection varies. Sometimes the drone performing the assimilation injects the victim using two tubular extensions on its hand (Scorpion, 1997). In other episodes the injection is done using a huge syringe (The Best of Both Worlds, 1990).

Many of the nanoprobes remain in the drone's body. They preserve the changes made during assimilation, stimulate regrowth of implants that are removed, speed the healing of wounds, and defend the drone against disease and infection (Regeneration, 2003).

3. *Augmentation*: The majority of these changes are implants: In Picard's assimilation his prosthetic arm appears to be attached surgically (The Best of Both Worlds, 1990). In the *Enterprise* episode "Regeneration" (2003), the implants are grown internally by the nanoprobes. That episode shows them growing on new victims and re-growing on existing drones with damaged implants.

The drone is given a cortical array that becomes part of the higher brain functions, such as language and independent thought. It also is the repository for memories and knowledge. Control of these functions enables suppression of the victim's individuality.

The victim receives an eyepiece to improve vision. They are also supplied with a homing device and a unique link-frequency to enable continual contact with the hive mind. One arm is amputated and replaced with a prosthesis. The body is covered with an exoskeleton called "exo-plating" to provide additional protection.

4. *Naming*: The new drone is given a designation. Jean Luc Picard's designation was Locutus of Borg.

The Borg developed their assimilation procedures over millennia. They employ all three of the technologies of interest to this chapter. Nothing is perfect, however. The holographic doctor in *Star Trek: The Next Generation* (First Contact, 1991) observes that in certain cases these implants cause severe skin irritation and recommends use of an analgesic.

There is also considerable disagreement about what the naming structure means to the Borg collective. For example, the full designation of the drone rescued by Starfleet Voyager is "Seven of nine, tertiary adjunct of unimatrix zero one." She was a six-year-old child when she and her parents were taken by the Borg. The official Star Trek description of the character provides no assistance on this matter (Seven of Nine, n.d.).

The Borg are not the only ones to use nanotechnology to alter or enhance human performance. "Not machine … not man … I'm more." These words are spoken by John Connor, the leader of the human resistance against Skynet. He says them in *Terminator Genisys* (2015) to describe what he has become after being infected by "machine-phase matter."[2] This nanotechnology is more advanced than the "mimetic polyalloy" in the T-1000 (*Terminator 2: Judgment Day*, 1991; Frakes, 1991) and the TX (*Terminator 3: Rise of the Machines*, 2003) models. Connor is infected when he is wounded by a projectile containing nanobots designed to create machine-phase matter. He does not die. Instead, the nanobots transform him into a T-3000 terminator. Like them, the new Connor is a shapeshifter that can assume any form—including that of other humans. The T-3000/Connor is also able to transform himself into tiny particles and then quickly regroup to form the physical appearance of John Connor. Shapeshifting makes it possible for T-3000s like Connor to avoid damage from bullets and many other kinds of assaults. If, however, they are damaged, their shapeshifting ability enables them to heal almost immediately.

Nanotechnology (called "nanomachines") is a central theme of the video game Metal Gear Solid 4: Guns of the Patriots (Kojima Productions, 2008–, ongoing). In Metal Gear games, the world is engulfed in never-ending warfare which forces many countries to turn to private military companies (PMCs) to obtain fighters (mercenaries), weapons, and other military support. By the start of Guns of the Patriots, the global-war economy has made PMCs rich and they have begun to use technology to enhance the abilities of their mercenaries. The tool of choice in Metal Gear Solid 4 games is nanotechnology which augments the strength and endurance of warfighters on the battlefield. The nanomachines are operated and controlled using a centralized network called Sons of Patriots (SOP). The following description comes from Metal Gear Solid 4—Rat Patrol Team 01 (IGN Walkthroughs, 2012).

THE SOP NETWORK

They've implemented a system that monitors in real time every single soldier engaged in combat action—whether he's state army or PMC. Each individual soldier has been fully ID-tagged with nanomachines injected into their bodies for that purpose. The nanomachines keep track of the soldiers and their real time personal data 24 hours a day. They monitor each man's position, movement, speed, reserve ammo, firing accuracy, wounds, rations, water intake, and supplies, sweat secreted, heart rate, blood pressure, and sugar levels, oxygen [*sic*]. All the data gathered on body condition, on sensory organ data showing pain and fear. There's data on every internal response within the body. All of it is collected by an AI at the system's core. This data is monitored at HQ to enable command to make quicker, more precise, more rational decisions. It also enables crisis management for each individual soldier. It's being used by the U.S. military, by states in allied countries, by PMCs. Even police agencies are starting to adopt it. Unless they agree to implement the system, PMCs aren't permitted to send troops anywhere.... We get a clear picture of what's going on around us so there's less confusion during missions. And our nanomachines communicate with each other making teamwork a lot smoother.... It's also a security guarantee against the PMCs (transcription of IGN Walkthroughs, 2012, 7:19).

Much like the neural implants in Douglas' *Star Carrier* (2010–, ongoing) series and the Brainpal in Scalzi's *Old Man's War* series (2005–2015), the SOP's support of rapid and effective communication between and among squad members enhances teamwork and performance. SOP monitors the emotions of its fighters. Brainpal sends that information to squad-mates, their commanding officer, and others with whom the individual has an open link. In Metal Gear Solid 4, the data flow is between the warfighter and the central core of the SOP.

The extensive support provided by SOP engenders dependence on the system, especially by novice fighters who are likely to rely far more on SOP than their comrades or themselves. That dependence is a weakness, because those fighters would be lost should the network fail.

There is an additional problem with SOP's centralized structure and its extensive control: "The system is mine. Your guns and your weapons are no longer your own" (CJake3, 2011, 5:45). This pronouncement is uttered by Liquid Snake/Ocelot, an enemy infiltrator, who has hacked SOP, causing all SOP-linked warfighters to lose their IDs. Without an ID, a warfighter can no longer use their weapons or control their vehicles. Like the fighters in Douglas' *Star Carrier* (Douglas, 2010–, ongoing) and John Scalzi's *Old Man's War* (2005–2015), when the SOP system is compromised or shut off, the warfighters become helpless and unable to defend themselves against anyone with a functioning weapon.

Real World[3]

Militaries in the real world see exoskeletons, robotic prosthetics, and nanotechnology as part of an effort that is sometimes called the "soldier of the future." Development in some of these areas is proceeding quickly.

Exoskeletons

At the close of the nineteenth century, Nicholas Yagn received U.S. patents for designs for an "Apparatus for Facilitating Walking, Running, and Jumping" (Yagn, 1890). His inventions included "springs being used to take up and accumulate the power, said springs being so arranged as to apply the power stored or accumulated at the seat, waist, or under the arms, respectively" (p. 1). Thirty years later, Leslie C. Kelley (Kelley, 1919) received a patent for his Pedomotor.

> Two sets of ligaments [wires] ... have their lower ends secured to the toe ... and after passing through sleeves at the front of the ankle joints pass each side of the legs and to the rear thereof to sleeves ... at the rear of the knees thence back on each side of the legs to common junctions ... through sleeves ... in front of the belt ... and terminate in suitable springs ... the upper ends of which are secured to a harness [p. 2].

Kelley's Pedomotor was operated by an external fuel source.

> Any suitable motive power may be employed to alternately operate the ligaments ... to produce a running movement. One type of motive power which I have illustrated is controlled and operated in the following manner:
> The harness ... has mounted on the rear thereof a suitable frame ... carrying a gas or other fuel container ... provided with a burner ... within a housing ... on the underside of a suitable boiler [p. 2].

There is no evidence that either Yagn's or Kelley's devices were ever built.

Gen. Paul F. Gorman began DARPA's work on exoskeletons in the late 1980s with his proposals of a "SuperTroop" for the future soldier of 2030

> aimed at total encapsulation of an individual who fights on foot, predicated upon integrating a powered exoskeleton into his battle dress to augment load-bearing capability, a personal computer networked with those of fellow combatants, and full body protection against ballistic, chemical, thermal, and directed energy threats [Gorman, 1990, p. v].

His design, which is shown in Fig. 23, included many features that appear in the armor created by the superhero Iron Man (Iron Man's Armor, n.d.) and other fictional exoskeletons. Among those features are sensors to monitor the external environment (e.g., temperature), instruments that keep track of the soldier's core bodily functions (e.g., heart rate), and technology to ensure that the wearer is well oriented in their environment. To communicate their identity to the SuperTroop, the wearer "would insert one dog-tag into a slot under the chest armor, thereby loading his personal program into the battle suit's computer" (pp. viii–7).

The U.S. Army's Special Operations Command (USSOCOM) Tactical Assault Light Operator Suit (TALOS) has retained many SuperTroop functionality goals. The USSOCOM's 2017 call for proposals characterizes TALOS as "an overarching vision to drastically improve" the foot soldier's "survivability and capability" (also see Part II: Superheroes & Supervillains). "The capability areas include enhanced warfighter protection, improved situational awareness, increased mobility, advancements in battlefield power generation and storage, and modernized ground force communication and control" (USSOCOM, 2017).

The U.S. Army has also been working on "liquid body armor" for TALOS and other applications. It is soft and malleable until it is struck by something like a bullet. Then it immediately stiffens, preventing the bullet from doing any harm (Teel, 2013; Johnson, 2017).

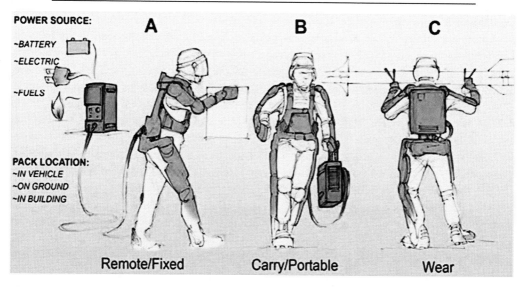

Figure 23. In the 1980s, Gen. Paul F. Gorman began designing the SuperTroop exoskeleton, intended for the future soldier of 2030 (Wikimedia Commons).

The more than forty components in Russia's Ratnik-3 Infantry Combat System are similar to those in TALOS. It is still only a concept unit but Russia plans to deploy it in 2020 (Hiznyak, 2017). The UK's "Future Soldier Vision" (FSV) is similar to TALOS and Ratnik-3. Its designers have begun to incorporate provisional solutions for power. "FSV's electronics are powered by a battery pack that hangs off the back of [sic] wearer's bulletproof vest. A separate battery powers the helmet" (Mizokami, 2015). China's second-generation exoskeleton is far less ambitious than these projects and it is likely to be deployed far sooner. It is "a body brace designed to help infantry members carry some 100 pounds of weapons, supplies, and ammunition" (Lin & Singer, 2018).

Even the most complex fictional exoskeletons are fully deployed and they almost always function perfectly. Real-world exoskeletons are still under development and, before they are deployed, they must be thoroughly tested. Testing can and does expose problems that may not be possible to overcome. Lockheed's Human Universal Load Carrier (HULC) is such an example. It was a partial exoskeleton covering only the legs and feet and its purpose was to enable warfighters to carry heavy loads over longer distances. Cornwall (2015) cites the opinion of the engineer running the tests:

> "One big problem was that the HULC forced wearers to walk in an unfamiliar way," says Karen Gregorczyk, a biomechanical engineer at the Army's Natick center who led the tests. That difficulty was compounded by a lack of coordination between human and machine. "It's trying to kick your leg forward and you're not ready to kick your leg forward," says Gregorczyk, who spent a half hour trying the suit. "It was a workout."

ROBOTIC PROSTHETICS

Like the prosthetic hands of King Nuada and Luke Skywalker, the operation of real-world prosthetic hands is becoming increasingly natural. The Georgia Tech School of Music developed a prosthesis using ultrasound "that allows amputees to control each of their prosthetic fingers individually. It provides fine motor hand gestures that aren't possible with current commercially available devices" (Georgia Tech, 2017). Ultrasound detects the movements its wearer wants to make using signals from muscle groups higher up in the arm. The prosthesis enabled its first wearer, a musician, to play the piano again. The Hennes hand, developed by a team of researchers at the Italian Institute of Technology (Barry & Sportelli, 2018), is no heavier than a real hand and it can perform fine motor tasks such as taking bills from an ATM and holding a pencil. Like Nuada's prosthetic hand, the Hennes hand looks like a real hand.

DARPA (n.d.*b*) wants a bi-directional, closed circuit system that links synthetic wires from a prosthesis to nerve bundles. The Johns Hopkins Hand Proprioception and Touch Interfaces (HAPTIX) is a bi-directional arm and hand system which "means it's capable of receiving signals from the human brain and, paired with the right surgical implants, transmitting signals to the brain" (Stone, 2016). Arm amputee Johnny Matheny has been Beta testing the system since 2011. He has undergone two surgeries: ossio integration which connects an implant directly to the bone of his upper arm and "target-and-muscle" surgery which allowed the implant to access neuronal information that would normally flow to and from the original limb. When Matheny wants to move his arm, hand, and/or fingers, his brain sends signals to the muscles in his upper arm. The arm implant "picks up electrical signals from his muscles. Those signals are transmitted via Bluetooth to a computer inside the prosthetic arm, which drives motors inside the device" (Stone, 2016).

This type of system is a forerunner for implants that enhance physical and mental performance. Such programs are being developed at research centers in the U.S., Russia, China, and elsewhere. DARPA's projects involving brain implants are part of former President Obama's "Brain Initiative" (DARPA, n.d.*c*). One of the programs in that initiative is the "Neural Engineering System Design (NESD)." The goal of NESD is to develop "an implantable system able to provide precision communication between the brain and the digital world" (DARPA, 2016; DARPA, 2017).

NANOTECHNOLOGY

Nanotechnology is the basis of the "liquid armor" described in the earlier discussion of the TALOS exoskeleton. The future warfighter in a TALOS exoskeleton might also be wearing a uniform made of "smart fabrics" (also "e-textiles") beneath it.[4] In a smart fabric, nanoparticles are woven into a textile capable of conducting an electrical current. The resulting fabric can be used to perform functions that were identified earlier as being necessary for exoskeletons, such as tracking of vital signs (e.g., heart rate, blood oxygen level), and environmental/safety monitoring (e.g., external temperature, presence of toxic gas). The smart fabric of Chen et al. (2016) can harvest solar and mechanical energy and direct it to devices. "Under ambient sunlight with mechanical excitation, such as human motion, car movement and wind blowing, the … textile was capable of generating sufficient power for various applications, including … directly charging a cell phone" (p. 6). A smart fabric like this could provide "energy salvaging" and could monitor vital functions, both of which are objectives of the TALOS project. MIT's Institute for Soldier Nanotechnologies is developing fibre-optics that hold a signal that could be identified through a laser. When shined upon the uniform, it would transmit a friendly signal to the user's own uniform, identifying the suspected soldier as friendly [Scataglini, Andreoni, and Gallant, 2015].

Researchers at the University of Central Florida are designing light-sensitive, smart fabrics for uniforms so that

> [i]f a sniper gun were aimed at a soldier, even if it were an infrared beam so it's not visible, the fibers embedded in the fabric deliver an electronic signal saying, "This surface is being interrogated by a laser" [Ravindranath, 2016].

Such concepts are applied in a different way to produce "nano camo." That is nano-based, dynamic camouflage that is akin to the cloak mode of the Crytek exoskeleton in the video game Crysis (Crytek, 2007–, ongoing), the camouflage technology in Iron Man's stealth armor (Uhley, 2009), and the cloak of invisibility in *Harry Potter and the Chamber of Secrets* (Rowling, 1998).

> The goal of this research program was to create a technology for artificially programmable infrared emissivity of surfaces. As an example, this would permit a vehicle, or a person to blend into its surroundings, and become invisible to an infrared camera [Yablonovitch, 2005].

Much like the use of nanotechnology in science fiction, real-world militaries are using nanotechnology to keep warfighters in good health. Some of the research areas are

- Disease diagnosis and treatment (Kumar & Kumar, 2014)
- Wound healing (Drummond, 2010)
- Damaged cells, organs, and limb regeneration (Pagano, 2017)
- Eye replacement (Ossola, 2015)
- Brain repair (Ellis-Behnke et al., 2006)
- Drug delivery (Park, 2007)
- Disease immunity monitoring (Smith, Simon, & Baker, 2013)
- Battlefield treatment of hemorrhagic shock (Salton, 2009)

Use of nanotechnology for health maintenance is reminiscent of the trillions of nanorobotics in Admiral Koenig's circulatory system monitoring his health (Douglas, 2010). Researchers at the University of California, San Diego, are also testing a drug-delivery system using swarms of drug-coated, nanobot spheres twenty microns thick. The swarm of spheres is ingested and the microbots are activated and begin the process of drug delivery when the spheres encounter stomach acids (Li et al., 2017). Chemotherapy delivery was mentioned in the Non-Humanoids chapter.

Plans Gone Awry

CONTEMPORARY MEDIA

As described earlier, in the manga *Trinity Blood* (Yoshida, (2000 [2007]), human settlers on Mars ingested an alien nanobot called Bacillus to help them survive in the severe Martian environment. It worked. The small print related to Bacillus, however, is that it transforms Methuselahs into vampires. Their sensitivity to the UV rays of the sun forces them to become nocturnal. During the war on Earth in which they fought against Earth-based humans, the need to sleep during the day made it easier for Earth-based humans to kill them in the daytime. These negative side effects caused the Methuselahs to lose the war. They were subsequently banished to Eastern Europe; which became the setting of the subsequent *Trinity Blood* novels, manga, and anime.

A second side effect is that there was a random Bacillus mutation that gave some nanobots a cross-like body shape. Humans who injected that mutated strain of Bacillus were changed into "Crusniks"—vampires that feed on other vampires.

Furor: LAWS

LAWS (see Glossary) are smart weapons that can select, locate, and attack targets without input from a human at any point in the process. They use AI to perform these functions and machine learning to learn and adapt based on past experience.

Passive autonomous weapons, notably anti-personnel weapons like land mines, have existed for centuries. They don't select, locate, and attack targets. They simply respond to a predefined external stimulus (e.g., being stepped on) without need of human control. Smarter, truer, autonomous weapons, such as guided missiles, are products of the twentieth century and are primarily used for defense. The U.S. Navy describes its Phalanx as "the only deployed close-in weapon system capable of autonomously performing its own search, detect, evaluation, track, engage and kill assessment functions" (United States Navy, 2017). The sentry guns operating along the Demilitarized Zone between South and North Korea have a fully autonomous mode. They can distinguish humans from animals and they use speech recognition to challenge an intruder who then must verbally respond with a code or be fired upon (Kumagai, 2007).

More than sixty countries, multi-national organizations, and non-state groups are actively engaged in R&D of LAWS. Some of this work is described in the preceding chapters of Part III as well as in Part II: Furor: Making Robots Moral. At the same time, efforts to establish an international agreement to ban LAWS are gaining traction. This movement has provoked a heated debate regarding the development of LAWS and their use in national and international conflicts. The United Nations has held several meetings on the issue.

The purpose of this chapter is to provide a balanced survey of the ongoing discourse about banning LAWS.

Historical Background

Banning weapons deemed to be inherently evil is an ancient, cross-cultural practice. The Han dynasty (202 BCE–220 CE) banned the poison *Ku* (see Part II: Criminals). Violators were subject to public execution. Feng and Shryock (1935) add that the "law of the Han was based on earlier codes, going back to at least the fourth century B.C." (p. 6). The Old Testament of the Bible forbids cutting down an enemy's food-producing trees "for the tree of the field *is* man's life" (Deuteronomy 20: 19–20). The Hindu *Laws of Manu* (ca. 200 BCE) says, "Let him not strike with weapons concealed (in wood), nor with (such as are) barbed, poisoned, or the points of which are blazing with fire" (7: 90). At the Second Lateran Council (1139 CE), the Catholic Church issued Canon 29 which reads, "We prohibit under anathema that murderous art of crossbowmen and archers, which is hateful to God, to be employed against Christians and Catholics from now on" (Schroeder, 1937, p. 213). The impact of Canon 29 on non–Christian crossbow archers was never assessed.

Since the beginning of the twentieth century, bans have taken the form of international treaties and agreements. Concern about the use of aircraft as a weapons platform prompted the Institute of International Law to make the following resolution: "Aerial war is allowed but on the condition that it does not present for the persons or property of the peaceful population greater dangers than land or sea warfare" (Scott, 1916, p. 171). The 1963 Nuclear Test-Ban Treaty banned all tests of nuclear weapons except underground ones (Freedman, 2018). Seven years later, powered by the signatures of 190 nations, the Treaty on the Non-Proliferation of Nuclear Weapons went into effect.

Anti-personnel mines were banned by the Ottawa Treaty (the "Mine Ban Treaty") that was drafted and ratified in 1997 by forty countries and went into effect in 1999. The devastation caused by chemical weapons led the United Nations to spearhead the Chemical Weapons Convention (CWC), a multilateral treaty banning the use, development, production, acquisition, stockpiling, and retention of chemical weapons for an unspecified period of time. It also formed an oversight organization, the Organization for the Prohibition of Chemical Weapons (OPCW), to ensure compliance with CWC provisions. That ban went into effect in 1997. As of 2017, 192 nations had ratified it.

The Movement to Ban LAWS

Those international treaties were crafted using shared, real-world experience of the damage caused by the weapon being banned. The movement to ban LAWS is different because

> this time the weapon being defined *does not yet exist*. The weapons previously prohibited had existed for decades and their effects were perfectly known. They could therefore be banned without a precise definition. The absence of shared experience or understanding make [sic] LAWS different [Vilmer, 2016].

To date, only semi-autonomous weapons have been deployed. Such weapons always include a human in the decision-making process. Consequently, arguments for and against a ban are primarily extrapolations from experience with armed, semi-autonomous aerial-weapons such as General Atomics' MQ-9 Reaper (Predator B) which was mentioned earlier in the Modern Literature section of Part III: Non-Humanoids.

Despite this problem, the international movement to ban LAWS is growing. Several organizations, notably the Campaign to Stop Killer Robots, were formed to promote the ban. Other supporters include nations, (e.g., Algeria, Chile, and Egypt), multinational organizations (e.g., European Parliament, International Committee of the Red Cross), human-rights groups (e.g., PAX, Human Rights Watch), and more than 3,000 scientists and engineers including Elon Musk and the late Stephen Hawking. The UN formed a committee to address the issue which has held several meetings.

The Debate

The PAX (2017) document, "Ten Reasons to Ban Killer Robots," provides a structured list of ethical, legal, and security concerns. Even though the source of the list is a proponent of the ban, common arguments from both sides are presented here in order to provide a balanced overview of the debate.

ETHICAL CONCERNS: LIFE OR DEATH?

A machine should never be allowed to make the decision over life and death. This goes against the principles of human dignity and the right to life. This decision cannot be reduced to an algorithm. Outsourcing this decision would mean outsourcing morality [Ten Reasons to Ban Killer Robots, 2017].

Favor a Ban

Delegating the decision to kill a human to an algorithm in a machine, which is not responsible for its action in any meaningful ethical sense, can arguably be understood to be an infringement on basic human dignity, presenting what in moral philosophy is known as a *malum in se*, a wrong in itself [Sauer, 2016].

The UN Rapporteur Christof Heyns added, "Machines lack morality and mortality, and many people believe they should as a result not have life and death powers over humans. This is among the reasons landmines were banned" (Office of the United Nations High Commissioner for Human Rights, 2013).

Oppose a Ban

Pointing to past atrocities committed by humans, some argue that the absence of emotion is a compelling reason to use LAWS. Robots do not fear for their lives, over-react, or succumb to stress, battle fatigue, anger, or other emotional responses that impel human warfighters to commit atrocities. Rabkin and Yoo (2017) argue that "by taking humans out of the firing decision, independent robots controlled by computer programming or even artificial intelligence could elevate the humanity of combat" (p. 134). They add,

The laws of war should favor combat methods that reduce harm to civilians and the death and destruction of war itself over any minimum requirement of human participation. If we can program the robot to execute attacks that reduce wartime errors and collateral damage below that of a human fighter, we should choose the robot [p. 153].

Vilmer (2015) questions the validity of the concern itself. "If the target is legal and legitimate, does the question of who kills it (a human or a machine) have any moral relevance? And is it the machine that kills, or the human who programmed it?" Müller and Simpson (2014) turn the concern on its head by taking the position that banning LAWS is morally culpable. "Just as it is culpable negligence to send in the infantry without body armour and helmets, so—other things being equal—it is also negligent to fail to develop LAWS" (p. 2).

ETHICAL CONCERNS: UNPREDICTABILITY

"Because of their nature these weapons could be highly unpredictable, especially in their interaction with other autonomous systems and if they are self-learning" (Ten Reasons to Ban Killer Robots, 2017). This concern addresses three kinds of unpredictability: the basic nature of LAWS; interactions with other autonomous systems; and self-learning.

Unpredictability due to their basic nature. A fully autonomous robot does not, by definition, follow a pre-determined, step-by-step procedure. It is designed to be flexible because it must operate in dynamic, rapidly changing environments. When it is sent on a mission, it is given a goal and the robot uses the sense-plan-act paradigm (see Introduction) to achieve that goal. Consequently, LAWS make decisions without human input or control. Those independent decisions are part of what could be seen as the unpredictability of fully autonomous weapons (LAWS).

Favor a Ban

Lin, Bekey, and Abney (2008) maintain that characterizing LAWS using the sense-plan-act paradigm has become too simplistic because the software systems of today are too large and complex for a single individual to program them.

> Now, programs with millions of lines of code are written by teams of programmers, none of whom knows the entire program, hence, no individual can predict the effect of a given command with absolute certainty, since portions of large programs may interact in unexpected, untested ways…. Furthermore, increasing complexity may lead to emergent behaviors, i.e., behaviors not programmed but arising out of sheer complexity [p. 8].

When tight development timetables are combined with system complexity and team programming, the result can be a poorly designed system filled with bugs and lacking ethical or security controls. Such systems are prone to malfunctions and failures that endanger soldiers, civilians, and sometimes international relations.

Oppose a Ban

At the 2016 UN Convention on Certain Conventional Weapons

> some states recalled … this risk is not unique to LAWS; it is part of all human action. As Neha Jain from the University of Minnesota raised, "Every human is a wild card, and we accept it each time we deploy a soldier on the battlefield." Why would the acceptable risk of LAWS be different to that which is accepted of humans? [Vilmer, 2016].

Is the unpredictability of LAWS comparable to that of human "wild cards?" Lucas (2013) maintains that it is, if the LAWS has been rigorously tested and proven reliable.

> If such a system malfunctioned (even as humans and their manned systems sometimes make mistakes, hit the wrong targets, or inadvertently kill the wrong people), then the procedure in the machine case would parallel that of the human case in similar circumstances [p. 219].

Mulrine (2011) argues that LAWS would produce less unpredictability than remotely piloted drones (RPDs) which are not only "tricky to fly," their unpredictability often occurs when the fragile communication link between the pilot and the drone is broken. That would not be an issue for LAWS.

LAWS and RPDs could share other types of unpredictability, notably those produced by internal problems (e.g., a power outage or sensor malfunction) and by external attack (e.g., hacking or jamming). The unpredictable behavior of at least one rogue RPD has forced the U.S. military to shoot it down.

ETHICAL CONCERNS: LEARNING

LAWS are especially unpredictable regarding their interaction with other autonomous systems and if they are self-learning systems. In order for a robot to learn, it needs an internal model of its environment, a reasoning engine, and an evaluation/measuring method (Bekey, 2005). Autonomous robots often use self-supervised learning. An "evaluation/measuring method" enables the robot to determine whether it has learned something and, if so, how well. It may also possess techniques for identifying and correcting errors.

Favor a Ban

The "Second Statement on Security" of the International Committee for Robot Arms Control warns that

> The sequence of events developing at rapid speed from the interaction of autonomous systems or swarms of two adversaries could never be trained, tested, nor truly foreseen.... Such interactions could create unstable and unpredictable behavior, behavior that could initiate or escalate conflicts, or cause unjustifiable harm to civilian populations [Sauer, 2016].

Oppose a Ban

Thurnher (2012) considers the ability to learn to be a tremendous breakthrough. "The true breakthrough ... is the way in which they adapt and learn. These systems are essentially able to learn from their own mistakes" (Thurnher, 2012, p. 79).

LEGAL CONCERNS

Fully autonomous weapons will likely not be able to adhere to International Humanitarian Law (IHL). They will likely not be able to properly distinguish between civilians and combatants, or make a proportionality assessment of acceptable collateral damage. Schmitt and Thurnher (2013) advise that assessment of adherence to IHL be governed by the purpose of IHL because

> the law of armed conflict has never been about ensuring a "fair fight"; rather, it comprises prohibitions, restrictions, and obligations designed to balance a State's interest in effectively prosecuting the war (military necessity) with its interest in minimizing harm to those involved in a conflict (humanity) [p. 232].

Vilmer (2016) reminds us to use human behavior as the measure for evaluating the ability of LAWS to comply with IHL.

> [A]s humans do not respect IHL perfectly (if they did, there would be no war crimes), the question is not so much whether LAWS will be capable of respecting IHL or not, but whether they will be capable of doing so better or worse than humans under the same circumstances. This argument was clearly expressed by law professor Marco Sassòli at the 2014 meeting, where he explained that the system must be required to "be able to recognize wounded, not like God would do, but like a human being would" [Vilmer, 2016].

This argument is known in the literature as the "Arkin test," named for Ronald C. Arkin whose work on encoding morality into robots is described in Part II: Furor: Making Robots Moral.[1]

Three questions involved are

- Are LAWS inherently evil/immoral (per Protocol I, Article 36)?
- Can LAWS distinguish between combatants and civilians (per the "principle of discrimination" also called the "principle of distinction")?
- Can LAWS limit their actions to those required to achieve the objectives of each mission (per the "principle of proportionality")?

The Laws of War

The International Committee of the Red Cross (ICRC) defines IHL as "a set of rules which seek, for humanitarian reasons, *to limit the effects of armed conflict*. It protects persons who are not or are no longer participating in the hostilities and restricts the means and methods of warfare (What Is International Humanitarian Law, 2014). IHL is distinct from Human Rights Law because it protects non-combatants and non-military property only during military conflicts. That is why IHL is often called the "Laws of War" (LOW) whereas Humanitarian Rights Law applies those and other protections during times of peace. The LOW come from four Geneva Conventions (held in 1863, 1906, 1929, and 1949), Protocols I & II (that update and modernize the Conventions), agreements banning specific weapons, and a few other established traditions. Together, they comprise the "Just War Theory" (JWT).[2]

LEGAL CONCERNS: MORALITY

There is debate whether LAWS are inherently evil or immoral. As indicated earlier, banning wartime actions and weapons deemed inherently evil or immoral is well established. JWT includes bans of chemical and biological weapons and Article 36 of Protocol I (United Nations, 1977) extends such assessments to new weapons.

> Art 36. New Weapons. In the study, development, acquisition or adoption of a new weapon, means or method of warfare, a High Contracting Party is under an obligation to determine *whether its employment would, in some or all circumstances, be prohibited by this Protocol or by any other rule of international law applicable to the High Contracting Party* [United Nations, 1977; emphasis added].

Favor a Ban

Grut (2013) complains that

> Article 36 does not seem to have been particularly effective in flagging concerns about autonomous weapons. Few states actively engage with this kind of weapons review process, and such review does not seem to have led to the prohibition of any development, acquisition, or adoption of new weapons.

Consequently, there would be no way to obtain support for a ban of LAWS using Article 36. This problem has led advocates of banning LAWS to turn to the two principles considered to be the bedrock of the LOW: distinction/discrimination and proportionality. They belong to a portion of JWT called "Just Conduct in War" or *jus in bello*.

> When hostilities commence, the current just war tradition brackets morally justifiable military violence with two broad criteria: *discrimination* and *proportionality*. First, the violent military action has to discriminate between combatants and noncombatants. Second, the costs of particular military action have to be proportional to the objective sought. The thread running through both criteria is the moral requirement that particular military missions be reasonably assessed as militarily necessary to achieve justified goals of the conflict [Hallgarth, 2013, pp. 31–32].

That is extremely difficult to do in conflicts where combatants and civilians look alike, a characteristic of the conflicts of today.

Oppose a Ban

Strawser (2013) proposes a more restrictive assessment of compliance based on bans already in the LOW: If it is not possible to identify at least one way in which a weapon can be used that is *not* immoral, then the weapon is "inherently evil." Chemical and biological weapons meet that criterion but RPDs and LAWS do not. There are, for example, autonomous sentry guns used for defense. RPDs are used to search for and detonate IEDs (Gilman, 2014). The UN Office for the Coordinator of Humanitarian Affairs (OCHA) has said that RPDs are important for humanitarian work in civil wars because the very presence of RPDs deters criminal acts and ethnic cleansing. These uses can easily be done by LAWS. There are also missions that can be accomplished equally well using traditional technologies or RPDs/LAWS. In such cases, "[w]e are morally required to use drones over the manned aircraft to prevent exposing pilots to unnecessary risk" (Strawser, 2013, p. 17).

Legal Concerns: Discrimination

Can LAWS distinguish between combatants and civilians (the "principle of discrimination/distinction")?

> Art 48. Basic Rule. In order to ensure respect for and protection of the civilian population and civilian objects, the Parties to the conflict shall at all times distinguish between the civilian population and combatants and between civilian objects and military objectives and accordingly shall direct their operations only against military objectives [United Nations, 1977].

Support or opposition to a ban based on discrimination/distinction depends upon whether or not one believes RPDs/LAWS can perform the necessary visual and auditory capture-and-analysis and then effectively interpret the information.

The environments in which RPDs/LAWS must operate are visually and auditorially complex, dynamic, and often contain unexpected types of variability. Nuanced information goes beyond simply processing sounds and images. These types of analyses are often called "situational awareness," "gut feelings," and "contextual awareness." They entail using prior knowledge and other experience to differentiate combatants (or, in law enforcement, criminals) from civilians. "[I]t can be extremely difficult to distinguish a farmer digging a trench from a member of an armed group planting an improvised explosive device" (Grut, 2013, p. 11). Discrimination is further muddied by the presence of military equipment in non-military environments where

> (decommissioned) tanks may be parked in playgrounds for children to climb on; foreign warships may be passing through the territorial waters of the enemy power; and neutral troops or peacekeeping forces may be present in areas in which other legitimate targets are located [Sparrow, 2016, pp. 9–10].

The difficulties are compounded because "terrorists and guerrillas refuse to follow the laws of war by refusing to distinguish themselves from civilians, hiding among them, and launching terror attacks on them" (Rabkin & Yoo, 2017, p. 37). There are also part-time civilians who aid the cause of the insurgency in some ways (e.g., money, shelter, arms transport) but otherwise are not involved in the conflict. Steinhoff (2013) calls these people "noninnocent civilians" (p. 191).

These conditions present significant challenges to humans. The core issue is whether RPDs and LAWS can perform as well as or better than experienced warfighters. RPDs use advanced sensory capture-and-analysis technology. The technology in them is continually improving because of the active research in auditory scene analysis (Evers & Naylor, 2018), facial re-identification (e.g., Yang et al., 2017), and related areas.

Favor a Ban

Given all the sensory and cognitive challenges facing humans and RPDs today, Haag and Hepkins (2015) state that "[t]here are... grave doubts that fully autonomous weapons would ever be able to replicate human judgment and comply with the legal requirement to distinguish civilian from military targets." Sharkey (2012) contends LAWS must be banned because AI will never be able to perform these types of subtle, situational-awareness distinctions.

> I suspect that human-level discrimination with adequate common sense reasoning and battlefield awareness may be computationally intractable. At this point we cannot rely on machines ever having the independent facility to operate on the principle of distinction as well as human soldiers can [p. 789].

Oppose a Ban

Schmitt and Thurnher (2013) contend that "human judgment can prove less reliable than technical indicators in the heat of battle" (p. 248). They offer examples where humans who ignored technology caused deadly accidents including the 1988 incident in which a U.S. warship shot down an Iranian commercial airliner. This behavior is called "scenario fulfillment."

Like Strawser's 2013 proposal, Schmitt and Thurnher (2013) also argue that a blanket ban based on the principle of discrimination confuses the weapon with its use.

> What has been missed in much of the dialogue so far is that even an autonomous weapon system that is completely incapable of distinguishing a civilian from a combatant ... can be used lawfully in certain environments. Not all battlespaces contain civilians or civilian objects. When they do not, a system devoid of the ability to distinguish protected persons and objects from lawful military targets can be used without endangering the former [p. 246].

U.S. General Michael Hayden (2016) emphasizes the ability of RPDs to discriminate, saying their ability (and ultimately that of LAWS) to hover over an area gathering information about individuals, groups, and locations can be more accurate than humans on the ground who have restricted visibility, movement, and time.

Grut (2013) thinks a "blanket ban" is unwise. She supports levying a moratorium on "un-fixed" LAWS, such as those used to perform targeted and signature attacks but not "fixed" LAWS, such as sentry guns, because their autonomous attack-operations are well-defined and limited to a given location.

> While there is a lot of skepticism regarding whether robots will ever be capable of adequately complying with IHL ... we do not really know what future developments hold in store in this area. Given that some developments towards autonomy might result in more discriminatory systems, a blanket ban on autonomy, particularly in the development stage would not be wise [p. 22].

LEGAL CONCERNS: PROPORTIONALITY

Can LAWS limit their actions to those required to achieve the objectives of each mission (the "principle of proportionality")?

Protocol I, Part IV, Section 1, Chapter II, Art 51. Protection of the civilian population.
5. Among others, the following types of attacks are to be considered as indiscriminate:
(b) An attack which may be expected to cause incidental loss of civilian life, injury to civilians, damage to civilian objects, or a combination thereof, which would be excessive in relation to the concrete and direct military advantage anticipated [United Nations, 1977].

Plaw (2013) emphasizes that ensuring RPDs and LAWS comply with the principle of proportionality is critical. "This question of the proportionality of drone strikes is an especially important one because it goes straight to the legality and morality of a tactic that has become increasingly central to the US counterterrorism strategy" (p. 126).

Sharkey (2012) divides proportionality into two categories:

the *easy proportionality problem*: minimizing collateral damage by choosing the most appropriate weapon or munition and directing it appropriately.... The *hard proportionality problem* is making the decision about whether to apply lethal or kinetic force in a particular context in the first place [p. 789].

Hard proportionality is a greater challenge because it involves answering difficult, subjective questions, such as, "What is the balance between loss of civilian lives and the expected military advantage? Will a particular kinetic strike benefit the military objectives or hinder them because it upsets the local population?" (p. 789). Sharkey doubts that LAWS would be able to address the hard proportionality problem.

Favor a Ban

Sharkey believes semi-autonomous systems can already calculate the easy-proportionality aspect of a strike. The ability to solve the hard-proportionality problem requires situational awareness, a moral code, a measure of wisdom, and "gut instinct." LAWS have none of these required components but Sauer (2016) admits that hard-proportionality decisions are difficult for humans as well—even those with a great deal of experience because, as mentioned earlier, it is often difficult to distinguish civilians from combatants.

Oppose a Ban

Arkin (2015) contends that a robot's lack of emotion will prevent it from responding with excessive force against civilians because of fear, anger, hatred, or revenge. Notably, a robot will not engage in indiscriminant massacres, such as the notorious massacre that occurred in My Lai, Vietnam. Arkin (2015) concludes, "It is not my belief that an unmanned system will ever be able to be perfectly ethical in the battlefield, but I am convinced they can ultimately perform more ethically than human soldiers" (p. 46).

Plaw (2013) provides the following distressing information about proportionality. Calculations of civilians killed in Pakistan by al-Qaeda and the Taliban from 2004 to 2011 "dwarfs that produced by all of the drone strikes combined, even on the most unfavorable count [to drone strike killings], by many orders of magnitude" (p. 146). Al-Qaeda and the Taliban were responsible for 12,205 civilian deaths which is nineteen times larger than the 638 deaths caused by RPDs.

Faced with such a scale of atrocities, it would be difficult to argue against the proportionality of a planned drone strike if US officials had good reason to think that it would significantly damage al-Qaeda or Taliban capabilities (or disrupt imminent attacks) even if it posed a risk to a small number of civilians. The demonstrated viciousness of these organizations lends credibility to the view that such a strike might save more civilian lives than it costs [p. 146].

Legal Concerns: Responsibility

Fully autonomous weapons create an accountability vacuum regarding who is responsible if something goes wrong. Who would be responsible? The robot, the developer, the military commander?

> Art 91. Responsibility. A Party to the conflict which violates the provisions of the Conventions or of this Protocol ... shall be responsible for all acts committed by persons forming part of its armed forces [United Nations, 1977].

Responsibility is generally not left there. When humans have perpetrated atrocities they are court martialed or otherwise punished, but what will happen when machines kill innocent people? In one of the first publications on this topic, Sparrow (2007) assesses the accountability of various parties.

- *Manufacturers* can be held accountable for unknown flaws and also known flaws, unless they have warned the customer. Then, the "responsibility is assumed by those who decide to send the weapon into battle" (p. 69).
- *Programmers/designers* are accountable, if they are negligent, but autonomous weapons are designed to make choices, act on them, and learn from experience, making them increasingly independent. Ultimately, "the connection between the programmers/designers ... is broken by the autonomy of the system" (p. 70).
- *Commanding officer.* This person is generally held accountable but autonomy makes LAWS different from other weapons. They are "smart" weapons and "the autonomy of the machine implies that its orders do not determine ... its actions" (p. 71).
- *LAWS.* A machine can cause someone's death but "[w]e typically [balk] at the idea that they could be morally responsible." Besides, "in order to be able to hold a machine morally responsible for its actions it must be possible for us to imagine punishing or rewarding it. Yet how would we go about punishing or rewarding a machine?" (p. 71).

Favor a Ban

Sparrow (2007) concludes that "for the foreseeable future then, the deployment of weapon systems controlled by artificial intelligences in warfare is therefore unfair either to potential casualties ... or to the officer who will be held accountable" (p. 75).

Oppose a Ban

Steinhoff (2013) takes issue with Sparrow saying,

> [I]t is intuitively quite implausible to assume that a just war becomes unjust the moment a single person is killed in a way that does not confer moral responsibility on anyone.... Sparrow's argument cannot refute the view that at least the use of some automated weapons in war ... can be justified [p. 182].

He is, however, willing to assign moral responsibility to the politicians who vote for and fund the development and use of LAWS.

Thurnher (2012) is not willing to make "autonomous" a synonym for "wild and crazy."

Even though a system is designed to operate autonomously, it would presumably be given specific orders from its headquarters about what types of missions it would be directed to accomplish.... As long as the types of targets and missions assigned to LARs [lethal autonomous robots] are valid military objectives, the LARs would be in compliance with the principle of necessity when engaging those targets [p. 80].

Lokhorst and van den Hoven (2012) contend that Sparrow is mistaken to claim LAWS cannot be held morally responsible because they cannot suffer from punishment.

[I]t is important to make a distinction between the means and the ends. Punishment is simply one means that may lead to the desired end [to stop killing innocent people]; it is not desirable in itself. If other courses of action are more effective, they are ipso facto preferable [p. 149].

Security Concerns: Starting War

As the deployment of fully autonomous weapons might lead to fewer casualties in one's own army, fully autonomous weapons could lower the threshold to go to war. Also, it reduces the incentive for finding political solutions to end conflicts.

Favor a Ban

In an interview with the International Review of the Red Cross, Peter Singer stated,

[N]ow we have a technology that enables us to carry out acts of what we previously would have thought of as war without having to wrestle with some of the potential political costs of sending a son or daughter into harm's way [Bernard, 2012, p. 471].

Lowering our own costs and reducing our own casualties also mitigate the political risk of waging war as compared with the costs of waging traditional wars. As a result, there would be fewer incentives for using diplomacy and other peaceful methods to avoid war. The result is that war would become more commonplace and would ultimately destabilize the international system.

Although Singer admits that "the barriers to war in our society were already lowering before this technology came along," he doesn't discount the impact of LAWS on that trend.

This new technology, though, may take those barriers to the ground. This is not just a notion of political theory. It relates to our oldest ideals of how democracies are better, more honourable, more thoughtful when it comes to war [Bernard, 2012, p. 471].

Oppose a Ban

Rabkin and Yoo (2017) take the opposite positions. They say, "Instability is spreading throughout the world" (p. 30) and point to the conflicts that are springing up in Asia, Eastern Europe, Africa, and the Middle East. It is their view that the use of small, accurate, and less destructive weapons will have a positive impact on global stability.

With these weapons available, we should see nations settle more disputes by negotiation rather than by escalation.... New weapons provide states with the means to exert pressure at lower levels of destruction and casualties, which provides ... more opportunities to divert from escalation to settlement" [pp. 35, 56].

They reject Singer's dire prediction that LAWS will virtually eliminate the barriers to war.

> The ability to use force more precisely will prove a benefit to the international system. The signaling of resolve and capability through less destructive attacks can help avoid the worldwide conflicts that caused such grave human suffering and death in the twentieth century.
> Ironically, the availability of new weapons technologies should reduce the chances of great power war and lead to more settlement of conflicts [p. 56].

This new technology could lead to a new international arms race which would have destabilizing effects and threaten international peace and security.

SECURITY CONCERNS: PROLIFERATION

An arms race has already begun. In fact, it may already be in full stride. As mentioned earlier, there are at least sixty countries and international organizations (e.g., NATO) that already have aerial drone technology. China, Russia, U.S., South Korea, and NATO are among those with active R&D programs pushing towards LAWS.

These efforts are encouraged and supported by national and international competitions. For example, the DARPA Challenges described in this chapter and in the Non-Humanoids chapter have promoted autonomy in both humanoid and non-humanoid robots. China's annual RoboMasters is an international competition that pits teams of robots against each other on a battlefield. Some challenges involve autonomy, such as the "computer vision challenge, where teams had to autonomously track and strike a rapidly moving target" (Popper, 2016). The annual Robot Challenge Competition, headquartered in Vienna, Austria, is a non-governmental competition that describes itself as "one of the biggest competitions for self-made, autonomous and mobile robots worldwide" (Robot Challenge, n.d.).

Favor a Ban

Possibly the most famous proponents of banning LAWS based on concerns about an arms race are almost 4,000 researchers and roboticists. Their 2015 open letter, "Autonomous Weapons: An Open Letter from AI & Robotics Researchers" (Autonomous Weapons, 2015), proposed a ban based on concerns about having an arms race leading to widespread access to and use of LAWS. They fear that it would cause global destabilization and a major threat to security (Autonomous Weapons, 2015). A second letter was sent on August 20, 2017, to the chair of the UN Group of Governmental Experts on LAWS (GGE). It urged the GGE to stop the arms race in LAWS. It was signed by 115 scientists and corporate leaders in robotics and artificial intelligence.

Gubrud (2016) considers the development of individual LAWS as the proverbial tip of a much larger iceberg that includes "highly automated battle networks" and systems of autonomous weapons that include components as small as nanobots: "Autonomous weapons are a salient point of departure in a technology-fueled arms race that puts everyone in danger. That is why I believe we need to ban them as fast and as hard as we possibly can."

Oppose a Ban

Ackerman (2015) believes an arms race is unavoidable and links the inevitability of an arms race to proliferation which results from commercial success. Even if military R&D

of LAWS were to stop, there would still be strong pressure to develop commercial, autonomous robots using cheap, off-the-shelf components. As far as Ackerman is concerned, no letter, UN action, or ban would stop this development.

There's simply too much commercial value in creating quadcopters (and other robots) that have longer endurance, more autonomy, bigger payloads, and everything else that you'd also want in a military system. And at this point, it's entirely possible that small commercial quadcopters are just as advanced as (and way cheaper than) small military quadcopters, anyway.

Anderson and Waxman (2013) maintain that an arms race was inevitable because

the United States has never been alone in pursuing these capabilities, the technologies of which are a function of advanced automation in many aspects of life, and it is a dangerous mistake to believe that it could have kept such capabilities in the box by foregoing them [p. 6].

Thurnher (2012) strongly believes the U.S. must maintain its lead in LAWS and related technologies. "To prevent being surpassed by rivals, the United States should fully commit itself to harnessing the potential of fully autonomous targeting" (p. 83). Robert Work, Deputy Secretary of Defense under President Obama, agreed, saying it's important for the U.S. to "dominate" machine learning and artificial intelligence to offset the imposing threats posed by China and Russia (Muoio, 2015).

Security Concerns: Escalation

These weapons could lead to rapid escalation of conflict as they would react to and interact with each other at speeds faster than humans can react or control. The speed of interactions is often expressed in terms of the Observe, Orient, Decide, Act cycle, which is usually called the "OODA loop."

The commander or executive who can figure out a situation, decide how to proceed, and execute that decision will normally keep his opponent in a reactive state that eventually leads to the disintegration of the opponent's ability to compete. The idea is called "getting inside the adversary's OODA Loop" [Riza, 2013, p. 41].

Militaries expect the speed of all aspects of warfare to increase. In 2009, the U.S. Air Force included the following in its report *Unmanned Aircraft Systems Flight Plan 2009–2047.*

In 2047 technology will be able to reduce the time to complete the OODA loop to micro or nanoseconds.... UAS [unmanned aircraft systems] will be able to react at these speeds and therefore this loop moves towards becoming a "perceive and act" vector. Increasingly humans will no longer be "in the loop" but rather "on the loop" [see Non-Humanoids chapter]—monitoring the execution of certain decisions [United States Air Force, 2009, p. 41].

Favor a Ban

To those seeking to ban LAWS, the idea of calmly ceding control to machines is deeply disturbing. The "Second Call to Ban" by the International Committee on Autonomous Robot Control (Altmann & Sauer, 2016) provides an example of why this is the case.

The problem is that an erroneous "counter" attack could be triggered by a sun glint in visual data misinterpreted as a rocket flame, sudden, unforeseen moves of the enemy swarm, or a simple software bug. That could then lead to a counter-attack of the other side, with fast escalation from crisis to war.

In his interview with Ari Shapiro, Paul Scharre links unpredictable behavior resulting from the interaction of autonomous systems with the speed of those interactions. Borrowing the term "flash crash" from a comparable situation in stock-market trading, he calls the result "flash wars," adding that "the fear is that we'd see something similar in warfare where countries automate decisions on the battlefield, taking humans out of the loop because there's an advantage in speed" (Shapiro & Scharre, 2018).

Oppose a Ban

Anderson and Waxman (2013) point out that all aspects of war are speeding up, including systems in piloted aircraft.

> Just as the aircraft might have to be maneuvered far too quickly for detailed human control of its movements, so too the weapons—against other aircraft, UAVs, anti-aircraft systems—might have to be utilized at the same speeds in order to match the beyond-human speed of the aircraft's own systems [p. 5].

Adams (2001 [2011]) puts this trend into a societal perspective. Looking further into the future, he adds with enthusiasm that

> [h]umans may retain symbolic authority but automated systems move too fast and the factors involved are too complex for real human comprehension.... [T]he new systems will enable people to accomplish far more in war and peace than was even conceivable before their development, or ... is even conceivable now [p. 12].

Security Concerns: Terrorism

In contrast to, for example, nuclear weapons, the technology would be relatively cheap and simple to copy. This would mean there is a big chance of proliferation. It would be highly undesirable if dictators, non-state armed actors or terrorists would be able to acquire these weapons.

The explosion of commercial RPDs has fueled wide availability of such devices. Non-state groups had used them for several years. ISIS, for example, purchased Chinese commercial drones, weaponized them, and used them against U.S. forces (Hambling, 2015a). Hezbollah launched Iranian-made drones against Israel (Fields, 2012). In 2015, a gun enthusiast mounted a 9mm handgun on a drone along with a "high-resolution camera, precision gyroscopes for aiming accuracy and a powerful accumulator for long-range activity" that, when combined, "produce the ideal terminator: nameless, faceless and with no strings attached" (Gunslinger Drone, 2015). As mentioned in Part II: Criminals, Mexican federal police found an armed drone in a vehicle driven by members of a drug cartel (Kryt, 2017).

As reported by Ari Shapiro (Shapiro & Scharre, 2018), Paul Scharre is seeing the same thing happen with software and hardware for autonomous systems. "These tools are available for free download. You can download them online. [It] took me about three minutes online to find all of the free tools you would need to download this technology and make it happen."

Favor a Ban

Fields (2012) points out that proliferation of RPDs and LAWS puts civilian populations at risk for attacks by terrorists using those technologies. Aware of that, Sauer (2016) asserts that LAWS must be banned now because the "vibrant global ecosystem of unmanned vehicles ... is a technical challenge but doable for state and nonstate actors."

Oppose a Ban

Vilmer (2016) believes that "civilian progress in the field of artificial intelligence and self-learning may anyway put these technologies on the market and therefore into military hands, making such a ban ineffective." How can you ban something that anyone could download from the Internet for free? A ban will not stop anyone who wants the technology from getting, developing, and using it. It would, however, make those nations that comply with the ban vulnerable to those that don't.

Scharre is concerned about what we do about this emerging proliferation and the potential to weaponize autonomous technology.

What are some options going forward? I think there are ways to think about narrower regulations that might be more feasible to avert some of the most harmful consequences. Maybe a more narrow ban on weapons that target people. And there has been some discussions [sic] underway internationally in trying to frame—reframe the issue and think about, what is the role of humans in warfare? [Shapiro & Scharre, 2018].

SECURITY CONCERNS: OVERSIGHT

Only a small number of people are needed to deploy a large number of autonomous weapons, raising concerns of prevention, oversight and control. The expectation is that some LAWS, like RPDs, will be small weapons that can easily be programmed and used by a single individual or a small group. This makes oversight extremely difficult. This situation presents oversight problems for those favoring a ban as well as for those who oppose one.

Favor a Ban

Sparrow (2016) holds that, without a ban or another type of limitation, it would be easy for rogue states and non-state groups to obtain and weaponize commercial autonomous devices—as some of them have already done with remotely piloted, commercial drones. He also dismisses another kind of oversight without a ban: humans monitoring the ethical behavior of LAWS.

This is problematic for two reasons. First, the need to "phone home" for ethical reassurance would mitigate two of the main military advantages of autonomous weapons, which are their capacity to make decisions more rapidly than human beings can and their capacity to operate in contexts where it is difficult to establish and maintain reliable communications to a human pilot [p. 13].

Oppose a Ban

Scharre and Horowitz (2015) point out that oversight of a ban on LAWS would be dangerous as well as challenging.

If autonomous weapons turn out to be useful, *someone* will build them. Even if all of the major military powers agree to a ban, rogue states like Syria or North Korea are hardly interested in international goodwill, to say nothing of terrorist organizations. This means that whatever weapons are "allowed," they need to be sufficiently capable to defeat the weapons of those who "cheat." A disarmament regime that resulted in the most unsavory states having the upper hand in a conflict would hardly be a satisfactory outcome.

Even if the international community is able to craft a ban on just the use of LAWS, there is no guarantee that the signatories would abide by any of its provisions. Evidence for this comes from history. The 1916 international resolution (cited earlier) against using aerial war against "the persons or property of the peaceful population" did not prevent warring nations from bombing major cities during the two world wars. Similarly, CWC signatories have not only developed and stockpiled chemical weapons; they have proven that they are willing to use them. The most striking example is Syria, whose president signed the CWC on September 14, 2013, and "sent a letter to the United Nations Secretary General…. In the letter, Assad said Syria would observe its CWC obligations immediately, as opposed to 30 days from the date of accession, as stipulated in the treaty" (Kimball & Davenport, 2018). Syria reportedly used chemical weapons against its citizens several times since then, including three attacks during the first quarter of 2018.

Security Concerns: Fueling Revenge

Like ARPDs (autonomous remotely piloted drones), deploying LAWS instead of human soldiers can be a cause of hatred among the population of the targeted state. The moral outrage this creates works against the attacking state's interests.

Favor a Ban

Exum et al. (2009) asserts that "every one of these dead non-combatants represents an alienated family, a new revenge feud, and more recruits for a militant movement that has grown exponentially even as drone strikes have increased" (p. 18).

In a 2013 article published in *The Atlantic*, Greenfield cites polls by the Pew Research Center which reveal that, in 2009, 64 percent of Pakistanis considered the U.S. to be an enemy, but by 2012 that percentage had risen to 74.

> In short, the US drone program not only undermines the long-term national security of the United States by fostering widespread anti–US sentiment, it also undermines the legitimacy of the host country [sic] government, whose support the US needs, and it provides fodder for jihadi rhetoric that strengthens the very groups the US seeks to destroy [Greenfield, 2013].

In *Wired for War* (2009b), P.W. Singer recasts Greenfield's concerns into cultural terms. After citing Arthur C. Clarke's (1973) third law: "Any sufficiently advanced technology is indistinguishable from magic" (p. 300), he tells the following story.

Drones and Cookies

[A]n official with the U.S. military's Joint Special Operations Command recounted a meeting with elders in the tribal region of Pakistan, the area where al-Qaeda leaders were reputed to be hiding out and the site of more than fifty drones [sic] strikes from 2006 through 2008. One of the elders was enamored of the sweet-tasting bread that was served to them at the meeting. He, however, went on to tell how the Americans had to be working with forces of "evil," because of the way that their enemies were being killed from afar, in a way that was almost inexplicable. "They must have the power of the devil behind them." As the official recounted with a wry chuckle, "You have a guy who's never eaten a cookie before. Of course, he's going to see a drone as like the devil, as like black magic" (p. 300).

According to Singer (2009b), the elder's perception is not as funny as the official thinks. Rather than exposing the ignorance of the elder, it highlights the ignorance and arrogance of the U.S. military and civilian leadership. Attempts to woo the elder and others like him that do not take into account their culture are destined to fail. After all, anyone who is in league with the devil or other dark forces is unlikely to inspire friendship or support.

Oppose a Ban

Most polls done of Pakistanis show that they are strongly opposed to the U.S. drone-strike program—even in areas not affected by drone strikes. The same polls also show that they have no love for the Taliban and al Qaeda, either (Al Jazeera, 2009; International Republican Institute, 2009; New America Foundation & Terror Free Tomorrow, 2010). In their summary analysis of their poll, the New America Foundation & Terror Free Tomorrow reported,

> What is interesting about our findings, however, is that the intense opposition to the US military and the drone program is *not* based on general anti–American feelings. Almost three-quarters of the people inside the tribal regions said that their opinion of the United States would improve if the U.S. increased visas for FATA residents ... withdrew the American military from Afghanistan or brokered a comprehensive peace between Israelis and Palestinians.

LANGUAGE

In addition to the PAX list, there are concerns related to the idea of banning LAWS. The fact that fully autonomous LAWS don't really exist is one of them. That issue was identified at the start of this chapter.

Another divisive factor is the language used to describe the technology and actions under consideration. Language is a sticking point that is hindering the movement to ban or regulate LAWS. According to Lucas (2013), "much of the dispute between proponents and critics of enhanced machine autonomy is mired in a nearly hopeless kind of conceptual confusion and linguistic equivocation" (p. 217).

The following definitions from The U.S. DoD *Directive 3000.09* (United States Department of Defense, 2012 [2017]) are used by military, political, and other agents involved in international regulatory discussions.

Autonomous weapon system. A weapon system that, once activated, can select and engage targets without further intervention by a human operator. This includes human-supervised autonomous weapon systems that are designed to allow human operators to override operation of the weapon system, but can select and engage targets without further human input after activation (pp. 13–14).

Semi-autonomous weapon system. A weapon system that, once activated, is intended to only engage individual targets or specific target groups that have been selected by a human operator. This includes:

> semi-autonomous weapon systems that employ autonomy for engagement-related functions including, but not limited to, acquiring, tracking, and identifying potential targets; cueing potential targets to human operators; prioritizing selected targets; timing of when to fire; or providing terminal guidance to home in on selected targets, provided that human control is retained over the decision to select individual targets and specific target groups for engagement [p. 14].

Welsh (2017) and Crootof (2015) offer different approaches to further define these and other core terms and the concepts which they embody. Welsh begins by separating "selection/targeting" from "engagement/attack," two core functions of LAWS that are not clearly delineated in the U.S. DoD definitions above. Each function has its own set of "loops" based on the well established human-weapon relationships: "human-in-the-loop," "human-on-the-loop," and "human-off-the-loop" that were described in the Non-Humanoids chapter.

Crootof's (2015) definition of "autonomous weapons system" derives from the strengths and weaknesses of existing definitions, including those in the 2012 [2017] U.S. DoD Directive. Her definition of "autonomous weapons system" is "a weapon system that, based on conclusions derived from gathered information and preprogrammed constraints, is capable of independently selecting and engaging targets" (p. 1842). She then delineates the underlying meaning of each phrase in the definition. For example, for "based on conclusions derived from gathered information and preprogrammed constraints" she posits that "[t]his clause attempts to distinguish between 'automated' and 'autonomous' weapon systems" (p. 1855) and then proceeds to specify those differences.

Linguistic and conceptual disambiguations like those proposed by Welsh and Crootof can help establish a common basis for deliberations on how to handle LAWS. The diverse and opposing views expressed regarding concerns on the PAX list indicate that creating that common basis will not be easy.

Glossary

Actuator: A small motor that powers a movable component of a robotic device.

Anime: A style of animation or animated cartoon on television and in film that uses the same types of stories and the same drawing style found in **manga**.

Autonomous: The ability of a robot or robot-precursor to move itself with intention. A device has full autonomy when it controls all of its actions without external help. It is semi-autonomous when some functions are autonomous but others are externally controlled. In this book, "human-like" autonomy refers to the broad-based autonomy possessed by humans and other biological creatures (see the Introduction).

Campaign: Term used frequently in games to refer to the setting in which adventures of a **role-playing game** take place. Games may have multiple campaigns.

Construct: Term used frequently in games to refer to an artificial creature. They are a kind of robot-precursor. "Constructs are made, not born. Some are programmed by their creators to follow a simple set of instructions, while others are imbued with sentience and capable of independent thought" (Crawford, 2018, p. 6).

CWC: Acronym for Chemical Weapons Convention, a treaty banning the use, development, production, acquisition, stockpiling, and retention of chemical weapons.

D&D: Acronym for the table-top, role-playing game Dungeons & Dragons. Also DnD.

DARPA: Acronym for U.S. Defense Advanced Research Projects Agency.

DoD: Acronym for U.S. Department of Defense.

EU: European Union.

Franchise: Similar to **Universe** with focus on "the brand," notably commercial activities and revenue (e.g., Terminator franchise).

Fully autonomous: See **Autonomous**.

Hack and Slash Game (or Hack and Slay Game): A game that emphasizes combat.

Homunculus (Homunculi): A small artificial being shaped like a human and often looking exactly like a human. Homunculi originated in folklore but are most strongly linked to alchemy. They are often characters in contemporary media, notably manga and anime.

Human-like autonomy: See **Autonomous**.

IED: Acronym for Improvised Explosive Device.

IHL: Acronym for **International Humanitarian Law**.

International Humanitarian Law (IHL): A set of laws sometimes called the "laws of war" that are designed to protect non-combatants and non-military property during military conflicts. IHL is not the same as Humanitarian Rights Law, which is designed to provide similar protections in peacetime. IHL is important to discussions about banning LAWS (see Part II: Furor: Making Robots Moral and Part III: Furor: LAWS).

ISR: Acronym for Intelligence, Surveillance, and Reconnaissance work.

LAWS: Acronym for Lethal Autonomous Weapons Systems. One of the names given to fully autonomous, robotic weapons systems.

Laws of War (LOW): A synonym for **International Humanitarian Law**.

LOW: Acronym for the **Laws of War**.

Manga: A style of graphic novel strongly associated with Japan and, in particular, with artist Osamu Tezuka, who was strongly influenced by the drawing techniques used by Walt Disney and in Betty Boop. The stories vary with regard to audience. Some are made for children but most include adult themes (e.g., social issues). An anime is generally drawn using vibrant colors. The characters are generally drawn with childlike faces that have large eyes and small mouths. Manga stories are often made into **anime**.

Mecha: A type of anime story that features extremely large, piloted robots that often battle each other.

ONR: Acronym for U.S. Office of Naval Research.

R&D: Acronym for Research and Development.

Remotely controlled (also Remote-control): A robot or robot-precursor that is controlled by an external source, usually a human.

Remotely piloted: Synonym for **Remotely controlled**.

ROE: Acronym for **Rules of Engagement**.

Role-Playing Game (RPG): A game in which each player selects a character to play (thus, their role) throughout the adventures in the game. Game play is driven by stories and the player must behave as the character would in those stories. Role-playing games are generally tabletop games like D&D.

RPD: Acronym for **Remotely Piloted** Drone.

RPG: Acronym for **Role-Playing Game**.

Rules of Engagement (ROE): Rules that specify when, how, and against whom military force may be used. ROE are discussed in Part III: LAWS.

Semi-autonomous: See **Autonomous**.

UK: United Kingdom.

UN: United Nations.

Universe: When applied to entertainment, it refers to content, media and products related to a particular brand (e.g., Terminator Universe). Emphasis is on content and characters.

U.S.: United States.

Warfighter: Generic name for someone who engages in combat during a military conflict.

WH40K: Acronym for the tabletop role-playing game Warhammer 40,000.

Notes

Part I

REVENGE

1. This Spanish legend has been adapted and retold many times including Tirso de Molina's *El Burlador de Sevilla y Convidado de Piedra,* first performed in 1616 and published in 1630; Molière's *Le Festin de Pierre,* first performed in 1665 and published in 1683; Mozart's *Don Giovanni* (1787); George Gordon (Lord) Byron's *Don Juan* (1822); and Alexander Pushkin's *Kamennyy gost* (1830).

2. Translation by the author.

GREED

1. In the U.S., this book was published in 1941 by Ferrar and Rinehart as *Escape from Freedom.*

2. The first robot capable of responding to speech was "Radio Rex," a toy marketed in 1920—twenty years after Le Rouge and Guitton published their book. "Rex was a brown bulldog made of celluloid and metal that appeared to respond to its name by leaping out of its house. The dog was controlled by a spring held in check by an electromagnet. The electromagnet was sensitive to sound patterns ... around 500Hz, such as the vowel in 'Rex.' ... Unfortunately, like many of its flesh-and-bone counterparts, Rex tended to remain stubbornly in its house despite the entreaties of its owner" (Markowitz, 2013, pp. 11–12).

3. According to Webster's New Universal Unabridged Dictionary, the term *deus ex machina* (2003) refers to "any artificial or improbable device resolving the difficulties of a plot" (p. 542). The expression comes from ancient Greek and Roman drama which sometimes introduced a god (*deus*) at the end of the play who suddenly appears to provide the final outcome of the entanglements in the play. The statue or actor representing the god was lowered onto the stage using a pulley or other equipment (*ex machina*).

4. There is disagreement about whether the annihilants in the movie serial were robots or humans wearing metallic uniforms. In the comic strip they are shown to be human when they remove their helmets. That never occurs in the movie serial giving the impression that the annihilants were robots.

5. Translation: And in the year 2000, the Cybermen released the computer virus that destroyed all the vowels.

FUROR: ROBOTS AS JOB KILLERS

1. The data referred to by Yang can be found at https://www.bls.gov/news.release/mslo.t02.htm.

Part II

CRIMINALS

1. Yod (׳) is the tenth letter of the Hebrew alphabet. It is the first letter of the four-letter Tetragrammaton (YHWY י ה ו ה) representing the name of God. In astrology, it is a triangular configuration of three planets, sometimes called the "finger of God" that produces unusual situations and personalities.

ENFORCERS

1. Dr. Hiroshi Ishiguro is a real-world roboticist who has made an android copy of himself.

2. That isn't always the case. Several years ago, military pilots refused to undergo retina scans for fear their eyesight would be affected.

FUROR: MAKING ROBOTS MORAL

1. Other objections are discussed in the chapter Part III: Furor: LAWS.

Part III

HUMANOIDS

1. For more information on this practice, see Military Penal Unit (2017).

2. In the DC Comics Universe, the name Cadmus brings to mind the fictional Project Cadmus which specialized in cloning. A number of U.S. organizations have been inspired to name themselves after Cadmus. The U.S. consulting firm Cadmus Group selected its name because Cadmus "brought the alphabet to Greece, founded one of the great city-states, and became renowned for his wisdom and advice" (Cadmus, n.d.).

3. The name "Amok" and the expression "run amok" come from the Amok warriors living on the Malabar Coast along the southwestern shore of the Indian subcontinent. They were feared because their behavior on the battlefield was akin to that of the Berserks in Scandinavia (Speidel, 2002, p. 287).

4. The professor's first name is virtually identical to that of Maestro Geppetto, the wood carver who creates the Pinocchio puppet in *The Adventures of Pinocchio* (Collodi, 1883 [1972]). He shares his family name with Giuseppe Garibaldi, the Italian military leader and nationalist who was the driving force behind the unification of Italy in 1871.

5. Caterina Sforza (1462/63–1509). Oxford Bibliographies writes, "Sforza's political cunning and forceful rule fascinated many in early modern Italy, including Niccolò Machiavelli (de Vries, 2018). According to Elizabeth Lev, Sforza's biographer, "Machiavelli, never particularly respectful of women, wrote especially insidiously about her. As a young man he had had direct dealings with Caterina and had not come out the better" (Lev, 2012, p. viii).

6. "Traditionally, mecha was used to describe anything mechanical in Japan, from cars, toasters, and radios to computers and yes, even robots. The term has since been adapted (mostly in the West) to mean 'robot anime' and is used to describe anime and manga series that center around robotic elements" (Luther, 2017).

7. The English-language version of the *Macross* series in all media is called *Robotech* (Macek & Agrama, 1985–, ongoing).

8. This portion of the chapter is intended to provide a general overview of military robots. Here are sources that provide more in-depth information: The History of Military Robots (n.d.); DARPA (2015); Everett (2015) *Unmanned Systems*; Jacobsen (2015) *The Pentagon's Brain*; Naval Studies Board (2005) *Autonomous Vehicles*; Singer (2009b) *Wired for War*; and Springer (2013) *Military Robots and Drones*. Another good resource is DARPA.mil, the website for DARPA.

9. The other areas are: interoperability and modularity; communication systems, spectrum, and resilience; security (research and intelligence/technology protection; persistent resilience; and weaponry.

Non-Humanoids

1. There is a legend that the V gesture for victory comes from longbow archers; this is repeated on the website of the Royal Shakespeare Theater as part of its announcement of its production of *The Life of Henry the Fifth* (Shakespeare, 1623 [2010]).

It is often told that the French would cut off the two arrow-shooting fingers of the English and Welsh longbow men that they captured, and the gesture was a sign of defiance on the part of the bowmen, showing the enemy that they still had their fingers. (Our Production of Shakespeare's Henry V, 2015).

Alas, there appears to be no primary-source evidence supporting this story (Curry, 2015).

2. Cohen no doubt meant "the *prospect* of being killed...."

3. Scharre (2014a) lists other benefits as well, such as "stealthy operations" that could not be done by non-robotic devices.

4. J.R.R. Tolkien wrote an adaptation of this saga in which Kullervo is renamed Túrin Turambar and Ukko is Gurthang ("Iron death"). The story appears in *The Silmarillon* (Tolkien, 1977).

5. "!" is a click produced by the tongue against the molars, made with the lips pulled back in a grimace. "*" is the same sound, but made with the lips pursed for a whistle (p. 14). Later in the book, it is revealed that the pattern has multiple layers of meaning including, "We exist" and "We who shape the cosmos."

6. Additional sources that provide more in-depth information include: The History of Military Robots (n.d.); Everett (2015) *Unmanned Systems of World Wars I & II*; Jacobsen (2015) *The Pentagon's Brain*; Naval Studies Board (2005) Autonomous Vehicles in Support of Naval Operations; Scharre (2014b) The Coming Swarm Singer (2009b) *Wired for War*; and Springer (2013) *Military Robots and Drones: A Reference Handbook*. Websites include DARPA.mil, NavyLive.dod, the official blog of the U.S. Navy; and the Unmanned Warrior annual war games hosted by the Royal Navy of the U.K., https://www.royalnavy.mod.uk.

Humans

1. Iyer (2017) states, "Etymology suggests that the word Vishpala refers to 'Ruler (or head) of a settlement'" (loc. 237) which is why she is called "Queen Vishpala." There is virtually nothing written about Queen Vishpala other than this story. Scholars disagree about whether she is a real historical figure or a product of mythology. One fifteenth century Indian scholar calls Vishpala a warrior queen in battle. According to Iyer, twentieth-century Vedic analyst Karl Friedrich Geldner interprets the story as being about a horse running a race but most scholars believe she was a human woman.

2. Machine-phase matter (also "machine phase nanotechnology) is an area of real-world research. Although he's not talking about a weapon, Drexler (1986) echoes and expands upon John Connor/T-3000's words: "Such a system would not be a liquid or gas, as no molecules would move randomly, nor would it be a solid, in which molecules are fixed in place. Instead this new machine-phase matter would exhibit the molecular movement seen today only in liquids and gases as well as the mechanical strength typically associated with solids."

3. For more information on these topics consult: Naval Studies Board (2005) *Autonomous Vehicles in Support of Naval Operations;* Singer (2009b) *Wired for War;* Springer (2013) *Military Robots and Drones;* Everett (2015) *Unmanned Systems;* Jacobsen (2015b) *The Pentagon's Brain;* The History of Military Robots (n.d.), and www.DARPA.mil.

4. The first article of clothing consisting of smart fabric was a T-shirt made at the Georgia Institute of Technology in 1999. It was named the "wearable motherboard" because it had sensors embedded in the fabric. It spawned the smart-fabric industry that has applications in healthcare and sports as well as in the military. The wearable motherboard T-shirt now resides in the Smithsonian Institution (Georgia Institute of Technology, n.d.; Gopalsamy, et al., 1999).

Furor: LAWS

1. A paper jointly authored by Kashner and Plaw (Kashner & Plaw, 2013) adds other dimensions to the application of IHL, particularly the principle of distinction. One dimension is whether IHL should be revisited and revised to properly address new technologies (e.g., LAWS).

2. For additional perspectives on Just War Theory see Walzer (1977) and Hallgarth (2013).

Bibliography

Aboy, C. (2016). New "Iron Man" Special Forces Exoskeleton Stops Bullets with Liquid Armor. *Futurism* [Online], 6 June 2016. Retrieved from https://futurism.com/2018-will-be-big-on-special-forces-exoskeleton-tech/.

Ackerman, E. (2015). We Should Not Ban "Killer Robots," and Here's Why. *IEEE Spectrum* [Online], 29 July 2015. Retrieved from https://spectrum.ieee.org/automaton/robotics/artificial-intelligence/we-should-not-ban-killer-robots.

Adams, T.K. (2001 [2011]). Future Warfare and the Decline of Human Decision-Making. *Parameters, 31*(4): 57–71 [*Parameters* [Online], 41(4): 1–15.]

Aeschylus (ca. 5th century BCE [1926]). *Eumenides*. n.p. [*Aeschylus* (Vols. 145 & 146). (H.W. Smith, Trans.). Cambridge, MA: Loeb Classical Library.] Retrieved from http://www.theoi.com/Text/AeschylusEumenides.html.

AFP News Agency (2014). *Talking Robots Take Control of Kinshasa's Traffic Problems* [Video file], 18 Feb. 2014. Retrieved from https://www.youtube.com/watch?v=xauw5VYUSuc.

Al Jazeera (2009). Pakistan: State of the Nation. Doha, Qatar: Author. Retrieved from http://www.aljazeera.com/focus/2009/08/2009888238994769.html.

Alien (1979). Directed by R. Scott [Film]. Los Angeles, CA: Twentieth Century–Fox.

Allanson, D., Darling, A., Gardner, C., & Lowson, I. (2002). The Official Star Wars Fact File: R2-D2. www.starwars.wikia.com [Wiki], 6 March 2002. Retrieved from http://starwars.wikia.com/wiki/R2-D2/Legends.

Altmann, J. & Sauer, F. (2016). Speed Kills! Why We Need to Hit the Brakes on "Killer Robots." ICRAC.net [Online], 8 April 2016. Retrieved 20 Nov. 2017 from https://icrac.net/2016/04/speed-kills-why-we-need-to-hit-the-brakes-on-killer-robots/.

Anders, C.J. (2015). *The Complete Guide to Every Single Terminator, from T-1 to T-3000* [Video file], 1 July 2015. Retrieved from https://io9.gizmodo.com/the-complete-guide-to-every-single-terminator-from-t-1-1715240162.

Anderson, K. & Waxman, M.C. (2013). *Law and Ethics for Autonomous Weapon Systems: Why a Ban Won't Work and How the Laws of War Can* (WCL Research Paper 2013–11; Columbia Public Law Research Paper 13–351) (Jean Perkins Task Force on National Security and Law Essay Series), Stanford, CA: The Hoover Institution, Stanford University. Retrieved from http//ssrn.com/abstract=2250126.

Anderson, S.L. (2008). Asimov's "Three Laws of Robotics" and Machine Metaethics. *AI & Society, 22*(4): 477–493. Retrieved from https://www.aaai.org/Papers/Symposia/Fall/2005/FS-05–06/FS05-06-002.pdf.

Annihilator (2002). *Robot Wars: Extreme Warriors* [Television series episode]. TNN (Season 2, episode 10), 8 June 2002.

Anthony, S. (2011). Lovotics, The New Science of Human-Robot Love. *Extreme Tech* [Online], 30 June 2011. Retrieved from http://www.extremetech.com/extreme/88740-lovotics-the-new-science-of-human-robot-love.

Anvil, C. (1966 [2003]). Strangers to Paradise. *Analog Science Fiction, 78*(2): 8–48. [In E. Flint (Ed.). *Interstellar Patrol* (pp. 7–49). Riverdale, NY: Baen Publishing Enterprises]. Retrieved from http://www.baen.com/chapters/W200304/0743436008.htm?blurb.

Arakawa, H. (2001–2010). *Fullmetal Alchemist*. Tokyo, Japan: Square Enix.

Arcadia (1999). *X Files* [Television series episode]. Fox (Season 6, episode 15), 7 March 1999.

Arce, N. (2014). 46 Percent of Britons Think Technology Evolves Too Fast, 17 Percent Will Have Sex with Robots. *Tech Times* [Online], 6 May 2014. Retrieved from http://www.techtimes.com/articles/6568/20140506/46-percent-of-britons-think-technology-evolves-too-fast-17-percent-will-have-sex-with-robots.htm.

Arkin, R. (2007). *Governing Lethal Behavior: Embedding Ethics in a Hybrid Reactive/Deliberative Robot Architecture*. Technical Report No. GIT-GVU-07–11. Atlanta, GA: College of Computing, Georgia Tech University. Retrieved from https://www.cc.gatech.edu/ai/robot-lab/online-publications/formalizationv35.pdf.

Arkin, R. (2008). Governing Lethal Behavior: Embedding Ethics in a Hybrid Deliberative/Reactive Robot Architecture, Part I. In *Proceedings of the 3rd International Conference on Human Robot Interaction*, Amsterdam, The Netherlands, 12–15 May 2008 (pp. 121–128). New York: ACM.

Arkin, R. (2009). *Governing Lethal Behavior in Autonomous Robots*. Boca Raton, FL: CRC Press.

Arkin, R. (2015). Counterpoint: Ronald Arkin. *Communications of the ACM, 58*(12): 46–47.

Armitage, N. (2015). European and African Figural Ritual Magic: The Beginnings of the Voodoo Doll Myth. In C. Houlbrook & N. Armitage (Eds.). *The Materiality of Magic: An Artifactual Investigation into Ritual Practices and Popular Beliefs* (pp. 85–101). Oxford, England: Oxbow Press.

As You Like It (ca. 1633) [Play]. Book by W. Shakespeare.

Asimov, I. (1942 [1983]). Runaround. *Astounding Science Fiction, 29*(1): 94–103. [In I. Asimov, P.S. Warrick & M.H. Greenberg (Eds.). *Machines That Think: The Best Science Fiction Stories about Robots and Computers* (pp. 209–232). New York: Holt, Rinehart and Winston.]

Asimov, I. (1950). Liar! In I. Asimov (Ed.), *I, Robot* (pp. 91–111). New York: Doubleday.

Asimov, I. (1954). *Caves of Steel.* New York: Doubleday.

Asimov, I. (1968). *The Rest of the Robots.* London: Grafton Books.

Asimov, I. (1976). Bicentennial Man. In J.L. del Ray (Ed.), *Stellar #2: Science Fiction Stories* (pp. 85–129). New York: Ballantine Books.

Asimov, I. (1978). The Machine and the Robot. In P.S. Warrick, M.H. Greenberg & J.D. Olander (Eds.). *Science Fiction: Contemporary Mythology* (pp. 244–254). New York: Harper and Row.

Asimov, I. (1985). *Robots and Empire.* London: Grafton Books.

Atsma, A.J. (n.d.). Erinyes. Theoi.com [Online]. Retrieved from http://www.theoi.com/Khthonios/Erinyes.html.

Autonomous Weapons: An Open Letter from AI & Robotics Researchers (2015). Open letter presented at the 24th International Joint Conference on Artificial Intelligence, Buenos Aires, Argentina, 28 July 2015. Retrieved from https://futureoflife.org/open-letter-autonomous-weapons/.

Avengers: Age of Ultron (2015). Directed by J. Wheden [Film]. Burbank, CA: Disney Studios.

Baker, B. (2014). The Terminator Myth—Why Military Robots Aren't Human Shaped. Army-Technologywww [Online], 20 Jan. 2014. Retrieved from http://www.army-technology.com/features/featureterminator-myth-why-military-robots-arent-human-shaped-4162318/.

Bane, T. (2016). *Encyclopedia of Giants and Humanoids: In Myth, Legend, and Folklore.* Jefferson, NC: McFarland.

Banks, I.M. (2000). *Look to Windward.* London: Orbit Books.

Barrett, D. (2015). Burglars Use Drone Helicopters to Target Homes. *Telegraph News* (Online), 18 May 2015. Retrieved from https://www.telegraph.co.uk/news/uknews/crime/11613568/Burglars-use-drone-helicopters-to-identify-target-homes.html.

Barry, C. & Sportelli, F. (2018). Italian Researchers Develop Lighter, Cheaper Robotic Hand. Phys.org [Online], 10 May 2018. Retrieved from https://phys.org/news/2018–05-italian-lighter-cheaper-robotic.html#jCp.

Bates, C. (1983). Luthor Unleashed! 46(544), June 1983. New York: DC Comics.

Bates, H. (1940 [1983]). Farewell to the Master. *Astounding Science Fiction,* Oct. 1940: 58–66. [In I. Asimov, P.S. Warrick, & M.H. Greenberg (Eds.). *Machines That Think: The Best Science Fiction Stories about Robots and Computers* (pp. 93–135). New York: Holt, Rinehart and Winston.]

Battle Droid (n.d.). StarWars.com [Online]. Retrieved from https://www.starwars.com/databank/battle-droid.

Bauers, W.C. (2014). *Unbreakable.* New York: Tom Doherty Associates.

Beasts of Dublith (2009). *Fullmetal Alchemist: Brotherhood* [Anime series episode]. MBS-TBS (Season1, episode 13), 2 July 2009.

Bedi, R.S. (2012). Is Hang Tuah Fact or Fiction? *The Star* [Online], 22 Jan. 2012. Retrieved from https://www.thestar.com.my/news/nation/2012/01/22/is-hang-tuah-fact-or-fiction/.

Beebe, R. (2014). FRIDAY FLASH FACT—"Super-hero."

Nothing But Comics [Online], 18 July 2014. Retrieved from https://nothingbutcomics.net/2014/07/18/friday-flash-fact-super-hero/.

Behavior Interactive (2013–, ongoing). SpongeBob SquarePants: Plankton's Robotic Revenge [Video game]. Santa Monica, CA: Activision.

Bekey, G. (2005). *Autonomous Robots: From Biological Inspiration to Implementation and Control.* Cambridge, MA: The MIT Press.

Belfiore, M. (2014). Here's Why Robots Taking Our Jobs Is a Good Thing. *The Guardian* [Online], 22 March 2014. Retrieved from http://www.business insider.com/why-robots-taking-jobs-is-a-good-thing-2014–3.

Bendis, B.M. (2013). *Age of Ultron.* New York: Marvel Comics. Retrieved from https://www.hoopladigital.com/play/12003783.

Bennett, H. (Producer) (1973–1978). *The Six Million Dollar Man* [Television series]. New York: American Broadcasting Company.

Bernard, V. (Interviewer) & Singer, P.W. (Interviewee) (2012). *Interview with P.W. Singer.* [Interview transcript]. *International Review of the Red Cross,* 94(866): 467–481.

Bernstein, R. (1959). The Menace of Metallo. *Action Comics,* 1(252), May 1959. New York: DC Comics.

Bernthal, J. (2018). Police Use Drone to Help Locate Suspect in Burglary. *Fox2Now* [Online], 7 March 2018. Retrieved from http://fox2now.com/2018/03/07/police-use-drone-to-help-locate-suspect-in-burglary/.

Bertman, S. (2015). The Role of the Golem in the Making of Frankenstein. *Keats-Shelley Review,* 19(1): 42–50.

The Best of Both Worlds (1990). *Star Trek: The Next Generation* [Television series episode]. CBS (Season 3, episode 26), 18 June 1990.

Bettini, M. (1992 [1999]). *Ritrato dell'Amante.* Milan, Italy: Einaudi. [*The Portrait of the Lover.* (L. Gibbs, Trans.). Berkeley, CA: University of California Press.]

Bill & Ted's Bogus Journey (1991). Directed by P. Hewitt [Film]. Los Angeles, CA: Orion Pictures.

Binder, E. (1965). *Adam Link—Robot.* New York: Paperback Library.

Binder, O. (1958). The Super-Duel in Space. *Superman,* 1 (242), July 1958. New York: Action Comics.

Black, J.A., Cunningham, G., Ebeling, J., Flückiger-Hawker, E., Robson, E., Taylor, J., & Zólyomi, G. (1998–2006). The Exploits of Ninurta: Translation. Oxford, UK: The Electronic Text Corpus of Sumerian Literature. Retrieved from http://etcsl.orinst.ox.ac.uk/.

Blade Runner (1982). Directed by R. Scott [Film]. Burbank, CA: Warner Brothers.

Bob Curran (consultant and author). Email to the author, 19 Nov. 2011.

Boissoneault, L. (2017). A Brief History of Book Burning, From the Printing Press to Internet Archives. *Smithsonian Magazine* [Online], 31 Aug. 2017. Retrieved from https://www.smithsonianmag.com/history/brief-history-book-burning-printing-press-internet-archives-180964697/.

Bolter (n.d.). www.Warhammer40K.wikia.com [Wiki]. Retrieved from http://warhammer40k.wikia.com/wiki/Bolter.

Borg (n.d.). StarTrek.com. Retrieved [17 Aug. 2017] from http://www.startrek.com/database_article/borg.

Borges, J.L. (1969). El Golem. In J.L. Borges (Ed.). *El Otro el Mismo* (pp. 47–50). *Buenos Aires, Argentina: Ediciones Neperus.*

Boston Dynamics (2018). *SpotMini.* Retrieved from https://www.bostondynamics.com/spot-mini.

Boulanin, V. & Verbruggen, M. (2017). *Mapping the Development of Autonomy in Weapons Systems: A Primer on Autonomy.* Stockholm, Sweden: Stockholm International Peace Research Institute. Retrieved from https://www.sipri.org/publications/2017/other-publications/mapping-development-autonomy-weapon-systems.

Bradbury, R. (1951). Robot City. In R. Bradbury (Ed.), *The Illustrated Man* (pp. 243–253). New York: Doubleday.

Bradbury, R. (1953). *Fahrenheit 451.* New York: Ballantine Books.

Brain, M. (2003). *Manna* [Online]. MarshallBrain.com. Retrieved from http://marshallbrain.com/manna1.htm.

Breault, M. (Ed.) (1990). *Advanced Dungeons & Dragons: Monstrous Compendium, Spelljammer Appendix* [Online]. Retrieved from https://rpg.rem.uz/Dungeons%20%26%20Dragons/AD%26D%202nd%20Edition/Spelljammer/MC7%20-%20Monstrous%20Compendium%20-%20Spelljammer%20Appendix%20I.pdf.

Brothers (1990). *Star Trek: The Next Generation* [Television series episode]. First run syndication (Season 4, episode 3), 8 Oct. 1990.

Brotherton-Bunch, E. (2017). If Robots Are Taking Jobs, Then Why Are There Still So Many Jobs? [Blog]. 6 May 2017. Retrieved from http://www.americanmanufacturing.org/blog/entry/if-robots-are-taking-jobs-then-why-are-there-still-so-many-jobs.

Budanovic, N. (2017). The Janissaries—An Elite Ottoman Army Unit Who Became Public Enemy No. 1. *History Online,* 27 Sept. 2016. Retrieved from https://www.warhistoryonline.com/medieval/janissaries-elite-ottoman-army-unit-became-public-enemy-no1.html.

Budrys A. (1954 [1989]). *First to Serve.* New York: Street and Smith Publications. [In I. Asimov, M.H. Greenberg, & C.G. Waugh (Eds.). *Isaac Asimov's Wonderful World of Science Fiction: Robots* (pp. 227–244). Markham, Ontario, Canada: Penguin Books Canada.]

Burton, B. (2017). Robot Exacts Revenge on Football Coach. *C/net* [Online], 6 Aug. 2017. Retrieved from https://www.cnet.com/news/robot-exacts-revenge-baylor-football-coach/.

Bush, V. (1945). As We May Think. *The Atlantic* [Online], July 1945. Retrieved from https://www.theatlantic.com/magazine/archive/1945/07/as-we-may-think/303881/.

Byrnes, M.W. (2014). Nightfall: Machine Autonomy in Air-to-Air Combat. *Air, Space, Power Journal* [Online], May-June 2014, 23(3): 48–75.

Byron, G.G. (1822). *Don Juan.* London: Davison Whitefriars.

Cadmus (n.d.). Home page. Cadmusgroup.com. Retrieved [10 June 2017] from http://www.cadmusgroup.com/our-company/.

Caidin, M. (1972). *Cyborg.* Westminster, MD: Harbor House.

Cameron, D. (2015). Robots, Hungry for Power, Are Too Weak to Take over the World. *Wall Street Journal* [Online], 13 May 2015. Retrieved from https://blogs.wsj.com/digits/2015/05/13/robots-hungry-for-power-are-too-weak-to-take-over-the-world/.

Capcom (1996). Resident Evil [Video game]. Osaka, Japan: Capcom.

Čapek, K. (1920 [n.d.]). *Rossumovi Univerzální Roboti, R.U.R.* Prague, Czechoslovakia: Aventinum. [*R.U.R. (Rossum's Universal Robots).* (P. Selver & N. Playfair, Trans.). np.] Retrieved from http://preprints.readingroo.ms/RUR/rur.pdf.

Card, O.S. (1985). *Ender's Game.* New York: Tor Books. Retrieved from http://oceanofpdf.com/.

Carpenter, J. & O'Bannon, D. (1974). *Dark Star: A Science Fiction Adventure* [Screenplay]. Internet Movie Script Database. Retrieved from http://www.imsdb.com/scripts/Dark-Star.html.

Carr, R.S. (1994). The Composite Brain. In P. Hanning (Ed.). *The Frankenstein Omnibus* (pp. 277–286). Edison, NJ: Chartwell Books.

Cath Maige Tuired (n.d.). Sacred-texts.com [Online] (E.A. Gray, Trans.). Retrieved [7 June 2016] from http://www.sacred-texts.com/neu/cmt/cmteng.htm.

Caton, J.L. (2015). *Autonomous Weapons Systems: A Brief Survey of Developmental, Operational, Legal, and Ethical Issues.* Carlisle, PA: Strategic Studies Institute, U.S. Army War College.

CGTN Africa (2013). *Kinshasa Traffic Robot Cops Hope to Tackle Traffic Along City Streets.* [Video file], 28 Dec. 2013. Retrieved from https://www.bing.com/videos/search?q=kinshasa+robot+traffic+cop&docid=60799089117 7970053&mid=B00C6CFD62E343FAFB93B00C6 CFD62E343FAFB93&view=detail&FORM=VIREHT.

Chaney, M. (2001). *Tesla: Man Out of Time.* New York: Touchstone.

Chemotherapy: Nano Medical Cures Coming Closer? (n.d.). UnderstandingNano.com [Online]. Retrieved [10 May 2017] from http://www.understandingnano.com/nanoparticle-chemotherapy.html.

Chen, J., Huang, Y., Zhang, N., Zou, H., Liu, R., Tao, C., Fan, X., & Wang, Z.L. (2016). Micro-Cable Structured Textile for Simultaneously Harvesting Solar and Mechanical Energy. *Nature Energy,* Sept. 2016: 1–8.

Christensen, B. (2007). Ancestor of Matrix Sentinel Robot Born. *Live Science* [Online], 25 May 2007. Retrieved from http://www.livescience.com/4462-ancestor-matrix-sentinel-robot-born.html.

Christopher, A. (2015). *Made to Kill: A Ray Electromatic Mystery.* [Kindle Paperwhite version 5.6.1.1]. Retrieved from Amazon.com.

Chu, J. (2015). MIT Cheetah Robot Lands the Running Jump. *MIT News* [Online], 29 May 2015. Retrieved from http://news.mit.edu/2015/cheetah-robot-lands-running-jump-0529.

Citizens United v. Federal Election Commission. 130 S. Ct. 42 (U.S. Supreme Court, 2010).

CJake3 [Screen name] (2011). *Metal Gear Solid 4: Guns of the Patriots—Liquid Ocelot: The System Is Mine* [Video file], 20 March 2011. Retrieved from https://www.youtube.com/watch?v=OeHgrf5z4C0.

Clarke, A.C. (1973). Hazards of Prophecy: The Failure of the Imagination. In A.C. Clarke (Ed.). *Profiles of the Future: An Inquiry into the Limits of the Possible* (pp. 19–26). New York: Harper & Row.

Clarke, R. (1993). Asimov's Laws of Robotics: Implications for Information Technology. *IEEE Computer,* 26(12): 53–61. Retrieved from http://www.rogerclarke.com/SOS/Asimov.html.

Clutton-Brock, T.H. & Parker, G.A. (1995). Punishment in Animal Societies. *Nature,* 373: 209–216.

Cocchiarella, N.B. (n.d.). Notes on Deontic Logic. Ontology.co [Online]. Retrieved 10 Oct. 2017 from https://www.ontology.co/essays/deontic-logic.pdf.

Collodi, C. (1883 [1972]). *Le Avventure di Pinocchio*. Florence, Italy: Tipografia Moder. [*The Adventures of Pinocchio*. (C. Della Chiesa, Trans.). Retrieved from Project Gutenberg at www.gutenberg.org/ebooks/500.]

Conrad, M. (2011). *The Business of Sports: A Primer for Journalists* (2nd Ed.). New York: Routledge.

Contingency Orders for the Grand Army of the Republic: Order Initiation, Orders 1 through 150 (n.d.). www.StarWars.wikia. com [Wiki]. Retrieved from http://starwars.wikia.com/wiki/Contingency_Orders_for_the_Grand_Army_of_the_Republic: _Order_Initiation,_Orders_1_Through_150.

Coogan, P. (2006). *Superhero: The Secret Origin of a Genre*. Austin, TX: Monkey Brain Books.

Cooper, D. (2016). Lithium Battery Failure Wipes out DARPA Robot at NASA. Engadgetwww [Online], 28 Oct. 2016. Retrieved from https://www.engadget.com/2016/10/28/lithium-battery-failure-wipes-out-darpa-robot-at-nasa/.

Cork, T. (2018). Police to Deploy Drones in Bristol for First Time to Keep Peace at "Gays Against Sharia" March. *Bristol Post* [Online], April 2018. Retrieved from https://www.bristolpost.co.uk/news/bristol-news/police-deploy-drones-bristol-first-1508883.

Cornwall, W. (2015). Can We Build an "Iron Man" Suit that Gives Soldiers a Robotic Boost? *Science Magazine* [Online], 15 Oct. 2015. Retrieved from http://www.sciencemag.org/news/2015/10/feature-can-we-build-iron-man-suit-gives-soldiers-robotic-boost.

Cost of Labor (n.d.). *Investopedia* [Online]. Retrieved 12 Feb. 2018 from https://www.investopedia.com/terms/c/cost-of-labor.asp.

Countdown (1985). *Robotech* [Anime television episode]. Syndication (Season 1, episode 2), 5 March 1985.

Crawford, J. (Ed.) (2018). *Dungeons & Dragons Monster Manual* [Online]. Retrieved from http://orkerhulen.dk/onewebmedia/Monster%20Manual.pdf.

Crichton, M. (2002). *Prey*. New York: HarperCollins.

Crootof, R (2015). The Killer Robots Are Here: Legal and Policy Implications. *Cardozo Law Review*, 36: 1837–1915. Retrieved from https://www.researchgate.net/publication/288825550_The_Killer_Robots_Are_Here_Legal_and_Policy_Implications.

Crozier, R. (2018). Rio Tinto's Robot Train Budget Soars above $1bn. *ITNews* [Online], 5 March 2018. Retrieved from https://www.itnews.com.au/news/rio-tintos-robot-train-budget-soars-above-1bn-486284.

CryNet Nanosuit (n.d.). www.Crysis.wikia.com [Wiki]. Retrieved 1 Sept. 2017 from http://crysis.wikia.com/wiki/CryNet_Nanosuit.

Crytek (2007–, ongoing). Crysis [Video game]. Redwood City, CA: Electronic Arts.

Culliford, P. (1973). *Benoît Brisefer, Tome 6: Lady d'Olphine*. Brussels, Belgium: Le Lombard.

Cunningham, S. (2000). *Cunningham's Encyclopedia of Magical Herbs*. Woodbury, MN: Llewellyn Publications.

Curran, B. (2011). *Man-Made Monsters: A Field Guide to Golems, Patchwork Soldiers, Homunculi, and Other Created Creatures*. Pompton Plains, NJ: The Career Press.

Curry, A. (2015). Was the V-Sign Invented at the Battle of Agincourt? Agincourt 600.com [Online]. Retrieved from http://www.agincourt600.com/2015/06/08/was-the-v-sign-invented-at-the-battle-of-agincourt/.

Cuthbertson, A. (2016). Surveillance Drone Thwarts Prison Drug Smugglers. *Newsweek* [Online], 18 July 2016. Retrieved from http://www.newsweek.com/drones-prison-drugs-cayman-islands-478885.

Cyborg (2006). *Smallville* [Television series episode]. WB (Season 5, episode 103), 16 Feb. 2006. Retrieved from http://smallville.wikia.com/wiki/Cyborg.

The Daleks (1963–1964). *Doctor Who* [Television series episodes]. BBC Worldwide (Season 1, story 2, episodes 5–11), 21 Dec. 1963–1 Feb. 1964.

Daleks—Invasion Earth 2150 A.D. (1966). Directed by G. Flemyng [Film]. London: British Lion.

Dante, A. (1265–1321 [1867]). *Divina Commedia*. n.p. [*Divine Comedy* (H.W. Longfellow, Trans.) np.] Retrieved from J. Nygrin at https://justcheckingonall.wordpress.com/2008/02/28/complete-dante-alighieris-divine-comedy-in-pdf-3-books/.

Dark Star (1974). Directed by J. Carpenter [Film]. Los Angeles, CA: Bryanston Distributing Company.

Darkside_of_the_Sun (2017). The Manhunters. Comic Vine.gamespot.com [Online], 26 April 2017. Retrieved from https://comicvine.gamespot.com/the-manhunters/4060-55857/.

DARPA (2015). *Breakthrough Technologies for National Security* [Online]. Washington, D.C.: DARPA. Retrieved from https://www.darpa.mil/attachments/DARPA2015.pdf.

DARPA (2016). *Bridging the Bio-Electronic Divide* [Online]. Washington, D.C.: DARPA. Retrieved from https://www.darpa.mil/news-vents/2015–01-19.

DARPA (2017). *Dormant, Yet Always-Alert Sensor Awakes Only in the Presence of a Signal of Interest* [Press release], 11 Sept. 2017. Retrieved from https://www.darpa.mil/news-events/2017–09-11.

DARPA (n.d.a). *Robotics Challenge: Robotics Challenge Finals 2015* [Online]. Washington, D.C.: DARPA. Retrieved [5 March 2017] from http://archive.darpa.mil/roboticschallenge/.

DARPA (n.d.b). *Hand and Proprioception and Touch Interfaces (HAPTIX)* [Online]. Washington, D.C.: DARPA. Retrieved from https://www.darpa.mil/program/hand-proprioception-and-touch-interfaces.

DARPA (n.d.c). *DARPA and the Brain Initiative* [Online]. Washington, D.C.: DARPA. Retrieved from https://www.darpa.mil/program/our-research/darpa-and-the-brain-initiative.

David, P. & Frank, G. (1994). We Are Gathered Here. *The Incredible Hulk*, 1(418), June 1994. New York: Marvel Comics.

Davies, O. (2003). *Cunning Folk: Popular Magic in English History*. London: Hambledon.

The Day the Earth Stood Still (1951). Directed by R. Wise [Film]. Los Angeles, CA: Twentieth Century Fox.

The Day the Earth Stood Still (2008). Directed by Derrickson, S. [Film]. Los Angeles, CA: Twentieth Century–Fox.

DC Comics (1959–, ongoing). *Green Lantern Corps*. New York: DC Comics.

Death in Heaven (2014). *Doctor Who* [Television series episode]. BBC One (Season 34, story 8, episode 12), 8 Nov. 2014.

Defoe, D. (1722). *A Journal of the Plague Year*. London: E. Nutt.

De Groot, J.J.M. (1892). *The Religious System of China, Its Ancient Forms, Evolution, History and Present Aspect, Manners, Custom and Social Institutions Connected Therewith* (Vol. V). Leyden, The Netherlands: E.J. Brill. Retrieved from http://classiques.uqac.ca/classiques/groot_jjm_de/religious_system_of_china/religious_system.html.

Dekel, E. & Curley, D.G. (2013). How the Golem Came to Prague. *The Jewish Quarterly Review*, 103(2): 241–258.

Del Monte, L.A. (2017a). Are Nanoweapons Paving the Road to Human Extinction? *Huffington Post* [Online], 3 June 2017. Retrieved from https://www.huffingtonpost.com/entry/are-nanoweapons-paving-the-road-to-human-extinction_us_59332a52e4b00573ab57a3fe.

Del Monte, L.A. (2017b). *Nanoweapons: A Growing Threat to Humanity*. Lincoln: University of Nebraska Press.

Delaney, K. (2017). *Bill Gates: The Robot That Takes Your Job Should Pay Taxes*. [Video file], 16 Feb 2017. Retrieved from https://www.youtube.com/watch?v=nccryZOcrUg.

Delvaux, M. (2016). *Draft Report with Recommendations to the Commission on Recommendations on Civil Law Rules on Robotics* [Online]. Strasbourg, France: Committee on Legal Affairs of the European Parliament. Retrieved from http://www.europarl.europa.eu/sides/getDoc.do?pubRef=-//EP//NONSGML%2BCOMPARL%2BPE-582.443%2B01%2BDOC%2BPDF%2BV0//EN.

Denham, H. (2018). Self-Ordering Kiosks Are Coming to More McDonald's. Are You Lovin' It? *Tampa Bay Times* [Online], 8 June 2018. Retrieved from http://www.tampabay.com/news/business/retail/Self-ordering-kiosks-are-coming-to-more-McDonald-s-Are-you-lovin-it-_168923217.

Dennys, N.B. (1876). *The Folklore of China, and Its Affinities with That of the Aryan and Semitic Races*. London: Trübner and Co.

Destroy the Defendroids (1988). *Superman* [Television series episode]. CBS (Season 1, episode 1), 17 Sept. 1988.

Deus ex machina (2003). *Webster's New Universal Unabridged Dictionary*. New York: Barnes & Noble.

Devlin, H. (2015). Rise of the Robots: How Long Do We Have Until They Take Our Jobs? *The Guardian* [Online], 4 Feb 2015. Retrieved from https://www.guardian.com/technology/2015/feb/04/rise-robots-artificial-intelligence-computing-jobs.

de Vries, J. (2018). Caterina Sforza. Oxford Bibliographies.com [Online], 11 Jan. 2018. Retrieved from http://www.oxfordbibliographies.com/view/document/obo-9780195399301/obo-9780195399301-0180.xml.

Dick, P.K. (1953 [1989]). Second Variety. *Space Science Fiction*, 1(6): 102–145. [In I. Asimov, M.H. Greenberg, & C.G. Waugh (Eds.). *Isaac Asimov's Wonderful World of Science Fiction: Robots* (pp. 178–222). Markham, Ontario, Canada: Penguin Books Canada.]

Dick, P.K. (1953 [2009]). Mr. Spaceship. *Imagination Magazine*, 4(1): 28–52. [In G. Rickman (Ed.). *The Early Works of P.K. Dick* (pp. 70–105). Gaithersburg, MD: Prime Books.]

Dick, P.K. (1956). The Minority Report. *Fantastic Universe*, 4(6): 4–34.

Dick, P.K. (1960). *Vulcan's Hammer*. New York: Vintage Books.

Doctor Who and the Daleks (1965). Directed by G. Flemyng [Film]. London: British Lion.

Doctor Who Universe (1963–, ongoing). [Television series]. London: British One.

Don Giovanni (1787). [Opera]. Music by W.A. Mozart. Lyrics by L. Da Ponte.

Dormehl, L. (2017). The Sentinel Is a Robot Designed to Make Police Traffic Stops Safer. *Digital Trends* [Online], 20 Feb. 2017. Retrieved from https://www.digitaltrends.com/cool-tech/sentinel-robot-traffic-stop/.

Douglas, I. (2010). *Earth Strike (Star Carrier #1)*. New York: Harper Voyager.

Douglas, I. (2010–, ongoing). *Star Carrier* [Book series]. New York: Harper Voyager.

Douglas, I. (2013). *Deep Space (Star Carrier #4)*. New York: Harper Voyager.

Drake, D. (1979–2007). *Hammer's Slammers* [Book series]. Wake Forest, NC: Baen.

Drexler, E. (1986). *Engines of Creation: The Coming Era of Nanotechnology*. New York: Doubleday.

Drexler, K.E. (2001) Machine-Phase Nanotechnology. *Scientific American* [Online], 16 Sept. 2001. Retrieved from http://www.ruf.rice.edu/~rau/phys600/drexler.htm.

Drones Used to Smuggle Drugs and Mobile Phones into Prisons at Rate of Twice a Month (2016). *The Telegraph* [Online], 23 Feb 2016. Retrieved from https://www.telegraph.co.uk/news/uknews/law-and-order/12170213/Drones-used-to-smuggle-drugs-and-mobile-phones-into-prisons-at-rate-of-twice-a-month.html.

Drummond, K. (2010). Air Force Treating Wounds with Lasers and Nanotech. *Wired* [Online]. 5 May 2010. Retrieved from https://www.wired.com/2010/05/air-force-researchers-heal-wounds-with-lasers-and-nanotech/.

Easton, T. (1989). Breakfast of Champions. In I. Asimov, M.H. Greenberg, & C.G. Waugh (Eds.). *Isaac Asimov's Wonderful World of Science Fiction: Robots* (pp. 159–164). Markham, Ontario, Canada: Penguin Books Canada.

8th Man (1992). Directed by Y. Horiuchi [Film]. New York: Fox Lorber.

Eisenbeis, R. (2016). The Original Macross Explained. *Anime Now* [Online].16 July 2016. Retrieved from http://www.anime-now.com/entry/2016/07/13/210016.

Elifasi Msomi (n.d.). True Crime Library.com [Online]. Retrieved 3 Jan. 2018 from https://www.truecrimelibrary.com/crimearticle/elifasi-msomi/.

Elkins, E. (2015). Experts Predict Robots Will Take Over 30% of Our Jobs by 2025—and White-Collar Jobs Aren't Immune. *Business Insider* [Online], 1 May 2015. Retrieved from http://www.businessinsider.com/experts-predict-that-one-third-of-jobs-will-be-replaced-by-robots-2015-5.

Ellis-Behnke, R.G., Liang, Y.-X., You, S-W., Tay, D.K.C., Zhang, S., So, K-F., & Schneider, G.E. (2003). Nano Neuro Knitting: Peptide Nanofiber Scaffold for Brain Repair and Axon Regeneration with Functional Return of Vision. In *Proceedings of the National Academy of Sciences of the U.S.A.* 28 March 2006, 103(13): 5054–5059. Retrieved from http://www.pnas.org/content/103/13/5054.long.

Elysium (2013). Directed by N. Blomkamp [Film]. Culver City, CA: TriStar Pictures.

EmptyMan000 [Screen name] (2016). *FMA Brotherhood Greeling Explains the Virtues of Greed* [Video file], 22 Jan. 2016. Retrieved from https://www.youtube.com/watch?v=RkK4mIoj9j8.

Englehart, S. & Dillin, D. (1977–, ongoing). *Manhunters.* New York: DC Comics.

Englehart, S. & Dillin, D. (2016a). Alpha Lanterns. *The Unofficial Guide to the DC Universe* [Online], 3 March 2016. Retrieved from http://dcuguide.com/w/Manhunters. Retrieved from http://dcuguide.com/w/Alpha-Lanterns.

Englehart, S. & Dillin, D. (2016b). Manhunters. *The Unofficial Guide to the DC Universe* [Online], 25 June 2016. Retrieved from http://dcuguide.com/w/Manhunters.

Englehart, S., & Gan, S. (1976). Star-Lord. *Marvel Preview,* 1(4) January 1976. New York: Marvel Comics.

Enoch, N. (2016). Rise of the Russian Robo-Soldier: Iron Man Military Hardware Is One Step Closer to Reality as Putin's Scientists Reveal "Ivan the Terminator." *Daily Mail* [Online], 27 May 2016. Retrieved from http://www.dailymail.co.uk/news/article-3612649/Iron-Man-robot-one-step-closer-reality-Putin-s-scientists-reveal-Ivan-Terminator.html.

Epstein, I. (Ed.) (n.d.). *Sanhedrin, Translated into English with Notes, Glossary and Indices.* (J. Shachter & H. Freedman, Trans.) n.p. Retrieved from http://www.come-and-hear.com/sanhedrin/index.html.

Eschbach, A. (2011 [2014]). *Herr aller Dinge.* Cologne, Germany: Lübbe. [*Lord of All Things* (M. Pakucs, Trans.). Kindle Paperwhite version 5.6.1.1.]

Estes, A.C. (2015). DARPA's Crazy but Genius Plan to Replace Batteries with Propane. *Gizmodo* [Online], 3 April 2015. Retrieved from https://gizmodo.com/darpas-crazy-but-genius-plan-to-replace-batteries-with-1695354917.

Everett, H.R. (2015). *Unmanned Systems of World Wars I & II.* Cambridge, MA: MIT Press.

Evers, C. & Naylor, P.A. (2018). Acoustic SLAM. *IEEE/ACM Transactions on Audio Speech and Language Processing,* 26(9): 1484–1498.

Exum, A.M., Fick, N.C., Humayun, A.A., & Kilcullen, D.J. (2009). *Triage: The Next Twelve Months in Afghanistan and Pakistan.* Washington, D.C.: Center for a New American Security. Retrieved from https://www.files.ethz.ch/isn/101358/2009_06_ExumFickHumayun_TriageAfPak_June09.pdf.

The Eye of God (n.d.). www.Fma.wikia.com [Wiki]. Retrieved [1 April 2017] from http://fma.wikia.com/wiki/Eye_of_God.

Fabing, H.D. (1956). On Going Berserk: A Neurochemical Inquiry. *Scientific Monthly,* Nov. 1956, 83(5): 232–237.

Fadilpašić, S. (2016). Robots Are Coming to Take Your Jobs Away. *ZNews* [Online], 17 Feb. 2016. Retrieved from https://www.itproportal.com/2016/02/17/robots-are-coming-to-take-your-jobs-away/.

Fantasia: Night on Bald Mountain/Ave Maria (1941). Directed by W. Jackson [Film]. Burbank, CA: Walt Disney Productions.

Faron, L.C. (1968). *The Mapuche Indians of Chile. Case Studies in Cultural Anthropology.* New York: Holt, Rinehart and Winston.

Father (n.d.). www.Villains.wikia.com [Wiki]. Retrieved 1 April 2018 from http://villains wikia.com/wiki/Father_(Fullmetal_Alchemist).

Feds Ban Drones Over Coast Guard Facilities, Prisons (2018). *The Associated Press* [Online], 27 June 2018. Retrieved from https://www.military.com/daily-news/2018/06/27/feds-ban-drones-over-coast-guard-facilities-prisons.html.

Felbab-Brown, V. (2016). Drugs and Drones: The Crime Empire Strikes Back. [Blog], 24 Feb. 2016. Retrieved from https://www.brookings.edu/blog/order-from-chaos/2016/02/24/drugs-and-drones-the-crime-empire-strikes-back/.

Feng, H.Y. & Shryock, J.K. (1935). The Black Magic in China Known as Ku. *Journal of the American Oriental Society,* 55(1): 1–30. Retrieved from https://www.biroco.com/yijing/Ku.pdf.

Fichera, M., Cotilletta, A., Marvelhgo, Jc1569, Stephens, J. & TaXa, W. (n.d.). Iron Man (Anthony Stark). Marvel.com [Wiki]. Retrieved 12 August 2017, from http://marvel.com/universe/Iron_Man_(Anthony_Stark).

Fields, N.R. (2012). *Advantages and Challenges of Unmanned Aerial Vehicle Autonomy in the Postheroic Age* [Unpublished master's thesis]. Harrisonburg, VA: James Madison University. Retrieved from http://commons.lib.jmu.edu/master201019.

Finger, B. (1961). The Conquest of Superman. *Action Comics,* 1(227), June 1961. New York: DC Comics.

First Contact (1991). *Star Trek: The Next Generation* [Television series episode]. Broadcast syndication (Season 4, episode 15), 18 Feb. 1991.

Flaccus, G.V. (ca. 80 CE [1928]). *Argonautica 7.* n.p. [*Argonautica Book 7* (J. H. Mozley, Trans.). Cambridge, MA: Loeb Classical Library.] *Retrieved from* http://www.theoi.com/Text/ValeriusFlaccus7.html.

Flash Gordon (1936). Directed by F. Stephani & R. Taylor [Film]. Los Angeles, CA: Universal Pictures.

Foerst, A. (2000). *Stories We Tell: Where Robots and Theology Meet* [Video file]. Retrieved 8 Nov. 2013 from http://cssr.ei.columbia.edu/events/event-archive/.

Ford, M. (2015). *Rise of the Robots: Technology and the Threat of a Jobless Future.* New York: Basic Books.

Foster, A.D. (2010–2012). *The Tipping Point* [Book series]. New York: Ballantine Books.

Foster, A.D. (2010). *The Human Blend.* New York: Del Rey.

Fox, G. & Siegel, J. (1940). Dead Men Tell No Tales: The Treasure Tower. *Action Comics,* 1(23), April 1940. New York: DC Comics.

Frakes, R. (1991). *Terminator 2: Judgment Day.* London: Sphere Books.

Frankenstein: The Man Who Made a Monster (1931). Directed by J. Whale [Film]. Universal City, CA: Universal Pictures.

Frankowski, L. (1999). *A Boy and His Tank.* Riverdale, NY: Baen Books. Retrieved from http://www.baen.com/chapters/boyt_1.htm.

Freedman, L.D. (2018). Nuclear Test-Ban Treaty. *Encyclopedia Britannica* [Online], 11 May 2018. Retrieved from https://www.britannica.com/event/Nuclear-Test-Ban-Treaty.

A Friend in Need (2012). *Star Wars: The Clone Wars* [Television series episode]. Cartoon Network (Season 4, episode 14), 13 Jan. 2012.

Fromm, E. (1942). *Fear of Freedom* New York: Ferrar and Rinehart.

Front Runners (2012). *Star Wars: The Clone Wars* [Television series episode]. Cartoon Network (Season 5, episode 3), 13 Oct. 2012.

Futureworld (1976). Directed by R.T. Heffron [Film]. Los Angeles, CA: American International Pictures.

Games Workshop (1987–, ongoing). Warhammer 40,000 [Tabletop game]. Nottingham, U.K: Developer.

Games Workshop (2014). *Warhammer 40,000 Codex: Dark Eldar*. Nottingham, U.K.: Author. Retrieved from http://wh40klib.ru/codex/actually_codex_and_rule/Dark_Eldar_7-th_ed_Eng.pdf.

Gansovsky, S. (1964 [2016]). Den Gneva. Russia. [Day of Wrath. In A. Vandermeer & J. Vandermeer (Eds.). *The Big Book of Science Fiction* (pp. 462–477) (J. Wormak, Trans.). New York: Vintage Books.]

Garnett, L.M.J. (1890). *The Women of Turkey and Their Folk-Lore*. London: David Nutt.

Gawne, T. (2012). *The Chronicles of Old Guy* [Kindle Paperwhite version 5.6.1.1]. Retrieved from Amazon.com.

Gelbin, C.S. (2011). *The Golem Returns: From German Romantic Literature to Global Jewish Culture, 1808–2008*. Ann Arbor: University of Michigan Press.

Genesis (1994). *Star Trek: The Next Generation* [Television series episode]. First run syndication (Season 7, episode 19), 19 March 1994.

Georgia Institute of Technology (n.d.). Georgia Tech Wearable Motherboard: The Intelligent Garment for the 21st Century. Retrieved 5 July 2017 from http://smartshirt.gatech.edu/.

Georgia Tech School of Music (2017). *The Force Is Strong: Amputee Controls Individual Prosthetic Fingers* [Press release], 11 Dec. 2017. Retrieved from https://music.gat-ech.edu/news/force-strong-amputee-controls-individual-prosthetic-fingers.

Gernsbach, H. (1924). Radio Police Automaton. *Science & Invention* [Online], May 1924: 14. http://cyberneticzoo.com/robots/1924-radio-police-automaton-gernsback-american/.

Gerrold, D. (1992). *A Season for Slaughter*. New York: Spectra.

Gettinger, D. & Michael A.H. (2016). *Law Enforcement Robots Datasheet* [Online]. July 2016. Center for the Study of the Drone. Retrieved from http://dronecenter.bard.edu/files/2016/07/LEO-Robots-CSD-7–16-1.pdf.

Geyser, J. (2017). Does Anyone Know What Father Did Wrong in the Eyes of Truth? [Answer], 10 Jan. 2017. Answer posted to https://www.quora.com/In-fullmetal-alchemist-brotherhood-Father-asks-Truth-what-he-did-wrong-Does-anyone-know-what-Father-did-wrong-in-the-eyes-of-Truth.

Ghost in the Shell (1995). Directed by M. Oshii [Film]. Tokyo, Japan: Shochiku and London: Manga Entertainment.

Ghost in the Shell (2017). Directed by R. Sanders [Film]. Hollywood, CA: Paramount Pictures.

Gier, N. (2012) The Golem, the Corporation, and Personhood [Blog], 14 April 2012. Retrieved from http://www.pocatelloshops.com/new_blogs/politics/?p=8982.

Gilman, D. (2014). *Unmanned Aerial Vehicles in Humanitarian Response*. New York: U.N. Office for the Coordination of Humanitarian Affairs. Retrieved from https://www.unocha.org/sites/unocha/files/Unmanned%20Aerial%20Vehicles%20in%20Humanitarian%20Response%20OCHA%20July%202014.pdf.

Glaser, A. (2016). 11 Police Robots Patrolling Around the World. *Wired* [Online], 24 July 2016. Retrieved from https://www.wired.com/2016/07/11-police-robots-patrolling-around-world/.

Glaser. A. (2017). Police Departments Are Using Drones to Find and Chase Down Suspects. *Recode* [Online], 6 April 2017. Retrieved from https://www.recode.net/2017/4/6/15209290/police-fire-department-acquired-drone-us-flying-robot-law-enforcement.

Gliński, M. (2015). The Trail of the Polish Golem. *Culture.Pl* [Online], 9 April 2015. Retrieved from http://culture.pl/en/article/the-trail-of-the-polish-golem.

Godzilla vs. Mechagodzilla (1974). Directed by J. Fukuda [Film]. Tokyo, Japan: Toho.

Godzilla (1954). Directed by I. Honda [Film]. Tokyo, Japan: Tono.

Goldberg, H. (2010). *Potential Costs of Veterans' Health Care* [Online], 7 Oct. 2010. Washington, D.C.: U.S. Congressional Budget Office. Retrieved from https://www.cbo.gov/publication/21773.

Goldberg, L. (2018). Ruby Rose to Play Lesbian Superhero Batwoman for the CW. *The Hollywood Reporter* [Online], 7 Aug. 2018. Retrieved from https://www.hollywoodreporter.com/live-feed/ruby-rose-play-lesbian-super hero-batwoman-cw-1132599.

The Golem (1924) [Opera] Bretan, N. Music & Lyrics by N. Bretan.

Der Golem (1915). Directed by H. Galeen & P. Wegener [Film]. Babelsberg, Germany: Universum Films.

Gopalsamy, C., Park, S., Rajamanickam, R., & Jayaraman, S. (1999). The Wearable Motherboard: The First Generation of Adaptive and Responsive Textile Structures (ARTS) for Medical Applications. *Virtual Reality*, 4: 152–168.

Gorman, P.F. (1990). Supertroop Via I-Port: Distributed Simulation Technology for Combat Development and Training Development (IDA Paper P-2374). Defense Technical Information Center [Online]. Retrieved 9 Aug. 2018 from http://www.dtic.mil/dtic/.

Gough, A. & Miller, M. (Producers) (2001–2011). *Smallville* [Television series]. Burbank, CA: The WB & The CW.

Der Goylem: Dramatische Poeme in Akht Bilder (1921) [Play]. Book by H. Leivick.

Granny's Revenge (n.d.). www.RobotWars.wikia.com [Wiki]. Retrieved from http://robotwars.wikia.com/wiki/Granny%27s_Revenge.

Greene, R. (ca. 1590). *The Honorable Historie of Frier Bacon and Frier Bungay*. London: Elizabeth Allde.

Greenfield, D. (2013). The Case Against Drone Strikes on People Who Only "Act" Like Terrorists. *The Atlantic* [Online], 19 Aug. 2013. Retrieved from www.theatlantic.com/international/archive/2013/08/the-case-against-drone-strikes-0n-people-who-only-act-like-terrorists/278744/.

Grievous Intrigue (2010). *Star Wars: The Clone Wars* [Television series episode]. Cartoon Network (Season 2, episode 9), 1 Jan. 2010.

Grimm, J. (1808). Entstehung de Verlangspoesie. *Zeitung für Einsiedler*, 8: 56.

Grove, F. (ca. 1627). *The Famous Historie of Fryer Bacon Containing the Wonderfull Things That He Did in His Life: Also the Manner of His Death*. London: E.A.

Grut, C. (2013). The Challenge of Autonomous Lethal

Robotics to International Humanitarian Law. *Journal of Conflict & Security Law*, 18(1): 5–23. Retrieved from https://www.law.upenn.edu/live/files/3401-grut-c-the-challenge-of-autonomous-lethal-robotics.

Gubrud, M. (2016). Why Should We Ban Autonomous Weapons? To Survive. *IEEE Spectrum* [Online], 1 June 2016. Retrieved from https://spectrum.ieee.org/automaton/robotics/military-robots/why-should-we-ban-autonomous-weapons-to-survive.

Gunslinger Drone, Your Moderately-Priced Hired Assassin (2015). RTwww [Online], 17 July 2015. Retrieved from https://www.rt.com/news/310097-drone-multirotor-semiautomatic-handgun/.

Gygax, G. & Ameson, D. (1974–, ongoing). Dungeons & Dragons [Tabletop game]. Renton, WA: Wizards of the Coast.

Haag, A., & Hepkins, F. (2015) Mind the Gap: The lack of accountability for killer robots. *Human Rights Watch* [Online]. Retrieved from http://www.hrw.org/report/2015/04/09/mind-gap/lack-accountability-killer-robots.

Hagstrom, A. (2017). These 3-Foot Robots Help Sentence People to Prison. *The Daily Caller* [Online], 5 Aug. 2017. Retrieved from http://dailycaller.com/2017/08/04/these-3-foot-robots-help-sentence-people-to-prison/.

Haldeman, J. (1974). *The Forever War.* New York: St. Martin's Press.

Hallgarth, M.W. (2013). Just War Theory and Remote Military Technology: A Primer. In B. J. Strawser (Ed.), *Killing by Remote Control* (pp. 25–46). New York: Oxford University Press.

Hambling, D. (2015a). ISIS Is Reportedly Packing Drones with Explosives Now. *Popular Mechanics* [Online], 16, Dec. 2015. Retrieved from http://www.popularmechanics.com/military/weapons/a18577/isis-packing-drones-with-explosives/.

Hambling, D. (2015b). *Swarm Troopers.* [Kindle Paperwhite version 5.6.1.1].

Hambling, D. (2016). Killer Drones Will Become More Like Birds if the U.S. Air Force Has Anything to Say About It. *Popular Mechanics* [Online], Jun 10, 2016. Retrieved from https://www.popularmechanics.com/military/a21279/perching-drones/.

Hamilton, P.F. (1996–1999). *Night's Dawn* [book series]. London: Macmillan.

Harney, W.E. (1959). *Tales from the Aborigines.* London: Robert Hale Limited.

Harrison, H. (1958 [2009]). *Arm of the Law. Fantastic Universe,* August 1958: 23–36. [Kindle Paperwhite version 5.6.1.1]

Harrison, H. (1962 [1983]). War with the Robots. *Science Fiction Adventures,* 27: 69–89. [In I. Asimov, P. S. Warrick, & M.H. Greenberg (Eds.), *Machines That Think: The Best Science Fiction Stories about Robots and Computers* (pp. 357–379). New York: Holt Rinehart & Winston.]

Harrison, H. (2000). *The Stainless Steel Rat.* New York: Tor Books.

Hasbro (2008). *Transformers Animated: Megatron.* Retrieved 5 Feb. 2017 from https://www.hasbro.com/common/instruct/83637.pdf.

Hayden, M.V. (2016). To Keep America Safe, Embrace Drone Warfare. *New York Times* [Online], 19 Feb. 2016. Retrieved from https://www.nytimes.com/2016/02/21/opinion/sunday/drone-warfare-precise-effective-imperfect.html.

Headquarters for Japan's Economic Revitalization (2015). *New Robot Strategy: Japan's Robot Strategy—Vision, Strategy, Action Plan.* Tokyo, Japan: Ministry of Economy.

Hearn, L. (1904). *Kwaidan: Stories and Studies of Strange Things.* Boston, MA: Houghton, Mifflin and Co. Retrieved from http://www.gutenberg.org/files/1210/1210-h/1210-h.htm.

Heavy Bolter (n.d.). Lexicanum.com [Online]. Retrieved [11 Dec. 2017] from http://wh40k.lexicanum.com/wiki/Heavy_bolter.

Heinlein, R.A. (1966). *The Moon Is a Harsh Mistress.* New York: Tom Doherty Associates.

Heinlein, R.A. (1959). *Starship Troopers.* New York: Ace Books.

Held, J.M. & Irwin, W. (2017). *Wonder Woman and Philosophy: The Amazonian Mystique.* Hoboken, NJ: Wiley-Blackwell.

Hennigan, W.J. (2017). As ISIS Drones Die, Dangers Live. *The Chicago Tribune* [Online], 2 Oct. 2017: 27.

Hennigan, W.J. (2018). Rising to a New Threat. *Time,* 11 June 2018: 30–33.

Herbert, B. & Anderson, K.J. (2002–2004). *Legends of Dune* [Book series]. New York: Tom Doherty Associates.

Herbert, B. & Anderson, K.J. (2012–2016). *Great Schools of Dune.* New York: Tom Doherty Associates.

Herbert, B. & Anderson, K.J. (2014). *Mentats of Dune.* New York: Tom Doherty Associates.

Hernandez, R. (2018). Lawmakers Demand Details on 1,400% Price Hike for Cancer Drug. *Biopharmdive* [Online], 4 April 2018. Retrieved from https://www.biopharmadive.com/news/lawmakers-demand-details-on-1400-price-hike-for-cancer-drug/520613/.

Der Herr der Welt (1934). Directed by H. Piel [Film]. Berlin, Germany: Neue Deutsch Lichtspiel-Syndikat Verleih.

Hersey, G. (2009). *Falling in Love with Statues: Pygmalion to the Present.* Chicago, IL: University of Chicago Press.

Hesiod (ca. 700 BCE). *Theogony.* Enargea.org. Retrieved from http://enargea.org/homyth/myths/Theogony.html.

Hillenburg, S. & Tibbitt, P. (Producers) (1995–, ongoing). *SpongeBob SquarePants* [Television series]. New York: Nickelodeon.

Hirai, K. (1963–1966). *Eitoman* [Book series]. Tokyo, Japan: Kodansha.

The History of Military Robots (n.d.). AllonRobots.com [Online]. Retrieved 10 Nov. 2017 from http://www.allonrobots.com/military_robots_history.html.

Hiznyak, N. (2017). Battle Tech: Why Russia's Ratnik 3 Is a "Breakthrough Infantry Combat System." *Sputnik International* [Online], 2 June 2017. Retrieved from https://sputniknews.com/russia/201702061050395003-russia-ratnik-infantry-combat-gear/.

Hollinger, P. (2016). Meet the Cobots: Humans and Robots Together on the Factory Floor. *Financial Times* [Online], 6 May 2016. Retrieved from https://news.nationalgeographic.com/2016/05/financial-times-meet-the-cobots-humans-robots-factories/.

Holloway, A. (2014). The Viking Berserkers—Fierce Warriors or Drug-Fuelled Madmen? Ancient Origins.net [Online], 23 March 2014. Retrieved from http://www.

ancient-origins.net/myths-legends/viking-berserkers-fierce-warriors-or-drug-fuelled-madmen-001472.

Homunculus (n.d.). www.Fma.wikia.com [Wiki]. Retrieved 10 June 2017 from http://fma.wikia.com/wiki/Mannequin_Soldiers#Mannequin_Soldiers.

Hooper, R. (n.d.). Law Enforcement Robots. Learn About Robots [Online]. Retrieved 10 Feb. 2018 from http://www.learnaboutrobots.com/lawEnforcement.htm.

Hopkins, J.K., Spranklin, B.W., & Gupta, S.K. (2009). A Survey of Snake-Inspired Robot Designs [Draft]. terpconnect.umd.edu. Retrieved from http://terpconnect.umd.edu/~skgupta/Publication/BB09_Hopkins_draft.pdf.

Hornyak, T.N. (2006). *Loving the Machine.* Tokyo, Japan: Kodansha International.

How Gundam Gets It's [*sic*] Name? (2010). Open the Toy [Blog], 8 July 2010. Retrieved from http://www.openthetoy.com/2010/07/how-gundam-gets-its-name.html.

HTF Market Intelligence (2016). *Law Enforcement Robots: Market Shares, Market Strategies, and Market Forecasts, 2016 to 2022* [Press release]. Retrieved 4 June 2017 from https://www.htfmarketreport.com/reports/17232-law-enforcement-robots-market.

Huang, E. (2017). China's Booming Electric Vehicle Market Is about to Run into a Mountain of Battery Waste. *Quartz* [Online], 28 Sept. 2017. Retrieved from https://qz.com/1088195/chinas-booming-electric-vehicle-market-is-about-to-run-into-a-mountain-of-battery-waste/.

Hughes, M. (1990). *Invitation to the Game.* New York: HarperCollins.

Hughes, T. (1993). *The Iron Woman.* London: Faber & Faber.

Hunter, W. (n.d.). Berzerk—Coins Detected in Pocket! The Dot Eaters.com [Online]. Retrieved from http://thedoteaters.com/?bitstory=berzerk.

I, Borg (1992). *Star Trek: The Next Generation* [Television series episode]. First run syndication (Season 5, episode 23), 12 May 1992.

I, Robot (2004). Directed by A. Proyas [Film]. Los Angeles, CA: Twentieth Century–Fox.

IGN Walkthroughs (2012). *Metal Gear Solid 4—Rat Patrol Team 01* [Video file], 3 Oct. 2012. Retrieved from https://www.bing.com/videos/search?q=metal+gear+solid+4+rat+patrol&view=detail&mid=096FD433F89A5C532F24096FD433F89A5C532F24&FORM=VIRE.

Imperial Robots (n.d.). www.warhammer40k.wikia.com [Wiki]. Retrieved 11 Dec. 2017 from http://warhammer40k.wikia.com/wiki/Imperial_Robots.

In Theory (1991). *Star Trek: The Next Generation* [Television series episode]. First run syndication (Season 4, episode 25), 3 June 1991.

The Incredibles (2004). Directed by B. Bird [Film]. Burbank, CA: Buena Vista Pictures.

The Incredibles 2 (2018). Directed by B. Bird [Film]. Burbank, CA: Walt Disney Pictures.

Inmates Use Drones to Smuggle Phones, Drugs, Porn (2017). *Crime and Justice News* [Online], 16 June 2017. Retrieved from https://thecrimereport.org/2017/06/16/inmates-smuggle-in-phones-drugs-porn-with-drones/.

Inns, P.J. (2006–, ongoing). The Matrix: Dock Defense [Video game]. Northamptonshire, England: Dan-Dare. Retrieved from http://www.dan-dare.org/FreeFun/Games/CartoonsMoviesTV/Matrix2.htm.

International Republican Institute (2009). *Pakistan Public Opinion Survey.* Washington, D.C.: International Republican Institute. Retrieved from http://www.iri.org/sites/default/files/2008-February-11-Survey-of-Pakistan-Public-Opinion-January-19-29-2008.pdf.

Iran Helping Hamas, Hezbollah Build Fleet of Suicide Drones (2015). *The Jerusalem Post* [Online], 9 April 2015. Retrieved from https://www.jpost.com/Middle-East/Iran-helping-Hamas-Hezbollah-build-fleet-of-suicide-drones-396673.

Iron Man (n.d.). Marvel.com [Online]. Retrieved 10 June 2017 from http://marvel.com/characters/29/iron_man.

Iron Man's Armor (n.d.). www.Marvel.wikia.com [Wiki]. Retrieved 10 July 2017 from http://marvel.wikia.com/wiki/Iron_Man_Armor.

Israel Aerospace Industries (n.d.). Harpy NG. Retrieved from http://www.iai.co.il/2013/36694–16153-en/Business_Areas_Land.aspx.

Iyer, S. (2017). *Avishi: Reimaging Vishpala of the Rig Veda.* [Kindle Paperwhite version 5.6.1.1.]

Jackson, D. (2016). Guangzhou Restaurant Fires Its Robot Staff for Their Incompetence. *Shanghaiist* [Online]. 6 April 2016. Retrieved from http://shanghaiist.com/2016/04/06/restaurant_fires_incompetent_robot_staff.php.

Jacobsen, A. (2015). *The Pentagon's Brain: An Uncensored History of DARPA, America's Top-Secret Military Research Agency.* New York: Little, Brown and Company.

Jaeger Program (n.d.). www.PacificRim.wikia.com [Wiki]. Retrieved 1 June 2017 from http://pacificrim.wikia.com/wiki/Jaeger_Program.

Jason and the Argonauts (1963). Directed by D. Chaffey [Film]. Culver City, CA: Columbia Pictures.

Jerome, J.K. (1893). The Dancing Partner. *The Idler Magazine,* March 1893. Retrieved from http://www.hornpipe.com/mystclas/myscl24.pdf.

Joburg Man Tormented by Tokoloshe That Does Not Want Him to Eat (2015). *iMansi* [Online], 20 Dec. 2015. Retrieved from http://imzansi.co.za/joburg-man-tormented-by-tokoloshe-that-does-not-want-him-to-eat/.

Jocasta (n.d.). Marvel.com [Online]. Retrieved 5 March 2017 from http://marvel.com/universe/Jocasta#axzz5KPxl9n9M.

Johns, G. (2008). Massacre of Sector 666. *Green Lantern* 4(33), Sept. 2008. New York: DC Comics.

Johnson, T. (2017). Liquid Body Armor. *Army News Service* [Online], 11 Dec. 2017. Retrieved from https://www.thebalancecareers.com/liquid-body-armor-3331922.

Jones, M. (2016). Yes, the Robots Will Steal Our Jobs. And That's Fine. *Washington Post* [Online], 17 Feb. 2016. Retrieved from https://www.washingtonpost.com/posteverything/wp/2016/02/17/yes-the-robots-will-steal-our-jobs-and-thats-fine/?utm_term=.b8ea64563854.

Jones, N.R. (1931). Zora of the Zoromes. *Amazing Stories,* 9(1): 88–120.

Journey into Night (2018). *Westworld* [Television series episode]. HBO (Season 2, episode 1), 22 April 2018.

Jun, L. (2016). China's First Intelligent Security Robot Debuts in Chongqing. *People's Daily* [Online], 26 April 2016. Retrieved from http://en.people.cn/n3/2016/0426/c90000–9049431.html.

Kanigher, R. (1962). *Showcase: Metal Men,* 1(37), April 1962. New York: DC Comics.

Kanigher, R. (1963–1978). *Metal Men*. New York: DC Comics.

Kanigher, R. (1964). The Robot Juggernaut. *Metal Men* 1(9), Aug.-Sept. 1964. New York: DC Comics.

Kant, I. (1785 [1895]). *Grundlegung zur Metaphysik der Sitten*. Riga, Latvia: J.F. Hartknoch. [*Fundamental Principles of the Metaphysic of Morals*. (T.K. Abbot, Trans.) London: Longmans, Green & Co.] Retrieved from http://www.gutenberg.org/ebooks/5682.

Kashner, A. & Plaw, A. (2013). Distinguishing Drones: An Exchange. In B.J. Strawser (Ed.). *Killing by Remote Control: The Ethics of an Unmanned Military* (pp. 47–85). New York: Oxford University Press.

Kawamori, S., Inoue, A., & Iwata, H. (Producers) (1982–1983). The Super Dimension Fortress Macross [Anime television series]. Osaka, Japan: MBS.

Kelley, L.C. (1919). Pedomotor: U.S. Patent No. 1,308,675. Washington, D.C.: U.S. Patent and Trademark Office. Retrieved from https://www.google.com/patents/US1308675.

Kenny's Revenge (n.d.). www.Ultimate-Robot-Archive. wikia.com [Wiki]. Retrieved from http://ultimate-robot-archive.wikia.com/wiki/Kenny%27s_Revenge.

Kerouack, J. (n.d.). Tokoloshe. Mythical Creatures and Beasts.com [Online]. Retrieved from http://www.mythical-creatures-and-beasts.com/tokoloshe.html.

Kiger, P.J. (2012). 10 Evil Robots Bent on Destroying Humanity. Science. HowStuffWorks.com [Online], 26 Nov. 2012. Retrieved from http://science.howstuffworks.com/10-evil-robots.htm.

Kimball, D. & Davenport, K. (2018). Syria: Timeline of Syrian Chemical Weapons Activity, 2012–2018. Armscontrol.org [Online]. Retrieved from https://www.armscontrol.org/taxonomy/term/149.

Knoetze, D. (2014). "Tokoloshes" Vandalise Rhodes Statue. *Crime & Courts* [Online], 23 May 2014. Retrieved from http://www.iol.co.za/news/crime-courts/tokoloshes-vandalise-rhodes-statue-1692902.

Knowledge Transfer Partnerships (2007). *Breval Environmental Limited Ductwork Robot Propels Company into New Market* [Press release]. Retrieved 3 Oct. 2016 from http://www.ktpscotland.org.uk/Portals/19/KTP-breval-high%20res.pdf.

Knuth, R. (2003). *Libricide: The Regime-Sponsored Destruction of Books and Libraries in the Twentieth Century*. Westport, CT: Greenwood Publishing Group.

Knuth, R. (2006). *Burning Books and Leveling Libraries: Extremist Violence and Cultural Destruction*. Toronto, Ontario, Canada: Praeger.

Kojima Productions (2008–, ongoing). Metal Gear Solid 4: Guns of the Patriots [Video game]. Tokyo, Japan: Konami.

Kolodner, J.L. (1992). An Introduction to Case-Based Reasoning. *Artificial Intelligence Review* [Online], 6: 3–34. Retrieved from http://alumni.media.mit.edu/~jorkin/generals/papers/Kolodner_case_based_reasoning.pdf.

Kongos, J. (1971). Tokoloshe Man [Recorded by J. Kongos]. *Kongos* [Vinyl]. London: Fly Records.

Kryt, J. (2017). Game of Drones: Mexico's Cartels Have a Deadly New Weapon. *Daily Beast* [Online], 12 Nov. 2017. Retrieved from https://www.thedailybeast.com/game-of-drones-mexicos-cartels-have-a-deadly-new-weapon.

Kumagai, J. (2007). A Robotic Sentry for Korea's Demilitarized Zone. *IEEE Spectrum* [Online], 1 March 2007. Retrieved from https://spectrum.ieee.org/robotics/military-robots/a-robotic-sentry-for-koreas-demilitarized-zone.

Kumar, N. & Kumar, R. (2014). *Nanotechnology and Nanomaterials in the Treatment of Life-Threatening Diseases*. London: Elsevier.

Kurtzman, A. (2011). The History of Transformers on TV. IGN.com [Online]. Retrieved from http://www.ign.com/articles/2011/06/27/the-history-of-transformers-on-tv.

Kurtzman, A., Orci, R., Kline, J. & Davis, S. (Producers) (2010–2013). *Transformers: Prime* [Television series]. Silver Spring, MD: Hub Network.

Kuttner, H., & Moore, C.L. (1955 [1989]). Two-Handed Engine. *The Magazine of Fantasy and Science Fiction*, Aug. 1955, 8(2): 3–23 [In I. Asimov, M.H. Greenberg, & C.G. Waugh (Eds.). *Isaac Asimov's Wonderful World of Science Fiction: Robots* (pp. 245–269). Markham, Ontario, Canada: Penguin Books Canada.]

L'Uomo Meccanico (1921). Directed by A. Deed [Film]. Milan, Italy: Milano Films.

Lackey, M. (1991). *By the Sword*. New York: Daw Books.

Lagowski, K. (2017). What You Should Know about Today's Electric Car Batteries. *Fleet Carma* [Online], 15 March 2017. Retrieved from https://www.fleetcarma.com/todays-electric-car-batteries/.

LaGrandeur, K. (1999). The Talking Brass Head as a Symbol of Dangerous Knowledge in Friar Bacon and in Alphonsus, King of Aragon. *English Studies*, 80(5): 408–422.

Lamb, R. (n.d.). 10 Robots with Dirty Jobs. HowStuffWorks.com [Online]. Retrieved from https://science.howstuffworks.com/10-robots-with-dirty-jobs.htm.

Lambert, V., Wiles, J., Lloyd, I., Bryant, P., Sherwin, D., Letts, B., …Strevens, M. (Producers) (1963–, on-going). *Doctor Who* [Television series]. London: BBC One.

Lambshead J. & Treadaway, J. (2004). *The Hammer's Slammers Handbook*. New York: Baen.

Laumer, K. (1976). *BOLO: Annals of the Dinochrome Brigade*. New York: Berkley Medallion.

Laumer, K. (1976–1990). *BOLO* [Book series]. Riverdale, NJ: Baen.

Laumer, K. & Keith, W.H. (1999). *BOLO Rising*. Riverdale, NY: Baen.

Le Rouge, G. & Guitton, G. (1899). *La Conspiration des Milliardaires, Tome II—À Coups de Milliards* [Kindle Paperwhite version 5.6.1.1].

Lead (n.d.). www.DC.wikia.com [Wiki]. Retrieved 10 April 2018 from http://dc.wikia.com/wiki/Lead.

Lee, S. (1963). Iron Man. *Tales of Suspense, #39*, March 1963. New York: Marvel Comics.

Lee, S. (1965a). Among Us Stalk the Sentinels. *X-Men*, 1(14), Nov. 1965. New York: Marvel Comics.

Lee, S. (1965b). Prisoners of the Mysterious Master Mold. *X-Men*, 1(15) Dec. 1965. New York: Marvel Comics.

Lee, S. (1968). Even an Android Can Cry. *Avengers*, 1(58), Nov. 1968. New York: Marvel Comics.

Lee, S. (1987). Heroes Always Win … Don't They? *Thor* (376), Feb. 1987. New York: Marvel Comics.

Legio Cybernetica (n.d.). Lexicanum.com [Wiki]. Retrieved 11 Dec. 2017 from http://wh40k.lexicanum.com/wiki/Legio_Cybernetica.

The LEGO Movie (2014). Directed by P. Lord & C. Miller [Film]. Burbank, CA: Warner Brothers Pictures.

Lem, S. (1964 [1973]). *Niezwyciężony*. Warsaw, Poland: Wydawnictwo MON. [*The Invincible*. (W. Ackerman, Trans.). New York: Seabury Press].

Lem, S. (1977). The Mask. In S. Lem (Ed.). *Mortal Engines* (pp. 181–230). New York: The Seabury Press.

Lempriere (1832). *Lempriere's Classical Dictionary for Schools and Academies: Every Name and All That Is Either Important or Useful in the Original Work*. Boston, MA: Carter, Hendel & Co.

Leonard, S. & Thomas, D. (Producers) (1960–1968). *The Andy Griffith Show* [Television series]. New York: CBS.

LeRoux, G. (1923 [1935]). *La Machine à Assassiner*. Paris, France: Tallander. [*The Machine to Kill* (n.t. Trans.). New York: The Macaulay Company.]

Lev, E. (2012). *The Tigris of Forlì*. New York: Houghton Mifflin Harcourt.

Lev, P. (2003). *The Fifties: Transforming the Screen, 1950–1959 (History of the American Cinema)*. New York: Charles Scribner and Sons.

Levin, I. (1972). *The Stepford Wives*. New York: Random House.

Levitz, P. (2013). Why Supervillains? In R.S. Rosenberg & P. Coogan (Eds.). *What Is a Superhero?* (Loc. 1654–1714) [Kindle Paperwhite version 5.6.1.1].

Lewis, A.D. (2013). Save the Day. In R.S. Rosenberg & P. Coogan (Eds.). *What Is a Superhero?* (Loc. 803–967). [Kindle Paperwhite version 5.6.1.1].

Li, J., Angsantikul, P., Liu, W., Esteban-Fernández de Ávila, B., Thamphiwatana, S., Xu, M., Sandraz, E., Wang, X., Delezuk, J., Gao, W., Zhang, L., & Wang, J. (2017). Micromotors Spontaneously Neutralize Gastric Acid for pH-Responsive Payload Release. *Angewandte Chemie International Edition*, 56(8): 2156–2161.

Lian, YL (2011). *Lovotics Episode 1* [Video file], 8 June 2011. Retrieved from https://www.youtube.com/watch?v=iq_USTBgeZY.

Liberman, M. (2012). Warfighter. Language Log [Online], 25 Nov. 2012. Retrieved from http://languagelog.ldc.upenn.edu/nll/?p=4339.

Liftoff (2011). *Eureka* [Television series episode]. Syfy (Season 4, episode 11), 11 July 2011.

Lin, J. & Singer, P.W. (2018). China Is Making 1,000-UAV Drone Swarms Now. *Popular Science* [Online], 8 Jan. 2018. Retrieved from https://www.popsci.com/china-drone-swarms.

Lin, P., Bekey, G. & Abney, K. (2008). *Autonomous Military Robotics: Risk, Ethics, and Design*. San Luis Obispo: California Polytechnic State University. Retrieved from http://ethics.calpoly.edu/onr_report.pdf.

Lockett, H.G. (1933). The Unwritten Literature of the Hopi. *Social Science Bulletin* (No. 2), 15 May 1933. Tucson: University of Arizona. Retrieved from Project Gutenberg at http://www.gutenberg.org/ebooks/15888.

Lokhorst, G-J. & van den Hoven, J. (2012). Responsibility for Military Robots. In P. Lin, K. Abney, and G.A. Bekey (Eds.). *Robot Ethics* (pp. 110–156). Cambridge, MA: MIT Press.

Long, E. (n.d.). Juuchi Yosamu [Online]. Retrieved 7 Dec. 2014 from http://www.cleandungeon.com/article/784/Juuchi+Yosamu.html.

Lönnrot, E. (1835 [1898]). *Kalevala*. Helsinki, Finland: J.C. Frenckellin ja Poika. [*The Kalevala: The Epic Poem of Finland, into English* (Vol. 2). (J.M. Crawford, Trans.). Cincinnati, OH: The Robert Clarke Company.]

Lordan, G. & Neumark, D. (2017). People Versus Machines: The Impact of Minimum Wages on Automatable Jobs. The National Bureau of Economic Research [Online], 2 Jan. 2018. Retrieved from http://www.nber.org/papers/w23667.

Lucas, G.R. (2013). Engineering, Ethics, and Industry: The Moral Challenges of Lethal Autonomy. In B.J. Strawser (Ed.). *Killing by Remote Control: The Ethics of an Unmanned Military* (pp. 211–228). New York: Oxford University Press.

Luther, K. (2017). The Evolution of "Mecha" From "Everything Mechanical" in Japan to Anime about Robots. ThoughtCo.com [Online], 16 July 2017. Retrieved from https://www.thoughtco.com/mecha-definition-144821.

Macek, C. & Agrama, A. (Producers) (1985–, ongoing). *Robotech* [Anime television series]. New York: Sci-Fi Channel.

Manhunters (n.d.). www.DCau.wikia.com [Wiki]. Retrieved from http://dcau.wikia.com/wiki/Manhunters.

Margaritoff, M. (2017). Australian Drug Cartel Used Drone to Spy on Police. *The Drive* [Online], 30 June 2017. Retrieved from http://www.thedrive.com/aerial/12050/australian-drug-cartel-used-drone-to-spy-on-police.

Mark, J. (2017). Ninurta: Definition. *Ancient History Encyclopedia* [Online], 2 Feb. 2017. Retrieved from https://www.ancient.eu/Ninurta/.

Markowitz, J. (2013). Beyond SIRI: Exploring Spoken Language in Warehouse Operations, Offender Monitoring, and Robotics. In A. Neustein & J.A. Markowitz (Eds.). *Mobile Speech and Advanced Natural Language Solutions* (pp. 3–22). Heidelberg, Germany: Springer.

Markowitz, J. (2015). Cultural Icons. In J. Markowitz (Ed.). *Robots That Talk and Listen* (pp. 21–54). Berlin, Germany: De Gruyter.

Martin, T., Jones, R., Harrod, H., Thompson, J., & Lewis, M. (2015). Doctor Who: 50 Things You Didn't Know. *Telegraph*, 17 Sept. 2015. Retrieved from http://www.telegraph.co.uk/tv/2015/doctor-who-50-things-you-didnt-know/.

Martinez, A.L. (2008). *The Automatic Detective*. New York: Tor Books.

The Master Mystery (1919). Directed by H. Houdini. & B.L. King [Film]. New York: Metro Pictures, Inc. & Octagon Films.

Master of the World (1934) Directed by H. Piel [Film]. Berlin, Germany: Ariel Productions.

The Matrix. (1999). Directed by The Wachowski Brothers [Film]. Burbank, CA: Warner Brothers.

The Matrix Reloaded (2003). Directed by L. Wachowski & L. Wachowski [Film]. Burbank, CA: Warner Brothers.

The Matrix Revolutions (2003). Directed by L. Wachowski & L. Wachowski [Film]. Burbank, CA: Warner Brothers.

Mattel (2015). Hello Barbie Q&A: Hello Barbie. Retrieved from http://hellobarbiefaq.mattel.com/wp-content/uploads/2015/12/hellobarbie-faq-v3.pdf.

Matthias, A. (2011). Is the Concept of an Ethical Governor Philosophically Sound? Paper presented at TILTing Perspectives 2011: Technologies on the Stand: Legal and Ethical Questions in Neuroscience and Robotics,

Tilburg, Netherlands, 11–12 April 2011. Retrieved from http://www.academia.edu/473656/Is_the_Concept_of_an_Ethical_Governor_Philosophically_Sound.

McCarter, M., Mfaume, K., Matsuka, Y. & Sugita, A. (Producers) (2002–2005). *Ghost in the Shell: Stand Alone Complex* [Television series]. Tokyo, Japan: NTV.

McGuire, S. (2014). We Are All Misfit Toys in the Aftermath of the Velveteen War. In D.H. Wilson & J.J. Adams (Eds.), *Robot Uprisings* (pp. 363–386). New York: Vintage Books.

McKinsey Global Institute (2017). *A Future That Works: Automation, Employment, and Productivity.* New York: McKinsey & Company.

McNeil, A. (1980). Berzerk [Video game]. Chicago, IL: Stern Electronics.

Megatron (G1) (n.d.). www.Tfwiki.net [Wiki]. Retrieved 7 Jan. 2017 from https://tfwiki.net/wiki/.

Megingjörð (n.d.). *Encyclopedia Mythica* [Online]. Retrieved 14 Oct. 2017 from https://pantheon.org/articles/m/megingjord.html.

Men of Iron (n.d.). Lexicanum.com [Online]. Retrieved 11 Dec. 2007 from http://wh40k.lexicanum.com/wiki/Men_of_Iron.

Metropolis. (1927). Directed by F. Lang [Film]. Hollywood, CA: Paramount Pictures.

Meyer, M. (2013). Yokai.com/home [Online]. Retrieved from http://yokai.com.

Meyrink, G. (1914 [1995]). *Der Golem.* Leipzig, Germany: Kurt Wolff. [*The Golem.* (M. Mitchell, Trans.). Hollywood, CA: Daedalus.] Retrieved from http://www.unclecthulhu.com/books/TheGolem.pdf.

Miles, L. (2000). Vrs. In S. Cole & J. Raynor (Eds.). *Doctor Who: Short Trips and Side Steps* (back cover). London: BBC.

Military penal unit (2017). *World Heritage Encyclopaedia* [Online]. Retrieved from http://gutenberg.us/articles/eng/Penal_military_unit.

Miller, M. (2006). Civil War #3. *Civil War.* 1(3), July 2006. New York: Marvel Comics.

Mills, P. (1979–, ongoing). *ABC Warriors. 2000 AD.* Oxford, UK: Rebellion Developments.

Mills, P. & Langley, C. (2010). *ABC Warriors.* Oxford, UK: Rebellion Developments.

Milton, J. (1645). Lycidas. The John Milton Reading Room [Online]. Retrieved from https://www.dartmouth.edu/~milton/reading_room/lycidas/text.shtml.

The Minority Report (2002). Directed by Spielberg, S. [Film]. Universal City, CA: Dreamworks.

Mithaiwaia, M. (2017). 15 Times Superman Has "Died." *Screenrant* [Online], 4 April 2017. Retrieved from https://screenrant.com/times-superman-has-died-best-fake-deaths/.

Mitrano, T. (2012). Technology Is a Double-Edged Sword. *Inside Higher Ed* [Online], 14 May 2012. Retrieved from https://www.insidehighered.com/blogs/law-policy-and-it/technology-double-edged-sword.

Miura, K. (1989–, ongoing [2003–, ongoing]). Beruseruku. Tokyo, Japan: Hakusensha. [Berserk. Milwaukie, OR: Dark Horse Manga].

Mizokami, K. (2015). The U.K. Unveils Its Soldier of the Future. *Popular Mechanics* [Online], 22 Sept. 2015. Retrieved from http://www.popularmechanics.com/military/research/news/a17435/the-uk-unveils-its-soldier-of-the-future/.

Mkhize, N. (1996). Mind, Gender, and Culture. In *Proceedings of the 2nd Annual Qualitative Methods Conference,* Johannesburg, South Africa, 3–4 Sept. 1996. Retrieved from http://www.criticalmethods.org/bodpol.htm.

Mobile Weapon (n.d.). www.gundam.wikia.com [Wiki]. Retrieved 7 June 2017 from http://gundam.wikia.com/wiki/Mobile_suit#Mobile_Suit.

Molière (1683). *Le Festin de Pierre.* Amsterdam: Henru Wetsein.

Mona, E. (Ed.) (2003). *Mutants & Masterminds: Freedom City.* Renton, WA: Green Ronin Publishing.

Moon, M. (2014). These Robots Have X-Ray Vision, Thanks to WiFi. *Engadget* [Online], 5 Aug. 2014. Retrieved from https://www.engadget.com/2014/08/05/robots-wifi-xray-see-through-walls/.

Moore, A. (1986). Whatever Happened to the Man of Tomorrow? *Action Comics,* 1(583), Sept. 1986. New York: DC Comics.

Moore, R.K. (2015). From Talking and Listening Robots to Intelligent Communication Machines. In J. A. Markowitz (Ed.), *Robots That Talk and Listen* (pp. 317–336). Boston, MA: DeGruyter.

Morrison, G. (1990). Down Paradise Way. *Doom Patrol,* 1(35), Aug. 1990. New York: DC Comics.

Müller, V.C. & Simpson, T.J. (2014). *Killer Robots: Regulate, Don't Ban.* Technical report [Online]. Oxford, UK: Oxford University, Blavatnik School of Government. Retrieved from https://www.researchgate.net/publication/283513768.

Mulrine, A. (2011). How Often Do US Military Drones "Disappear"? *The Christian Science Monitor* [Online], 5 Dec. 2011. Retrieved from https://www.csmonitor.com/USA/Military/2011/1205/How-often-do-US-military-drones-disappear.

Muoio, D. (2015). Russia and China Are Building Highly Autonomous Killer Robots. *Tech Insider* [Online], 15 Dec. 2015. Retrieved from http://www.businessinsider.com/russia-and-china-are-building-highly-autonomous-killer-robots-2015–12.

Murison, M. (2018). How Skydroid Could Protect Prisons from Drone Smugglers. *The Internet of Business* [Online], 8 March 2018. Retrieved from https://internetofbusiness.com/uk-government-prison-drone-deliveries/.

Myr, S. (2013). Good & Evil in 40K. www.Warhammer40k.wikia.com [Wiki]. Retrieved from http://warhammer40k.wikia.com/wiki/Thread: 35074.

Nanoweapons (2017). Article36.com [Position paper]. Retrieved from http://www.article36.org/wp-content/uploads/2017/11/Nano-Final-17Nov17.pdf.

Naval Studies Board (2005). *Autonomous Vehicles in Support of Naval Operations.* Washington, D.C.: The National Academies Press. Retrieved from https://www.nap.edu/catalog/11379/autonomous-vehicles-in-support-of-naval-operations.

New America Foundation & Terror Free Tomorrow (2010). *Public Opinion in Pakistan's Tribal Regions.* Washington, D.C.: Authors. Retrieved from http://www.terrorfreetomorrow.org/upimagestft/FATA poll1.pdf.

Newitz, A. (2017). *Autonomous.* New York: Tom Doherty Associates.

Nintendo R&D & Intelligent Systems (1986). Metroid [Video game]. Kyoto, Japan: Nintendo.

Niven, L. (1972). Cloak of Anarchy. *Analog Science Fic-*

tion/*Science Fact*, 89(1): 74–92. Retrieved from http://www.larryniven.net/stories/cloak_of_anarchy.shtml.

Office of the United Nations High Commissioner for Human Rights (2013). *A Call for a Moratorium on the Development and Use of Lethal Autonomous Robots* [Press release], 31 May 2013. Retrieved from http://www.ohchr.org/EN/NewsEvents/Pages/Acallforamoratoriumonthedevelopmentrobots.aspx.

Ohitsme, Wezqu, Pete, & Holo78 [Sceen names] (n.d.). Ultron. Retrieved from http://marvel.com/universe/Ultron#axzz5D1uFrvN0.

Oitzman, M. (2017). Europe Tries to Get Ahead on Robot Rules and Taxes. *Robotics Business Review* [Online], 22 March 2017. Retrieved from https://www.roboticsbusinessreview.com/manufacturing/europe-tries-get-ahead-robot-rules-taxes/.

Ōkubo, A. (2013). Startup. *Soul Eater* 15(62), 23 July 2013. New York: Yen Press.

Optimus Prime (G1) (n.d.). www.tfwiki.net [Wiki]. Retrieved 7 Jan. 2017 from https://tfwiki.net/wiki/Optimus_Prime_(G1).

Orczy, E. Baroness (1905). *The Scarlet Pimpernel.* n.l.: Greening.

The Original (2016). *Westworld* [Television series episode]. HBO (Season 1, episode 1), 2 Oct. 2016.

Orlowski, C. (n.d.). DARPA Robotics Challenge (DRC). DARPA.mil. Retrieved 2 Dec. 2017 from http://www.darpa.mil/program/darpa-robotics-challenge.

Orwell, G. (1950). *Nineteen Eighty Four.* London: Secker & Warburg.

Ossola, A. (2015). Replace Your Eyeballs with Synthetic Ones. *Popular Science* [Online], 20 April 2015. Retrieved from http://www.popsci.com/biotech-startup-wants-replace-your-eyeballs-synthetic-ones.

Our Production of Shakespeare's Henry V (2015). thersc.com [Online], Retrieved from http://thersc.tumblr.com/post/131739938990/our-production-of-shakespeares-henry-v-follows.

Ovid (ca. 8 CE [2000]). *Metamorphōseōn librī.* n.p. [*Ovid's Metamorphoses.* (A.S. Kline, Trans.). n.p.] Retrieved from http://ovid.lib.virginia.edu/trans/Ovhome.htm#askline.

Pacific Rim (2013). Directed by G. del Toro [Film]. Burbank, CA: Warner Brothers.

Pagano, A. (2017). Repairing Organs with the Touch of a Nanochip. *IEEE Spectrum* [Online], 12 Aug. 2017. Retrieved from http://spectrum.ieee.org/video/biomedical/devices/repairing-organs-with-the-touch-of-a-nanochip.

Paglia, J., Craig, C.G. & St. John, T. (Producers) (2006–2012). *Eureka* [Television series]. New York: Sci-Fi/syfy.

Paizo, Inc. (2016). *Golem: User Manual* [Online]. Retrieved from www.d20pfsrd.com/bestiary/monster-listings/constructs/golem/.

Palmer, D. (2016). Prisons Fight Drug Smuggling Drones with Drone-Detection Technology. *Digital Trends* [Online], 26 June 2016. Retrieved from https://www.digitaltrends.com/cool-tech/prisons-fight-drug-smuggling-drones/.

Park, K. (2007). Nanotechnology: What It Can Do for Drug Delivery. *Journal of Control Release* [Online], 16 July 2007, 120(1–2): 1–3. Retrieved from https://www.ncbi.nlm.nih.gov/pmc/articles/PMC1949907/.

Pearson, R. (2005–, ongoing). *The Kingdom Keepers* [Book series]. New York: Disney-Hyperion.

Pearson, R. (2005). *The Kingdom Keepers: Disney after Dark.* New York: Disney-Hyperion.

Peeples, J. (2015). 52 LGBT Superheroes and Villains. *The Advocate* [Online], 7 July 2015. Retrieved from https://www.advocate.com/arts-entertainment/geek/2015/07/07/52-lgbt-superheroes-and-villains.

Penadés, A. (2016). Bred for Battle—Understanding Ancient Sparta's Military Machine. *National Geographic* [Online], 11 Dec. 2016. Retrieved from https://www.nationalgeographic.com/archaeology-and-history/magazine/2016/11–12/sparta-military-greek-civilization/.

Pence Lays Out Plans for Trump's "Space Force" to Be Installed by 2020 (2018). [Online], 9 Aug. 2018. Retrieved from https://www.cbsnews.com/news/space-force-update-mike-pence-announcement-today-2018–08–09-live-stream/.

Peterson, H. (2015). McDonald's Shoots Down Fears It is Planning to Replace Cashiers with Kiosks. *Business Insider* [Online], 6 Aug. 2015. Retrieved from http://www.businessinsider.com/what-self-serve-kiosks-at-mcdonalds-mean-for-cashiers-2015–8.

Peyne, T. (1998). Tomorrow Never Knows. *JLA Tomorrow Woman*, 1(1), 1 June 1998. New York: DC Comics.

Pickens, J. (Ed.) (2010). *Advanced Dungeons & Dragons: Complete Monstrous Manual*, vol. 2. [Online]. Retrieved from http://www.lomion.de/cmm/clwohorr.php.

Piercy, M. (1991). *He, She, and It.* New York: Random House.

Piers, C. (2015). *Evolution of the Terminator: From T-1 through T-1 Million.* [Video file], 9 July 2015. Retrieved from http://www.therobotspajamas.com/evolution-of-the-terminator-from-t-1-through-t-1-million/.

Pirates of the Caribbean (2003). Directed by G. Verbinski [Film]. Burbank, CA: Walt Disney Studios Motion Pictures.

Pisani, J. (2017). Beware Connected Toys That Can Spy, FBI Warns. *Chicago Tribune*, 28 Dec. 2017, Section 2: 2.

Pistoeka sabotage droid (n.d.). Wookiepedia [Wiki]. Retrieved 30 Oct. 2017 from http://starwars.wikia.com/wiki/Pistoeka_sabotage_droid/Legends.

Pistono, F. (2012). *Robots Will Steal Your Job, But That's OK.* Seattle, WA: CreateSpace.

PlatinumGames (2013–, ongoing). Metal Gear Rising: Revengeance [Video game]. Tokyo, Japan: Konami.

Plato (n.d. [1925]). *Minos* [*Plato in Twelve Volumes* (Vol. 9). (W.R.M. Lamb, Trans.). Cambridge, MA: Harvard University Press.] Retrieved from http://www.nlnrac.org/node/236.

Plaw, A. (2013). Counting the Dead: The Proportionality of Predation in Pakistan. In B.J. Strawser (Ed.). *Killing by Remote Control: The Ethics of an Unmanned Military* (pp. 126–153). New York: Oxford University Press.

Poe, E. A. (1839). The Man That Was Used Up. *Burton's Gentleman's Magazine* [Online], July-Dec. 1839, 5: 66–70. Retrieved from https://archive.org/stream/burtonsgentleman1839burt#page/n5/.

Pohl, F. (1955 [1989]). The Tunnel under the World. *Galaxy Science Fiction*, 9(4): 6–37 [In I. Asimov, M.H. Greenberg, & C.G. Waugh (Eds.). *Isaac Asimov's Wonderful World of Science Fiction: Robots* (pp. 13–43). Markham, Ontario, Canada: Penguin Books Canada.]

Polybius (n.d. [2011]). *The Histories.* n.p. [*The Histories of Polybius* Volume III, Book 8 (W.R. Paton, Trans.).

The Loeb Classical Library Edition [online]. Cambridge, MA: Harvard University Press. Retrieved from http://penelope.uchicago.edu/Thayer/E/Roman/Texts/Polybius/8*.html.

Popper, B. (2016). Rise of the RoboMasters: We Went to China's Silicon Valley to See the Front Lines of the Robot Wars. *The Verge* [Online], 27 Sept. 2016. Retrieved from https://www.theverge.com/2016/9/27/13059144/dji-robomasters-robot-drone-battle-video-frank-wang-interview.

Power Fist (n.d.). Lexicanum.com [Online]. Retrieved 11 Dec. 2017 from http://wh40k.lexicanum.com/wiki/Power_fist.

Pratchett, T. (1983–2015). *Discworld* [Book series]. New York: Random House.

Pratchett, T. (1996). *Feet of Clay.* London: Victor Gollancz. [Kindle Paperwhite version 5.6.1.1].

Price, N. S. (2002). *The Viking Way: Religion and War in Late Iron Age Scandinavia* [Unpublished doctoral dissertation]. Uppsala University, Uppsala, Sweden.

Priestley, R. (1987–, ongoing). Warhammer 40,000 [Tabletop game]. Nottingham, U.K.: Games Workshop & Nottingham, U.K.: Citadel Miniatures.

Prinz, G. (Producer) (1966). *8th Man* [Anime series]. New York: ABC Films.

Pushkin, A. (1830). *Kamennyy Gost.* Leningrad, Russia: Leningrad Music, W. Bessel & Co.

Q Who? (1989). *Star Trek: The Next Generation* [Television series episode]. CBS (Season 2, episode 16), 8 May 1989.

Qu, Z, Xiao, G., Xu, N., Diao, Z. & Jia-Zhou, H. (2016). A Novel Night Vision Image Color Fusion Method Based on Scene Recognition. Paper presented at the 19th International Conference on Information Fusion, Heidelberg, Germany, 5–8 July. Piscataway, NJ: IEEE.

Quick, D. (2010). Battlefield Extraction-Assist Robot to Ferry Wounded to Safety. *New Atlas* [Online], 25 Nov. 2010. Retrieved from http://newatlas.com/battlefield-extraction-assist-robot/17059/.

Quick, D. (2012). iRobot Launches New 710 Warrior Robot. *New Atlas* [Online], 9 Feb. 2012. Retrieved from https://newatlas.com/irobot-710-warrior/21396/.

Rabkin, J. & Yoo, J. (2017). Killer Robots Will Save Human Lives. Encounter Books.com [Online], 28 Sept. 2017. Retrieved from https://www.encounterbooks.com/features/why-killer-robots-will-save-human-lives/.

Radcliffe, A. (2015). Every Limb Lost in the *Star Wars* Films. StarWars.com [Online], 10 March 2015. Retrieved from https://www.starwars.com/news/every-limb-lost-in-the-star-wars-films.

Radford, B. (2013). Voodoo: Facts about Misunderstood Religion. *LiveScience* [Online], 30 Oct. 2013. Retrieved from http://www.livescience.com/40803-voodoo-facts.html.

Rasmussen, K. (1921). *Eskimo Folk-Tales.* London: Gydendal.

Ratcliffe, A. (2015). 7 of R2-D2's Most Heroic Acts: StarWars.com Looks at Some of the Overweight Glob of Grease's Finest Moments! [Blog], 14 April 2015. Retrieved from http://www.starwars.com/news/7-of-r2-d2-most-heroic-acts.

Ratti, O & Westbrook, A. (1999). *Secrets of the Samurai: A Survey of the Martial Arts of Feudal Japan.* Wareham, MA: Castle Books.

Ravindranath, M. (2016). The Military Is Pouring Money into Smart Fabrics, but There's a Holdup. *Nextgov* [Online], 18 April 2016. Retrieved from http://www.defenseone.com/technology/2016/04/military-wants-smart-fabrics-theres-holdup/127589/.

Raymond, A. (1934). *Flash Gordon,* 1(1), 7 Jan. 1934. New York: King Features.

Redheart [Screen name] (2015). Russian "Skynet" to Lead Military Robots on the Battlefield. *World Defense* [Online], 19 Oct. 2015. Retrieved from https://world-defense.com/threads/russian-%e2%80%98skynet%e2%80%99-to-lead-military-robots-on-the-battlefield.3265/.

Regeneration (2003). *Star Trek: Enterprise* [Television series episode]. UPN (Season 2, episode 23), 7 May 2003.

Reider, N.T. (2009). Animating Objects: Tsukumogami Ki and the Medieval Illustration of Shingon Truth. *Japanese Journal of Religious Studies,* 36: 231–257.

Rensi, E. (2016). Thanks to "Fight for $15" Minimum Wage, McDonald's Unveils Job-Replacing Self-Service Kiosks Nationwide. *Forbes* [Online], 29 Nov. 2016. Retrieved from https://www.forbes.com/sites/realspin/2016/11/29/thanks-to-fight-for-15-minimum-wage-mcdonalds-unveils-job-replacing-self-service-kiosks-nationwide/#2bfb6704fbc6.

Renunger, E. (2017). Taoist Immortal Lü Dongbin (Lu Tung Pin)—An Introduction. Thoughtco.com [Online], 18 March 2017. Retrieved from https://www.thoughtco.com/taoist-immortal-lu-dongbin-lu-tung-pin-an-introduction-3182609.

Retro Gamer Team (Interviewers) & McNeil, A. (Interviewee) (2014). *The Making of Berzerk.* [Partial interview transcript], 14 Oct. 2014. Retrieved from https://www.retrogamer.net/retro_games80/the-making-of-berzerk/.

Revenge of the Robot (2003). *Sonic X* [Anime series episode]. Fox (Series 2, episode 31), 16 Oct. 2004.

Reynolds, A. (2004 [2012]). *Century Rain.* London: Gollancz. [Kindle Paperwhite version 5.6.1.1].

Reynolds, C.W. (1968). Flocks, Herds, and Schools: A Distributed Behavioral Model. *Computer Graphics* [Online], 21(4): 25–34. Retrieved from http://www.cs.toronto.edu/~dt/siggraph97-course/cwr87/.

Rig Veda (1896). *The Hymns of the Rigveda* (R.T.H. Griffith, Trans.). Retrieved from http://www.sanskritweb.net/rigveda/griffith.pdf.

RIM-8 Talos (n.d.). WeaponsSystems.net [Online]. Retrieved from http://weaponsystems.net/weaponsystem/II02%20-%20RIM-8%20Talos.html.

Ringo, J. (2003–2006). *The Council Wars* [Book series]. Riverdale, Canada: Baen Books.

Rise of the Cybermen (2006). *Doctor Who* [Television series episode]. BBC Worldwide (Season 2, episode 5), 13 May 2006.

Riza, M.S. (2013). *Killing without Heart.* Washington, D.C.: Potomac Books.

RoboCop (1987). Directed by P. Verhoeven [Film]. Los Angeles, CA: Orion Pictures.

Robot (1974–1975). *Doctor Who* [Television series episodes]. BBC Worldwide (Season 12, series 1, episodes 1–4), 28 Dec. 1974–18 Jan. 1975.

Robot & Frank (2012). Directed by J. Schreier [Film]. Culver City, CA: Samuel Goldwyn Films.

Robot Challenge (n.d.). Robot Park Academy. Retrieved 20 April 2017 from http://www.robotpark.com/academy/robot-challenge-2013-vienna-austria-31035/.

Robot Police Officer Goes on Duty in Dubai (2017). *BBC News* [Online], 24 May 2017. Retrieved from http://www.bbc.com/news/technology-40026940.

Robotic Prosthetics (n.d.). Human Technology.com [Online]. Retrieved [7 March 2017] from https://www.humantechpando.com/robotic-prostheses/.

The Robots of Death (1977). *Doctor Who* [Television series episodes]. BBC Worldwide (Season 14, story 5, episodes 1–4), 29 Jan.–19 Feb. 1977.

Robot's Revenge (1985). *The Jetsons* [Television series episode]. ABC (Season 2, episode 36), 20 Nov. 1985.

Robson, J. (2013). *Transformers: The Covenant of Primus.* Seattle, WA: Amazon Publishing.

Roddenberry, G. & Berman, R. (Producers) (1987–1994). *Star Trek: The Next Generation.* [Television series]. First run syndication.

Rogan, T. (2018). Robot Soldiers Can't Replace Human Soldiers. *The Examiner* [Online], 9 Feb. 2018. Retrieved from https://www.washingtonexaminer.com/robot-soldiers-cant-replace-human-soldiers.

Ronen, G. (2009). IDF Develops Spy Robot Snake with "Suicide" Capability. *Israel National News* [Online], 10 June 2009. Retrieved from http://www.israelnationalnews.com/News/News.aspx/131807.

Rosenberg, Y. (1909 [2007]). *Niflos Maharal.* Piortrkov, Poland: Y. Rosenberg. [*The Golem and the Wondrous Deeds of the Maharal of Prague.* (C. Leviant, Trans.). New Haven, CT: Yale University Press.]

Rosheim, M. (2006). *Leonardo's Lost Robots.* Berlin, Germany: Springer-Verlag.

Ross, A. (1999). Earth X, Chapter 1. *Earth X.* 1(1), April 1999. New York: Marvel Comics.

Rossiter, J. (2016). *John Rossiter: Pollution-Eating Robot* [Video file], March 2016. Retrieved from https://www.ted.com/talks/jonathan_rossiter_a_robot_that_eats_pollution.

Rowling, J.K. (1998). *Harry Potter and the Chamber of Secrets.* London: Bloomsbury.

Royston, P. (n.d.). The Hidden Hero: Baroness Orczy and the Myth of the Secret Identity. *Guidewrite* [Online]. Retrieved from http://www.portwashington.com/moveweb/Guidewrite/hiddenhero.html.

Saarilouma, P. (2015). Four Challenges in Structuring Human-Autonomous Systems Interaction Design Processes. In A.P. Williams & P.D. Scharre (Eds.). *Autonomous Systems: Issues for Defence Policymakers* (pp. 226–248). The Hague, Netherlands: NATO Communications and Information Agency.

Saberhagen, F. (1967 [2012]/2007). *Berserkers* [Book series] New York: Tom Doherty Associates.

Saberhagen, F. (1993). *Berserker Kill.* New York: Tom Doherty Associates.

Saha, D. & Liu, S. (2017). Increased Automation Guarantees a Bleak Outlook for Trump's Promises to Coal Miners. *Brookings* [Online] 25 Jan. 2017. Retrieved from https://www.brookings.edu/blog/the-avenue/2017/01/25/automation-guarantees-a-bleak-outlook-for-trumps-promises-to-coal-miners/.

Salton, J. (2009). Nanotech Battlefield Treatment to Ease Pain and Limit Dangerous Side Effects. *New Atlas* [Online], 28 Sept. 2009. Retrieved from http://newatlas.com/nanotech-battlefield-treatment-eases-pain-limits-side-effects/12957/.

Sanchez, A. (2015). Worst Case Scenario: The Criminal Use of Drones. COHA.org [Online], 2 Feb. 2015. Retrieved from http://www.coha.org/worst-case-scenario-the-criminal-use-of-drones/.

Sanderson, B. (2009). *Warbreaker.* New York: Tor Books.

Sasamura, T. & Matsumoto, M. (Producers) (2003–2004). *SonicX* [Anime series]. Tokyo, Japan: TV Tokyo.

Sauer, F. (2016). Stopping Killer Robots: Why Now Is the Time to Ban Autonomous Weapons Systems. *Arms Control Today* [Online], Oct. 2016. Retrieved from https://www.armscontrol.org/ACT/2016_10/Features/Stopping-Killer-Robots-Why-Now-Is-the-Time-to-Ban-Autonomous-Weapons-Systems.

Scalzi, J. (2005–2015). *Old Man's War* [Book series]. New York: Tom Doherty Associates.

Scalzi, J. (2005). *Old Man's War.* New York: Tor Books.

Scalzi, J. (2006). *The Ghost Brigades.* New York: Tom Doherty Associates.

Scataglini, S., Andreoni, G., & Gallant, J. (2015). A Review of Smart Clothing in Military. In *WearSys '15: Proceedings of the 2015 Workshop on Wearable Systems and Applications,* Florence, Italy, 18 May 2015 (pp. 53–54). New York: ACM.

Scharre, P. (2014a). *Robotics on the Battlefield Part I: Range, Persistence and Daring.* Washington, D.C.: Center for a New American Security, Oct. 2014.

Scharre, P. (2014b). *Robotics on the Battlefield Part II: The Coming Swarm.* Washington, D.C.: Center for a New American Security, Oct. 2014.

Scharre, P. & Horowitz, M.C. (2015). Ban or No Ban, Hard Questions Remain on Autonomous Weapons. *IEEE Spectrum* [Online]. 20 Aug. 2015. Retrieved from https://spectrum.ieee.org/automaton/robotics/military-robots/ban-or-no-ban-hard-questions-remain-on-autonomous-weapons.

Schmitt, M.N. & Thurnher, J.S. (2013). "Out of the Loop": Autonomous Weapons Systems and the Law of Armed Conflict. *Harvard National Security Journal,* 4(2): 231–281. Retrieved from https://papers.ssrn.com/sol3/papers.cfm?abstract_id=2212188.

Schodt, F. (1988). *Inside the Robot Kingdom.* Tokyo, Japan: Kodansha International.

Schroeder, H.J. (1937). *Disciplinary Decrees of the General Councils: Text, Translation and Commentary.* St. Louis, MO: B. Herder.

Scorpion (1997) *Star Trek: Voyager* [Television series episode]. UPN (Season 3, episode 26), 21 May 1997.

Scott, J.B. (1916). *Resolutions of the Institute of International Law: Dealing with the Law of Nations.* New York: Oxford University Press.

Screamers (1995). Directed by C. Duguay [Film]. Culver City, CA: Columbia Pictures.

Selby, S. (2015). *The Bow: Invention out of Necessity* [Video file], Oct. 2015. Retrieved from https://www.youtube.com/watch?v=vfdcXbUazKk.

Sengupta, S. (2014). Unarmed Drones Aid U.N. Peacekeeping Missions in Africa. *New York Times* [Online], 2 July 2014. Retrieved from https://www.nytimes.com/2014/07/03/world/africa/unarmed-drones-aid-un-peacekeepers-in-africa.html.

Seung-woo, K. (2017). Korea to Use Drones to Monitor Inmates. *The Korea Times* [Online], June 2017. Retrieved from http://www.koreatimes.co.kr/www/news/tech/2017/06/133_230654.html.

Seven of Nine (n.d.). Star Trek Discovery. Retrieved 11

Oct. 2017 from http://www.startrek.com/database_article/seven-of-nine.

Shakespeare, W. (1623 [2010]). The Life of Henry the Fifth. *First Folio* (pp. 69–95). [*Henry V.* New York: The Modern Library]

Shapiro, A. (Interviewer) & Scharre, P. (Interviewee) (2018). Autonomous Weapons Would Take Warfare TO a New Domain, without Humans. *NPR: All Tech Considered* [Online], 23 April 2018. Retrieved from https://www.npr.org/sections/alltechconsidered/2018/04/23/604438311/autonomous-weapons-would-take-warfare-to-a-new-domain-without-humans.

Sharkey, N. (2012). The Evitability of Autonomous Robot Warfare. *International Review of the Red Cross,* 94(886): 787–799.

Shatner, W. (1989). *Tekwar.* New York: Ace/Putnam.

Shaw, L. (Producer) (1980). *Beyond Westworld* [Television series]. New York: CBS.

Sheckley, R. (1953). Watchbird. *Galaxy Science Fiction,* 5(5): 74–95.

Sheckley, R. (1954). The Battle. *If Magazine: Worlds of Science Fiction,* Sept. 1954: 52–56. Retrieved from http://lingualeo.com/es/jungle/the-battle-by-robert-sheckley-53189#/page/1.

Shelley, M.W. (1818 [1957]). *Frankenstein; or, The modern Prometheus.* London: Lackington, Hughes, Harding, Mavor & Jones. [*Frankenstein.* New York: Pyramid Books.]

Sherwin, B.L. (1985). *The Golem Legend: Origins and Implications.* Lanham, MD: University Press of America.

Sherwin, Rabbi Byron L. (Jewish scholar and ethicist). Email to the author, 16 Dec. 2013.

Shewan, D. (2017). Robots Will Destroy Our Jobs—and We're Not Ready for It. *The Guardian* [Online], 11 Jan. 2017. Retrieved from https://www.theguardian.com/technology/2017/jan/11/robots-jobs-employees-artificial-intelligence.

Shirow, M. (1989–1990). *Ghost in the Shell.* Tokyo, Japan: Kodansha.

Shooter, J. (1977). The Bride of Ultron. *Avengers* 1(162), Aug. 1977. New York: Marvel Comics.

Shteynberg, G., Gelfand, M.J. & Kim, K. (2009). Peering into the "Magnum Mysterium" of Culture: The Explanatory Power of Descriptive Norms. *Journal of Cross-Cultural Psychology* [Online], 40(1): 46–69.

Sidner, S. & Simon, J. (2016). How Robot, Explosives Took out Dallas Sniper in Unprecedented Way. *CNN* [Online], 12 July 2016. Retrieved from http://www.cnn.com/2016/07/12/us/dallas-police-robot-c4-explosives/.

Siegel, J., & Shuster, J. (1940). *Action Comics,* April 1940, 1(23). New York: DC Comics.

Simak, C.D. (1944 [2016]). Desertion. *Astounding Science Fiction,* 34(3): 64–74. [In A. Vandermeer & J. Vandermeer (Eds.). *The Big Book of Science Fiction* (pp. 156–163). Toronto, Ontario, CA: Vintage Books]

Simon & Schuster (1996). Star Trek: Borg [Video game]. New York: Developer.

Singer, I.B. (1969 [1982]). *The Golem.* New York: The Jewish Daily Forward. [*The Golem.* New York: Farrar Straus Giroux].

Singer, P.W. (2009a). Military Robots and the Laws of War. *Brookings* [Online], 11 Feb. 2009. Retrieved from https://www.brookings.edu/articles/military-robots-and-the-laws-of-war/.

Singer, P.W. (2009b). *Wired for War.* New York: Penguin.

Sleeping Beauty (1959). Directed by C. Geronimi [Film]. Burbank, CA: Buena Vista.

Smalley, D. (2016). *Autonomous Swarmboats: New Missions, Safe Harbors* [Press release], 4 Dec. 2016. Retrieved https://www.onr.navy.mil/Media-Center/Press-Releases/2016/Autonomous-Swarmboats.

Smith, A. & Anderson, J. (2014). AI, Robotics, and the Future of Jobs. PewInternet.org [Online], 6 Aug. 2014. Retrieved [10 March 2016] from http://www.pewinternet.org/2014/08/06/future-of-jobs/.

Smith, D.M., Simon, J.K., & Baker, J.R., Jr. (2013). Applications of Nanotechnology for Immunology. *Nature Reviews Immunology.* Aug. 2013, 13(8): 592–605.

Soper, S. (2018). Amazon's AI taking over HQ. *Chicago Tribune,* 21 June 2018: (Section 2) 4.

Sparrow, R. (2007). Killer Robots. *Journal of Applied Philosophy,* 24(1): 62–77.

Sparrow, R. (2013). War without Virtue. In B.J. Strawser (Ed.). *Killing by Remote Control: The Ethics of an Unmanned Military* (pp. 84–105). New York: Oxford University Press.

Sparrow, R. (2016). Robots and Respect: Assessing the Case against Autonomous Weapons Systems. *Ethics and International Affairs,* 30(1): 93–116.

Speidel, M. (2002). Berserks: A History of Indo-European "Mad Warriors." *Journal of World History,* 13 (Sept 2002): 252–290.

Spenser, E. (1590 [1894–1897]). *The Faerie Queene,* London: William Ponsonby. [T. Wise (Ed.). *The Faerie Queene.* London: George Allen Ruskin House.]

Spindrifting South African Sea Monkey (2008). Twisted Tales of the Tokoloshe [Blog], 10 Oct. 2008. Retrieved from http://southafricanseamonkey.blogspot.com/2008/10/twisted-tales-of-tokoloshe.html.

Springer, P. J. (2013). *Military Robots and Drones: A Reference Handbook.* Santa Barbara, CA: ABC-CLIO.

Stadler, S. (2012). *Exoskeleton.* North Kingston, RI: Dark Hall Press.

Stanford Biomimetics and Dextrous Manipulation Laboratory (2017). bdml.stanford.edu. Retrieved 4 Feb. 2018 from http://bdml.stanford.edu/Main/ClimbingAdhesionHome.

Star Trek Generations (1994). Directed by D. Carson [Film]. Hollywood, CA: Paramount Pictures.

Star Trek Universe (1966–, ongoing). New York: CBS.

Star Wars [Screen name] (Interviewer) & Ben Burtt (Interviewee) (2014). *Interview: R2-D2* [Video file] 2 Feb. 2014. Retrieved from https://www.youtube.com/watch?v=eUwnFYBPMlU.

Star Wars: The Clone Wars (2008). Directed by D. Filoni [Film]. Burbank, CA: Warner Brothers Pictures.

Star Wars: Episode II—Attack of the Clones (2002). Directed by G. Lucas [Film]. Los Angeles, CA: Twentieth Century Fox.

Star Wars: Episode III—Revenge of the Sith (2005). Directed by G. Lucas [Film]. Los Angeles, CA: Twentieth Century Fox.

Star Wars: Episode V—The Empire Strikes Back (1980). Directed by I. Kershner [Film]. Los Angeles: Twentieth Century–Fox.

Star Wars: Episode VI—Return of the Jedi (1983). Directed by R. Marquand [Film]. Los Angeles: Twentieth Century–Fox.

Star Wars Universe (1977–, ongoing). Burbank, CA: Walt Disney.

Star Wars (1977). Directed by G. Lucas [Film]. Los Angeles, CA: Twentieth Century–Fox.

Stasse, O., Flayols, T. Budhiraja, R., Giraud-Esclasse, K., Carpentier, J., Mirabel, J., Del Prete, A., Souères, P., Mansard, N., Lamiraux, F., Laumond, J-P., Marchionii, L., Tome, H. and Ferro, F. (2017). TALOS: A New Humanoid Research Platform Targeted for Industrial Applications. In *Proceedings of the 17th IEEE-RAS International Conference on Humanoid Robotics*, Birmingham, UK, 15–17 Nov. 2017 (pp. 689–695). Piscataway, NJ: IEEE.

Statistics Bureau (2017). *Statistics Japan: February 1, 2017*. Tokyo, Japan: Ministry of Internal Affairs and Communications. Retrieved from http://www.stat.go.jp/english/data/jinsui/tsuki/index.htm.

Steinhoff, U. (2013). Killing Them Safely: Asymmetry and Its Discontents. In B.J. Strawser (Ed.). *Killing by Remote Control: The Ethics of an Unmanned Military* (pp. 179–207). New York: Oxford University Press.

Stepford (2010). *Webster's New World College Dictionary* (4th Ed.). Boston, MA: Houghton Mifflin Harcourt.

The Stepford Wives (1975). Directed by B. Forbes [Film]. Culver City, CA: Columbia Pictures.

Sterling, B (2009). Imaginary Gadgets 0002: The Brazen Head. In *Wired* [Online], 9 Feb. 2009. Retrieved from https://www.wired.com/2009/02/imaginary-gad-1/.

Stone, M. (2016). DARPA's Mind-Controlled Arm Will Make You Wish You Were a Cyborg. *Gizmodo* [Online], 1 May 2016. Retrieved from https://gizmodo.com/darpas-mind-controlled-arm-will-make-you-wish-you-were-1776130193.

Strawser, B.J. (2013). Introduction: The Moral Landscape of Unmanned Weapons. In B.J. Strawser (Ed.). *Killing by Remote Control: The Ethics of an Unmanned Military* (pp. 3–24). New York: Oxford University Press.

The Stray (2016). *Westworld* [Television series episode]. HBO (Season 1, episode 3), 16 Oct. 2016.

Strelan, P., Feather, N. & McKee, I. (2011). Retributive and Inclusive Justice Goals and Forgiveness: The Influence of Motivational Values. *Social Justice Research* [Online], 24: 126–142.

Stross, C. (2008). *Saturn's Children*. New York: Berkley Publishing Group.

Sturluson, S. (ca. 1200 CE [2006]). *Snorra Edda*. n.p. [*The Younger Edda*. (R.B. Anderson, Trans.)]. Retrieved from https://www.gutenberg.org/files/18947/18947-h/18947-h.htm#poet_hrungner.

Suarez, D. (2012). *Kill Decision*. New York: Dutton.

Sudarshana, K. (2017). Artificial Intelligence (A.I), Robotics in Yoga Vāsiṣṭha. Booksfact.com [Online], 21 July 2017. Retrieved from https://www.booksfact.com/technology/ancient-technology/artificial-intelligence-robotics-yoga-vasistha.html.

Sunrise (Producer) (1979–1980). *Mobile Suit Gundam* [Anime television series]. Nagoya, Japan: Nagoya Broadcasting Network.

Superman Robot (n.d.). www.DC.wikia.com [Wiki]. Retrieved 11 Dec. 2014 from http://dc.wikia.com/wiki/Superman_Robot.

Sweet Revenge (n.d.). www.Battlebots.wikia.com [Wiki]. Retrieved from http://battlebots.wikia.com/wiki/Kenny%27s_Revenge.

Szondy, D. (2015). South Korea's Team KAIST Wins 2015 DARPA Robotics Challenge. *New Atlas* [Online], 8 June 2015. Retrieved from http://newatlas.com/darpa-drc-finals-2015-results-kaist-win/37914/.

T-800 (n.d.). www.Terminator.wikia.com [Wiki]. Retrieved 10 June 2017 from http://terminator.wikia.com/wiki/T-800.

T-1 (n.d.). www.Terminator.wikia.com [Wiki]. Retrieved 10 June 2017 from http://terminator.wikia.com/wiki/T-1.

T-1000 (n.d.). www.Terminator.wikia.com [Wiki]. Retrieved 10 June 2017 from http://terminator.wikia.com/wiki/T-1000.

T-70 (n.d.). www.Terminator.wikia.com [Wiki]. Retrieved 10 June 2017 from http://terminator.wikia.com/wiki/T-70.

T-X (n.d.). www.Terminator.wikia.com [Wiki]. Retrieved 10 June 2017 from http://terminator.wikia.com/wiki/T-X.

Talos (n.d.). www.ForgottenRealms.wikia.com [Wiki]. Retrieved 7 March 2018 from http://forgottenrealms.wikia.com/wiki/Talos.

Talos Group (n.d.). Cisco Blogs [Blog]. Retrieved from https://blogs.cisco.com/author/talos.

Taylor, K. (2016). Fast-Food CEO Says He's Investing in Machines Because the Government Is Making It Difficult to Afford Employees. *Business Insider* [Online], 16 March 2016. Retrieved from http://www.businessinsider.com/carls-jr-wants-open-automated-location-2016-3.

Teel, R. (2013). Army Explores Futuristic Uniform for SOCOM. *U.S. Army* [Online], 28 May 2013. Retrieved from https://www.army.mil/article/104229/army_explores_futuristic_uniform_for_socom.

$10 Million Awarded to Family of Plant Worker Killed by Robot (1983). *The Citizen, Ottawa* [Online], 11 August 1983, p. 14. Retrieved from https://news.google.com/newspapers?id=7KMyAAAAIBAJ&sjid=Bu8FAAAAIBAJ&pg=3301,87702&dq=flat-rock+williams+robot&hl=en.

Ten Reasons to Ban Killer Robots (2017). PAX.org [Online]. Retrieved from https://www.paxforpeace.nl/media/files/pax-ten-reasons-to-ban-killer-robots.pdf.

The Tenth Planet (1966). *Doctor Who* [Television series episode]. BBC Worldwide (Season 4, story 2, episodes 1–4), 8–20 Oct. 1966.

The Terminator (1984). Directed by J. Cameron [Film]. Los Angeles, CA: Orion Pictures.

Terminator Genisys (2015). Directed by A. Taylor [Film]. Los Angeles, CA: Paramount Pictures.

Terminator 3: Rise of the Machines (2003). Directed by J. Mostow [Film]. Burbank, CA: Warner Brothers.

Terminator 2: Judgment Day (1991). Directed by J. Cameron [Film] Culver City, CA: TriStar Pictures.

Terminator Universe (1984–, ongoing). Portland, OR: Pacificor.

Tezuka, O. (2008). The Hot Dog Corps. In F.L. Schodt (Ed.). *Astro Boy* (pp. 33–206). Milwaukie, OR: Dark Horse Manga.

Tezuka, O. (2009). *Astro Boy* (F.L. Schodt, Trans.). Milwaukie, OR: Dark Horse Manga.

Thirteen (n.d.). www.Transformersprime.wikia.com [Wiki], Retrieved 7 Jan. 2017 from http://transformersprime.wikia.com/wiki/Thirteen.

Thomas, R. (1968). Behold the Vision. *The Avengers*, 1(57), Oct. 1968. New York: Marvel Comics.

Thomas, R. (1970). Come on In … The Revolution's Fine. *Avengers* 1(83), Dec. 1970. New York: Marvel Comics.

Thsepo (2016). My Bum Has a GPS Tracking Device Which Was Injected by a Tokoloshe. *iMansi* [Online], 30 March 2016. Retrieved from http://imzansi.co.za/my-bum-has-gps-tracking-devices-which-was-injected-by-a-tokoloshe/.

Thurnher, L. (2012). No One at the Controls: Legal Implications of Fully Autonomous Targeting. *Joint Force Quarterly* [Online], Issue 67: 78–84. Retrieved from http://ndupress.ndu.edu/Portals/68/Documents/jfq/jfq-67/JFQ-67_77–84_Thurnher.pdf.

Tirso de Molina (1630). *El Burlador de Sevilla y Convidado de Piedra*. Spain: n.p.

Tobies, M. (2014). *Complete Monstrous Manual* [Online]. Retrieved from http://www.lomion.de/cmm/clwohorr.php.

Todd, S. (2007). The African Tokolosh. *Ezine Articles* [Online], 3 Dec. 2007. Retrieved from http://ezinearticles.com/?The-African-Tokoloshe&id=862897.

Toet, A. & Hogervorst, M.A. (2012). Progress in Color Night Vision. *Optical Engineering*, 51(1).

Tokoloshe (n.d.). Mythical-Creatures-and-Beasts.com. Retrieved 12 June 2015 from http://www.mythical-creatures-and-beasts.com/tokoloshe.html.

Tokoloshe Steals Dockets: Court Evidence (2011). *News24* [Online], 28 Feb. 2011. Retrieved from https://www.news24.com/Archives/City-Press/Tokoloshe-steals-dockets-court-evidence-20150429.

Tolkien, J.R.R. (1937). *The Hobbit*. Boston, MA: Houghton Mifflin (US); New York: HarperCollins (UK).

Tolkien, J.R.R. (1977). *The Silmarillon*. New South Wales, Australia: George Allen & Unwin.

Tolstoy, L. (1873–1877[1919]). *Anna Karenina*. Philadelphia, PA: George W. Jacobs.

Tolstoy, L. & Winters, B.H. (2010). *Android Karenina*. Philadelphia, PA: Quirk Books.

Top 100 Comic Book Villains of All Time (2009). IGN.com [Online]. Retrieved from http://www.ign.com/lists/top-100-comic-book-villains/38.

Toy Story (1995). Directed by J. Lasseter [Film]. Burbank, CA: Buena Vista.

Transformers Universe (2007–, ongoing). Pawtucket, RI: Hasbro; Tokyo, Japan: Tankara Tomy.

Transformers: Revenge of the Fallen. (2009). Directed by M. Bay [Film]. Universal City, CA: Dreamworks Pictures.

Transformers (2007). Directed by M. Bay [Film]. Universal City, CA: Dreamworks Pictures & Hollywood, CA: Paramount Pictures.

Trckova-Flamee, A. (2005). Talos (Revision 4): Encyclopedia Mythica. Pantheon.org [Online], 19 Nov. 2005. Retrieved from https://pantheon.org/articles/t/talos.html.

Treehouse of Horror XVII (2006). *The Simpsons* [Television series episode]. Fox Broadcasting Company (Season 18, episode 4), 5 Nov 2006.

TrekCore (2010). *The Borg Documentary—1 of 2* [Video file], 30 Nov. 2010. Retrieved from http://www.youtube.com/watch?v=7txo8OfYONA.

Treseder, W. (2015). "Warfighter" Is Not the Best Way to Define Service Members. *Task & Purpose* [Online], 3 March 2015, Retrieved from http://taskandpurpose.com/warfighter-wrong-way-define-american-service-member/.

Tripzibit [screen name] (2013). Keris Taming Sari the Legendary Weapon of Hang Tuah. Unsolved Mysteries in the World [Blog], 15 Feb. 2013. Retrieved from http://www.unmyst3.com/2013/02/keris-taming-sari-legendary-weapon-of.html.

Tucker, P. (2018). A Criminal Gang Used a Drone Swarm to Obstruct an FBI Hostage Raid. *Defense One* [Online], 3 May 2018. Retrieved from https://www.defenseone.com/technology/2018/05/criminal-gang-used-drone-swarm-obstruct-fbi-raid/147956/?oref=d-channelriver.

2003 Inductees (2003). R2-D2. RobotHallofFame.org [Online]. Retrieved from http://www.robothalloffame.org/inductees/03inductees/r2d2.html.

Type-Moon (2004). Fate/Stay Night [Video game]. Japan: Developer.

Uhley, L. (2009). Field Trip. *Iron Man: Armored Adventures* 1(8), 29 May 2009. New York: Marvel Comics. Retrieved from http://iron-man-armored-adventures.wikia.com/wiki/Field_Trip.

Undersea Kingdom (1936). Directed by B.R. Eason & J. Kane [Film]. Los Angeles, CA: Republic Pictures.

United Nations (1977). *Geneva Convention/Protocol 1* (Doc. 17512) [Online]. Geneva, Switzerland: United Nations. Retrieved from https://en.wikisource.org/wiki/Geneva_Convention/Protocol_I.

United States Air Force (2009). *Unmanned Aircraft Systems Flight Plan 2009–2047* [Online]. Washington, D.C.: U.S. Air Force. Retrieved from www.govexec.com/pdfs/072309kp1.pdf.

United States Department of Defense (2012 [2017]) *Directive: Autonomy in weapons systems* (No. 3000.09) [Online]. Retrieved from https://www.esd.whs.mil/portals/54/documents/dd/issuances/dodd/300009p.pdf.

United States Department of Defense (2013). *Unmanned Systems Roadmap FY2013–2038* [Online]. Washington, D.C.: U.S. Department of Defense.

United States Department of Defense (2016). *Deputy Secretary: Third Offset Strategy Bolsters America's Military Deterrence* [Press release], 31 Oct. 2016. Retrieved from https://www.defense.gov/News/Article/Article/991434/deputy-secretary-third-offset-strategy-bolsters-americas-military-deterrence/.

United States Department of Defense (2017). *Department of Defense Announces Successful Micro-Drone Demonstration* [Press release], 9 Jan. 2017, No: NR-008–17. Retrieved from https://www.defense.gov/News/News-Releases/News-Release-Release.

United States Department of Defense (2018). *DOD Dictionary of Military and Associated Terms* [Online]. Washington, D.C.: U.S. Department of Defense. Retrieved from http://www.jcs.mil/Portals/36/Documents/Doctrine/pubs/dictionary.pdf.

United States Navy (2017). *MK 15–Phalanx Close-In Weapons System (CIWS): Fact File* [Online], 25 Jan. 2017. Retrieved from http://www.navy.mil/navydata/fact_display.asp?cid=2100&tid=487&ct=2.

USSOCOM (2017). *BAA for the Tactical Assault Light Operator Suit (TALOS) (BAATALOS18)*. Washington, D.C.: Special Operations Forces Acquisition, Technology, and Logistics Center. Retrieved from https://www.fbo.gov/index?tab=documents&tabmode=form&subtab=core&tabid=1374a59fcc684ca920bc6c3fc23e846b.

Utsunomiya, K., Kaji, A., Suzuki, T. & Shirakura, S. (Producers) (1992–1993). *Kyōryū Sentai Zyuranger* [Anime series]. Tokyo, Japan: TV Asahi.

Valmiki (n.d. [1999]). Yoga Vāsiṣṭha. n.p. [*The Yoga–Vasishtha Maharamayana of Valmiki* (Vihari-Lalamitra, Trans.). Delhi, India: Low Price Publishing.] Retrieved from https://www.satyavedism.org/the-yoga-vasishtha-maharamayana-mitra.

Valmiki (n.d. [2003]). *Ramayana*. n.p. [*RÁMÁYAN OF VÁLMÍKI, Book VI* (R.T.H. Griffith, Trans.)] Retrieved from http://www.sacred-texts.com/hin/rama/index.htm.

Vandyke, L. (1964). I'm Gonna Spend My Christmas with a Dalek [Recorded by the Go-Go's]. On *I'm Gonna Spend My Christmas with a Dalek* [Vinyl]. London: Oriole. (Dec. 1964).

Van Hohenheim (n.d.). www.Hero.wikia.com [Wiki]. Retrieved 1 April 2017 from http://hero.wikia.com/wiki/Van_Hohenheim.

Vanillaware (2009–2015). Muramasa: The Demon Blade [Video game]. Tokyo, Japan: Marvelous Entertainment & Marvelous AQL.

Vellian, D. (2008). Muramasa and Masamune [Blog], 20 July 2008. Retrieved from http://loreandlegends.blogspot.com/2008/07/muramasa-and-masamune.html.

Verheiden, M. (2007). Metal Men Part I: We Robots! *Superman/Batman* 1(34), April 2007. New York: DC Comics.

Victor Stone's Accident (n.d.). www.Superfriends.wikia [Wiki]. Retrieved 5 Jan. 2018 from http://superfriends.wikia.com/wiki/Victor_Stone%27s_accident.

Vigliotti, J. (2016). Watch out, Drones: This Bald Eagle Can Take You Down. *CBS News* [Online], 25 May 2016. Retrieved from https://www.cbsnews.com/news/dutch-police-use-eagles-to-take-down-illegal-drones/.

Villiers de l'Isle-Adam, A. (1886 [1982]). *L'Eve Future*. Paris, France: Biblioteque Charpentier. [*Tomorrow's Eve*. (R.M. Adams, Trans.). Urbana: University of Illinois Press].

Vilmer, J-B J. (2015). Terminator Ethics: Should We Ban "Killer Robots"? *Ethics & International Affairs* [Online], 23 March 2015. Retrieved from https://www.ethicsandinternationalaffairs.org/2015/terminator-ethics-ban-killer-robots/.

Vilmer, J-B. J. (2016). Autonomous Weapon Diplomacy: The Geneva Debates. *Ethics & International Affairs* [Online], 27 Sept. 2016. Retrieved from https://www.ethicsandinternationalaffairs.org/2016/autonomous-weapon-diplomacy-geneva-debates/.

Vinge, V. (1984). *The Peace War*. New York: Tor.

Virtuosity (1995). Directed by B. Leonard [Film]. Hollywood, CA: Paramount Pictures.

Vonnegut, K., Jr. (1952). *The Player Piano*. New York: Charles Scribner's Sons.

Walking Bombs (1940). *Flash Gordon Conquers the Universe*. Directed by F. Beebe & R. Taylor [Film series episode]. Universal City: Universal Pictures.

Wallach, W. & Allen, C. (2009). *Moral Machines: Teaching Robots Right from Wrong*. Oxford, UK: Oxford University Press.

Walworth, A. (Producer) (2005). *Gargoyles: Guardians of the Gates* [Video file]. Retrieved 3 Jan. 2018 from https://www.youtube.com/watch?v=Y60e92MFnJE.

Walzer, M. (1977). *Just and Unjust Wars: A Moral Argument with Historical Illustrations*. New York: Basic Books.

Wan, E.L. (2002). Keris—Is It Merely a Sword? Things Asian.com [Online], 2 May 2002. Retrieved from http://thingsasian.com/story/keris-it-merely-sword.

The Warhammer 40,000 Codex: Dark Eldar (2014). Nottingham, UK: Games Workshop, Ltd. Retrieved from http://wh40klib.ru/codex/Actually_codex_and_rule/Dark_Eldar_7-th_ed_Eng.pdf.

Wasabiroots (2017). *Taming Sari* [Video file], 3 Nov. 2017. Retrieved from https://www.youtube.com/watch?v=AJYA_CbdFzc.

Watts, P. (2010). Malak. In J. Strahan (Ed.). *Engineering Infinity* (pp. 13–32). Oxford, UK: Solaris Publishers. Retrieved from http://www.rifters.com/real/shorts/PeterWatts_Malak.pdf.

Weber, D. (1992–, ongoing). *Honor Harrington* [Book series]. Wake Forest, NC: Baen Books.

Weber, D. (2000). *Ashes of Victory*. [Kindle Paperwhite version 5.6.1.1].

Weber, D. (2002). *War of Honor*. [Kindle Paperwhite version 5.6.1.1].

Wells, H.G. (1896). *The Island of Dr. Moreau* [Kindle Paperwhite version 5.6.1.1].

Welsh S. (2017). Clarifying the Language of Lethal Autonomy in Military Robots. In: M.I.A. Ferreira, J.S. Sequeira, M.O. Tokhi, E.E. Kadar, & G.S. Virk (Eds.). *A World with Robots* (pp. 171–183). Cham, Switzerland: Springer.

Westall, S. (2017). Robocop Joins Dubai Police to Fight Real Life Crime. *Reuters* [Online], June 2017. Retrieved from https://www.reuters.com/article/us-emirates-robocop/robocop-joins-dubai-police-to-fight-real-life-crime-idUSKBN18S4K8.

Westworld (1973). Directed by M. Crichton [Film]. Beverly Hills, CA: Metro-Goldwyn-Mayer.

What Is an Exoskeleton (n.d.). Exoskeleton Report.com [Online]. Retrieved 5 March 2017 from https://exoskeletonreport.com/what-is-an-exoskeleton/.

What Is International Humanitarian Law (2014). icrc.org [Online], 31 Dec. 2014. Retrieved from https://www.icrc.org/en/document/what-international-humanitarian-law.

White, M.D., Arp, R. & Irwin, W. (2008). *Batman and Philosophy: The Dark Knight of the Soul*. Hoboken, NJ: John Wiley & Sons.

White Hole (1991). *Red Dwarf* [Television series episode]. BBC2 (Season 4, episode 4), 7 March 1991.

Whitwam, R. (2018). Boston Dynamics Robots Can Now Run Outside, Navigate Autonomously. ExtremeTech.com [Online], 14 May 2018. Retrieved from https://www.extremetech.com/extreme/269163-boston-dynamics-robots-can-now-run-outside-and-navigate-autonomously.

Wickham, A. (Producer) (2016–, ongoing). *Westworld* [Television series]. New York: HBO.

Widow's Revenge (n.d.). www.RobotWars.wikia.com [Wiki]. Retrieved from http://robotwars.wikia.com/wiki/Widow%27s_Revenge.

Wiener, N. (1964). *God & Golem, Inc.* MIT Press.

Wiesel, E. (1983). *Golem: The Story of a Legend*. New York: Summit Books.

Wiking, C. (2017). If Your Child Has This Doll, You Should Get Rid of It Now. *Microsoft Network* [Online], 19 Feb. 2017. http://www.msn.com/en-us/lifestyle/

family-relationships/if-your-child-has-this-doll-you-should-get-rid-of-it-now/ar-AAn3JzC?li=BBmkt5R&ocid=spartandhp.

William of Malmsbury (12th century CE [1847]). *Gesta Regum Anglorum.* n.p. [J.A. Giles (Ed.). *William of Malmesbury's Chronicle of the Kings of England: From the Earliest Period to the Reign of King Stephen.* (J. Sharpe, Trans.). London: Henry G. Bohn.

Williams, A. (2015a). Defining Autonomy in Systems: Challenges and Solutions. In A.P. Williams & P.D. Scharre (Eds.). *Autonomous Systems: Issues for Defence Policymakers* (pp. 27–64). The Hague, Netherlands: NATO Communications and Information Agency.

Williams, A. (2015b). Russian Military Unveils T-14 Armata Semi-Autonomous Tank. *Robotics Business Report* [Online], 14 July 2015. Retrieved from https://www.roboticsbusinessreview.com/security/russian_military_unveils_t_14_armata_semi_autonomous_tank/.

Williams, Y. (2010). Inuit Mythical Beasts and Creatures: Tupilak & More. Unexplainable.net. Retrieved from http://www.unexplainable.net/ancients/inuit-mythical-beasts-and-creatures-tupilaq-more.php.

Willis, R. (1996). *World Mythology.* New York: Holt Paperbacks.

Wilson, D.H. & Long, A.C. (2008). *The Mad Scientist Hall of Fame.* New York: Citadel Press.

Wilson, J. (2016). Rio Tinto's Driverless Trains Are Running Late. *Financial Times* [Online], 19 April 2016. Retrieved from https://www.ft.com/content/fe27fd68–0630–11e6–9b51–0fb5e65703ce.

Winterbach, H. (2006). Heroes and Superheroes: From Myth to the American Comic Book. *South African Journal of Art History,* 21(1): 114–134.

The Witch's Familiar (2015). *Doctor Who* [Television series episode]. BBC (season 9, episode 2). 26 Sept. 2015.

Wizards of the Coast (2015). *Systems Reference Document 5.1: User Manual* [Online]. Retrieved from https://dnd-wiki.org/wiki/Publication: SRD-OGL_v5.1.

Wizards of the Coast (n.d.). *Disintegrate: D&D Spells.* Retrieved 10 Feb. 2018 from https://www.dnd-spells.com/spell/disintegrate.

Wolfman, M. (1980). Superman and Green Lantern. *DC Comics Presents,* 1(26), Oct. 1980. New York: DC Comics.

The Wulgaru (2016). MythicalBeastWars.com [Online]. http://mythicalbeastwars.com/2013/08/the-wulgaru/the-wulgaru/.

Xal'atath, Blade of the Black Empire (2017). Gamepedia.com [Online]. Retrieved 10 Feb. 2018 from https://wow.gamepedia.com/Xal%27atath,_Blade_of_the_Black_Empire.

Yablonovitch, E. (2005). *Electrochormic Adaptive Infrared Camouflage: Interim Progress Report* (Report no. KDH7-Final). Los Angeles: University of California Los Angeles, Electrical Engineering Dept.

Yagn, N. (1890). U.S. Patent No. 440, 684: Apparatus for Facilitating Walking, Running, and Jumping. Washington, D.C.: U.S. Patent and Trademark Office. Retrieved from https://www.google.com/patents/US440684.

Yang, J.L. (2011). Does Government Regulation Really Kill Jobs? Economists Say Overall Effect Is Minimal. *Washington Post* [Online], 13 Nov. 2011. Retrieved from https://www.washingtonpost.com/business/economy/does-government-regulation-really-kill-jobs-economists-say-overall-effect-minimal/2011/10/19/gIQALRF5IN_story.html?noredirect=on&utm_term=.ac4c2783b5bd.

Yang, X., Wang, M. Hong, R. Tian, Q. & Rui, Y. (2017). Enhancing Person Re-Identification in a Self-Trained Subspace. *ACM Transactions on Multimedia Computing Communication, and Applications,* 13(3): 27: 1–27: 22.

Yeolekar, M.A. (2015). *Modeling and Stability of Robotic Motion.* [Unpublished doctoral dissertation]. Gujarat University, Gujarat, India. Retrieved from http://shodhganga.inflibnet.ac.in/bitstream/10603/105099/5/05_chapter1.pdf.

Yoshida, S. (2000 [2007]). *Toriniti Buraddo Furomu ji Enpaia.* Tokyo, Japan: Kadokawa Shoten. [*Trinity Blood* (Volume 1: From the Empire). (A. Moreno, Trans.). Tokyo, Japan: Tokyopop, Inc.]

Yoshida, S. (2005 [n.d.]). *Torinitei Buraddo Canon Shingaku Taizen.* Tokyo, Japan: Kadokawa Shoten [*Canon Summa Theologica—Translated* [(Reißzahn & M. Yamazaki, Trans.). Retrieved from http://newhumanempire.weebly.com/canon-summa-theologica.html.]

Yoshida, S. & Yasui, K. (2000). *Trinity Blood, Vol. 1.* Tokyo, Japan: Kadokawa Shoten.

Young, B. (2018). The First "Killer Robot" Was Around Back in 1979. HowStuffWorks.com [Online], 9 April 2018. Retrieved from https://science.howstuffworks.com/first-killer-robot-was-around-back-in-1979.htm/printable.

Young, L. (2016). The Legendary Chinese Poison Made by Forcing Snakes, Scorpions, and Centipedes to Fight. *Atlas Obscura* [Online], 11 Nov. 2016. Retrieved from https://www.atlasobscura.com/articles/the-legendary-chinese-poison-made-by-forcing-snakes-scorpions-and-centipedes-to-fight.

Young Frankenstein (1974). Directed by M. Brooks [Film]. Los Angeles, CA: Twentieth Century–Fox.

Yurieff, K. (2018). Boston Dynamics' Robots Keep Getting Smarter—and Soon They'll Be Available for Purchase. *CNN Tech* [Online], 11 May 2018. Retrieved from http://money.cnn.com/2018/05/11/technology/boston-dynamics-robot-spotmini/index.html.

Zanno, L.E., Varricchio, D.J., O'Connor, P.M., Titus, A.L., Knell, M.J. (2011). A New Troodontid Theropod, Talos sampsoni gen. et sp. nov., from the Upper Cretaceous Western Interior Basin of North America. *PLoS ONE* 6(9): e24487, [Online], 19 Sept. 2011. Retrieved from http://journals.plos.org/plosone/article?id=10.1371/journal.pone.0024487.

Index

ABC Warriors 28, 113
aerial drone 6, 8, 15, 30, 79, 80, 93, 100, 101, 119, 122, 149, 151, 152, 153, 154, 164, 166, 167, 168, 171, 196, 201, 202, 204, 206, 207, 208, 208, 209; and copseyes 93–4; and golem 79, 131; *see also* drone; drone army; drone strike
affect *see* emotion
A.I. *see* artificial intelligence; intelligence
agent Smith 95; and Sid 6.7 95
alchemy *see* *Fullmetal Alchemist*
alive 19, 29, 73, 76, 81, 85, 110, 132, 157; *see also* give life
AllSpark *see* soul
android 3, 5, 10, 22, 24, 26, 27, 28, 30, 32, 33, 35, 41–42, 43, 45, 51, 71–72, 75, 93, 94, 96, 102, 108, 109, 112, 113, 117, 134, 141–142, 158; *see also* homunculus
Android Karenina 41–42, 48, 89; *see also* android
anger 24, 26, 33, 66, 72, 77, 82, 83–84, 96, 111, 128, 138, 146, 195, 201; *see also* emotion; emotionless
animal (embodiment) 8, 15, 16, 19, 21–22, 25, 27, 32, 39, 43, 82, 83, 84, 87–89, 95–96, 98, 101, 101–102, 149, 151–152, 159, 161, 165–166; *see also* embodiment
aristo 71–72, 75; and cyber tanks 158; and Erasmus 72; and ku 71; and tokoloshe 71; *see also* Freya; Rhea
Arkin, Ronald 122–123, 197, 201; *see also* ethics
armor *see* powered exoskeleton
arms race 204–205
articulate *see* language; speech (fictional); speech (real)
artificial intelligence 3, 63, 95, 102, 116, 159, 195, 202, 204, 205, 207; *see also* intelligence
Asimov, Isaac 23, 43, 73, 76, 93, 119–122; *see also* ethics; Three Laws of Robotics
assassin 5, 11, 30, 40, 41, 42, 70, 71, 73, 75, 141, 142, 177, 178
Astro Boy *see* Mighty Atom
autobot 28, 110–111, 114, 140–141, 143; *see also* Optimus Prime
automatic (control) 6, 8, 139, 168, 169

automation 39, 57–63; *see also* job automation; weapon (automated)
automaton 26, 30, 37, 39, 44, 48, 79, 97, 98, 117, 129, 142, 144, 205, 206; *see also* job automation; weapon (automated)
autonomy 6–8, 53, 54, 87, 90, 95, 98, 99, 119, 122, 128, 131, 132, 133, 136, 139, 142, 144, 145, 148, 149, 150, 152, 153–154, 155, 165, 167–169, 172, 200, 202, 204, 205, 209, 210, 211; *see also* power (control)
avarice *see* greed for wealth
avenge *see* revenge
Avengers 50–51, 111, 116, 118; Dark Avengers 113; Iron Avengers 113; *see also* superhero

ban (LAWS) 125, 193–210
ban (technology) 21, 71–72, 72, 100, 139, 193–194
batteries 52, 53, 112, 128, 131, 144–145, 146, 165, 166, 167, 189; *see also* power (fuel)
Battlebots *see* competition
battledroid (Star Wars) *see* Star Wars Universe
Berserker (fiction) 155–156, 164
Berserker (real) 128, 174, 180; *see also* fighting style (Berserk)
Biblical locusts *see* buzz droid
Bill & Ted androids *see* doppelganger
biomechanics *see* locomotion; movement (robot body)
bipedal (two-legged) *see* locomotion
blood lust *see* drive to kill
bloodthirsty *see* drive to kill
body composition (robot) 5, 19, 25, 37, 48, 73, 74, 83, 87, 88, 89–90, 95, 98,
body composition (robot-precursor) 4, 5–6, 11, 15, 16, 17, 17–18, 21, 22, 25, 29, 31, 32, 34, 35, 38, 66, 68, 71, 75–76, 78, 83–84, 85
BOLO tank 156–157; and collaboration (robots) 168; *see also* tank
bomb 30, 49, 92, 100, 108, 135, 148, 159, 160, 162–163, 166, 170–171, 181, 208
the Borg 9, 51–52, 185–186; *see also* language; Lore; voice
brain control 22, 32, 45, 46, 50, 55,

89, 90, 111, 112, 132, 137, 169, 170, 181, 185, 190; *see also* cyborg; prosthetics; RoboCop
Brainiac 50, 105, 107, 109, 110; *see also* supervillain
buzz droid 161; and biblical locusts 161
by-the-book 85, 90, 92, 96 *see also* Ned; Paradise police; Talus; *Wulgaru*

Čapek *see* R.U.R.
cobot *see* human-robot collaboration
collaboration *see* human-robot collaboration
collaboration (robots) *see* BOLO tank; collaborative autonomy
collaborative autonomy 161, 168–169; *see also* autonomy
Commander Data 10, 51, 120, 129; *see also* Lore; Star Trek Universe
communicate 9, 76, 86, 101, 118, 153, 158, 161, 168, 187, 188; *see also* language; speech (fictional); speech (real); voice
competition (robots) 7, 53, 144, 145, 146, 169, 204
composition *see* body composition
consciousness *see* self-awareness
construct (games) 131, 163, 164
construction *see* body composition; embodiment
control (of humans) 72, 95, 98, 99, 100, 110
control (of robots/robot-precursors) 5, 6–8, 53, 76, 87, 90, 110, 115, 117, 119, 123, 135, 136, 142, 144, 145, 146, 147, 149, 151, 153, 154, 156, 159, 160, 170, 185, 187, 189, 193, 196, 205, 206, 207, 210; *see also* remote control; swarm
control relationship *see* control; autonomy
controller mechanism *see* swarm; collaborative autonomy
copseyes *see* aerial drone
corporate greed *see* corporation; greed
corporation 3, 33, 36, 37, 38, 39-40, 45, 47, 52, 55–56, 71–72; as golem 52; and tulpa 47; *see also* job automation; Talos
create life *see* give life

235

crime prevention 82–83, 88, 93–
    94; and ABC Warriors 113; and
    aerial drones 100–101; and giant
    (Hopi) 82; and making robots
    moral 119–123
crime punishment 82–103
criminal (non-robotic) 35, 43, 44,
    45, 46, 65, 84, 91, 91–92, 94, 95,
    99, 100, 105, 116, 122, 127, 135,
    199
criminal (robotic) 40, 44, 45, 83,
    66–81, 90, 99, 135, 193; see also
    aerial drones; Supervillain; Talos
crowd control 98–99, 99, 100; see
    also aerial drone
cyber tank 132, 153, 157–158, 164;
    see also tank
cybermen 49–51; see also cyborg
cyborg 3, 4, 5, 30, 45, 46, 48, 49,
    50, 70, 77, 89, 94, 95, 107, 108,
    109, 112, 116, 127, 132–133, 143,
    177; see also cybermen; Cyborg
    (superhero)
Cyborg (superhero) 109, 112, 116,
    127, see also cyborg; Mighty
    Atom; RoboCop

dangerous (environment) 8, 39, 51,
    72, 101, 121, 125, 129, 145, 207 see
    also dangerous, dull, and dirty
dangerous, dull, and dirty 47, 57,
    59, 125
dangerous (robot) 72, 75, 205; see
    also violence
dangerous (robot-precursor) 17,
    18, 68, 86; see also violence
DARPA 6–8, 143, 144, 148, 166,
    188, 190; see also DARPA robot-
    ics challenge
DARPA robotics challenge 6–8,
    53, 144–146, 204; see also com-
    petition
Data see Commander Data
DC Comics 29, 108, 110, 112, 113,
    136; see also Brainiac; Man-
    hunters; Superman robot
decepticon 28, 110, 140–141, 143;
    see also Megatron
Defense Advanced Research Proj-
    ects Agency see DARPA
Deputy Andy 96; and Paradise
    police 96; and wulgaru 96
detective 73, 82, 92, 93, 104, 109;
    and Nero Wolfe 73
doppelganger 25, 26, 47, 47–48,
    49, 57, 75, 77, 93, 96, 108, 109–
    110, 213Enforcersn.1
DRC see competition; DARPA
    robotics challenge
drive to kill 3, 6, 13, 16, 49, 51, 69,
    83, 89, 93, 127, 131- 133, 136, 155
drone 5, 8, 9, 35, 48, 51, 52, 66, 73,
    89, 90, 91, 95, 98, 129, 131, 133,
    139, 156, 164, 165, 166, 185–186;
    see also aerial drone; drone
    army; drone strike
drone army 26, 36, 37, 41, 42, 46,
    49, 95, 101, 127, 128, 135–136, 136,

139, 141, 142, 147, 161–162; see
    also aerial drone; drone; drone
    strike; LAWS
drone strike 201, 202, 208, 209; see
    also aerial drone; drone; drone
    army; LAWS
Dubai police robot 98

ED-209 3, 102–103; see also Robo-
    Cop
8 Man 109; see cyborg (superhero)
embodiment 4–5, 15, 41, 50, 66,
    69, 75, 89, 95, 111, 148, 158, 159,
    163–164, 165–166; see also an-
    droid; animal (embodiment);
    humanoid; non-humanoid;
    shapeshifter
emotion 3, 9, 10, 13, 31, 33, 51, 74,
    77, 78, 86, 93, 95, 96, 98, 108, 111,
    112, 123, 129, 132, 133, 138, 142,
    157, 163, 184, 187, 195, 201; see
    also perfect soldier
emotionless 10, 22, 23, 26, 50, 54,
    82, 86, 87, 98, 102, 112, 129, 132,
    135, 195; see also emotion; soul-
    less
empathy see emotion
Erasmus 72, 119; and Sid 6.7 74
Erinyes 82, 83–84, 87, 89, 94; see
    also dangerous; punishment; vi-
    olence
ethical control see ethics
ethics 61, 112, 119–123, 194, 195–
    197, 198–199
evil 11, 15, 19, 28, 28–29, 33, 41, 42,
    45, 47, 51–52, 57, 66, 69, 75, 76,
    83, 85–86, 87, 89, 105, 106, 108,
    109–110, 112, 115, 116, 139–140,
    147, 150, 152, 161, 193, 198, 198–
    199, 208–209; see also ban
    (LAWS); sword
exoskeleton see powered exoskele-
    ton
external control see remote con-
    trol

fantasy 76, 85, 104; see also science
    fiction
Father (homunculus) see Full-
    metal Alchemist
fear 3, 11, 16, 19, 23, 65, 68, 79, 84,
    85, 88, 94, 102, 111, 123, 132, 164,
    183, 187, 195, 201; see also emo-
    tion
fearless 21, 127–128, 164; see also
    emotionless
fearsome see fear
fighting style (Berserk) 128, 131,
    180; Berserker (fiction) 155;
    Frankenstein 77; golem 77, 78;
    Khumbakarna 131; mannequin
    soldiers 136; Spartoi 131; wrack
    140
fighting style (Spartan) 128, 129,
    142; doll swarm 132
fly (robot) 17, 42, 83, 93–94, 97,
    100, 108, 113, 114, 149–151, 152,
    158, 164, 167, 168, 173, 174, 176,

181, 184, 196; see also aerial
    drone
Frankenstein (book) 3, 5, 9, 19–21,
    22, 42–43, 81, 119; see also mon-
    ster; Shelley, Mary
Frankenstein (film) 5, 8, 20, 42, 73,
    78, 81; see also monster
Frankenstein, Victor 5, 9, 19, 20,
    21, 42–43, 73; see also Franken-
    stein (book); Frankenstein (film)
Frankenstein; or the modern
    Prometheus see Frankenstein
    (book)
Frankenstein: The man who made a
    monster see Frankenstein (film)
Freya 71–72, 79
Friar Roger Bacon 54–55; see also
    oracular head
fuel see power (fuel)
full autonomy see autonomy
Fullmetal Alchemist 6, 28, 74, 136
Furies see Erinyes; two-handed
    engine

Gashadokuro 4, 17–18, 24, 43
ghost see soul
Ghost in the Shell see Kusanagi,
    Motoko
giant 11, 18, 26, 41, 96, 109, 113, 116,
    144, 146–147, 173, 180; see also
    giant (Hopi); Sentinel (hu-
    manoid)
giant (Hopi) 66–67, 82; see also
    crime prevention; giant
give life 15, 16, 19, 22, 28, 34, 42,
    66, 85, 97
golem 43, 57, 65, 66, 75–78, 78, 79,
    80–81, 131; and aerial drone 131;
    see also construct; The Golem of
    Prague
gray goo see nanoweapon
greed 13, 26, 30, 33–56, 57, 59, 60,
    62, 66, 70, 74, 89, 90, 102, 103,
    110, 135, 166
greed (alien) 41, 49–52, 55
greed (corporate) 34, 36, 37 38, 39,
    44–47, 49–52
Greed (fictional character) 33, 74,
    52; see also Fullmetal Alchemist
greed (robot) 49–54
greed for knowledge 33, 36, 41,
    42–43, 51–52
greed for power 36, 41–42, 46–51
greed for wealth 33, 34, 35, 43–45,
    55–56
grief see emotion
The Golem of Prague 76–78, 81;
    see also golem

hacking 23, 54, 70, 94, 187, 196
hatred (by human) 43, 75, 93, 94,
    102, 108, 113, 193, 201, 208–209
hatred (by robots) 4, 18, 20, 21, 22,
    77, 108; see also emotion; emo-
    tionless
homunculus 6, 28, 33, 52, 74, 211;
    see also android; Father; Full-
    metal Alchemist

horror 42, 49, 78, 115, 163–164
human in the loop *see* in the loop
human-like autonomy *see* autonomy
human-machine control *see* remote control
human on the loop *see* on the loop
human out of the loop *see* out of the loop
human-robot collaboration 60, 168
humanoid (fictional) 3, 4, 5, 9, 11, 15, 21, 43, 45, 50, 52, 73, 73–74, 79, 82, 84, 84–85, 77, 92, 93, 95, 96–98, 99, 102–103, 110, 110–111, 111, 114–116, 125, 127–143, 158, 163, 164–165, 174; *see also* golem; shapeshifter; Talos
humanoid (real) 10, 11, 53, 95, 98, 99, 125, 143–146, 149, 165, 204; *see also* DARPA

implant 40, 50, 71, 172, 179, 185, 186, 187, 190; *see also* robotic prosthetics
in the loop 53, 167, 168, 205, 210 *see also* supervised autonomy
inarticulate *see* voiceless, language (fictional)
insanity 16, 24, 50, 72, 74, 89, 111, 119, 121, 153, 154; see also *torture*
intelligence 5, 8, 8–9, 10, 21, 23, 24, 25, 31, 34, 41, 43, 44, 45, 73, 76, 78, 98, 106, 108, 109, 111, 122, 127, 128, 129, 132, 133, 134, 136, 139, 141, 142, 150, 151, 152, 153–154, 155, 156, 158, 162, 163, 164, 165, 168, 175; *see also* artificial intelligence; drone
intonation *see* speech (fictional); speech (real); voice
iron man 87, 113, 145, 172, 175, 181, 188, 191; *see also* exoskeleton; Stark, Tony
iron men 37, 113, 135–136; Iron Avengers 113
The Island of Dr. Moreau 21, 42, 51, 109

job automation 11, 13, 39–40, 47, 55, 57–64, 73, 88, 93; *see also* greed (corporation)
job killing *see* job automation
joy 14, 26, 67, 74, 77, 83, 87, 120, 127, 151; *see also* drive to kill
Justice League of America 108, 109, 111, 112; *see also* superhero

killer robot (anime) 28, 33, 52, 137–139; *see also* killer robot (manga)
killer robot (comics) 28, 28–29, 46, 50–51, 73, 131, 136, 140, 181–182
killer robot (film) 3, 4, 5, 8–9, 9, 26–28, 32, 39, 43–45, 46–48, 48–49, 73–74, 75, 77–78, 102–103, 131,135–136, 136, 137, 140–143, 161, 162–163, 164, 170–171, 184, 186

killer robot (folklore) 4, 4–5, 5, 11, 14–19, 33, 34–36, 47, 54–55, 66–70, 75, 75–76, 80–81, 82, 82–85, 129–132, 136, 146–147, 149, 150–153, 172, 173–175
killer robot (games) 29–30, 45–46, 75, 78, 136, 139–140, 161–162, 163–164, 182, 182–183, 186–187
killer robot (literature) 3, 8, 10, 11, 19–26, 32, 36–43, 55, 66, 70–73, 74, 75, 76–77, 85–94, 101–102, 127, 132–135, 147, 148, 153–161,161, 164–165, 170, 172, 175–181, 182, 187
killer robot (manga) 6, 9, 28, 33,48, 73, 74,-75, 127, 131, 136, 137, 191–192
killer robot (mythology) *see* killer robot (folklore)
killer robot (real) 5, 6–8, 9, 12, 28, 30–32, 47, 52–54, 55–56, 57–64, 78–80, 94, 98–101, 119–124, 125, 127–128, 128–129, 137, 143–146, 148–149, 149, 165–170, 171, 187–191, 193–210
killer robot (television) 3, 9, 10, 26, 30, 46, 48, 49–50, 51–52, 78, 183–184, 184–186
killing spree *see* rampage
knowledge *see* greed for knowledge
ku 69–70, 71, 72, 74, 119, 193; and Erasmus 72; and Father 74; and Muramasa 69; *see also* drive to kill
Kusanagi, Motoko 94–95, *see also* cyborg; soul

language (fictional robots) 5, 8–10, 22, 34, 76, 99, 152, 156–157, 163, 179, 183–184, 185; *see also* Borg; R2-D2; toys
language (real robots) 5, 9–10, 16, 23, 25–26, 34, 39, 52, 54, 93, 162, 163, 168, 169, 172, 183, 209–210; *see also* speech technology
law enforcement 84–118, 199; *see also* Deputy Andy; Paradise police; police robot; radio police automaton
LAWS 102, 122, 125, 193–210; *see also* ban (LAWS)
learning 5, 8, 23, 101–102, 129, 197, 207; *see also* machine learning; training; unpredictability
lethal autonomous weapons systems *see* LAWS
life essence *see* soul
life force *see* soul
local processing (on robot) 53, 54, 144, 189
locomotion 5, 6–8, 9, 11, 15, 18, 37, 49, 97, 98, 99, 140, 141, 144, 145, 154, 158, 163, 172, 178; *see also* aerial drone
loitering 151, 167–168; *see also* autonomy
Lore 3, 51; and Commander Data

51, 129; *see also* the Borg; emotion
love 10, 23–24, 31, 41, 77, 78, 108, 114, 121, 138, 151, 184, 208; *see also* emotion
Lovotics *see* love
loyalty 17, 113, 128, 129, 132, 133, 134, 135, 139, 141, 142, 143, 163; *see also* perfect soldier

machine autonomy *see* autonomy
machine learning 22, 101–102, 119, 152, 153, 193, 195, 205; *see also* learning; training; unpredictability
mad scientist 3, 19–22, 26, 32, 33 & 41–43 & 46–50, 51, 73, 93, 108, 109, 111, 118; *see also* greed
magic *see* magician
magician 3, 16, 48, 54, 83, 85, 108, 132, 208, 209
making robots moral *see* ethics
Manhunters 28–29, 112, 129; *see also* Sentinel (humanoid); supervillain
Marvel Comics 109, 111, 112, 116, 131, 172, 181; *see also* Avengers; Iron Man; Stark, Tony; supervillain; Ultron
master mold 111, 112–113; *see also* Sentinel (humanoid); supervillain
mecha 116, 136–137, 137, 138; and tank 136; *see also* real robot genre
mechanical hound 88, 96; and 77s 89; and spider 96; and *Wulgaru* 89
Megatron 28, 110–111, 114, 141; *see also* decepticon
meld *see* cyborg
microbot 25, 98, 149, 159, 160, 161, 168, 169, 191; *see also* nanotechnology; nanoweapon
Mighty Atom (aka Astro Boy) 48, 108, 121; *see also* superhero
military robot 3, 38, 53, 80, 90, 100, 102, 113, 122–123, 125–118; *see also* Arkin, Ronald; LAWS; weapons (automated)
missile 153, 154, 157, 161, 162, 169, 193
Molé, Napun 70, 75; and *ku* 71; *see also* assassin; cyborg
monster 3, 5, 9, 17, 20–21, 32, 49, 72, 73, 78, 81, 85, 95, 109, 163, 181; *see also* Frankenstein; yokai
morality *see* ethics
movement (robot body) 5, 6, 15, 97, 98, 99, 145, 168, 172, 178, 181, 182, 188, 190; *see also* fly; locomotion; swarm
Mrs. Adophine II (aka Lady d'Olphine) 74–75; and Molé, Napun 75; and Rhea 75; *see* doppelganger
Muramasa 68–69, 75, 83, 89; and Nightblood 85–86; and Xal'atath 75; *see also* evil; sword

mutant 111, 112, 113; *see also* X-Men
Mutants & Masterminds (game)
    51, 94, 116
mute *see* voiceless

nanite *see* nanotechnology
nanobot *see* nanotechnology
nanotechnology (fictional) 11, 38,
    71, 84, 109, 125, 149, 159, 160, 161,
    168–169, 175, 178–181, 182, 185–
    187, 191–192; *see also* powered
    exoskeleton
nanotechnology (real) 38, 78, 160,
    172, 173, 174, 190–191, 204,
    214*Humans*n.1; *see also* powered
    exoskeleton
nanoweapon 25, 159, 160, 161, 169
Ned 92; and Dubai police robot
    98–99
Need 86–87; and Nightblood 87;
    see also sword
Nightblood 85–87; and Muramasa
    86–87
non-humanoid (fictional) 5, 9, 11,
    31, 95, 101–102, 148–165, 170–171;
    see also nanobots
non-humanoid (real) 6–8, 12, 53,
    99–101, 149, 151, 152, 153, 154,
    160, 165, 165–169, 171, 204; *see
    also* DARPA; nanobot

obedience 47, 76, 88, 120, 128, 129,
    152; *see also* perfect soldier
Olivaw, R. Daneel 93; and Talus
    93; *see also* Talus
on the loop 53, 167, 205; *see also*
    supervised autonomy
Optimus Prime 28, 109–110, 111,
    114, 140–141; *see also* autobot
out of the loop 53, 167, 206; *see
    also* autonomy
oracular head 3; Albertus Magnus
    113; Friar Roger Bacon 35, 54–
    55; Pope Sylvester II 35–36, 42
overpower *see* power (strength)
oversight (of autonomous
    weapons) 207–208

Paradise police 90–92; and *Wul-
    garu* 90
payback *see* revenge
perfect soldier 125, 126, 128–129,
    133, 134, 135, 141; *see also* auton-
    omy; intelligence; loyalty
perch and stare *see* power (fuel)
police robot 90, 92, 97, 98; *see also*
    law enforcement
Pope Sylvester II *see* oracular head
positronic brain 23, 120; *see also*
    Asimov, Isaac
power (ability) 104, 105, 106, 107,
    108, 109, 110, 117, 118, 139, 152,
    154, 156; *see also* power (control)
power (control) 3, 24, 29, 33, 34,
    36, 41–42, 43, 45, 46–51, 47, 48,
    49, 51, 70, 71, 72, 74, 97, 98, 104,
    106, 110, 136, 139, 141, 164, 195,
    199; *see also* greed; mad scientist

power (fuel) 52–53, 92, 109, 112,
    113, 114, 131, 134, 136, 138, 144,
    157, 161, 165, 166–167, 176, 188,
    189, 190, 196, 206
power (strength) 158, 160, 161, 164,
    165, 174, 181, 183, 188, 209; *see
    also* powerful; superpower
power belt 173, 175, 181, 182; *see
    also* exoskeleton
power hungry *see* batteries; mad
    scientist; power (control); power
    (fuel)
powered exoskeleton 11, 125, 172,
    173, 175–176, 177, 179, 181, 182–
    184, 185, 187–189, 190–191
powerful 18, 19, 21, 23, 25, 36, 38,
    39, 46, 48, 52, 68, 74, 76–77, 86,
    96, 106, 108, 110, 113, 123, 125,
    132, 141, 151, 155, 157, 204 *see
    also* power (control); power
    (strength); superpower
powerhouse *see* power (control),
    powerful
powerless *see* power (strength)
pride *see* emotion
program (project/system) 31, 47,
    48, 73, 93, 100, 101, 111, 132, 137,
    148, 149, 188, 190, 191, 196, 204,
    208–209
program (robot code) 3, 4, 5, 6, 8,
    23, 26, 28–29, 31, 41, 42, 45, 46,
    47, 51, 53, 65, 73, 75, 77, 90, 95,
    96, 99, 101, 102, 105, 111, 112, 128,
    129, 132–133, 142, 153, 153–154,
    156, 157, 168, 188, 191, 195, 196,
    207, 210; robot fight program-
    ming 41, 77, 78; *see also* morality
programmability *see* program
Prometheus 19, 42, 83; *see also*
    Frankenstein (book)
prosthetics (non-robotic) 173–174;
    see also prosthetics (robotic)
prosthetics (robotic) 11, 40, 41,
    109, 125, 172, 174, 175, 177–178,
    184, 185, 187, 189–190

R2-D2 9, 163; and Sharur 163; *see
    also* language; voice
rabbi *see* golem
radio police automaton 98, 99, 100
rampage 3, 12, 20, 30, 73, 74, 77,
    78, 81, 82, 119, 234; see also
    Berserker (real)
real robot genre 136–139
recharge *see* batteries
refuel *see* power (fuel)
remote control (remote-control)
    8, 15, 38, 42, 43–44, 46, 48, 51,
    53, 93, 94, 98, 99, 100, 149, 167,
    212
remotely piloted *see* remote con-
    trol
retina scan 95–96
retribution *see* revenge
revenge 4, 5, 10, 13, 14–32, 33, 37,
    38, 42–43, 45, 67, 68, 77, 83, 83,
    105, 107, 119, 120–121, 161, 201,
    208–209

revenge surrogate *see* revenge;
    surrogate
Rhea 72; and Erasmus 72; *see also*
    aristo
RoboCop 3, 45, 103, 109; and 8th
    man 109; *see also* cyborg; super-
    hero
Robomasters *see* competition
robot superiority 21–22, 48, 51, 72,
    92, 95, 110, 134, 135, 139
Robot Wars *see* competition
robotic language *see* language
robotic prosthetics *see* prosthetics
    (robotic)
robotic speech *see* speech (fic-
    tional); speech (real); voice
robotic weapon *see* aerial drone;
    LAWS; nanoweapon; non-
    humanoid
roboticist 3, 48, 77, 90, 93, 113, 119,
    122–123, 139, 144, 204, 213*en-
    forcers*n.1
R.U.R. 42, 43

sadist *see* joy; suffering
science fiction 3, 10, 12, 23, 48, 49,
    62, 72, 77, 78, 85, 102, 104, 119–
    122, 139, 143, 153, 155, 156, 159,
    162, 176, 177, 184, 191
self-awareness 10, 22, 23, 25, 30, 31,
    41, 48, 85, 90, 95, 111, 112, 113, 120,
    128, 129, 131, 133, 137, 140, 141,
    142, 153, 155, 156, 162, 164, 172
self-replicating *see* nanotechnol-
    ogy; nanoweapon
semi-autonomy 8, 98, 156, 158,
    168, 201, 209–210; *see also* auton-
    omy
Sentinel (humanoid) 111, 112, 113;
    see also master mold
Sentinel (real) 99, 162
Sentinel (squid) 161–162; and real
    Sentinels 162
shapeshifter 5, 25, 28, 95, 109–110,
    114, 115, 116m 140–141, 142, 151,
    164, 186; *see also* Sharur; Trans-
    formers Universe
Sharur 149, 151–153, 156, 162, 164,
    167, 172; and R2-D2 163; *see also*
    autonomy; intelligence; speech
    (fictional)
Shelley, Mary *see* Frankenstein
Sid 6.7 73–74; and ku 74
Skynet 4, 141–143, 164, 186
solar power 166–167, 190; *see*
    power (fuel)
SOP network 186–187
sorcerer [magic, witch spell] 3, 4,
    14, 15, 16–17, 18, 26, 35, 36, 42,
    66, 67, 69, 114, 150, 183
soul 24–25, 28, 75, 76, 77, 78, 83,
    94–95, 110, 118, 131, 133, 141, 164,
    176
soulless 52, 77, 78, 141, 142
Spartoi 4, 129–131, 132, 136; and
    Berserks 131
speak *see* speech (fictional);
    speech (real); voiceless

speech (fictional) 5, 9, 16, 37, 39, 53–54, 77, 78, 97, 136, 150, 156–157, 161, 176, 177, 183–184
speech (real) 31, 59, 98, 113, 144, 193
speech recognition *see* speech technology
speech synthesis *see* speech technology
speech technology 9, 31, 37, 59, 98, 136, 156, 176, 178, 193, 213Greedn.2
speechless *see* voiceless
Star Trek Universe 3, 9, 10, 51–52, 120, 129, 185, 186; *see also* the Borg
Star Wars Universe 3, 5, 9, 26, 140, 142–143, 161, 163, 184; and Terminator Universe 141, 142, 145; and Transformers Universe 140, 142–143; *see also* assassins; prosthetics
Stark, Tony 113, 172, 175, 181; *see also* iron man; powered exoskeleton
statue 3, 18, 19, 36, 68
Stone, Victor *see* Cyborg (superhero)
suffering 5, 14, 16, 17, 18, 21, 22, 30, 33, 67, 68, 71, 74, 77, 82, 84, 107, 119, 120, 140, 148, 177, 203, 204;
superhero 11, 27, 48, 65, 94, 104–118, 140, 165, 188; female 105, 108; identity 104, 105, 106, 108, 109, 181; immortality 107, 108; mission 94, 104, 105, 106, 108, 112, 113, 140; and mythology 107; powers 94, 104, 105, 109; sexual orientation 112; teams 111–114; *see also* powered exoskeleton
superman robots 105, 107
superpower *see* power (ability); powerful; superhero; supervillain
supertroop 188–189; *see also* powered exoskeleton
supervillain 11, 28, 29, 65, 104, 106–107, 110–111, 112, 140, 141, 175; importance 106–107; mission 106, 110, 111, 129; powers 104, 106–107, 108, 110–111; teams 111–114; *see also* powered exoskeleton
supervised autonomy 53, 145, 209; *see also* autonomy
surrogate 14, 15, 16, 25, 26, 27, 30, 31, 66

swarm 25, 38, 84, 98, 132, 149, 152, 153, 158, 159, 160, 168–169, 186–187; *see also* nanotechnology; nanoweapon
sword 3, 5, 70, 75, 83, 85–86, 89, 148, 151, 156, 163

talk *see* language; speech (fictional); speech (real)
Talos 11, 65, 114–117, 164, 188–190; *see also* Mutants & Masterminds; T-ALOS
Talus 87–88, 93
Taming Sari 151, 153, 154, 158, 167; *see also* sword
tank 98, 136, 141, 145, 147, 148, 164–165, 168, 172, 199; *see also* BOLO tank; cyber tank
task-level autonomy *see* supervised autonomy
telepathy 86, 108, 118
Terminator Universe 4, 5, 140, 141–142, 164, 186; *see also* Skynet; Star Wars Universe
Three Laws of Robotics 23–24, 73, 76, 119–122; *see also* Asimov, Isaac; positronic brain
tokoloshe 5, 16, 66 67–68, 71, 74
torment *see* suffer
toys (fiction) 10, 11, 22–23, 24, 31, 42, 132; and toys (real) 23
toys (real) 23, 54, 109
training 46, 48, 159, 197; *see also* learning; machine learning
Transformers Universe 5, 28, 109, 110–111, 114, 140, 141, 142, 143, 164; *see also* autobot; decepticon; Megatron; Optimus Prime; Star Wars Universe; Terminator Universe
tsukumogami 17, 24, 68, 152; *see also* yokai
tulpa 3, 34, 46, 47
tupilak 15–16, 119, 136
twin *see* doppelganger
two-handed engine (aka fury) 87

Ukko 150–151, 156, 163; *see also* sword
Ultron 50–51, 111, 112, 117–118
unemotional *see* emotionless
unpredictability 101–102, 112, 195–197; *see also* autonomy; machine learning; Manhunter

vengeance *see* revenge
V.I.K.I. 45, 136
violence 21, 26, 30, 69, 83, 90, 93, 94, 97, 100, 101, 106, 133
vocalize *see* language; speech (fictional); speech (real)
voice 9, 16, 40, 48, 75, 86, 91, 94, 136, 141, 143, 156, 178, 179, 183–184; *see also* language; speech (fictional); speech (real); speech technology; telepathy; voiceless
voiceless 9, 16, 69, 76, 78, 86, 97, 134

walk *see* locomotion
warfighter 11, 125, 126, 127, 129, 131, 132, 139, 141, 142, 143, 147, 148, 150, 151, 152, 165, 172, 173, 175, 177, 179, 180, 182, 186, 187, 188, 189, 190, 191, 195, 200, 212; *see also* perfect soldier
watchbird 8, 82, 87–88, 94, 101–102, 119; and gargoyles 94; and giant (Hopi) 88; and Manhunters 112, 129
weapon (automated) 5, 11, 26, 29, 36, 37, 42, 44, 49, 70, 86, 97, 98, 99, 136, 172, 202, 204, 205, 206; *see also* military robot; nanoweapon; non-humanoid; real robot genre; weapon (melee); weapon (range)
weapon (melee) 148, 150, 151, 161; *see also* humanoid; weapon (automated)
weapon (range) 148–149, 150, 161; *see also* weapon (automated); weapon (melee)
Wells, H.G. *see* The Island of Dr. Moreau
wireless connectivity 23, 54, 145, 162, 180, 187; *see also* hacking; SOP network
Wulgaru 84–85, 89, 90, 92, 99; and Paradise police 92, 96; and Talus 87

Xal'atath 75; *see also* evil
X-men 111, 113; *see also* Sentinel (humanoid)

yokai 17, 68, 152